Miles Walker Mattinson, Stuart Cunningham Macaskie

The Law relating to corrupt and illegal Practices

At Parliamentary, Municipal and other Elections

Miles Walker Mattinson, Stuart Cunningham Macaskie

The Law relating to corrupt and illegal Practices
At Parliamentary, Municipal and other Elections

ISBN/EAN: 9783337153359

Printed in Europe, USA, Canada, Australia, Japan

Cover: Foto ©Suzi / pixelio.de

More available books at **www.hansebooks.com**

THE LAW RELATING TO

CORRUPT AND ILLEGAL PRACTICES

AT PARLIAMENTARY, MUNICIPAL AND OTHER ELECTIONS,

AND THE

PRACTICE ON ELECTION PETITIONS,

WITH AN APPENDIX OF STATUTES, RULES AND FORMS.

BY

MILES WALKER MATTINSON,
OF GRAY'S INN, BARRISTER-AT-LAW; JOINT AUTHOR OF "PRECEDENTS OF PLEADINGS,"

AND

STUART CUNNINGHAM MACASKIE,
OF GRAY'S INN, BARRISTER-AT-LAW; AUTHOR OF "LAW OF EXECUTORS AND ADMINISTRATORS,"
AND A "TREATISE ON BILLS OF SALE."

THIRD EDITION.

LONDON:
WATERLOW AND SONS LIMITED, LONDON WALL, E.C.
1892.

PREFACE TO THE THIRD EDITION.

IN offering the Third Edition of this work to the Profession and the Public, the Authors have only to say that they have sought to bring the treatment of the subject down to date by such additions to, and amendments of, the text as late cases and late statutes render necessary.

The recent establishment of County Councils in England and Wales, and the application of the Corrupt Practices Acts to the elections of all County Councillors has widened still further the area of interest taken in the matters discussed in this book.

M. W. M.
S. C. M.

1, Garden Court, Temple, E.C.,
    16th June, 1892.

A HANDBOOK OF THE LAW RELATING TO THE MANAGEMENT OF PARLIAMENTARY, COUNTY COUNCIL AND MUNICIPAL ELECTIONS. A statement of the Law relating to the machinery of Elections. Second Edition. By H. STEPHEN, Barrister-at-Law. In cloth, 1s.

PREFACE TO THE FIRST EDITION.

THE sweeping changes in the Law for the Prevention of Corrupt Practices at Elections effected by the Act of 1883 have rendered obsolete existing works on the subject, at the same time that the increased stringency of punishment enacted has heightened the importance of a clear comprehension of the whole subject by all persons concerned in the conduct of elections. In these circumstances the Authors present to the Profession and the Public this work, in which they have sought to engraft what has been newly enacted by the Legislature upon such of the old learning as has been retained, and so to offer a complete view of the whole law relating to Corrupt Practices at Elections as it will prevail throughout the United Kingdom on the 15th of October, 1883.

The Act of 1883 is not a code of the Laws against Corruption: it is only an Amending Act. To grasp the subject resort must be had to four distinct sources, viz., the Common Law of Parliament, the unrepealed sections of the Acts for the Prevention of Corruption prior to the legislation of this year, the Act of 1883 itself, and the reported decisions of the Election Judges.

There were two methods open to the Authors in treating of the Laws relating to Corrupt Practices at Elections. One was to follow a course, not uncommon, of merely editing the Act of 1883 and presenting it with notes appended to its sections explanatory of their meaning and indicative of the changes in the law. But the Authors felt that this would be but an inadequate and confusing treatment of a subject of great inherent complexity, and would have the necessary effect of making their work a sealed book to all save lawyers. They accordingly discarded this method, and, instead, arranging and methodising the whole learning of the subject in what has seemed to them the most intelligible order, they have inserted the provisions of the new Act in those parts of the Statement into which they seemed naturally to fall.

The Authors hope it will be found that a discussion of no part of the law has been omitted by them, and that they have not failed to note in its appropriate place any decision of authority; while they trust their anxiety to give all the references in contemporary reports to cases quoted will add to the practical usefulness of the book in the hands of the Profession.

M. W. M.
S. C. M.

September, 1883.

CONTENTS.

	PAGE
TABLE I.	XI
Showing the Offences which avoid a Parliamentary Election.	
TABLE II.	XII
Showing the Offences which avoid the Election of Councillors.	
TABLE III.	XIII
Showing the Punishments, Incapacities, and Penalties inflicted on Offenders at Parliamentary Elections.	
TABLE IV.	XIV
Showing the Punishments, Incapacities and Penalties inflicted on Offenders at the Election of Councillors.	
TABLE OF CASES .	XV

PART I.

THE FORFEITURE OF THE SEAT.

CHAPTER I. . . .	3
Corrupt Practices.	
Section I.—Bribery	4
Section II.—Treating	41
Section III.—Undue Influence	56
Section IV.—Personation, and Aiding and Abetting Personation	64
Section V.—False Declaration .	66
CHAPTER II.	67
Illegal Practices which avoid a Parliamentary Election.	
Section I.—When committed by the Candidate or any Agent	67
Section II.—When committed by the Candidate or the Election Agent . .	76

	PAGE
CHAPTER III.	90

Illegal Practices which avoid a Municipal Election.

    Section I.—When committed by the Candidate or any Agent 90

    Section II.—When committed by the Candidate, or with his knowledge and consent 92

CHAPTER IV. 98

The Employment by the Candidate at a Parliamentary Election of a Corrupt Agent.

CHAPTER V. . 101

General Corruption.

CHAPTER VI. 106

The General Prevalence of Illegal Practices at a Municipal Election.

CHAPTER VII. 109

The Candidate's Agents within the meaning of Chapters I., II. and III.

CHAPTER VIII. 131

The Office and Duties of the Election Agent at a Parliamentary Election, and Parliamentary Election Expenses.

    Section I.—His Appointment 131

    Section II.—The Nature and Amount of the Expenses at an Election 137

    Section III.—The Payment of Election Expenses . . 149

    Section IV.—The Return and Declaration of Election Expenses . . . 154

CHAPTER IX. . . . 159

Election Expenses at Municipal Elections.

CHAPTER X. . . 164

Practice and Procedure.

    Section I.—On Application for Relief . . 164
    Section II.—On Election Petitions . . 172
    Section III.—On a Scrutiny . . . 193
    Section IV.—Evidence on Election Petitions . . 201
    Section V.—The Awarding and Taxation of Costs . 213

CONTENTS.

PART II.

THE PUNISHMENT OF OFFENDERS.

	PAGE
CHAPTER I.	227
Their Detection and Prosecution.	
CHAPTER II. .	233
Their Punishment.	
Section I.—By Election Commissioners .	233
Section II.—By the Election Court . . .	237
Section III.—By a Court of Summary Jurisdiction .	246
Section IV.—By the Court of Assizes . . .	250
Section V.—By the High Court in Suits for Penalties .	254

PART III.

THE APPLICATION OF THE ACT OF 1884 TO CERTAIN OTHER ELECTIONS IN ENGLAND AND WALES.

CHAPTER I.	258
Elections of Mayor, Alderman, Elective Auditor, or Revising Assessor in any Borough.	
CHAPTER II.	260
Elections of Members of Local Boards, Improvement Commissioners, Poor Law Guardians, Members of School Boards, and Members of County Councils.	
CHAPTER III.	267
Municipal Elections in the City of London.	

THE FRANCHISE ACTS, 1884-5, being the Representation of the People Act, 1884; Registration Act, 1885; Parliamentary Elections (Redistribution) Act, 1885, and Medical Relief Disqualification Removal Act, 1885, with introduction and NOTES. By MILES WALKER MATTINSON, Barrister-at-law, Joint Author of "Mattinson and Macaskie on Corrupt Practices." In boards, 2s. 6d.

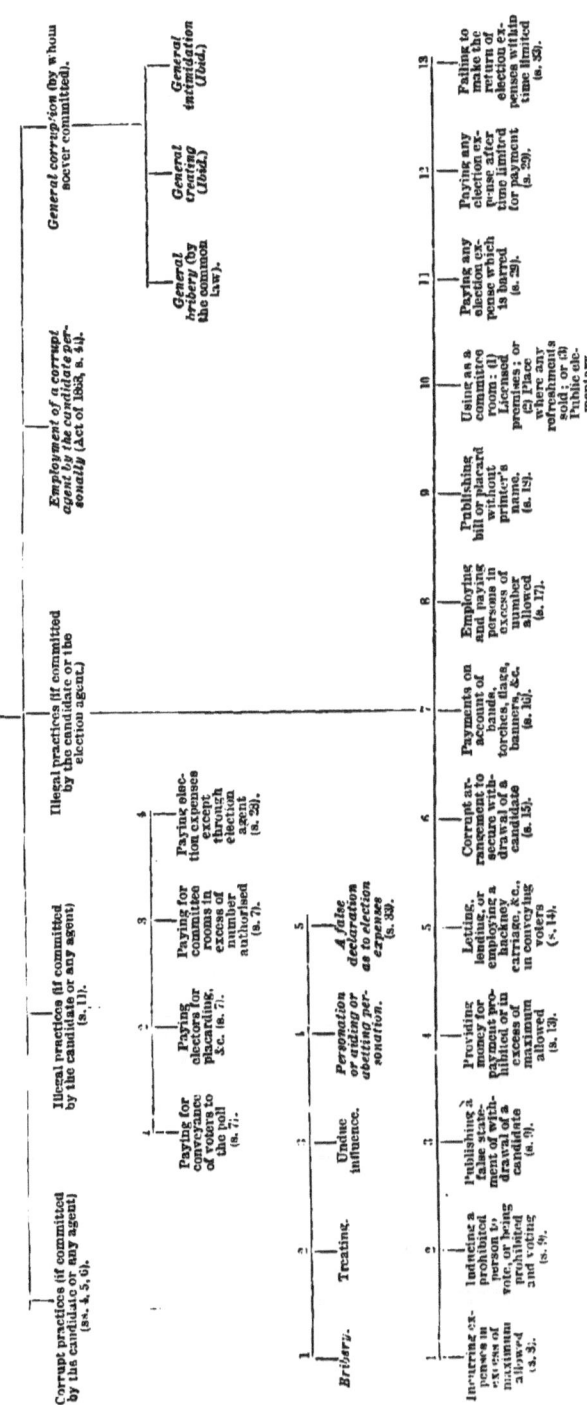

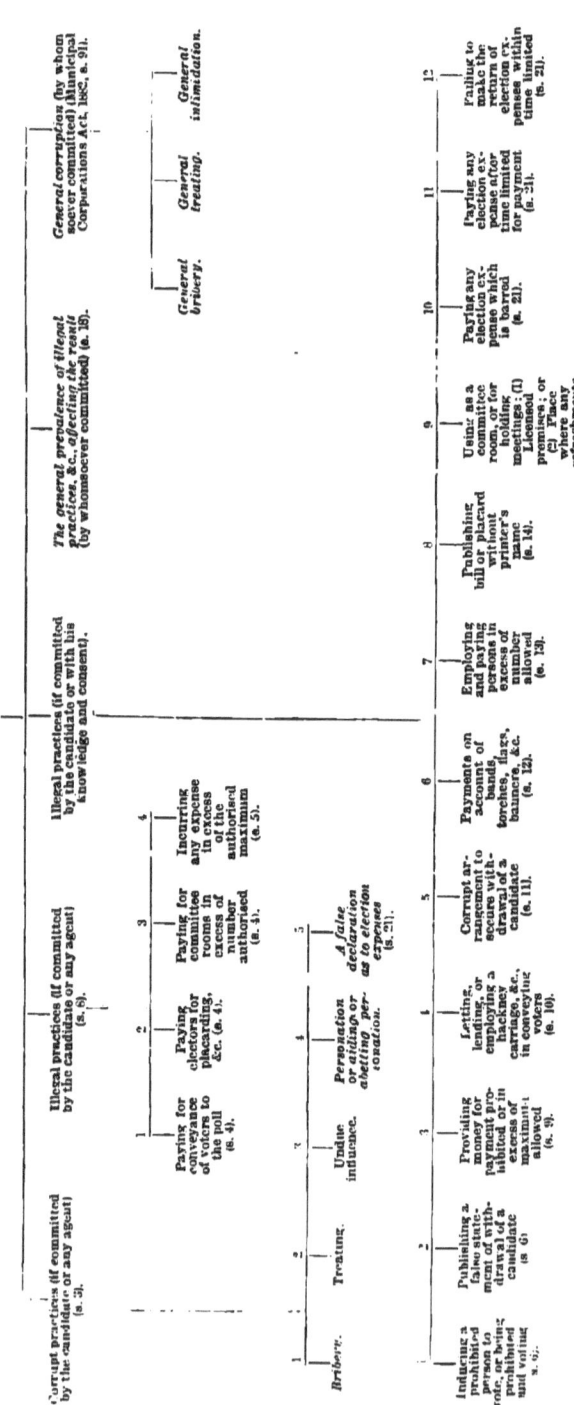

TABLE II., RELATING TO THE ELECTION OF COUNCILLORS.

GIVING A COMPLETE LIST OF ALL CORRUPT AND ILLEGAL PRACTICES WHICH AFFECT THE SEAT, AND INDICATING THE SECTION OF THE ACT OF 1884, UNDER WHICH THEY DO SO.

N.B.—The offences in italics are so emphasised because the court has no power in any of those cases to grant relief, either under ss. 19 or 20 of the Act of 1884, or at all.

TABLE III.

Showing Maximum Punishments, Incapacities and Penalties to which Persons are exposed for Offences at Parliamentary Elections.

Offence.	Maximum Punishment.	Incapacities.	Penalties in Civil Court.
Knowingly making a false Declaration as to election expenses	7 years' penal servitude, and	(1) Incapacity to sit in House of Commons for 7 years (2) Incapable of being registered as elector or voting at any election (Parliamentary or otherwise) for 7 years (3) Incapable for 7 years of holding any public or judicial office (4) If a justice of the peace, barrister, &c., liable to further consequences under s. 38.	
Personation, or aiding, abetting, or inciting to the commission of personation	2 years' hard labour, and	All the above incapacities.	
Any other Corrupt Practice (viz., bribery, treating or undue influence)	1 year with or without hard labour, or fine of £200, and		
A Corrupt Arrangement for the withdrawal of a petition (s. 41 of the Act of 1883)	1 year's imprisonment and a fine of £200	No incapacities.	
Election Agent failing to make Return of Expenses after being ordered by the Court	Fine of £500 .	No incapacities.	
Illegal Practices	Fine of £100 .	Incapable of being registered and voting at any election in the constituency, *where illegal practice committed*, for 5 years.	
Illegal Payment, Hiring or Employment	Fine of £100 .	No incapacities.	
Returning officer or his deputy, partner or clerk, acting as Agent for any Candidate (30 & 31 Vict., c. 102, s. 59)	Fine or imprisonment as for a common law misdemeanour		£100 a day to any person who sues for the same.
A Member Sitting and Voting after the expiration of the time limited for transmitting return of election expenses, when the return is not made	.	.	.
Providing or Giving Cockades, Ribbons, &c., to persons in constituency during election	.	.	40s. and full costs of suit to any person who sues for the same.

N.B.—The above *incapacities* apply to any and every person convicted of or reported as guilty of any of the offences named; but if a Candidate is reported by an *Election Court* as personally guilty of any *corrupt practice*, *in addition* to all those incapacities he becomes incapable of ever being elected to or sitting in the House of Commons for the constituency in which he offended (s. 4), and if he is reported as personally guilty of any *illegal practice* he is incapable for the next seven years of sitting in the House of Commons for the constituency in which he offended (s. 11).

TABLE IV.

SHOWING MAXIMUM PUNISHMENTS, INCAPACITIES AND PENALTIES TO WHICH PERSONS ARE EXPOSED FOR OFFENCES AT THE ELECTION OF COUNCILLORS.

Offence.	Maximum Punishment.	Incapacities.	Penalties in Civil Court.
Knowingly making a false DECLARATION as to election expenses	7 years' penal servitude	(1) Incapacity to sit in the House of Commons for any place for 7 years (2) Incapable of being registered and voting at any Parliamentary or other election (3) Incapable for 7 years of being elected to any public, municipal or judicial office. (4) If a justice of the peace, barrister, &c., liable to further consequences under s. 38 of Act of 1883 and s. 23 of Act of 1884	
PERSONATION, or aiding, abetting, or inciting to the commission of personation	2 years' hard labour, and	All the above incapacities.	
Any other CORRUPT PRACTICE (viz., bribery, treating or undue influence)	1 year's imprisonment or a fine of £200, and	All the above incapacities.	
CORRUPT ARRANGEMENT for the withdrawal of a petition	1 year's imprisonment and a fine of £200	No incapacities.	
Any ILLEGAL PRACTICE	Fine of £100	Incapable for 6 years of being registered as an elector or voting at any election within the borough.	
Any ILLEGAL PAYMENT, HIRING or EMPLOYMENT	Fine of £100	No incapacities.	
AGENT FAILING TO MAKE A RETURN OF HIS EXPENSES to the candidate within specified time	Fine of £50	No incapacities.	
COUNCILLOR Sitting and VOTING after the expiration of the time limited for transmitting return of election expenses, when the return is not made			£50 for every day in which he sits and votes to any person who may sue for the same.

N.B.—In addition, if any *candidate* is convicted of, or reported by, an Election Court as guilty of any *corrupt practice*, he becomes incapable of *ever* holding any corporate office in the borough in which he offended. (S. 3 of the Act of 1884.) And if the report of an Election Court is that any *candidate* has been guilty *by his agent* of any corrupt practice, such candidate becomes incapable of holding any corporate office in the borough for 3 years.

TABLE OF CASES.

Aldridge v. Hurst	178, 180, 193
Arch v. Bentinck	185, 196
Archer v. McGirr	191
Athlone	65
Aylesbury	27, 30, 52
Ayres, ex p.	245
Barnstaple	222
Barrow	47, 48, 71, 83, 88
Barstow	88
Beale v. Smith	182
Belfast	31, 40
Berwick	182, 193, 194, 197, 199, 200, 215
Beverley	13, 208
Bewdley	43, 48, 111, 115, 117, 119, 125, 182, 214
Blackburn	8, 10, 60, 109, 112, 120, 208
Bodmin	54, 112
Bolton	22, 68, 183, 215
Boston	17, 35, 214
Bradford	13, 47, 48, 101, 204, 209
Bradlaugh v. Clarke	158
Brecon	13, 50, 180
Bridgwater	128, 206
Bristol	15, 183, 188
Brett v. Robinson	15, 46
Buckrose	70, 73, 77, 83, 84, 155, 166, 178, 215, 231
Cambridgeshire	142
Carrickfergus	20, 35
Carter v. Mills	173
Cashel	119, 211
Clark, ex p.	165
Clark v. Wallond	178, 182
Clark's Case	65
Cheltenham	8, 25, 210, 204
Chester	184, 204, 212
Chorlton v. Lings	87
Cooper v. Slade	21, 43
Coventry	22, 39, 65, 183, 202, 213, 215
Darlington, ex p.	169
Dover	210
Down	57, 63
Drinkwater v. Deakin	199
Drogheda	102, 209, 215
Dublin	22, 112
Dudley	104
Durham	18, 112, 113
Earl of Beauchamp v. Overseers of the Parish of Madresfield	87
Evesham	183, 202
Galway	59, 100, 104, 174, 211
Gloucester	63, 65, 180, 194
Goodwin's Case	208
Gravesend	25, 32, 124, 193, 213, 214
Greenock	202
Guildford	8, 203, 215
Hackney	2, 107, 215
Harwich	113, 114, 117, 118, 122, 183, 207, 210
Hartlepool	180
Hargreaves v. Scott	221
Hargreaves v. Simpson	257
Hastings	14, 21, 23, 30, 208
Hempson, ex p.	165
Hereford	118, 176, 181
Hill v. Peel	220, 222
Hindle v. Waring	173
Horsham	22
Hughes v. Meyrick	223
Huguenin v. Baseley	61
Hutchinson, ex p.	168
Ipswich	18, 22, 73, 83, 103, 240
Ives, ex p.	169
James v. Henderson	194
Joyce v. O'Donnel	196
Kennington	140, 186, 220, 224
Kidderminster	8, 46, 174
King's Lynn	205, 206, 210
Kingston-upon-Hull	177
Kirkwood v. Webster	220
Knaresborough	202
Launceston	27, 32
Lenanton	88, 164, 166, 168
Lenham v. Barber	182
Lichfield	57, 101, 205
Limerick	103, 126
Line v. Warren	191, 192
Longford	46, 61, 102, 182, 215

TABLE OF CASES.

Lord Rendlesham v. Haward . 87
Londonderry 116, 124, 205, 206, 211
Louth 46, 49

Mackley v. Chillingworth . . 223
Malcolm v. Parry . 128, 197, 200
Mallam v. Bear . . . 181
Mallow 8, 185
Maidstone 52
Maude v. Lowley . . . 178
Marshall v. James . . . 173
Mayo 215
McLaren v. Home . . 189, 223
Moore v. Kennard . . . 181
Moore v. Scully . . . 199
Morton v. Mitchell . . . 173

Neild v. Batty . . . 196
North Durham 61, 103, 104, 179, 180, 206
North Norfolk 58, 59, 60, 63, 98, 112, 127, 130, 204, 210
Northallerton . . 61, 62, 209
Norwich 11, 18, 45, 71, 73, 99, 103, 112, 120, 127, 129, 138, 139, 155, 182, 196, 199, 208, 214, 224
Nottingham . . 104, 215

Oldham . . 25, 197, 200
Oxford 18

Pascoe v. Puleston . . . 224
Pease v. Norwood . . 173, 176
Pembroke, ex p. . . . 170
Penrhyn . . . 28, 214
Perry, ex p. 166
Petersfield . . . 60, 213
Pickering v Startin . . . 177
Plymouth . . . 21, 36, 39
Poole . . . 10, 51, 103, 214
Pontefract 52

R. v. Barnewell . . . 61
R. v. Fox 65
R. v. Holl 228
R. v. Mansel-Jones . 185, 236, 240
R. v. Price 228
R. v. Riley . . . 246, 250
R. v. Shellard . . . 246
R. v. Stroulger . . . 251
Renfrew 197
Robson, ex p. . . . 154
Rothwell's Case . . . 65

Salford . 10, 103, 129, 174, 183, 209
Salisbury (1) . 103, 117, 181, 212

Salisbury (2) . . 18, 37, 117,
Sandwich 20
Shrewsbury . . . 10, 117, 177
Simpson v. Yeend . . . 21
Sligo 11, 101
Southampton . 9, 14, 129, 196, 210, 221
Stafford . . 33, 38, 63, 128, 129
St. Ives 102
Staleybridge . . 21, 63, 116, 184
Stepney . 10, 63, 64, 65, 81, 138, 185, 186, 197, 199, 200, 215, 231
Stevens, ex p. 165
Stevens v. Tillett . . . 16
Stowe v. Jolliffe . . 194, 198
Stroud 12, 13, 16, 25, 118, 184, 193, 212
Tamworth . 10, 17, 32, 46, 102, 127, 209, 221
Taunton (1) . . 23, 117, 122
Taunton (2) . . . 117, 207
Tewkesbury . . . 118, 183
Thirsk 193, 211
Thomas v. Wylie . . . 176
Thornbury 105
Tillett v. Stracey . . 220, 221
Tipperary 205
Trench v. Nolan. . . 199, 221
Turnbull v. Janson . . . 223
Tyrone 194

Unwin v. Macmullen 192

Wakefield 124
Walker, ex p. . . . 168, 266
Wallingford . . 44, 46, 48, 214
Waterford . . . 28, 184
Wells v. Wren . . . 181
Wentworth v. Lloyd . . . 220
West Belfast 183, 186, 188, 203, 206
Westbury 31, 49, 58, 60, 112, 116, 121, 214
Westminster 8, 20, 47, 116, 119, 121, 184, 206, 207, 209
Wigan 37, 49, 121, 183, 204, 211, 214
Wigtown . . . 199, 215
Wilks, ex p. . . . 165
Wills' Case . . . 65
Windsor . 12, 32, 33, 34, 51, 56, 59, 112, 116, 205, 207, 215
Woodward v. Sarsons . 199, 215
Worcester . . . 205, 215

Yates v. Leach . . . 172, 199
Yorkshire, S.W. Riding . 183, 196
Youghal . 33, 48, 49, 129, 172, 209

THE LAW RELATING TO
CORRUPT AND ILLEGAL PRACTICES AT ELECTIONS.

WE purpose treating of the law relating to corrupt and illegal practices at Parliamentary and Municipal elections, *first*, with reference to the effect of corrupt and illegal acts upon the Seat, and, *secondly*, with reference to their consequences to Individuals. PARLIAMENTARY & MUNICIPAL.

PART I.

THE FORFEITURE OF THE SEAT.

A PARLIAMENTARY ELECTION IN ENGLAND, SCOTLAND, OR IRELAND, upon petition, is avoided and the seat forfeited by :

I. Any corrupt act committed by the sitting member or *any one of his agents*, or by—

II. Any of the illegal practices enacted by ss. 7 and 28 of the Act of 1883, committed by the sitting member or *any one of his agents*, or by—

III. Any illegal practice enacted by the Act of 1883, committed by the sitting member, *or by his election agent*, or by—

IV. The employment, by the candidate *personally*, of an agent convicted of or reported for corrupt practices, or by—

V. General corruption by *whomsoever committed* ;

subject, in *some of these cases* to the possibility of relief under ss. 22, 23, or 34 of the Act of 1883.

THE ELECTION OF A COUNCILLOR IN A MUNICIPAL BOROUGH IN ENGLAND, upon petition, is avoided, and the seat forfeited by :

I. Any corrupt act committed by the sitting member, *or any one of his agents*, or by—

II. Any of the illegal practices enacted by ss. 4 and 5 of the Act of 1884, whether committed by the sitting member, *or any one of his agents*, or by—

III. Any illegal practice enacted by the Act of 1884, committed by the sitting member *personally*, or by—

IV. General corruption by *whomsoever committed*, or by—

V. The general prevalence of illegal practices, payments, hirings, or employments by *whomsoever committed;*

subject in *some of these cases*, to the possibility of relief under ss. 19 and 20 of the Act of 1884.

Parliamentary and Municipal elections, held under the provisions of the Ballot Act, are also liable to be set aside, on the ground that they have not been conducted in accordance with the principles laid down in that Act and that the result of the election has been affected thereby (s. 13 of the Ballot Act, 1870, and the *Hackney Case*, 2, O'M & H., 77). Any discussion, however, of the circumstances under which the return will be invalidated on this ground is foreign to the scope of this work, which relates to corrupt and illegal practices at elections. But the matter is mentioned here that the reader may have before him, in a single view, all the possible grounds upon which an election may be upset.

CHAPTER I.

CORRUPT PRACTICES.

CORRUPT Practices are thus defined by the Act of 1883 :— <small>PARLIAMENTARY & MUNICIPAL.</small>
"The expression 'corrupt practice,' as used in this Act, <small>Definition of Corrupt Practices.</small> means any of the following offences, namely: Treating and undue influence, as defined by this Act, and bribery and personation as defined by the enactments set forth in Part 3 of the 3rd Schedule to this Act, and aiding and abetting counselling and procuring the commission of the offence of personation, and every offence which is a corrupt practice within the meaning of this Act shall be a corrupt practice within the meaning of the Parliamentary Elections Act, 1868" (s. 3).

A later section of the same Act makes it a corrupt practice for a candidate at a Parliamentary Election knowingly to make a false declaration accompanying the return of election expenses (s. 33).

The Act of 1884 relating to Municipal elections expressly adopts the above definition of corrupt practices given in s. 3 of the Act of 1883 (s. 2), and further, its 21st section contains a provision similar to the 33rd of the earlier Act, constituting the act of knowingly making a false declaration a corrupt practice.

The result is that so far as the definition of corrupt practice is concerned the law relating to Parliamentary and Municipal elections is the same; and an election—Parliamentary or Municipal—is liable to be defeated, and the sitting member to lose his seat, if any one of the following acts is proved against him, viz., either

1. BRIBERY;
2. TREATING:
3. UNDUE INFLUENCE,

THE LAW RELATING TO

Parliamentary & Municipal.

4. Personation and Aiding, Abetting, Counselling, and Procuring the Commission of Personation ; or,

5. A False Declaration :

whether any of these corrupt acts is committed by him personally, or by anyone whom the law construes as his agent for the purposes of the election.

It is proposed, in the first instance, to examine the authorities as to the definition of the offences named, and later to discuss the meaning which has been given to the word "agent" in this connection.

Section 1.—Bribery.

Statutory definitions of bribery, 17 & 18 Vict. c. 102, s. 2.

The Acts of 1883 and 1884 contain no new definition of bribery. On the contrary, s. 3 of the Act of 1883 already quoted, expressly incorporates the definitions of bribery contained in former Corrupt Practices Prevention Acts into the Act of 1883, and in the third part of the third schedule those definitions are set out in detail. It is necessary in this place to give their full text. S. 2 of the Corrupt Practices Prevention Act, 1854 (the 17 & 18 Vict., c. 102), provides :

" The following persons shall be deemed guilty of bribery, and shall be punishable accordingly—

Sub-sec. 1.

" 1. Every person who shall, directly or indirectly, by himself or by any other person on his behalf, give, lend, or agree to give or lend, or shall, offer, promise, or promise to procure, or endeavour to procure any money or valuable consideration to or for any voter, or to or for any person on behalf of any voter, or to or for any other person in order to induce any voter to vote or refrain from voting, or shall corruptly do any such act as aforesaid on account of such voter having voted or refrained from voting at any election :

Sub-sec. 2.

" 2. Every person who shall, directly or indirectly, by himself or by any other person on his behalf, give or promise, or agree to give or procure, or offer, promise, or promise to procure or to endeavour to procure any office, place, or employment to or for any voter, or to or for any person on behalf of any voter, or to or for any other person in order to induce such voter to vote or refrain from voting, or shall corruptly do any such act as aforesaid on account of any voter having voted or refrained from voting at any election : [Parliamentary & Municipal.]

"3. Every person who shall, directly or indirectly, by himself or by any other person on his behalf, make any such gift, loan, offer, promise, procurement, or agreement as aforesaid to or for any person in order to induce such person to procure or endeavour to procure the return of any person to serve in Parliament, or the vote of any voter at any election : [Sub-sec. 3.]

"4. Every person who shall, upon or in consequence of any such gift, loan, offer, promise, or procurement or agreement procure, or engage, promise, or endeavour to procure the return of any person to serve in Parliament, or the vote of any voter at any election : [Sub-sec. 4.]

"5. Every person who shall advance or pay or cause to be paid any money to or to the use of any other person with the intent that such money or any part thereof shall be expended in bribery at any election, or who shall knowingly pay or cause to be paid any money to any person in discharge or repayment of any money wholly or in part expended in bribery at any election. Provided always, that the aforesaid enactment shall not extend, or be construed to extend to any money paid or agreed to be paid for or on account of any legal expenses *bona fide* incurred at or concerning any election. [Sub-sec. 5.]

S. 3 of the same Act provides : [Sec. 3.]

PARLIAMENTARY & MUNICIPAL.

"The following persons shall also be deemed guilty of bribery, and shall be punishable accordingly—

Sub-sec. 1.

"1. Every voter who shall, before or during any election, directly or indirectly, by himself or by any other person on his behalf receive, agree, or contract for any money, gift, loan, or valuable consideration, office, place or employment for himself or for any other person, for voting or agreeing to vote, or for refraining or agreeing to refrain from voting at any election :

Sub-sec. 2.

"2. Every person who shall, after any election, directly or indirectly, by himself or by any other person on his behalf, receive any money or valuable consideration on account of any person having voted or refrained from voting, or having induced any other person to vote or refrain from voting at any election."

30 & 31 Vict., c. 102, s. 49.

Section 49 of the Representation of the People Act, 1867 (the 30 & 31 Vict., c. 102) is as follows :—

"Any person, either directly or indirectly, corruptly paying any rate on behalf of any ratepayer for the purpose of enabling him to be registered as a voter, thereby to influence his vote at any future election, and any candidate or other person, either directly or indirectly, paying any rate on behalf of any voter for the purpose of inducing him to vote or refrain from voting, shall be guilty of bribery, and be punishable accordingly ; and any person on whose behalf and with whose privity, any such payment as in this section is mentioned, is made, shall also be guilty of bribery and punishable accordingly."

The Act of 1884 incorporates ss. 2 and 3 of the 17 & 18 Vict., c. 102, and s. 49 of the 30 & 31 Vict., c. 102, and applies them to municipal elections, so that a definition of bribery common to parliamentary and municipal elections is thus obtained.

There are two other Acts further creating the offence of bribery. They have, however, no application to municipal

CORRUPT PRACTICES AT ELECTIONS.

elections, and their practical importance with reference to parliamentary elections is not great. They are: <small>PARLIAMENTARY & MUNICIPAL.</small>

1st. The Representation of the People (Scotland) Act, 1868 (the 31 & 32 Vict., c. 48, s. 49), which contains a provision in the case of Scotch elections similar to the provisions of s. 49 of the 30 & 31 Vict., c. 102, and

2nd. The Universities Elections Amendment (Scotland) Act, 1881 (44 & 45 Vict., c. 40, s. 2), which provides:— <small>44 & 45 Vict., c. 40, s. 2.</small>
"Any person, either directly or indirectly, corruptly paying any fee for the purpose of enabling any person to be registered as a member of the general council and thereby to influence his vote at any future election, and any candidate or other person, either directly or indirectly, paying such fee on behalf of any person, for the purpose of inducing him to vote or refrain from voting, shall be guilty of bribery, and shall be punishable accordingly; and any person on whose behalf and with whose privity, any such payment as in this section mentioned, is made, shall also be guilty of bribery and punishable accordingly."

Applying the statutory definitions of bribery given in the above sections to the subject under consideration, viz., the effect of bribery upon the seat, the general result is, that if a candidate or any one of his agents, gives or lends, or offers, or promises to procure, or to endeavour to procure (1) any money; or (2) valuable consideration; or (3) office, place, or employment, to or for any voter or to or for any person on behalf of any voter, or to or for *any other person*, in order to induce such voter to vote or refrain from voting, or if he shall *corruptly* do any of the above-mentioned acts on account of any voter having voted or refrained from voting at any election, then the offence of bribery is complete and the seat is lost. There are other special acts which are defined as amounting to bribery. They will be treated of in due course; but the effect of the more material sections is as we have stated. <small>Effect of statutory definition of bribery.</small>

It will be observed that to constitute the full offence of bribery, it is not necessary that the person bribed should actually have received anything. "Every person who <small>Bribery, though nothing received.</small>

shall " . . . . merely "*agree to give*," &c., or even "*offer*, *promise*," &c., is guilty of bribery. Nor is it even necessary that the person to whom the offer is made should accept the promise, or be in any way influenced by the corrupt overture.

<small>Motive of the briber the test.</small> "When bribery is alleged," said Martin, B., in the *Westminster Case* (20 L.T., n.s., 238; 1 O'M. & H., 89), "the question is as *to the motive of the briber* and not as to the effect on the bribed. It is whether the alleged briber intended to influence or induce the vote, not whether the vote was actually influenced." Therefore, to adopt the illustration used by Willes, J., in the *Blackburn Case* (1 O'M. & H., 202; 20 L.T., n.s., 826), if a voter is bribed with half-a-crown and he accepts the bribe and then goes and votes *against* the party from which he received it, still the corrupt act of giving the money (or promising it) will defeat the whole election. So it has been held that giving, or offering to give, a bribe to a person who was on the register, but who, owing to a disqualification arising from non-residence, was not (as the law then stood) entitled to vote, and did not vote, is none the less bribery (*Guildford Case*, 1 O'M. & H., 15; 19 L.T., n.s., 729).

<small>Stronger evidence requisite when offer only.</small> It should be noted that, in one or two cases learned judges have pointed out that where the bribery charged is that of corrupt *offers* merely, the evidence required to prove it should be stronger than where money actually passed. (*Cheltenham Case*, 1 O'M. & H., 64; *Mallow Case*, 2 O'M. & H., 22.) This, however, is only a suggestion as to the light in which evidence, on a subject where misunderstanding is so possible, should be viewed, and it must not be taken as in any way infringing upon the well-established law that where the fact of a corrupt *offer* is once established, the consequence <small>But offer may be bribery.</small> is the loss of the seat. The *Kidderminster Case* (2 O'M. & H., 170) affords a good illustration of a corrupt offer amounting to bribery, though the persons to whom it was made received nothing under it. There the respondent the night *before* the election, in the course of a speech, said: "When we have won the election we will have an entertainment together." He repeated this *after* the election, and in pursuance of his

promise sent down a large sum of money to be spent in organising a *fête*. The entertainment was not, in fact, held, but Mellor, J., decided that the corrupt promise made on the night before the polling constituted bribery, and the respondent was unseated.

It is not necessary that the bribe should be made *directly* to the voter or to the person sought to be bribed. The words of the section are : " Every person who shall . . . . give . . . . to or for any voter or to or for any person on behalf of any voter, *or to or for any other person in order to induce any voter to vote or refrain from voting,*" shall be guilty of bribery. If, though it be given or made to some third person, the Court is satisfied that through such third person it is intended that the voter shall be influenced by it, that is enough ; as where colourable payments are made to the children of voters for fancied services in order that their parents may be induced to vote in a particular way or to refrain from voting. Willes, J., in the *Southampton Case* (1 O'M. & H., 223), referred to such a case and drew this distinction. If payments are made to young children forming part of a family in respect of services really rendered by them, the payments are to be regarded as made to their parents, and if the latter vote at the election, their votes must come off on a scrutiny. But if payments are made to young children who have rendered no services, or merely nominal services, with the view of influencing their parents who are voters, that will be bribery which will affect the seat. No doubt the latter proposition is as sound now as when the learned judge laid it down some years ago ; but with regard to the first it must be remarked that s. 17 of the Act of 1883, makes it an illegal practice involving the loss of the seat, when committed by the candidate *or his election agent*, to employ for payment any persons over and above the limited number specified in the Schedule. The Act of 1884 attaches a similar penalty to the payment of more than a limited number of persons in connection with a municipal election, with this difference that the seat is only forfeited when it is shown that the payment was made with the knowledge or

Parliamentary & Municipal.

Bribe need not be given directly.

Payments to children may be bribes to their parents.

consent of the sitting member. The prohibitions contained in these Acts against the employment of paid agents at elections are general in their terms, and would seem to include children and to affect the election when they are employed in excess of the number allowed.

In the *Stepney Case* (4 O'M. & H., 38), decided after the new legislation, it was held in accordance with the *Southampton Case* (*supra*) that, upon a scrutiny, the vote of a voter whose children had been employed and paid as messengers must be disallowed; but there was no suggestion that the total number of messengers employed was in excess of the legal limit and no opinion was given upon the point above discussed.

In another case it was laid down that treating (and *à fortiori* bribing) women with a view of influencing their husbands, brothers or sweethearts, who were voters, would avoid the election (per Willes, J., in the *Tamworth Case*, 1 O'M. & H., 86; the *Poole Case*, 31 L.T., n.s. 171).

The *amount* of the bribe is of no importance when the fact that it was given as a bribe is established. It is strange that there was once some doubt on this point. Martin, B., intimated in the *Salford Case* (1 O'M. & H., 142; 20 L.T., n.s. 127) that when the sum spent in bribery did not exceed half-a-crown and it was not brought home to the candidate *personally*, that such bribery would not be sufficient to forfeit the seat. The doubt which has arisen on the subject and crept into some works of authority is entirely founded upon this *dictum*, which, however, was *obiter*, as his lordship found the particular bribes suggested had not in fact been proved. On the other hand Willes, J., in the *Blackburn Case* (1 O'M. & H., 202; 20 L.T., 823), distinctly stated that in his view a bribe of half-a-crown given to a voter, though it did not in fact influence his vote, would upset the election. Channell, B., in the *Shrewsbury Case* (2 O'M & H., 37), said that he agreed with Willes, J., rather than with Martin, B., and that in his opinion, when once the act of bribery is made out, the Court cannot consider whether it is significant in amount or insignificant. And in the

Norwich Case (2 O'M. & H., 41), Keating, J., decided that a single act of bribery without reference to the sum given, avoided the election. Taking the plain words of the Act of 1854, which defines bribery as the giving, &c., of *any money or valuable consideration*, and the current of authorities quoted above, it cannot be doubted that the law now is that if the sitting member or his agent has given a bribe, no matter how small the sum or comparatively valueless the thing, the election is defeated. This inference is the stronger since the passing of the Acts of 1883 and 1884, as it must be carefully noted that the 22nd section in the one case and the 19th in the other, which under very stringent conditions, relieve a candidate from the consequences of an agent's misconduct where the same is of a "trivial, unimportant and limited character," apply only to cases of treating, undue influence and illegal practices, and have no application to a case of bribery. <small>PARLIAMENTARY & MUNICIPAL.</small>

The above view, expressed in the earlier editions of this work, has been entirely confirmed by the *Norwich Case* (54 L.T., n.s. 625). There the Court (Denman and Cave, JJ.) held that a single act of bribery—the amount given was only 2s.—brought home to an agent of the successful candidate avoided the election, and they held further that there was no power to grant relief under section 22 of the Act of 1883.

With regard to the time at which the bribery is committed, it is immaterial how long *before* the election the bribe is given, provided it was given with a view to the election petitioned against, or to an election of which it is the continuance. The law on this point was stated emphatically and clearly in the *Sligo Case* (1 O'M. & H., 302): Any act committed previous to an election, no matter at what distance of time, *with a view to influence a voter at a coming election*, whether it is one, two or three years before, is just as much bribery as if it was committed the day before the election; nay more, if a man commits bribery in the first week of a Parliament, and if he sues for the suffrages of that constituency in the last week of the seven years which precede <small>Time when bribe given.</small> <small>Immaterial how long before.</small>

PARLIAMENTARY & MUNICIPAL. the dissolution, that act committed six years before can be given in evidence against him, and his seat will not hold an hour." So, to adopt the case put by Bramwell, B., in the *Stroud Case* (2 O'M. & H., 183), suppose "the respondent had said to a voter, 'Here is £5 for you if you will promise to vote for me when I am a candidate'—if he does not come forward for the next ten years, his act will still be bribery within the Act of Parliament," and an election held many years after the corrupt practice might be invalidated by it. The same learned judge, in the *Windsor Case* (31 L.T., n.s. 136), suggested a limitation to the generality of this rule—viz., that a bribe given a long time before the election only invalidates the subsequent election if it is *possible* that it may still be operating on the mind of the voter. Therefore in the cases put by his lordship, where (1) a bribe is given to a voter and he dies before the election : or (2), where a bribe is given but before the election both the briber and the voter repent and the money is returned, he stated the election would not be avoided ; but having regard to the stringency of ss. 4 and 5 of the Act of 1883, which, without any qualification whatever, incapacitate a person from sitting in Parliament for a term specified therein who has been guilty of any corrupt practice in reference to an election, it is doubtful whether in the cases put the seat would now be safe.

Suggested limitation.

Effect of bribe given *after* election. When something is given to a voter *after* he has voted, it must be noted that in the words of the Act the giving of the thing is only bribery where it is given "corruptly." The distinction which has been drawn is this : Where money or money's worth is given to a voter before he votes in order to induce him to do so, the law infers the corrupt act, which is the material element in bribery ; but where money or money's worth is given to a man after he has voted the burden of proving a corrupt arrangement or understanding between him and the candidate or his agent prior to the voting is thrown upon those suggesting bribery. " If money is given to a man before an election to induce him to vote or refrain from voting, it is *ipso facto* bribery, and has the effect of disqualifying the candidate from being elected ; but if the money is given after the man has voted it must be shown to have been given corruptly." (Martin, B., in the second *Bradford Case*, 19 L.T., n.s. 723; *Brecon Case*, 2 O'M. & H., 44.) It may well be doubted, however, whether in the practical conclusion to be drawn from the giving of money to a voter immediately after an election there is much distinction between such a case and the case where it is given before. Possibly the fact of the gift in the former case may be explained consistently with the honesty of the giver; but apart from some satisfactory explanation, the mere circumstance that a voter received money or money's worth for voting would afford a very strong presumption that he received it in fulfilment of a corrupt bargain. In the case suggested by Bramwell, B., in the *Stroud Case* (2 O'M. & H., 184), the inference of a corrupt arrangement would not be drawn. "For instance," said his lordship, "such a thing as this might happen, if a man voted and got turned out of his situation and went to anybody for charity, and a man said, 'I am sorry for you, here is a sovereign,'" that would not be a corrupt payment, though it might be said to have been given on account of the man having voted a particular way. Nevertheless, in almost every case where a payment is made in consequence of a voter having voted, it would be a corrupt giving, unless some reason, such as I have suggested, could be given."

<small>Parliamentary & Municipal.</small>

<small>Little practical difference.</small>

Again, with reference to the time at which the bribe is given, an election may be invalidated by acts of bribery proved to have been committed upon the occasion of *another*, and even *different kind* of, election to that under investigation. Thus a parliamentary election may be upset by bribery at a municipal election, and it is presumed the converse case will equally hold. The test is—Was the bribe, though given at the municipal election and nominally with reference to it, really intended to influence the parliamentary election?

<small>Effect of bribery at municipal election.</small>

In the *Beverley Case* (1 O'M. & H., 143; 20 L.T, n.s. 792) there was little or no bribery suggested at the parliamentary election, but the case for the petitioners was that a

<small>The *Beverley Case*.</small>

PARLIAMENTARY & MUNICIPAL.

wholesale system of corruption prevailed at the municipal election, held a fortnight before the parliamentary election. It was proved that bribery at municipal elections in Beverley was so common and notorious that the price which votes brought upon such occasions was well known. The ordinary bribe was 5s. a vote, and the sum usually spent at a municipal election in corruption was £130. At the election in question, however, it was shown (1) that sums three or four times in excess of the ordinary bribes were paid to each voter; (2) that about £800 was disbursed in this way; (3) that nearly 1,000 persons were bribed; and (4) that after the municipal elections were practically decided, the respondent's agents went on bribing as extensively as before. The learned judge held, that though these bribes were nominally given with reference to the municipal election, they were really intended to influence the parliamentary election, which was known to be imminent, and indeed was held in a fortnight, and he unseated the sitting members accordingly. In this case the facts were clear, and the whole proceeding most flagrant and gross.

It is necessary, however, to connect the two elections—the municipal and parliamentary—together, and to show that though nominally they are two contests, in fact they are regarded by the parties bribing as one. And in the *Southampton Case* (1 O'M. & H., 226), and the *Hastings Case* (1 O'M. & H., 217; 21 L.T., n.s. 234), where the evidence

Must be connection between municipal and parliamentary election.

failed on this point, bribery at a municipal election which preceded the parliamentary by a very short while, was held not to affect the validity of the latter. "These elections" said Willes, J., in the former case, "are *primâ facie* distinct: there is no necessary connection between them, and it is not enough to show misconduct with reference to the municipal election *without connecting that election in some way with the parliamentary election*. There have been cases in which it was clear that the municipal and the parliamentary election were part of one political contest, and that corrupt action at the municipal election either was intended expressly to operate upon parliamentary elections, or that the necessary result of what was done at the municipal election was to affect the parliamentary election ; where, upon the principle being applied that persons must contemplate the natural consequences of their acts, an intention to affect the parliamentary election ought to be attributed both to people who were shown to have misconducted themselves with reference to the municipal election, and to agents of the members who have been guilty of corrupt practices in the course of the municipal election, but with a view to the effect of such practices upon the parliamentary election. In such cases the judges have held that the two elections were, under the circumstances, really parts of one and the same political contest, and that the members in the parliamentary contests were bound by the acts of their agents in the course of the municipal contest."

The principle that where two elections are so connected as really to form part of a single contest, bribery at the one is bribery at the other has been applied to the case of corrupt practices at a test ballot *preceding the formal election. The point arose and was decided in the* Bristol Case *(2 O'M. & H. 2), reported as* Brett v. Robinson *in the Common Pleas, (L.R. 5, C.P. 503 ; 39 L.J. C.P., 265 : 23 L.T., n.s. 188, 18 W.R., 866). The facts were that there being a vacancy in the representation of the city of Bristol, three Liberal candidates offered themselves. To avoid a split in the Party they agreed that there should be a test ballot to determine who should stand at the election as the candidate of the whole Party. Mr. Robinson, one of the three, was at the head of the test ballot, stood at the election, and was returned to Parliament ; but it appeared, on petition, that his agents had given money to voters to vote for him at the test ballot, without, however, making any stipulation as to their votes at the election. It was held by the Court of Common Pleas, upon a case reserved, that the corrupt acts at the test ballot were calculated to have so immediate an influence upon the election held immediately afterwards, that they destroyed the validity of the latter.*

It is conceived that the principle of this decision will fully

_{PARLIAMENTARY}
_{& MUNICIPAL.}

The *Southampton Case*

Bribery at a test ballot.

16 THE LAW RELATING TO

Parliamentary & Municipal. cover the case of bribes given to members of a Committee of Selection or other persons to secure the adoption of a person as the candidate of a Party at a particular election—at least where the Party is the dominant party in the Constituency.

Bribery at previous parliamentary election. So bribery at one parliamentary election may be fatal to the return at another; but this is only where the two elections are connected, and form part of one contest in the sense that the seat was not filled by a good return at the first election, which thus has become abortive, and the second contest is held to supplement and complete it, and fill the original vacancy. This principle was fully acted upon in the *Norwich Case* (reported as *Stevens* v. *Tillett* in the Common Pleas, L.R. 6, C.P. 147; 40 L.J., C.P. 58), where the facts were that the respondent Tillett was a candidate for Norwich at the General Election of 1868, and was defeated. His successful opponent was unseated upon petition, and for the vacancy thus created the respondent became a candidate and was elected. A petition was filed against his return, and the bribery relied on was bribery committed at the election of 1868. It was held by the Court that inasmuch as the contests were for the same seat, which had never been filled by a good return, they were so connected that bribery at the one was in law bribery at the other. See also the three *Stroud Cases* (2 O'M. & H., pp. 107, 179, and 181.)

The form of the bribe immaterial. The *form* in which the bribe is given is immaterial. If, though the money is given under the name of a payment for services rendered, it is really a reward for voting, the offence is proved. The Court will look at the substance of the transaction, and not allow itself to be hoodwinked by a mere name. One common way in which the law against bribery has been sought to be evaded has been by payments made to voters for services alleged to have been rendered in connection with the election, as where the voters or the relatives of voters have been appointed canvassers, messengers, watchers, clerks, and so forth, and paid at a rate generally in excess of the remuneration ordinarily given to persons in their station. From the earliest times the law

Paying voters for services may be bribery.

has been that this "colourable" employment of voters with the view of paying them for their votes was bribery.

A leading case on this subject is the *Boston Case* (44 L.T., n.s. 288; 3 O'M. & H., 153). There the acts of bribery complained of in the petition consisted mainly of the employment on the polling day of a large number of persons to act as watchers, the bulk of whom were voters. They were paid at rates varying from 10s. to 2s. 6d. a day, and there appear to have been about 300 or 400 of them. The Court was of opinion, on the facts, that the object in employing all these persons was not to obtain *bonâ fide* services from them but to influence their votes, and the sitting member was unseated accordingly. The judgment, which was given by Lush, J., with the concurrence of the other judge (Mr. Justice Manisty), is worth a perusal as well for the review of the authorities it contains as for the clear and emphatic language in which the law on the subject is expressed. "In view of all these circumstances, can we come to any other conclusion than that the employment of this large body of voters was a colourable employment and a pretext for finding them a day's wages in order to induce them to vote? It is immaterial whether the object was to gain over voters from the other side or to prevent them going over to that side. The Act forbids and makes penal any attempt to influence a vote by such means. We need hardly say that it is no answer to a charge of violating the Bribery Act in this way, that it is a common practice, or that it was resorted to in self-defence and as a means of counteracting illegal practices on the other side. Sitting here in a court of justice we cannot accept such a plea. We have reason to fear that the practice is too common, notwithstanding the warnings which have been given in previous decisions. In 1869, Blackburn, J., reported the employment of voters as watchers, who rendered no service of any value, as a corrupt practice. In the same year, in the *Tamworth Case*, Willes, J., had to consider a case where the agent had been authorised to engage a few men, none of whom were to be voters, whereas the man on

THE LAW RELATING TO

Parliamentary & Municipal. the polling day engaged 130, of whom 29 only were voters. He came to the conclusion that the agent employed them, not to advance the interests of his employer, but to gain popularity for himself; but he emphatically said, that if he had arrived at the conclusion that the object was to engage one voter to vote for his employer, who would otherwise have voted for his opponent, he should have declared the election void. In 1874, Bramwell, B., deprecated the practice as shown in the *Durham Case*, and warned future candidates of the danger they incurred by following such a practice. And in 1875 I had to declare in the *Norwich Case* that the election was void, solely on the ground of the colourable employment of voters as messengers on the polling day." (See also the *Oxford Case*, 3 O'M. & H., 154.)

In the *Ipswich Case* (4 O'M. & H., 72; 54 L.T., N.S., 620) it was proved that a number of men were employed and paid to keep order at meetings. It was not necessary to decide whether the payments made to them were colourable bribes, because the Court held that their employment was illegal under the Act of 1883, and further that payments made to them were election expenses, which ought to have been returned, and upon that and a number of other grounds the election was declared void.

Payment of voters not necessarily bribery. On the other hand, the *mere* employment and payment of a considerable number of voters in connection with an election, when there was *bonâ fide* work for them to do, and they were not paid substantially in excess of the ordinary remuneration, did not, *prior to the Act of 1883*, invalidate the election. (The *Salisbury Case*, 4 O'M. & H., 23). Nor is it now a *corrupt practice*, defeating the election, when committed by any agent, though as will be seen later on (except under certain strict limitations), it is an illegal employment, avoiding the election, when committed by the candidate or his *election agent* in the case of a parliamentary election (*Ipswich Case supra*), and in the case of a municipal election when committed by the candidate *personally*.

Law prior to Act of 1883. Prior to the new legislation, the law was this: If persons were colourably employed and paid for work they never did,

CORRUPT PRACTICES AT ELECTIONS. 19

in order to influence their votes, this was bribery, and if done PARLIAMENTARY
& MUNICIPAL. by any agent of the candidate, the election was defeated. But if persons were *bonâ fide* paid for work they really did, it was not bribery, though inasmuch, as by the 30 & 31 Vict., c. 102, s. 11, voters who have received any payment in connection with the election, are disqualified from voting, on a scrutiny, their votes were struck off. As the law now stands it is conceived that the colourable employment and payment of voters to secure their votes, is as much bribery as ever, and when it is committed by *any* agent, the seat is lost. On the other hand, when the employment and payment of voters is *bonâ fide*, and when they are not employed by the candidate *himself or with his knowledge, or by his* Law on this
point now. *election agent*, though the votes given must come off on a scrutiny, and though the persons employing and the persons knowingly employed, are liable to certain penalties mentioned later on, it is submitted the seat will not be affected.

But though this is so, it must be borne in mind that under the Acts of 1883 and 1884, to employ and pay any voters except the very limited number authorised by the express terms of these Acts, is an illegal employment. The punishment to the individual convicted of an illegal employment is the same, whether the election at which the offence was committed was a parliamentary or a municipal election; but the effect on the election varies. In the case of a parliamentary election an illegal employment, when committed by a candidate, *or his election agent*, becomes an illegal practice, and vitiates the election. In the case of a municipal election an illegal employment only becomes an illegal practice when committed by or with the knowledge of the candidate *personally*, and it is only, therefore, in such an event that the seat is lost. The way in which the law The present
law illus-
trated. will now operate may be illustrated thus: Case I. A is an agent of the sitting member at the election (though not his election agent). He *bonâ fide* employs B, who is a voter, and pays him for work he really performs. The election, whether parliamentary or municipal, is not defeated; though on a scrutiny, B's vote must come off, and both A and B are liable to punishment. Case II. A is an agent of the sitting member at the election (though not his election agent). He pays B a sum of money under the name of wages, but really to get his vote. This is bribery, and any election is vitiated. Case III. A is the election agent of the candidate at a parliamentary election. He *bonâ fide* (but in excess of the proper number) employs B, who is a voter, and pays him for services he really rendered. This is an illegal practice, and the election is defeated. Case IV. A is an agent of the sitting member at a municipal election. He *bonâ fide* (but in excess of the proper number) employs B, who is a voter, and pays him for services rendered in connection with the election. This is an illegal employment, rendering A and B liable to punishment; but unless it is proved that the offence was committed with the knowledge and consent of the sitting member, the seat is not affected.

Other instances of bribery, cloaked under the pretence of payment, are payments of excessive prices for things bought, and the hiring of rooms which are not wanted, with a view of influencing the votes of the persons who receive the money. Thus, in the *Westminster Case* (1 O'M. & H, 90 ; 20 L.T., n.s. 238) it was suggested that the respondent through his agents had paid unusual sums for the right of placarding, in order to secure the votes of the persons paid. The Judge was not satisfied that the charge was made out, but he stated emphatically that if it were proved that money had been paid with such an object, it would be bribery. So, where cabs are colourably hired for the purpose of procuring the votes of their owners (the *Carrickfergus Case*, 3 O'M. & H., 91); or as in the *Sandwich Case* (3 O'M. & H., 158) where a large number of rooms were hired in public-houses with a view of securing the vote and interest of the innkeepers, the offence of bribery is made out. "There is no difference," said Lush, J., in the last case, " in substance between a colourable hiring of the voter's room as a committee room and the colourable hiring of the voter himself as a messenger. The object in each case is to secure his vote. The only difference between the two cases is the form of

CORRUPT PRACTICES AT ELECTIONS. 21

the disguise." It should be mentioned that the three cases last given are all specially dealt with by the Acts of 1883 and 1884. The hiring of windows and boards from electors, payments for cabs in connection with the conveyance of voters to and from the poll, and the hiring of committee rooms in excess of the limit allowed, are now illegal practices (s. 7 of the Act of 1883, and s. 4 of the Act of 1884), which avoid the election if committed by any agent. Parliamentary & Municipal.

Analogous to bribery under the colour of paying wages for work done, or the price of goods supplied, is bribery under the pretence of compensating a voter for loss of time or for travelling expenses. It has always been held that promising to pay a voter his day's wages, so that he may be no loser by coming to vote, is an act of bribery (the *Staleybridge Case*, 20 L.T., n.s., 75; 1 O'M. & H., 67; *Hastings Case*, 1 O'M. & H., 219; 21 L.T., n.s., 234). "It is clear that as the law is framed, and as the statute is worded, to pay a person for coming to vote, giving him his day's wages or making up to him his loss of time for the purpose of voting at an election, would be a bribe. The words of the Act are clear beyond all question on this point." (Per Blackburn, J., in *Hastings Case*, quoted *supra*.) So it is bribery to promise a voter that he will be "remunerated for any loss of time" (*Simpson* v. *Yeend*, L.R. 4 Q.B 626). Equally the payment of a substitute to do the voter's work while he is away voting is bribery. (The *Plymouth Case*, 3 O'M. & H., 107.) *Bribery to compensate voter for loss of time.*

Or pay for a substitute.

So with regard to travelling expenses, to promise to pay a voter his travelling expenses if he comes and votes for a particular candidate is bribery. This was decided in the case of *Cooper* v. *Slade*. (6 H.L.C. 747; 27 L.J. Q.B., 442; 4 Jur., n.s., 791.) The action was brought to recover penalties from the defendant, who had been a candidate at the Cambridge election; and the question which came before the Lords for decision was whether a letter written to an outvoter requesting him to come to the borough and record his vote, and adding in a postcript "your railway expenses will be paid," was an act of bribery. The House *Bribery to promise to pay travelling expenses.*

PARLIAMENTARY & MUNICIPAL. of Lords, after consulting the judges, held that such a promise amounted to bribery.

In the *Coventry Case* (1 O'M. & H., 109; 20 L.T., n.s., 405), *Dublin Case* (1 O'M. & H., 273), the *Horsham Case* (3 O'M. & H., 54), and still more lately and since the new legislation, the *Ipswich Case* (54 L.T., n.s. 620), this view of the law was acted upon; and there can be no doubt that a promise to pay the *bare* travelling expenses of a voter if he will come and give his vote is an act of bribery. But when a circular was sent to an outvoter asking him to come over and record his vote and enclosing a railway pass, but annexing no condition to its use, it was held that this did not come within the doctrine of *Cooper* v. *Slade*, and though (as the law then stood with regard to borough elections) it was an illegal act, it was not bribery (the *Bolton Case*, 31 L.T., n.s. 194;

But unconditional payment is not bribery.
2 O'M. & H, 138). In giving his decision the learned judge (Mellor, J.) carefully distinguished the case before him from *Cooper* v. *Slade*. In the latter he pointed out the travelling expenses were promised conditionally upon the voter voting for Mr. Slade. In the case before him, the railway pass was sent and received by the voter without any condition. All control over the pass was gone after it left the office of the respondent's agent, and the voter if he liked could avail himself of it without being under any compulsion to vote for the respondent.

Now all payments for travelling expenses illegal.
However, the *Bolton Case* (*supra*) has now ceased to be of much practical importance on the question of the safety of the seat. No doubt the ruling of the learned judge in that case is still law to the extent that merely sending a railway pass to a voter, or giving him his bare travelling expenses *unconditionally*, will be held to fall short of a corrupt practice; but, as we have already stated, s. 7 of the Act of 1883, and s. 4 of the Act of 1884, make the payment of any money on account of the "conveyance of electors to or from the poll" an illegal practice, which if committed by a candidate, or *any one of his agents*, will avoid either a parliamentary or a municipal election. (The *Ipswich Case*, 54 L.T., n.s., 620.)

We have seen that paying a voter for his loss of time in *Parliamentary & Municipal.* attending to vote is bribery. On the other hand, paying him for his loss of time in attending at the Registration Court to claim and support his vote is not *necessarily* bribery. It may or may not be so according to the time when, and the circumstances under which the money was paid, and the amount paid. The *Taunton Case* (1 O'M. & H., 353; 21 L.T., n.s., 129, where Blackburn, J., decided that payments in respect of loss of time at the Registration Court *did* amount to bribery, and the *Hastings Case* (1 O'M. & H. 219; 21 L.T., n.s., 234), where the same learned judge held that such payments *did not* establish bribery, may profitably be examined in this connection. In the *Taunton Case* it was proved that the Registration Court was held in September. The election came off in November. The payments were not made till November and upon the eve of the election, and they were made without any precautions being taken that persons who had really attended the Registration Court alone got it. Under these circumstances, it was held that the money was not paid *bonâ fide* to recoup the recipients for their loss of time at the registration, but to influence their votes at the election. *When payments for attending Revision Court bribery.*

"It may well be," said the learned judge, "that there may be a payment for an attendance at the Barrister's Court, which should be *bonâ fide* for that purpose, and no other, and which is not meant by the Act of Parliament. From the fact of paying a person money for attending to be put upon the register, it is a matter of inference that doubtless the persons who put the voter on the register expected him to vote for their party. No doubt that would be in their minds at the time. Doubtless, if you were to pay a man direct for being put upon the register, and to offer a reward for every person who would himself come and be registered by the Conservative Association or the Liberal Association, as the case might be, it would not be as a matter of law that would be a bribe for a vote; but it would be a matter of very strong observation, and there would be reasonable grounds for inferring that those who paid people *The Taunton Case.*

PARLIAMENTARY & MUNICIPAL.

The test is whether payment is really made for loss of time at Revision Court.

Or was intended to influence vote at election.

The *Hastings Case.*

belonging to any particular political party for coming and being put upon the register did expect, as part of what they were paying for, that they were to vote for that party when the election came. It would be a matter of fact, not of law, but the inference would be strong. When it is merely repaying them what might be called money out of pocket, the loss of a day's work, the inference is by no means so strong. It might be so, or it might not be. In each case it would be a matter of inference looking at the facts, and a very important fact would be whether or not an election was pending or close approaching. It would require looking at that to see whether it was really paid to induce the votes, or whether it was really and *bonâ fide* a repayment for money out of pocket. I certainly think it would be a wise thing on the part of all people to avoid making such payments at any time, because, certainly it is always open to the observation and inference that it may be for the corrupt practice of inducing the vote, and may, therefore, be considered bribery. In the present case, however, we have to go a great deal further than that. *I think, where it was bonâ fide, it would not be a bribe; where it was intended to induce a vote, which would be a matter to be collected from the whole of the facts, it would be a bribe."*

On the other hand, in the *Hastings Case* (quoted *supra*), the payments were made at the time of the registration, they did not exceed the sums the voters were out of pocket, and some precautions were taken that only persons entitled got the money. The learned judge held that in this case the payments did not amount to bribes, pointing out that the important elements in determining whether the money was a payment for the vote were (1st), whether the payments were really and truly made contemporaneously with the registration; and (2ndly), whether they were honestly intended to be merely a remuneration for what the man was out of pocket, so that he should not be a loser, or whether the intention was that he should make a profit. Although his lordship decided that the payments in that case fell short of bribes, yet, in concluding his judgment, he said that payments made for a registration, *especially when the registration is coming closely before an election*, were suspicious things, and a very little additional evidence in such a case as that before him, would lead him to the conclusion that the intention of the payment was to influence the election.

While on the subject of the payment of registration expenses, it is well to recall that by the express words of the 30 & 31 Vict., c. 102, s. 49, corruptly paying any rate on behalf of a ratepayer for the purpose of enabling him to be registered as a voter, and for the purpose of influencing his vote at any future election is bribery. The mere fact of paying the ratepayer's rates is not enough to constitute the offence. It must be proved that it was done to influence his vote (the *Cheltenham Case*, 1 O'M. & H., 64), though, apart from any evidence of a direct arrangement, the court will, when the surrounding circumstances point to it, infer the corrupt intention with which the thing was done. In the *Oldham Case* (1 O'M. & H., 165), it was proved that an alleged agent paid a voter's rates in order that he should get him on to the register; but it was also proved as a fact that there was no arrangement or understanding as to how he was to vote. The learned judge held upon the particular facts of the case that this payment of rates was not corrupt. Payments made to a freeman, or on his behalf, to enable him to take up his freedom, and so be placed upon the register, do not come within the provisions of the 30 & 31 Vict., c. 102, s. 49 ; and, therefore, whether or no such payments amount to bribery will turn upon the question of the existence of any arrangement or understanding as to the vote.

Giving workmen a holiday on the polling day, and paying them as if they had worked, *may be* an act of bribery. In the *Gravesend Case* (3 O'M. & H., 84 ; 44 L.T., n.s., 64) it was held to amount to bribery. In the *Stroud Case* (2 O'M. & H., 181) it was held to fall short of it. In the former it was proved that on the day *before the polling* a communication was made to all the workmen in the respondent's employment that they would have a holiday on the next day, but that they would be paid as usual, and that they

Parliamentary & Municipal.

Corrupt payment of rates is bribery.

Giving a holiday may be bribery.

Gravesend Case.

must come the next morning and give in their time. It was also proved that on the occasion of previous elections a holiday had been given to the respondent's men, *but no payment was made to them in respect of that day.* In giving judgment, Denman, J., said : " It was contended that Weeks (the respondent's agent) made the above-mentioned communication to the men with the intention of influencing their votes. It was urged on the other side that it was a mere act of benevolence or justice, and had no connection with the pending election. We cannot adopt this latter view. We think it beyond all question that Weeks had the election in view when he made his communication to the men on the night preceding the polling day, and intended it to influence the votes of all who might be doubtful." On the other hand, in the *Stroud Case* (quoted *supra*), it was also proved that the men at certain mills belonging to the respondent's agents received a holiday on the polling day, and were paid for that day ; but, unlike the *Gravesend Case*, there was no evidence that *previous* to the polling day they were promised their wages. It was argued for the petitioners that there was an implied promise, inasmuch as at an election held three months before the men also had a holiday, and afterwards got their wages ; but Bramwell, B., held that a single instance of prior payment did not warrant the inference that payment would be made a second time, and he declined to hold that the act of paying the wages after the election, disconnected from any promise made before, was bribery.

Since the above decisions, the 48 & 49 Vict., c. 56, has been passed, which in s. 1 enacts as follows :—" Nothing in the law relating to parliamentary elections shall make it illegal for an employer to permit parliamentary electors in his employment to absent themselves from such employment for a reasonable time for the purpose of voting at the poll at a parliamentary election, without having any deduction from their salaries or wages on account of such absence, if such permission is, so far as practicable, without injury to such business of the employer, given equally to all persons alike, who are at the time in his employment, and if such permission is not given with a view of inducing any person to record his vote for any particular candidate at such election, and is not refused to any person for the purpose of preventing such person from recording his vote for any particular candidate at such election."   *Parliamentary & Municipal.*

The conditions under which it is safe to grant a holiday to voters to record their votes would seem to be: (1) that the time allowed is reasonable; (2) that the holiday is given equally; and (3) that it is not given with a view of inducing the voter to vote in any particular way. (See the *Aylesbury Case*, 4 O'M. & H., 59.)

The principle of the *Gravesend Case* seems to be that a promise of some advantage to an elector, made with a view of influencing his vote, is bribery, though it is not proved that any express condition is annexed to the fulfilment of the promise. And in full accordance with this principle is the decision in the *Launceston Case* (2 O'M. & H., 129; 30 L.T., n.s. 823). There it was proved that the respondent was a large landowner in the borough. During the progress of the contest some clamour was raised with reference to his preservation of the rabbits on his estate. A night or two before the polling the respondent, addressing a public meeting, said: "I give authority for you, everyone of you, to kill every rabbit upon my estate; kill them, ferret them, shoot them, trap them, do whatever you like, send them to market." At other meetings the respondent and his agent used similar language, and they took special measures to secure the wide circulation of a local paper containing the public declaration of the respondent's views on this subject. Mellor, J., who tried the case, decided that this was an offer of a "valuable consideration" within the statutes, and that an act of bribery had been committed by the respondent personally. His lordship drew the distinction between the case where the motive for the act was the *bonâ fide* desire of a landlord to give his tenants a privilege, and where the object was to influence the election, as he believed was the object in the case before him.   *Promising an advantage bribery, though no condition annexed.*   *Launceston Case.*

PARLIAMENTARY & MUNICIPAL.

A promise to give an office bribery.

Bribery is not limited to the giving or lending of money or some valuable thing. It is, by the clear words of the statute, equally bribery to give or promise or to agree to endeavour to procure any office, place or employment, as an inducement to an elector to vote or refrain from voting. In the *Waterford Case* (2 O'M. & H., 25), it was held that an offer made by an agent of the respondent to vacate a seat in the town council in favour of a certain person if he would vote for the respondent was a bribe within the meaning of the Act. But to give a man *bonâ fide* employment unconnected with the election is not bribery, merely because the man happens to be a voter. "A man is not bound to refuse to take into his service a man of his way of thinking if he is going to set up for the borough. He must not do that as a reward for the vote he hopes to obtain, and he must not make the vote a condition of employment. But the employment of persons to do work must go on in election times as well as in others; the affairs of life cannot be brought to a standstill." (*Per* Willes, J., in the *Penryn Case*, 1 O'M. & H., 128.) But, of course, paid employment *at an* election is a different thing, and, except to a very limited extent, it is now entirely prohibited by the Acts of 1883 and 1884.

A question of practical importance is: To what extent does a candidate bring himself within the law against bribery by lavish expenditure or hospitality in his constituency, by subscriptions to institutions and public charities and political party objects, by charitable benefactions to individuals and classes of persons connected with the constituency.

The effect of a candidate's expenditure in the constituency.

Profusion *at* an election is now under the ban of the Legislature. The expenditure of a candidate in connection with the election—*i.e.*, with the conduct and management of the election—is circumscribed within the narrowest bounds, and any excess beyond the limit is fatal. But there is no statutory limit imposed upon his general expenditure in the constituency during the interval between elections. His liability for such expenditure remains to-day very much as it was prior to the new law. It is true there is increased punishment if he transgresses, but recent legislation has in no way widened and enlarged the definition of the particular offence of bribery now under consideration. And a candidate can lawfully spend as much as he likes in his constituency before the election provided such expenditure is not made under circumstances amounting to bribery or treating, and provided also that it is not of such a character and made at such a time as to lead the Court to regard it as an election expense. It is impossible to prevent wealth having a considerable weight in the determination of elections. A man may use his wealth in a manner to ingratiate himself with a considerable portion of the constituency, and so powerfully influence their votes, and yet not bring himself within the law. Suppose a person of wealth to set up a great establishment in or near a constituency and spend large sums among the tradesmen in the place. In that way he will, in all probability, create an interest in his favour, which will be felt at the election. So if a man were to establish some form of industry in a town he aspired to represent which involved, in addition to the employment of the people, a considerable expenditure of money in the place. In that way again he would influence opinion in his favour; but in neither of the cases mentioned would there be any violation of the law. To put even a stronger case. Suppose a man purchased all the house property in a constituency and became the employer of all the labour, with the distinct view and object of rendering himself more acceptable and securing his return. Even in that case it is conceived there would be no breach of the law. The mere fact that a man holds a position in which it is in his power to confer great benefits upon the constituency—even though he acquired that position and keeps it in the belief that it will advantageously affect his election—matters nothing. If people are led spontaneously to support him from the desire of standing well with one who may advance their individual interests or the interests of their community, there is no violation of the law. But if directly or indirectly he approaches them and makes the distribution of his favours *dependent* upon political support, or by any act or word on

PARLIAMENTARY & MUNICIPAL. his part creates the opinion in their minds that it will be the better or the worse for them in their private affairs according as they support or oppose him, that will be evidence of bribery.

Lavish expenditure. The only case in the books upon the subject of lavish expenditure and its effect upon an election is the *Hastings Case* (1 O'M. & H., 217; 21 L.T., n.s , 234). In giving judgment Blackburn, J., said: "It was shown that Mr. and Mrs. Brassey had bills with the tradesmen and spent a very considerable sum of money in the town ; and it was said as part of the petitioner's case, that that expenditure had been increased and was the more lavish, because the election was coming on ; in short, that there was a lavish household expenditure, with a view of influencing the election with the same intention and in the same way as would, if it had been an expenditure of meat and drink to influence the election, have come within the definition of treating

Not necessarily illegal. *But there is no law yet which says that any lavish expenditure in a neighbourhood with a view of gaining influence in the neighbourhood and influencing an election is illegal at all.* In order to constitute anything that would be a corrupt practice in respect of expenditure of that sort, it must be made with a view of *influencing a particular vote*. If such an expenditure is made at a place with a tacit understanding of this kind, ' I will incur bills and spend my money with you if you will vote for me, that being not the side on which you intended to vote,' if it is intended to produce that effect upon the vote, it amounts to bribery. In the present case there is nothing to show that in either of the cases there was such an understanding or such an arrangement made. Whether or not the expenditure was more lavish than it would otherwise have been is no matter for me to enquire into, because that would not affect the election if it was made out.

The law thus laid down fourteen years ago is, it is submitted, law still. And, in a word, the result is this : There is no reason why a man who is a candidate for a constituency should not live and spend his money there. That is legal. (See the *Aylesbury Case* (4 O'M. & H., 59), which, though strictly a case of alleged treating, is in accordance with this view, and seems to cover the statement in the text.) But if he makes the spending of his money with any particular persons conditional on their voting for him, he is guilty of bribery.

Parliamentary & Municipal.

Again, a person who is a candidate may lawfully give subscriptions to institutions and charitable and other objects in his constituency, including subscriptions to political associations and clubs. On the other hand, subscriptions may unquestionably be given under circumstances which will amount to bribery. For instance, if a man gave a considerable sum, say to a burial club, on condition that all the members of the club voted for him, that would be as clear bribery as if he had distributed the sum in question among the individual members of the club upon a like condition. The common case, however, of a person subscribing to the philanthropic and public objects of a place without condition annexed to his gifts, or moderate subscriptions to political party objects (not in themselves illegal) is not struck at by the law as it now stands.

Charitable subscriptions.

There are only two reported cases where subscriptions were charged as corrupt acts. In the *Westbury Case* (1 O'M. & H., 49) it was proved that one of the candidates had sent a cheque for £10 as a subscription to a dissenting chapel almost at the same time that he issued his address. Willes, J., said: "I have myself often observed that people who mean to become candidates subscribe to things they would otherwise not have subscribed to; but I think that is a step off corrupt practices; it is charity stimulated by gratitude or hope of favours to come." So, in the *Belfast Case* (1 O'M. & H., 282; 21 L.T., n.s., 475), where it was proved that the respondent had subscribed to an Orange Lodge, although his principles were not identical with those of the lodge, Baron Fitzgerald declined to hold that this was an act of bribery.

Subscriptions.

In both these cases it is clear that the motive of the donor was not an unmixed charitable motive. He had in his mind the hope that some persons would be favourably affected towards him at the election by his liberality. But the court held that this desire to win popularity with a certain section of the constituency by evincing a sympathy with the objects they supported was a very different thing to a corrupt influence brought to bear upon individual electors in their private affairs.

So a person who is a candidate may lawfully give charitable benefactions to individuals or classes of persons in the constituency; but it is obvious that he is treading upon dangerous ground here. Acts which candidates call acts of charity, may be interpreted by an Election Court as bribes. There is no case where an election has been upset merely by reason of a candidate's lavish expenditure, or the number and amount of his subscriptions; but there are many cases where the seat has been forfeited by acts which were held to be bribes under the cloak of charity. It will be convenient here to review some of the authorities on this subject.

In the *Windsor Case* (1 O'M & H., 2; 19 L.T., n.s., 613) the respondent gave a pound to a voter who had previously promised him his vote, and who subsequently came to him in distress. Willes, J., held that upon all the facts this was not a bribe. This case must not be misunderstood. It by no means settles that giving a pound to a voter who is in distressed circumstances is necessarily an innocent act. On the contrary, unexplained, it raises a strong presumption of bribery against the person who gives the money. In the *Windsor Case* it must be assumed that the learned judge who saw and heard the parties was satisfied that the respondent acted from motives of pity merely. In this view the case is an authority for saying that a gift of money by a candidate during an election is not necessarily bribery. If, however, several benevolences of the same kind were established against the respondent, he would seem to come within the *Gravesend Case* (44 L.T., n.s., 64; 3 O'M. & H., 84), and the *Launceston Case* (2 O'M. & H., 129; 30 L.T., n.s., 823).

In the *Tamworth Case* (20 L.T., n.s., 181) it was proved that the respondent, on the night of nomination, visited one of the cottages on his property, in company with a person whose name was not known, for the purpose of canvassing the tenant. He saw the tenant's wife, who complained that she was in pain and distress and about to be confined, and that the roof of the cottage was out of repair and it was raining in. At the respondent's request his companion gave her 5s. Willes, J., held that this was not a corrupt act, but charity, natural under the circumstances. The observations we have applied to the *Windsor Case* apply to this case. It is a dangerous, but not necessarily a fatal, thing for a candidate during the contest to give money to a person who appears to be in distressed circumstances.

The *Youghal Case* (21 L.T., n.s., 307; 1 O'M. & H., 294) is a somewhat singular case. It was proved that on and immediately before the polling day, large sums of money were distributed in shillings and half-crowns to poor people in the streets of the borough. As much as £160 was so given away by one person, £130 by another, and £50 by a third. None of this money was given to voters. The learned judge unseated the respondent on other grounds, but as to this part of the case, suggested that bribery was not made out. It will be observed that this is only a *dictum*, and not a decision. It is difficult to criticise a judgment given in an abbreviated form and with only a bald summary of the facts. But the expression of opinion above cited should be accepted with great caution. It is hard to think that such a proceeding as the open distribution of money on the polling day among poor persons, though none of them may be voters would now pass with impunity.

In the *Stafford Case* (1 O'M. & H., 230; 21 L.T., n.s., 210) it was proved that at the Christmas before the election the sitting member, through his agent, distributed £720 in charity. At the corresponding period of the year before—when the election was more distant—he only distributed £300 in this way. The election was avoided on other grounds, but in giving judgment, Blackburn, J., said: "I do not for a moment mean to say that there may not be many excellent charities distributed to these amounts and more by many people, but where I find that charities are distributed in a borough, by those who are expecting to contest it as candidates, and distributed, without check, by the election agent of the borough, I am not charitable enough to draw any other conclusion than that they do it with the intention of giving the voters money in the hope and expectation that it will influence the future election. And there is the further and great danger attending it, that the knowledge that they have been doing it will cause men at the future elections to give their votes in the expectation and hope that they will hereafter receive payment. When that is brought home to any one, I think it would undoubtedly mean corruption."

Windsor Case In the second *Windsor Case* (2 O'M. & H., 89; 31 L.T., n.s., 133) *some long time* before the election, and upon the occasion of distress caused by a flood, the respondent gave away about £100 *among his tenants*, some of whom were voters and some not, and who paid him altogether about £3,000 a year in rent. This money was spent in coals, beef, and tea, and the respondent on being asked whether, when he made these gifts, he had in view the election for the borough, hesitated to say that to a certain extent he had not. Bramwell, B., held that, under the circumstances, the gifts were not corrupt. He said, " It is certain that the coming election must have been present to the respondent's mind when he gave away these things. But there is no harm in it if a man has a legitimate motive for doing a thing, although in addition to that he has a motive, which if it stood alone, would be an illegitimate one. He is not to refrain from doing that which he might legitimately have done on account of the existence of this motive, which by itself would have been an illegitimate one. If the respondent had not been an intending candidate for the borough, and yet had done as he has done in respect of these gifts, there would have been nothing illegal in what he did, and the fact that he did intend to represent Windsor, and thought good would be done to him, and that he would gain popularity by this, does not make that corrupt which otherwise would not be corrupt at all." These remarks of his lordship have given rise to a good deal of discussion, and while some judges have expressed their approval of them, others have thought they were too wide, and calculated to mislead candidates into acts which would be held corrupt. The decision itself is probably sound enough, for it is to be observed (1) That the money was given a long time before election; (2) upon a legitimate occasion; (3) it was given merely to the respondent's tenants, from whom he received a large rental, and (4) the amount was not great. *Parliamentary & Municipal*

In the *Carrickfergus Case* (3 O'M. & H., 90), Dowse, B., read the passage from the judgment of Bramwell, B., in the *Windsor Case* that we have given, and said that he quite approved of it. *Approved in Carrickfergus Case.*

The *Boston Case* (2 O'M. & H., 161), is important in this connection. There it was proved that the respondent, who lived in the neighbourhood of Boston and had been in the habit of giving largely to the local charities through the medium of other persons, and of entrusting sums of money to the clergy to distribute among the poorer classes, in the December preceding the general election of 1880 directed his agent to distribute 150 tons of coal among the poor of Boston. The person to whom the respondent entrusted the distribution of the coal had cards printed with these words on them, "Please deliver   cwts. of coal to   for Thomas Parry (the respondent), B. B. Dyer (the agent)," and on the back of the cards the words "With Mr. Parry's compliments." The cards were distributed among the electors and non-electors of Boston, and the coals were obtained upon them. Grove, J., held, that having regard to the circumstances under which the charity was conferred, there was on the part of the respondent's agent an intention to influence the votes of the recipients. His lordship said, "It has been over and over again held that an unfair and improper donation with the view, motive, and intention of securing a vote, is corrupt within the meaning of the Act of 1854. It might be a doubtful question (and it is one which was discussed in the *Windsor Case*) whether assuming two motives to exist, the one being pure and the *Boston Case. Distribution of coal on eve of election. Judgment of Mr. Justice Grove.*

other with the intention to corrupt, you could exclude the corrupt intention and rely wholly upon the pure intention. I think that must be rather a question of degree. A man may wish to be charitable in a neighbourhood, but at the same time he may have an eye to his own interests, and there must be in fact some limiting line, incapable of being defined in words, where the two things come to a nearly equal balance. We know, for instance, that persons looking forward to be candidates for Parliament are generally pretty liberal to the charities in the district, and such liberality, so far as I am aware, has never been held to vitiate the election." His lordship then proceeded to say that if it had been known that Parliament would be dissolved upon the 26th of January, and these gifts of coal had been made on the 14th of January with that knowledge, he would have had great difficulty in holding that the respondent was not personally guilty of bribery. He thought, however, that at the time the respondent did not think the election was imminent, and though his agent had carried out the dispensing of the charity in a way which showed that he meant to influence votes and the seat must be forfeited, yet he would refrain from reporting him as guilty of personal bribery.

Plymouth Case. In the *Plymouth Case* (3 O'M. & H., 107) it was proved that the respondent ever since he was returned as member had been in the habit of sending to the mayor and other persons in the borough sums of from £250 to £500 to be distributed among the poor. These gifts were usually made on occasions like that of the marriage of one of his children, and they were made in other districts with which the respondent was connected as well as Plymouth. One such distribution was made in 1874 and another in 1876. On the election being called in question, in 1880, it was argued that the gifts were merely colourable charity and were intended to influence votes. The court (Lush and Manisty, JJ.) refused to draw any such conclusion from the evidence. They said they were of opinion that the respondent was a man of large-hearted benevolence, whose disposition was to share his large means among the poor and needy of the places with which he was connected, and that in making those gifts he acted from a laudable sense of duty. But at the same time the learned judges were emphatic in pointing out that charitable gifts may be nothing more than a specious and subtle form of bribery, a pretext adopted to veil the corrupt purpose of gaining or securing the votes of the recipients, and " if this is found to be the object of the donor it matters not under what pretext or in what form, to what persons, or through whose hands the gift may be bestowed, or whether it has proved successful in gaining the desired object or not."

The *Wigan Case* (4 O'M. & H., 14) is one in which treating, rather than bribery, un ler the pretext of charity, was suggested ; but the following remarks made by Bowen, J., are of general application : " Charity at election times ought to be kept by politicians in the background. No doubt the distress was great in Wigan at the time, and there was, probably, many a fireless and breadless house throughout the town, but the persons who ought to have relieved the distress were not the politicians of Wigan ; they ought to have stood aloof, they had another duty to discharge on that day, and they could not properly discharge both duties on the same day. In truth, I think it will be generally found that the feeling which distributes relief to the poor *at election times*, though those who are the distributors may not be aware of it, is really not charity, but party feeling following in the steps of charity, wearing the dress of charity and mimicking her gait."

The second *Salisbury Case* (4 O'M. & H., 21) is the last authority on the subject. There it was proved, that very shortly *after* the election the respondent gave £100 to be spent in coals and blankets among the poor ; but it was also proved, that after the election of 1880, when he was defeated, he gave a similar gift, and that it was a tradition in the borough for each of the members to give £100 a year for distribution among the poor. On these facts the court (Pollock, B., and Manisty, J.) held that the fair inference to be drawn was, that the gift was not given with the intention of corrupting the minds of future voters, or as a reward for past voting, but that it was done honestly as a matter of charity, and with the view of keeping up that sort of good feeling which it is desirable should exist between the rich and the poor. Pollock, B., referred to the dictum of Bramwell, B., in the *Windsor Case* already quoted, and remarked: "If it were necessary to consider this as a new matter, I am not quite sure that I should be prepared to go so far as Lord Bramwell went in that proposition. I should prefer, myself, to say we must take the whole of the evidence into consideration, and consider whether the governing principle in the mind of the man who gave such gifts was, that he was doing something with a view to corrupt the voters, or whether he was doing something which was a mere act of kindness and charity."

<small>Result of the authorities.</small>

We have set out the authorities on this subject at some length, but at no greater length than the difficulty and importance of the question discussed warrants. The conclusions to be deduced, it is submitted, are as follows:—

1. *Bonâ fide* charitable benefactions in a constituency which a person represents, or aspires to represent, do not constitute bribery.

2. But benefactions made under the colour and name of charity, with the view of influencing the votes of the recipients, or other persons through them, are bribes.

<small>The motive of the donor the test.</small>

3. What was the motive of the donor in each case is a question of fact to be determined by the court from an examination of all the evidence. But, in determining such question, attention must be paid to the time when, with reference to the election, the gifts were made, the habit and practice of the donor with regard to charities elsewhere and before he became a candidate, even to the traditions of the constituency, and to the amount of the gift. If the distribution of charity is made shortly before an election, a strong presumption of a corrupt motive arises (the *Boston Case* and the *Stafford Case*, quoted *supra*): if, on the other hand, it is made some

time before, there is no such presumption (the *Plymouth Case* and the *Windsor Case*, quoted *supra*). [Parliamentary & Municipal.]

S. 2 of the 17 & 18 Vict., c. 102 (already quoted) makes it bribery for any person, directly or indirectly to make any gift, loan, offer, promise, procurement or agreement to or with any person in order to induce such person to *procure* or *endeavour to procure* the return of any person to Parliament or the vote of any voter at any election, "provided always that the aforesaid enactment shall not extend or be construed to extend to any money paid or agreed to be paid for or on account of any legal expenses *bonâ fide* incurred at or concerning any election." This provision, which is substantially a re-enactment of a statute of George III., was primarily devised to strike against corrupt arrangements by which patrons of close boroughs sold their influence in them. But it would seem to have a larger scope than this, and to make it an act of bribery to pay or promise anything to any person (though a stranger to the borough) with a view of securing that person's assistance or influence in the election unless such payment was in the nature of "legal expenses *bonâ fide* incurred at or concerning the election." The only case in which this section has come before any of the judges was the *Coventry Case* (1 O'M. & H., 97 ; 20 L.T., n.s., 405). [Coventry Case.] In that case there were two respondents, and it was proved that there was an arrangement between them by which one of them agreed, in the event of the other consenting to stand in conjunction with him, that he would pay all the other's expenses. The latter had previously contested the constituency and, it was said, was popular in it. It was suggested that this promise to pay the election expenses was within the section. Willes, J., said that the question for him was, whether the one respondent intended by this promise to purchase the influence of the other in the constituency, or was the promise merely made with the view of serving the party. His lordship came to the latter conclusion, and refused to avoid the election; but his [Judgment of Willes, J.] language was very precise as to the operation of the section in a case which really comes within it. "It would

[To pay for influence or bribery.]

PARLIAMENTARY & MUNICIPAL.

be bribery in the case of the person who gave, as well as in the case of the person who received the benefit, and if the respondent E agreed to give the respondent H £5, I may say a farthing in point of law—if he agreed to give him anything, if only a peppercorn, for the purpose of purchasing any influence which the respondent H had with the electors of Coventry, and of advancing the respondent E's interest as a candidate at the election—that would be bribery within the statute."

The last sub-section of the 17 & 18 Vict., c. 102, s. 2, makes it bribery to advance or pay any money *with the intent* that such money should be expended in bribery or to knowingly pay any money in repayment of any money, wholly or in part, expended in bribery at any election.

Subscriptions towards expenses of candidates legal.

This provision in no way strikes at subscriptions towards defraying the expense of any particular candidate or of candidates belonging to a particular party. Such subscriptions are very common. They have never been called in question, and in the *Belfast Case* (1 O M. & H., 285; 21 L.T., 475) Fitzgerald, B., intimated an opinion that they were perfectly legal and constitutional.

There are cases in the reports of the proceedings before Election Committees where the latter have held that a bet made by a voter on the event of an election invalidates his vote and necessitates its being struck off on a scrutiny. (Rogers on Elections, 12th edition, 386.) It is difficult to understand these decisions on the facts presented in the meagre reports preserved. But, apart from authority, if the court is satisfied that a bet or wager made by a candidate or any one of his agents is merely a corrupt contrivance to influence a voter, and to induce him to cast his vote in one direction or another, or to abstain from voting, that is bribery which will defeat the election.

Wagers may be bribes.

Section II.—Treating.

Treating is the second of those corrupt acts, which if committed by a candidate or any one of his agents, will avoid either a Parliamentary or a Municipal election. Various statutes from the 7 and 8 Wm. III., c. 4, onwards, have prohibited the giving of meat, drink and entertainment with the view of influencing votes, and there are innumerable cases where the seat has been forfeited for corruption of this description. Those statutes were all repealed by the Corrupt Practices Act, 1854 (the 17 & 18 Vict., c. 102), which in its 4th section enacted as follows:— *[Parliamentary & Municipal.]*

"Every candidate at an election who shall corruptly by himself, or by or with any person, or by any other ways and means on his behalf, at any time, either before, during, or after any election, directly or indirectly give or provide, or cause to be given or provided, or shall be accessory to the giving or providing, or shall pay, wholly or in part, any expenses incurred for any meat, drink, entertainment or provision, to or for any person, in order to be elected, or for the purpose of corruptly influencing such person, or any other person to give or refrain from giving his vote at such election, or on account of such person having voted or refrained from voting at such election, shall be deemed guilty of the offence of treating, and shall forfeit the sum of £50 to any person who shall sue for the same, with full costs of suit; and every voter who shall corruptly accept and take any such meat, drink, entertainment or provision, shall be incapable of voting at such election, and his vote, if given, shall be utterly void and of non-effect." *[Old definition of treating.]*

And by the joint operation of the Act of 1854, s. 36, and the 46th section of the 31 & 32 Vict., c. 125, the election of any person who was guilty by himself or his agent of treating was avoided. S. 23 of the Act of 1854 also made it an illegal act, rendering the person guilty of it liable to a penalty of 40s. (though the seat was not affected), merely to

Parliamentary & Municipal. give any meat, drink, &c., to any voter on the nomination day or the polling day.

S. 1 of the Act of 1883 repeals s. 4 of the Act of 1854, and by s. 66 of the same Act the 23rd s. is also repealed, and in lieu of the provisions of the old law the following section **Definition of treating in Act of 1883.** is substituted: "Whereas, under s. 4 of the Corrupt Practices Act, 1854, persons other than candidates at Parliamentary elections are not liable to any punishment for treating, and it is expedient to make such persons liable; be it therefore enacted: Any person who corruptly by himself, or by any other person, either before, during, or after an election, directly or indirectly, gives or provides, or pays wholly or in part the expense of giving or providing, any meat, drink, entertainment or provision to or for any person for the purpose of corruptly influencing that person, or any other person, to give or refrain from giving his vote at the election, or on account of such person, or any other person having voted or refrained from voting, or being about to vote, or refrain from voting at such election, shall be guilty of treating. And every elector who corruptly accepts or takes any such meat, drink, entertainment or provision shall also be guilty of treating."

The Act of 1884 applies to municipal elections the above definition of treating, and it may be taken that whatever is treating at a Parliamentary election is treating at a Municipal election.

Although the wording of s. 1 of the Act of 1883 is different from the wording of s. 4 of the Act of 1854, there is no material alteration in the definition of the offence of treating. The latter section includes in its definition the causing to be given or provided meat, &c., but inasmuch the former forbids the giving or providing directly or indirectly of any meat, &c., and it is a principle of law that a man does that himself which he does through another, it would seem that the words of s. 1 are comprehensive enough to include **No material alteration between old and new definition.** every act in this connection which the repealed section was directed against. Again, s. 4 of the old Act contained the words, "or shall be accessory to the giving or providing."

Those words are omitted from s. 1, but evidence that a PARLIAMENTARY & MUNICIPAL. candidate knew that meat, &c., was to be given and consented to the giving, which would constitute him an accessory, would also be evidence that he actually gave it within the meaning of s. 1. Towards the end of the definition in s. 1 some words are added which were not in s. 4. It is treating to give . . . "on account of such person *or any other person* having voted." The words in italics are new, and they somewhat enlarge the sweep and scope of the description of the offence. But subject to the minor variations we have mentioned, the old definition of treating is preserved, and substantially all that the legislature has done is to increase the penalties for the offence, and make subject to them classes of persons who before escaped.

It will be noted that in the definition of treating contained in the Act of 1854 the word "corruptly" is introduced. "Every candidate who *corruptly*," &c. . . . is guilty of treating." This word is preserved in the definition given in the Act of 1883. "any person who *corruptly*," &c., &c. There *Meaning of the word "corruptly."* has been a good deal of discussion as to the precise effect which ought to be given to the word "corruptly," and the extent to which it distinguishes the liability of a candidate for the act of giving a glass of beer from his liability for the act of giving a shilling. However, it is now well settled that the word "corruptly" in this connection does not mean wickedly, or immorally, or dishonestly, or anything of that sort, but means *with the object and intention of doing that which the legislature plainly means to forbid*. (See the judgment of Willes, J., in *Cooper* v. *Slade*, 6 H.L.C., 747; 27 L.J., Q.B., 449; and the *Bewdley Case*, 1 O'M. & H., 19; 19 L.T., n.s., 676.) "In fact, giving meat or drink *Remarks of Lord Blackburn.* is treating when the person who gives it has an intention of treating—not otherwise; and in all cases where there is evidence to show that meat or drink has been given, it is a question of fact for the judge whether the intention is made out by the evidence, which in every individual case must stand upon its own grounds, and although each individual case may be a mere feather's weight by itself and so small

44 THE LAW RELATING TO

PARLIAMENTARY & MUNICIPAL. that one would not act upon it, yet if there is a large number of such cases, a large number of slight cases will together make a strong one; and consequently it must always be a very important inquiry what was the scale, the amount and the extent to which it was done." (Per Blackburn, J., in the *Bewdley Case, supra.*)

Essence of offence of treating. The essence of the offence of treating is the *intention* with which the meat or drink is given. If it is given with an intention to influence a vote, that is treating, and the effect upon the election is exactly the same as the effect of a bribe, subject to the possibility of the Court in case of a parliamentary election granting relief under s. 22 of the Act of 1883, and in the case of a municipal election granting relief under s. 19 of the Act of 1884, in the circumstances to be presently discussed. "Whenever a candidate," said Blackburn, J., in the *Wallingford Case* (1 O'M. & H., 59), "is either by himself or by his agents in any way accessory to providing meat, drink, or entertainment for the purpose of being elected, with an intention to produce an effect upon The test is the intention. the election, that amounts to corrupt treating. Whenever, also, the intention is by such means to gain popularity, and thereby to affect the election; or, if it be that persons are afraid that if they do not provide entertainment and drink to secure the strong interests of the publicans and of the persons who take drink whenever they can get it for nothing, they will become unpopular, and they therefore provide it to affect the election—when there is an intention in the mind either of the candidate or his agent to produce that effect, then I think that it is corrupt treating. But everything is involved in the question of intention, and it becomes important to see what is the amount of the treating. The statute does not say or mean that it shall depend upon the amount of the drink. *The smallest quantity given with the intention will avoid the election.* But, when we are considering, as a matter of fact, the evidence, to see whether a sign of that intention does exist, we must as a matter of common sense, see on what scale and to what extent it is done."

There is one obvious distinction between bribery and

treating in regard to the light in which evidence of the giving of money and drink should respectively be viewed. As soon as it is proved that money was *given*, only one of two inferences is possible—it is either a case of charity or a bribe. But when it is proved that drink or meat has been *given*, you are not driven to one or other of these alternatives. There is another possible explanation of the transaction, for it is a common knowledge that good fellowship, and friendly relations, and the customs of the country lead to an interchange of treating between persons where both charity and bribery are out of the question. Therefore, it may be said that, as a rule, it requires stronger evidence of an intention to influence the vote in the case where the thing given is meat or drink, than where the thing given is money or some other valuable consideration.

Parliamentary & Municipal. Distinction between bribery and treating.

In a recent case (the *Norwich Case*, 4 O'M. & H., 91), Cave, J., made the following remarks with regard to the definition of treating: "In my judgment the statute does not apply to that form of treating which exists occasionally between socials and equals, where first the one treats and then the other treats, and which is only one form of ordinary hospitality. Neither does it apply to certain kinds of treating which exist in relation to business matters; it is not at all uncommon for persons when they have struck a bargain to cement it with a little drink, and it is obvious that the treating referred to in s. 1 of the Act has no reference to treating of that sort. It applies, in my judgment, to that sort of treating which exists where the superior treats his inferior, the treating which gives the treater influence over the person treated, and secures to the former the goodwill of the latter—not, however, to all cases of this kind does the corrupt treating spoken of in the Act apply. It does not apply where the treating is in return for small services, as where a man may treat a railway guard or porter, or he may treat his own servants; nor does it apply where the object is to acquire general goodwill. It must have reference to some election, and it must be for the purpose of influencing the vote of the person treated.

<small>PARLIAMENTARY & MUNICIPAL.</small> What the object is in each particular case must depend upon the circumstances of the case.

<small>To offer drink, &c., not treating.</small> It will be observed that, in the statutory definitions of treating, it is not made an offence to *offer*, or *promise*, or *agree to give* meat, &c. Still, it is right to remind the reader that <small>But may be bribery.</small> to offer, promise, or agree to give any valuable consideration is bribery (see the *Kidderminster Case*, 2 O'M. & H., 366); therefore, it is doubtful whether the omission of these words from the statutory definition adds anything to the protection of candidates.

<small>Treating need not be direct.</small> As in the case of bribery, so in that of treating, it is not necessary that the meat or drink should be given *directly* to the voter whose vote it is sought to influence. Drink given to women with the view of influencing their husbands, brothers and sweethearts, was in the *Tamworth Case* (1 O'M. & H., 80), held to be treating, and so in the *Longford Case* (2 O'M. & H., 15), the treating of non-electors was held to be within the statute. In the *Wallingford Case* already quoted, Blackburn, J., seemed to intimate that treating of all classes with a view to obtaining popularity would avoid the election, though, as to the latter proposition, it must be stated that in a later case (*Louth Case*, 3 O'M & H., 161), Dowse, B., expressed a contrary view.

<small>Treating at municipal may affect parliamentary election.</small> It has been stated that bribery at a Municipal election may be construed to be bribery at a Parliamentary election held shortly afterwards, and the same principle applies to the case of treating. See the *Hastings Case* (1 O'M. & H.; 21 L.T., n.s., 234), when, though on the facts before him, Blackburn, J., did not think that the treating at the Municipal election in any way influenced the Parliamentary contest, yet he clearly intimated that if it had such an effect the seat would have been forfeited. Equally, treating at a test ballot to determine which of three candidates shall be accepted as the nominee of the party, is as fatal to the election as bribery on a similar occasion. (*Brett v. Robinson*, L.R., 5 C.P., 503; 39 L.J., C.P., 265; 23 L.T., n.s., 188; 18 W.R., 866.)

Again, just as payments made to persons in respect of

their loss of time attending the Registration Court may be bribery, so treats of meat and drink to persons who attend the court to support their votes may be treating affecting the election "when its object is to procure popularity and votes at the Parliamentary election." (Per Blackburn, J., in the *Hastings Case*, 21 L.T., n.s. 234.) On the other hand, if it is shown that the treating has reference merely to the proceedings in connection with the registration, it will not affect the election, as where a supper is held to celebrate a triumph at the Revision Court, and the entertainment is paid for by the sitting member or his agent. This was held in the *Coventry Case* (1 O'M. & H., 106) not to affect the election, though such a proceeding is obviously most dangerous. *[Parliamentary & Municipal. Treats given at time of registration.]*

To what extent may a candidate lawfully give refreshments to voters and others employed by him in connection with the work of an election? It is submitted that the law on this point is as follows:—Meat and drink given *in moderation* by a candidate to persons really engaged in the work of the election was not, and it is submitted is not, necessarily corrupt treating though it may amount to an employment of the persons and so be illegal under s. 17 of the Act of 1883 and s. 13 of the Act of 1884. (See *Barrow Case* 54 L.T. n.s., 618 : 4 O'M. & H. 79.) On the other hand, meat and drink given to persons who do no real service in connection with the election, though as a cloak and screen they are called committeemen and canvassers, will be regarded as corrupt treating. The law was clearly laid down by Martin, B., in several cases in 1869, and his statement of it has never been judicially questioned. *[Refreshments to voters.]*

In the second *Bradford Case* (19 L.T., n.s., 723 ; 1 O'M. & H., 35), it was proved that on the polling day refreshments were provided in the committee rooms for all persons who were necessarily there for the purposes of the election. Those persons were voters, but inasmuch as they were all partisans honestly engaged in the work of the election, his lordship held that there was no treating to secure their votes.

So in the *Westminster Case* (1 O'M. & H., 90 ; 20 L.T.,

n.s., 236) the same learned judge held that providing refreshments on the polling day for persons *bonâ fide* engaged in the work of the election was not corrupt treating.

Blackburn, J., in the *Wallingford Case* (1 O'M. & H., 58; 19 L.T., n.s., 766) apparently had this statement of the law present to his mind when without in any way impugning it, he said it would be very much better if candidates left their agents and those who were working gratuitously in their behalf to provide their own refreshments. In the *Barrow Case (supra)* where the successful candidate openly provided refreshments for all canvassers and others working on the polling day, the court (Field and Day, JJ.) refused to find that this amounted, *in that case*, to treating, but they held that it constituted an employment of the persons who received the refreshments, within the meaning of sec. 17 of the Act of 1883, and on that ground they avoided the election.

The grosser forms of treating are where public-houses are opened, as it is called, and persons, whether voters or not, allowed to go in and out and drink or eat what they want with little limit imposed. This was what happened in the *Youghal Case* (21 L.T., n.s., 306; 1 O'M. & H., 291), where it was proved that crowds of electors and non-electors were gratuitously supplied with drink at the bar of the hotel in which the respondent's committee met, whenever they asked for it. The election was upset. So in the first *Bradford Case* (19 L.T. n.s., 720; 1 O'M. & H., 33) it was proved that the respondent's agents opened 115 public-houses in the borough, and in these houses all persons who came there and went through the farce of having their names put down as committeemen were supplied with drink. The election was upset. In the *Bewdley Case* (1 O'M. & H., 16; 19 L.T. n.s., 676) it was shown that a large number of public-houses—about 20—were habitually open during the election, that whoever went in there got drink as he wished, and that all the drink was ordered and controlled by a clerk of the respondent's agent. The judge was clearly of opinion that this treating invalidated the election. There are many other cases where the seat has been forfeited where treating has been carried on on a similar scale. Indeed, where such general and widespread treating as this is established, the election is in peril at common law apart altogether from proof that the corruption was the act of the respondent or any of his agents. {PARLIAMENTARY & MUNICIPAL.}

It cannot be stated too precisely that when once the Court is satisfied that meat or drink was given with the corrupt intention of influencing a vote, the offence of treating is complete, utterly regardless of the amount of meat or drink given. The authorities establishing this proposition are consistent from the *Westbury Case* in 19 L.T., n.s., 24, to the *Wigan Case* (4 O'M. & H., 13). And it is further fortified by s. 22 of the Act of 1883, and s. 19 of the Act of 1884, which clearly contemplate that treating may be of a "trivial, unimportant, and limited character," and so far as the seat is concerned give relief in such cases only under stringent conditions. {Amount of drink, &c., given generally immaterial.}

On the other hand, there are many cases in the books where it has been proved that meat and drink have been given to voters by a candidate or his agent, and yet the election has been upheld. These cases all go on the principle, which is a perfectly sound one, that the giving of the meat and drink is not in itself corrupt treating; it is giving it with the intention of influencing the vote which makes the offence. In the cases we mention the Court has considered all the surrounding circumstances, and come to the conclusion, *as a fact*, that the candidate or his agents did not mean to affect the votes of the recipients of his or their hospitality. See the *Louth Case* (3 O'M. & H. 161), where the cases on this point are carefully collated and discussed by Dowse, B. {Giving drink, &c., to voters may not be treating.}

It is clear that treating *before* an election, with a view of influencing it, is as much an offence as treating at the election. (The *Youghal Case*) 21 L.T., n.s., 317.) Whether treating *after* an election will invalidate it depends upon whether or no the treating was in pursuance of any arrangement, express or implied, made during the course of {Treating after an election.}

the election. The leading authority here is the *Brecon Case* (2 O'M. & H., 43). There it was proved that after the election an entertainment was given by the mother of the respondent, but with his knowledge and concurrence, to a large number of persons, among whom were many who had voted for the respondent at his election, and some who had voted against him. It was not, however, proved that this entertainment had been mentioned or even thought of until the election was over, neither was it proved that any such entertainment had ever been given before, or that it was intended thereby to influence the voters at a future election. The learned judge (Lush, J.) upheld the election. In giving judgment, he said: "In what then does corrupt treating after the election consist? It is easy enough to state what would be corrupt treating before the election. Indeed, the Act itself defines it, but what is that ingredient which must enter into the treating in order to make it corrupt with reference to an election which is over and past, and when it can no longer influence the voting, or have any effect upon the election. I do not agree that treating with a view to attach the voters to the candidate, and secure their future support, is within this branch of the section. Treating for such a purpose may peril the future election which it is designed to influence, but we are now dealing with a past election, and the treating charged is, therefore, a proceeding which reflects back and taints that by-gone election. Nor can it be merely giving an entertainment as an expression of gratitude, or by way of rewarding the voters. So to hold, would be to give no meaning to the word 'corruptly,' for the Act says that the offence shall consist, not in the giving meat, drink, &c., to a voter, 'on account of his having voted,' but the doing so corruptly on account of his having voted. I am, therefore, driven to the conclusion that the treating which the Act calls corrupt, as regards a by-gone election, must be connected with something which preceded the election, must be the complement of something done or existing before and calculated to influence the voter while the vote was in his power. An invitation given before to an entertainment to take place afterwards, or even a promise to invite, or a practice of giving entertainments after an election, which it may be supposed the voters would calculate on, would, if followed up by the treating afterwards, give to it the character of corrupt treating."

It will be seen that the learned judge intimated that a practice of giving entertainments after an election which the voters might be supposed to calculate upon, might be equivalent to a promise made before or during an election, so as to make the subsequent treating corrupt. This very point arose in the *Poole Case* (2 O'M. & H., 123), and was decided by Grove, J., in accordance with Lush's, J., opinion. There it was proved that after the election there was considerable treating of voters by the respondent's agents. No previous promise was suggested, but it was proved that after the last election, at which the respondent was also a candidate, a great deal of drink was given away by his agents, and the learned judge held that, having regard to what took place then, there was a tolerably clear understanding among the voters of Poole, that drink would be distributed as soon as the poll was over. His lordship fully adopted the doctrine of the *Brecon Case*, in cases where it was proved that the entertainment was given on a spontaneous rejoicing.

It is thus reasonably clear that the hospitality of a member *after* an election, if entirely unconnected with any promise before or previous conduct from which a promise can be implied, will not amount to corrupt treating and avoid the election.

Hospitality *before* an election, admits to some extent of different considerations. There is no law to prevent a man being hospitable in the place he aspires to represent ; but if the Court is satisfied that he dispenses his hospitality with a view of securing particular votes, he comes within the statute. It is entirely a question of intention ; and each case must stand upon its own bottom. In the *Windsor Case* (1 O'M. & H., 3 ; 19 L.T., n.s., 613) it was proved that the respondent

PARLIAMENTARY & MUNICIPAL.

Standing drink at public dinner.

was in the chair at a dinner of a non-political society—the Oddfellows—some two or three weeks before the election began. He ordered champagne to be served to all the persons present, many of whom were voters, and he paid for it. The question was whether, under the circumstances, this was an act of corrupt treating. Mr. Justice Willes held it was not. He described it as a "questionable" proceeding, and as being of an "objectionable" character, but acting upon a decision of an Election Committee, he, apparently with some reluctance, upheld the election. The Election Committees on this point drew a distinction which is not very intelligible. In the *Pontefract Case* (W. & D., 71) the respondent stood a quantity of drink at a dinner of the Oddfellows, and the committee held that this was not treating within the Act, as the society, at whose dinner he gave the treat, was not a political one. The *Maidstone Case* (W. & D., 104), on the other hand, is an authority that exactly similar treating, at the dinner of a political society, would be corrupt treating. We confess we cannot understand the distinction. If anything, treating at the dinner of a non-political society is likely to be more pernicious, and have a greater effect upon the election. In the one case, the candidate is treating partizans, whose votes in nine cases out of ten, are already secured. In the other case he is treating persons, many of whom have no fixed views, and who are probably open to influences of the kind. It must be carefully noted with reference to the *Windsor Case*, that it is merely a decision upon the facts. It lays down no principle of law, and it is no authority for saying that a candidate can, with impunity, dispense gratuitous drink or meat on the eve of an election.

The *Aylesbury Case* (4 O'M. & H., 62) is the latest case. There the respondent some few months before the election and after he had announced himself as a candidate, gave a large treat in the grounds of his mansion. Several thousand persons were entertained, and tickets of admission were given without reference to the politics of the persons who received them. On the other it was proved that in

previous years the respondent had given similar entertain- <small>PARLIAMENTARY & MUNICIPAL.</small>
ments, though not to so large a number of persons. An
explanation of the more liberal scale of this entertainment
was given which the Court thought reasonable, and finally
the Court (Field and Day, JJ.) held that the corrupt
motive of influencing the election was not established.

It has been already stated, that the quantity of meat or <small>Amount of treating material</small>
drink given, where the corrupt intent is made out, is im-
material, so far as the offence of treating is concerned; but <small>where relief sought under s. 22 of Act of 1883.</small>
the quantity of the meat or drink given is most material in
the connection we have now arrived at. Judges have again
and again expressed their sense of the hardship of the law
which compelled them to unseat a member who had done
his best to conduct his election purely, but who had been
compromised by some trifling act of treating committed
by an agent. Until the Act of 1883 they had no option.
Now by the 22nd section of that Act in the case of parliamentary elections, and by the 19th section of the Act of
1884 in the case of municipal elections, a limited power of
granting relief to a sitting member is given to the Court
trying a parliamentary or municipal petition. The two
sections, with two differences to be presently mentioned,
and some necessary verbal variations, are the same. The
22nd section of the Act of 1883 is as follows:—

"When upon the trial of an election petition, respecting
an election for a county or borough, the Election Court report
that a candidate at such election has been guilty by his
agents of the offence of *treating*, and undue influence and
illegal practice, or of any such offences in reference to such
election, and the Election Court further report that the
candidate has proved to the Court:—

"(*a.*) That no corrupt or illegal practice was committed
at such election by the candidate or his election
agent, and that the offences named in the said
report were committed contrary to the orders, and
without the sanction or connivance of such candidate or his election agent; and

"(*b.*) That such candidate and his election agent took all

54 THE LAW RELATING TO

<small>PARLIAMENTARY & MUNICIPAL.</small>

reasonable means for preventing the commission of corrupt and illegal practices at such election; and

"(c.) That the offences mentioned in the said report were of a trivial, unimportant, and limited character; and

"(d.) That in all other respects the election was free from any corrupt or illegal practice on the part of such candidate, and of his agents,

then the election of such candidate shall not, by reason of the offences mentioned in such report, be void, nor shall the candidate be subject to any incapacity under this Act."

A glance at this section is sufficient to show that the indulgence it permits is so hedged round with restrictions and limitations that it cannot have any very wide application. It has no application to any act of *bribery*, or to any act of *personation*, though the bribe given be trifling in amount, and though there be every circumstance of extenuation in the case. But it does apply to treating, and this curious result may follow. To promise a glass of beer as an inducement for a vote is bribery. (The *Bodmin Case* 1 O'M. & H. 124). To actually give a glass of beer is treating. If it is proved that an agent of a candidate (not being his election agent) *has given* a glass of beer, and if the other conditions of s. 22 are satisfied, the Court cannot unseat the sitting member. But if it is proved that the agent merely *promised* a glass of beer, has the Court any power to relieve from this trifling act of bribery? It is submitted it has not.

<small>Section applies to treating but not to bribery.</small>

<small>What the respondent must prove to obtain relief.</small>

Assuming, however, that the act or acts in respect of which the candidate wishes relief, under s. 22 is or are acts of treating merely, the only subject with which we are now concerned, the candidate is not entitled to such relief unless he affirmatively proves, (1), that the said acts were not done by *himself* or *his election agent*; or (2), with his or the election agent's knowledge or consent, and (3), that he and his agent took all reasonable means to prevent the commission of corrupt and *illegal practices*; (4), that the acts in question were committed contrary to his orders and the orders of his election agent; (5), that in all other respects the election

<small>Relief under the Act of 1883.</small>

was free from any corrupt or *illegal practice* on the part of the candidate or any of his agents ; (6), that no corrupt or illegal practice was committed at the election by the candidate or his election agent ; and (7), that the acts in question were of a trivial, unimportant and limited character.

<small>PARLIAMENTARY & MUNICIPAL.</small>

The 19th section of the Act of 1884 gives an exactly similar power in the case of municipal elections, exercisable by the Court trying a municipal petition under the same conditions, with two important differences. The Act of 1884 does not require, nor contemplate the appointment of an election agent in connection with a municipal election. Therefore, the 19th section in setting out the conditions upon compliance with which a candidate may obtain relief, omits all mention of the election agent. Again, one of the things a candidate at a parliamentary election has to prove to entitle him to relief is that the acts in question were committed contrary to his orders. It will be seen that the Act of 1884 requires the fullest proof that the acts were committed without his knowledge, consent, and connivance, and that he took reasonable means to prevent their commission ; but it does not require it to be proved that they were committed contrary to his orders. The result is that a candidate at a municipal election seeking relief from the Election Court, has to prove merely (1), that the act or acts in question was or were not committed by him personally or (2), with his knowledge, consent, or connivance, and that (3), he took all reasonable means to prevent the commission of corrupt or illegal practices. (4), that in all other respects the election was free from any corrupt or illegal practice, and (5), that the acts in question were of a trivial, unimportant and limited character. The procedure to obtain relief is treated of hereafter.

<small>Under the Act of 1884</small>

Section III.—Undue Influence.

Parliamentary & Municipal.

Definition of undue influence.

The offence of undue influence is thus defined by s. 2 of the Act of 1883 (which is incorporated by s. 2 of the Act of 1884):

"Every person who shall, directly or indirectly, by himself or by any other person on his behalf, make use of or threaten to make use of, any force, violence or restraint, or inflict, or threaten to inflict, by himself or by any other person, any temporal or spiritual injury, damage, harm or loss upon or against any person in order to induce or compel such person to vote or refrain from voting, or on account of such person having voted or refrained from voting at any election, or who shall, by abduction, duress, or any fraudulent device or contrivance, impede or prevent the free exercise of the franchise of any elector, or shall thereby compel, induce or prevail upon any elector either to give or to refrain from giving his vote at any election, shall be guilty of undue influence."

The corresponding section under the old law was s. 5 of the Corrupt Practices Act, 1854, which was almost identical in terms, but the words "temporal and spiritual" are new, and the general words "in any other manner practise intimidation" and "or otherwise interfere with" the free exercise of the franchise, are omitted. These modifications do not appear to alter the law.

Antiquity of the law.

This portion of the law is as old as Parliament itself. By 3 Edwd. I. c. 5: "Because elections ought to be free, the king commandeth, under pain of great forfeiture, that no great man nor other *by force of arms nor by malice or menacing*, shall disturb any to make free election." A vote, to be a good vote, must be freely given, and the question whether a man gives a free vote is much the same as the question whether a man has made a free will (*Windsor*, 1 O'M. & H., 6; 19 L. T., 43).

"The proper definition of that undue influence which was dealt with in 17 & 18 Vict, c. 102, s. 5, is using any violence or threatening any damage, or resorting to any fraudulent contrivance to restrain the liberty of a voter so as PARLIAMENTARY & MUNICIPAL. either to compel or frighten him into voting or abstaining from voting otherwise than as he freely wills" (*Lichfield,* 1 O'M. & H., 25; 20 L.T., 11). Yet the statute leaves entirely untouched influences which operate upon the mind of a voter and coerce him in the exercise of his franchise *without any act being committed* on the part of the person from whom the influence emanates. For example, a shopkeeper fears to incur the displeasure of profitable customers, a workman fears to incur the displeasure of his employer, a Silent and tenant fears to incur the displeasure of his landlord, and they legitimate influence. will be influenced by these considerations although neither the landlord, nor the employer, nor the customer either intends or threatens, or does any act of injury whatever in consequence of their exercise of the franchise (*Down,* 3 O'M. & H., 136).

"The law cannot strike at the existence of influence. The law can no more take away from a man who has property, or who can give employment, the insensible but powerful influence he has over those whom, if he has a heart, he can benefit by the proper use of his wealth, than the law can take away his honesty, his good feeling, or any other qualities which give a man influence with his fellows. It is the abuse of influence with which alone the law deals. Influence cannot be said to be abused because it exists and operates. (Per Willes, J., *Lichfield,* 1 O'M. & H., 22; 20 L.T., 11.)

Legitimate influence might be abused, although no injury Illegitimate canvassing. were actually done or threatened in so many words, and in such a case the abuse of it might amount to undue influence. At Lichfield, a very influential person, who was a magistrate, a poor law guardian, a town councillor, and a trustee of several local charities, stationed himself in the yard in front of the polling place and there exhorted and persuaded poor voters coming to the poll, and ticked off their names on the register. His servant, who was also there, on seeing an elector come up wearing adverse colours, cried "We will remember him another day." No other persons but special constables were allowed in the yard. The Court was of

PARLIAMENTARY & MUNICIPAL.

opinion that what had been done exceeded the bounds of legitimate canvassing and reprehended it, but, with some doubt, declined to avoid the election. (*Lichfield*, 3 O'M. & H. 136).

The "undue influence" clause is to be read by the light thrown upon it by the "bribery" clause, and that of which it would be bribery to promise the enjoyment, it is intimidation to threaten the deprivation of. (*Westbury*, 1 O'M. & H., 52).

"Bottling" voters.

The use of "force, violence or restraint," or a threat to use it, to prevent the free exercise of the franchise, is rare. Either under the first, or under the concluding words of the section, would be included the practice of making voters drunk in order to prevent their voting, shutting them up, driving or sending them away from the polling place with a like object, or, as was done in some old cases, taking out voters to Norway under the pretence that they were being taken to the place of polling. Any such act done by any agent avoids the election. (*North Norfolk*, 1 O'M. & H., 236; 21 L.T., 264).

The case becomes more difficult when the act charged is the utterance of expressions which may mean to imply a threat to inflict some temporal or spiritual injury in order to influence the voter or because he has voted or refrained from voting, but an ambiguous act may generally be interpreted by surrounding circumstances.

Undue influence by landlords.

The law does not strike at the legitimate influence of any person. Thus, where a nobleman said to a number of his tenants: "If you can vote for my friend, Captain T., I shall be delighted if you will do so. If you cannot vote for him, at all events stay at home and do not vote against him" Keogh, J., first brushed aside a suggestion that any resolution of the House of Commons could make it illegal for a peer so to interfere in an election, or make law at all, and then continued : "It would be a sorry day for this country (and for none more than for the tenant class themselves) if landlords, noblemen or gentlemen, were entirely shut off from the exercise of that legitimate influence which a landlord has a right to use." (*Galway*, 2 O'M. & H., 55.) It is to be noted that in that case it was not suggested that the nobleman in question evicted or threatened to evict or injure any recalcitrant tenant.

So where it merely appeared that all Mr. M's tenants who were in arrear with their rent had voted as he asked them to do, the seat was not affected. "The mere fact of a person having influence and intentionally retaining it is not alone evidence of unduly exercising that influence." (*Windsor*, 1 O'M. & H., 6; 19 L.T., 43). A case much nearer the line was the second *Windsor Case*. (2 O'M. & H., 88; 31 L.T., 133). There it was proved that the respondent had evicted a number of his tenants after the election of 1868 because they had voted against him, but it was not proved that this conduct did, as a fact, influence any elector at the election of 1874, which was the one in question. Nor so far as can be gathered from the reports, does it seem that the respondent went to his tenants in 1874, saying, "I want you to promise me." Bramwell, B., declined to unseat the respondent, because it was not proved that the threat which was practically held out to the tenants in 1868—that if they voted against their landlord in future they also would be evicted—was operative in 1874. Probably it would have been otherwise if in 1874 the respondent had canvassed his tenants. That would have been equivalent to saying. "I have come to ask for your vote, and if you don't give it you had better remember what happened in 1868." The learned judge marked his disapproval of the respondent's conduct by depriving him of the costs of the petition, but admitted that there was a legitimate mode of influence, and that a landlord having a choice between two tenants—one agreeing with him in politics and the other not—might legally select the person agreeing with him.

The result seems to be that a landlord or his agent may canvass his tenants and exhaust every argument in order to persuade them to vote as he wishes, provided that he neither inflict nor threaten to inflict any injury upon any tenant who holds out. (*North Norfolk*, 1 O'M. & H., 237; 21 L.T.,

264.) If the tenant became such on his promise to vote for his landlord's party, it would be exceedingly dangerous for the landlord in canvassing him to remind him of his promise (*Petersfield*, 2 O'M. & H., 94).

Undue influence by employers.

Undue influence by employers is often difficult to prove, when it takes the form of dismissal after the election on account of the workmen having voted, as it may be suggested that the dismissal was for some other reason. At *Westbury* (1 O'M. & H., 50) the employer told his workpeople, "No man shall remain in my employment who votes for L.," and afterwards dismissed some of his workpeople who voted for L., after promising not to vote at all. It was ingeniously but vainly suggested that they were dismissed because of their untruthfulness in voting after promising not to vote and not because of their political opinions. The wrongful dismissal by an employer of a single voter from his employment shortly before an election, upon the ground of his political opinion, is *evidence* of intimidation. (*Blackburn*, 1 O'M. & H., 203 ; 20 L.T., 823.) But where an employer has a mixed motive for dismissing his man, where he has a reason for getting rid of him apart from his politics, is the employer bound to abstain from discharging him merely because an election is at hand? At *Blackburn* (*supra*) Willes, J., thought not, but recommended employers so acting to preserve clear evidence of the non-political ground for dismissing the workman. (See also *North Norfolk*, 1 O'M. & H., 241 ; 21 L.T , 264.) When the majority of the workpeople in certain mills, just before the election, drove out some of the minority who held unpopular opinions and prevented them from continuing their work, the masters looking on and not attempting to interfere, the election, agency being proved, was avoided (*Blackburn*, *supra*).

Undue influence by workmen.

Withdrawal of custom.

The case of withdrawal of custom stands upon the same ground. A man may deal with a tradesman because he is of the same political opinions, and not because he sells commodities cheap or good. But to withdraw, or to threaten to withdraw, custom from a tradesman because of his voting or not voting is using undue influence. (*North Norfolk*,

1 O'M. & H., 241; 21 L.T., 204; *North Durham*, 2 O'M. & H., 159; *R.* v. *Barnwell*, 5 W.R., 557.) There are some observations of Blackburn, J., made in the first case to the effect that the loss threatened or inflicted by the withdrawal of custom must be a substantial loss. "It must be so serious that one could direct a jury in a criminal court to find that a person was guilty of misdemeanour." The tendency of the law during the last 15 years has been, however, to increased stringency, and no one could be recommended to presume upon the chance of these *dicta* being adopted. In election matters the maxim *de minimis non curat lex* seldom applies. _{PARLIAMENTARY & MUNICIPAL. Whether the injury must be substantial.}

It has been held to be intimidation to threaten a dissenting minister to give up a pew in his chapel if he will not vote as his congregation or any of the congregation desire him to do. (*Northallerton*, 1 O'M. & H., 168; 21 L.T., 113.)

The limits of the exercise of spiritual influence by ecclesiastics and others have never been very exactly fixed, and while the subject was under debate in Parliament it seemed to be assumed that a great deal must be left to the common sense of the election court. But it is not too much to say that threats of spiritual harm uttered by an ecclesiastic will be viewed more seriously than when uttered by one layman to another. Yet even the clergy may exercise their legitimate influence. It is not unlawful for a body of clergymen to meet together to select a candidate (*Longford*, 2 O'M. & H., 14), nor for any clergyman to canvass for his favourite candidate. But he must not, either in dealing with members of his flock, or with any elector, use the influence which his position confers upon him, in the words of Sir S. Romilly in *Huguenin* v. *Baseley*, 14 Ves. 273, "to work upon the passions, to excite superstitious fears or pious hopes, to inspire, as the object may be best promoted, despair or confidence, to alarm the conscience by the horrors of eternal misery, or support the drooping spirits by unfolding the prospect of eternal happiness, that good or evil, which is never to end." A priest may, said Fitzgerald, J., at *Longford* (2 O'M. & H., 16), "counsel, advise, recommend, entreat. _{Spiritual intimidation.}

Parliamentary & Municipal.

Threats by ecclesiastics.

and point out the true line of moral duty and explain why one candidate should be preferred to another." All that is merely advice and argument. But " he must not hold out *hopes of reward* here *or hereafter*, and he must not use threats of temporal injury, or of disadvantage, or *of punishment hereafter*. He *must not*, for instance, *threaten to excommunicate*, or to withhold the sacraments, or to expose the party to any other religious disability, or *denounce the voting for any particular candidate as a sin*"—(per Fitzgerald, J., in the *Longford Case, supra*.) And Keogh, J., at *Galway County* (2 O'M. & H. 47), declared that if the meanest freeman who crawled about the town were shown to have been refused the rites of the church by an agent of the sitting member on account of his vote, or the vote of any one of his family, the election would have been avoided instantly.

These principles are not confined to Ireland. They are of general application. It cannot be doubted that if any clergyman or ecclesiastic, whether of the established church or of any dissenting community, were to threaten his flock generally or any elector liable to be influenced by the threat, with the refusal of any rite of the church, or that his (the ecclesiastic's) influence would be exerted to prevent the election to any office in the church (as churchwarden, deacon or elder) of any person who should not vote in a particular way, or were, in sermons or otherwise, to speak of voting in a particular way as a sin, he would be guilty of using undue influence, and if he were an agent of the candidate returned, that the election would be avoided.

Attempts to intimidate.

"A *mere attempt* on the part of an agent to intimidate a voter, even though it were unsuccessful, would avoid an election." (Willes, J., at *Northallerton*, 1 O'M. & H., 168; 21 L.T., 116.)

Hasty words.

But if there is no act done after a threat, but the case rests on a threat alone, although that makes no difference in law, the election court will require to be satisfied that the threatening words were serious and deliberate, intended to affect the vote, and not merely hasty expressions by an angry man. (*North Norfolk*, 1 O'M. & H., 240; 21 L.T., 267, per Blackburn, J.) {Parliamentary & Municipal.}

If an agent were to bring a mob into a constituency to terrify hostile electors, or were to exhort a mob, or any persons not to allow hostile voters to vote, the election would be avoided, although it may not be shown that the writing or violence prevailed to such an extent as to prevent the election being entirely free. (*Staleybridge*, 1 O'M. & H., 72; 20 L.T., 75; *Stafford*, 1 O'M. & H., 228; 21 L.T., 210; *North Norfolk*, 1 O'M. & H., 240; 21 L.T., 264.) {Violence short of general intimidation.}

As to "fraudulent devices or contrivances used" to impede or prevent the free exercise of the franchise, it would seem that these words would cover an agreement by A to pair with B, A intending all the while to vote, and voting accordingly. (See *Northallerton*, 1 O'M. & H., 169.) Possibly also an agreement by a paid agent, who cannot vote, to pair with an elector, who is ignorant of the former being a paid agent, would be within the section. And it would be a "fraudulent device" to issue cards of instruction for voting, marked with a cross opposite one candidate's name, and stating that any other mark would invalidate the vote, if the Court should think that the cards were *intended* to mislead ignorant voters, but not otherwise. (*Gloucester*, 2 O'M. & H., 60. The *Stepney Case* 4 O'M. & H. 39.) Whether it was "undue influence" for an agent to advertise that the ballot was a sham, and that he would be able to ascertain how each elector voted, and to distribute among the electors 10,000 copies of a newspaper containing an article taking the same view was a question on which Fitzgerald, B., and Barry, J., differed. (*Down*, 3 O'M. & H., 122.) As the voting of some electors would certainly be different according as the voting was to be secret or open, it is certainly not easy to understand on what grounds it can be said that such a contrivance does not "impede or prevent the free exercise of the franchise." Then as such a statement is untrue and calculated to mislead ignorant voters, surely it is fraudulent? {Fraudulent devices.}

Undue influence is one of the offences against the con- {Relief against consequences}

PARLIAMENTARY & MUNICIPAL. *of undue influence.* sequences of which, on an election petition, relief may be granted by the Court, upon the conditions already stated in dealing with the subject of treating. (S. 22 of the Act of 1883, and s. 19 of the Act of 1884.)

SECTION IV.—PERSONATION AND ABETTING PERSONATION.

Personation defined. The offence of personation or of aiding, abetting, committing, or procuring the commission of the offence of personation is a corrupt practice and felony, and if committed by any candidate or agent of a candidate will avoid his election. (ss. 3 and 5 of the Act of 1883, and s. 3 of the Act of 1884.) The offence is thus defined by the Ballot Act, 1872, s. 24: "A person shall for all purposes of the laws relating to Parliamentary and municipal elections, be deemed to be guilty of the offence of personation who at an election for a county or borough or at a municipal election, applies for a ballot paper in the name of some other person, whether that name be that of a person living or dead or of a fictitious person, or who having voted once at any such election applies at the same election for a ballot paper in his own name."

The effect of this section is that the offence is committed if the application for a ballot paper is made in the name of any other person than the applicant, or if the applicant, having voted already at the election, applies for a second ballot paper in his own name. The latter words of the section would extend to cases in which a person happens to be twice on the register, whether for the same or different qualifications, for a double entry on the register gives no right to vote twice, or where a person happens to be on the register of different divisions of the same county or borough. (*Stepney Case*, 4 O'M. & H., 43.) Under the former words of the section, "applies for a ballot paper in the name of *some other person*," it has been held, when there were two persons named R.R., one only of whom was on the register, and the other voted, that the act of the other in voting was an act of personation and that the vote must be struck off.

(*Rothwell's Case*, 20 L.T., 314; *Clark's Case*, 44 L.T., 290.) <small>PARLIAMENTARY & MUNICIPAL.</small> The application is none the less in the name " of some other person," because the applicant happens to bear the same name as the person on the register.

But if a man applies for a ballot paper in a name other than his name of origin, or the name by which he is generally known, but in a name which appears on the register and which was inserted by the overseer in the belief it was *his* name, and for the purpose of putting him on the register, he is not guilty of personation. (*R.* v. *Fox*, 16 Cox C.C., 166.)

It would seem that the offence is not committed if the person voting or attempting to vote, *bonâ fide* and upon reasonable grounds of belief, but erroneously, believes that he is the person entitled to vote; nor would it be committed if an agent, who instigated another to vote, in a similar way, and on similar grounds, erroneously believed the person instigated to be entitled to vote. (*Athlone*, 3 O'M. & H., 59; *Gloucester*, 2 O'M. & H., 63; *Stepney Case*, 4 O'M. & H., 43.) But if the act is an innocent one, the person voting believing that he was the person on the register, the vote should be attacked in the petition and particulars, as being given by a person not on the register. To treat the case merely as one of personation may be insufficient. (*Athlone*, *supra*.) <small>Innocent personation</small>

If two persons are improperly on the register in respect of the same premises both of them may vote, and the offence of personation is committed by neither (20 L.T., 315). If A, who is entitled to vote, chooses to be called B, and so votes, that does not vitiate his vote. (*Wills's Case*, 20 L.T., 310.)

If an agent of the candidate returned should knowingly instigate the commission of the offence of personation it would seem that the election would be bad at common law as well as under the statute. (*Coventry*, 1 O'M. & H., 100; 20 L.T., 405; *Gloucester*, 2 O'M. & H., 64.)

It is important to remember that the offence of personation is complete upon the *application* for a ballot paper being made. <small>When offence complete.</small>

Section V.—A False Declaration.

Parliamentary & Municipal.

A false declaration a corrupt practice.

S. 33 of the Act of 1883 requires the election agent of the candidate to transmit a true return of the election expenses to the returning officer within a time specified. This return must be accompanied by two declarations, one made by the candidate, and the other by the election agent, in the forms set forth in the schedule, in effect stating that the return is a true one, and that the sums mentioned in it are the only sums which have been paid in connection with the election. The nature of the return and declaration are fully discussed in chapter VIII. Sub-s. 7 of the 33rd s. provides: "If any candidate or election agent *knowingly* makes the declaration required by this section falsely, he shall be guilty of an offence, and on conviction thereof, on indictment, shall be liable to the punishment for wilful and corrupt perjury; *such offence shall also be deemed to be a corrupt practice within the meaning of this Act.*" And being a corrupt practice it avoids the election.

In municipal elections also the making by the candidate returned of a wilfully false declaration respecting election expenses is a corrupt practice which avoids the election. (S. 21, sub-s. 5 of the Act of 1884.)

CHAPTER II.

ILLEGAL PRACTICES WHICH AVOID A PARLIAMENTARY ELECTION.

SECTION I.—WHEN COMMITTED BY THE CANDIDATE OR ANY AGENT.

THESE are four in number. Three are contained in s. 7 of the Act, of 1883, and one in s. 28; and by s. 11 of the same Act, if the Election Court reports that a candidate at any election has been guilty by *his agents* of any illegal practice "in reference to such election, that candidate shall not be capable of being elected to or sitting in the House of Commons for the said county or borough during the Parliament for which the election was held, and if he has been elected, his election shall be void." *[Parliamentary — Such illegal practices four in number.]*

S. 7 is as follows:—

"(1.) No payment, or contract for payment, shall for the purpose of promoting or procuring the election of a candidate at any election be made, *[Section 7 of Act of 1883.]*

"(*a*.) On account of the conveyance of electors to or from the poll, whether for the hiring of horses or carriages, or for railway fares, or otherwise; or

"(*b*.) To an elector on account of the use of any house, land, building, or premises for the exhibition of any address, bill, or notice, or on account of the exhibition of any address, bill, or notice; or

"(*c*.) On account of any committee room in excess of the number allowed by the first schedule to this Act.

"(2.) Subject to such exception as may be allowed in pursuance to this Act, if any payment or contract for payment is knowingly made in contravention of this section either before, during, or after an election, the person making

Parliamentary such payment or contract shall be guilty of an illegal practice, and any person receiving such payment, or being a party to any such contract, knowing the same to be in contravention of this Act, shall also be guilty of an illegal practice.

Sub-s. 3 proviso. "(3.) Provided that where it is the ordinary business of an elector, as an advertising agent, to exhibit for payment, bills and advertisements, a payment to or contract with such elector, if made in the ordinary course of business, shall not be deemed to be an illegal practice within the meaning of this section."

Illegal to pay for conveyance of voters to the poll. The first offence consists in actually paying, or contracting to pay (whether to an elector or a non-elector) any money on account of the conveyance of electors to or from the poll, and it is specifically stated that the offence is complete, whether the payment or contract for payment relates to the hiring of horses or carriages, or is for railway fares, *or otherwise*. This is a material change upon the old law. Prior to the new Act, in *county elections* it was lawful to convey electors **The old law on the subject** to or from the poll in hired carriages, or to bring them from a distance by means of free passes on the railway, or otherwise; and the almost uniform practice was for both sides to avail themselves to the full of this right. In the case of *borough* elections, while the conveyance of voters to or from the poll in hired conveyances was legal within the limits of the boroughs themselves (43 & 44 Vict., c. 18, s. 2), any payment on account of their conveyance outside the boroughs was illegal, though it did not avoid the election. (The *Bolton Case*, 2 O'M. & H.; 31 L.T., n.s., 194.)

Now, counties and boroughs are placed upon exactly the same footing, and not only is the conveyance of electors at the candidate's expense to or from the poll in *hired* conveyances, or upon the railway, made illegal; but if any agent **Contract with livery stablemen for conveyance of voters.** of the candidate makes any payment, or contract for payment, with a view to their conveyance, the election is avoided. That is unquestionably the general effect of the first part of the s. 7. The wording of a later section raises, however, a question whether this is so in every case. S. 14, sub-s. 1

forbids any person to *let*, lend, or employ for the conveyance of voters to or from the poll, any carriage, horse, or animal, *which he keeps or uses for the purpose of letting out to hire*, and the second sub-section goes on : "A person shall not *hire*, borrow, or use for the purpose of the conveyance of electors to or from the poll any carriage, horse, or other animal which he knows the owner thereof is prohibited by this section to *let*, lend, or employ for that purpose, and if he does so, he shall be guilty of an *illegal hiring*." An illegal hiring is treated in the Act as a less heinous offence than an illegal practice, and does not avoid the election, unless it is committed by the candidate personally, or *his election agent*. Now, suppose a person who is held to be an agent of the candidate, though he is not an election agent, hires all the carriages and horses in the stables of a livery stableman, and uses them for the conveyance of voters to and from the poll, is he only guilty of an illegal hiring ? If so, the election will stand. On the other hand, if he hires a single horse, from a person who is not a livery stable keeper, he clearly comes within s. 7, sub-s. 1, and committing an illegal practice, the election is avoided. If this be so, the result is curious, for then, to make a contract for the hire of carriages with persons whose business it is to supply horses and carriages, and who can supply them wholesale, would *not* defeat the election, but to make a contract with other persons *would*. It can hardly be supposed that the legislature meant this, but it is open to argument that it has enacted it. S. 7 contains a merely general prohibition against entering into contracts for the hire of conveyances, and annexes a heavy penalty to any breach of it. S. 14 specifically deals with the hiring of conveyances from one class of persons, and prohibits this under a lighter penalty. Unless the view is adopted that the penalty under s. 14 is cumulative and that, therefore, the persons mentioned in it are guilty *both* of an illegal practice and an illegal hiring, the other construction is that the latter section qualifies the former, and takes the persons specifically dealt with by it out of the general words of s. 7. However this may be, it should be noted in connection

PARLIAMENTARY

The effect of a contract with livery stablemen for conveyance of voters. Ss. 7 & 14.

Parliamentary Proviso to sub-s. 11 engrafted on s. 7.

with the prohibition contained in s. 7 against payments and contracts for the conveyance of voters to the poll, that sub-s. 3 of the 14th ·s. provides that 'nothing in this Act shall prevent a carriage, horse, or other animal being *let to*, or *hired*, or employed, or used by an elector, or several electors, at their joint cost, for the purpose of being conveyed to or from the poll."

In the *Buckrose Case* (4 O'M. & H., 117) it was held that where a voter had driven to the poll in a cab, paying nothing to the driver, and being ignorant that the use of the cab was prohibited by law, no offence had been committed and that his vote was good. But query whether *his* use of the cab was prohibited by law. See s. 14 (3).

Illegal to pay electors for placarding.

The second offence consists in paying *to any elector*, or contracting to pay to him, any sum on account of the use of any house, land, building or premises, for the exhibition of any address, bill or notice, or on account of the exhibition of address, bill or notice, with the proviso that if it is the ordinary business of an elector as an advertising agent, to exhibit them, any payment to him shall not be illegal. This section speaks for itself. It strikes at a form of corruption suggested in the *Westminster Case* (referred to at p. 20), where it was charged that the respondent sought to influence voters by paying them sums of money for the privilege of exhibiting his placards in their windows or upon their shutters. That was held to be a corrupt practice only where the payment was made with the corrupt view of influencing the vote of the person who got the money; but under this section it is an illegal practice to make these payments *to any elector* without reference to the motive which dictates the payment. It would seem, however, that it is lawful to pay non-electors for the right of exhibiting placards, &c., unless it be shown that by excessive payments to such persons it is sought to influence the votes of electors connected with them. Then it would probably be bribery.

But not illegal in case of non-electors.

Schedule I., Part II., makes it lawful to pay "the expenses of printing, the expenses of advertising and the expenses of publishing, issuing and distributing addresses and notices." It is, therefore, permissible to employ persons to distribute and post ordinary election bills and placards. See the *Barrow Case* (4 O'M. & H., 76) where the documents printed were copies of a letter written by a distinguished statesman and exhortations to "Vote for D——." But it would be illegal for a volunteer to make such payments, except, perhaps, to the extent of a few shillings, for by s. 28 no election expense may be paid except by or through the election agent. *The Norwich Case* (4 O'M. & II., 89.) Parliamentary

The third offence consists in paying, or contracting to pay, for any committee rooms in excess of the number allowed in the first schedule to the Act. The second part of the first schedule prescribes the number of committee rooms, which may legally be paid for in the cases respectively of borough and county elections. Illegal to pay for committee rooms in excess of number allowed.

In a borough, *at least* one committee room is allowed. If the number of electors exceed 500, then one extra committee room for every complete 500 is allowed, and if there is a number of electors over and above any complete 500, then another committee room for such extra number. Thus where the number of electors is, 1,501, it would seem four committee rooms are permitted, and so on. Legal number of committee rooms in boroughs.

In the case of counties, the following committee rooms are allowed—(1.) One central committee room; (2.) One committee room for each polling district; and (3.) Where the number of electors in any polling district exceeds 500 one additional committee room for every *complete* 500 electors over and above the first 500. Thus if there is a county with polling-districts A, B, C, and D, and in A there are 400 electors, in B 600, in C 1,000, and in D 1,060, the committee rooms which may be legally hired will be as follows (*a.*) One central committee room; (*b.*) One committee room in A; (*c.*) One committee room in B, for though there are more than 500 electors there is not a second *complete* 500; (*d.*) Two committee rooms in C; and (*e.*) Two committee rooms in D. It is important to have a clear view of the number of committee rooms which may be hired and *paid for*, because, under the section we are considering, In counties.

any payment or contract for payment made in respect of any committee room in excess of the number allowed is an illegal practice which will defeat the election if made by any agent.

What is a committee room.   There is no definition in the Act of what constitutes a committee room. Is a committee room a single room or a suite of rooms ? Is it an illegal practice for the election agent to have in addition to the room in which the general work of the election is conducted, another room contiguous in which he sits himself, and uses for necessary purposes of the election ? We think not; but the only attempt at a definition of a committee room is a negative one in the general interpretation clause, " the expression committee room shall not include any house or room occupied by a candidate at an election as a dwelling, by reason only of the candidate there transacting business with his agents in relation to such election ; nor shall any room or building be deemed to be a committee room for the purposes of this Act by reason only of the candidate, or any agent of the candidate, addressing therein electors, committee men, or others." What the Act strikes at is *payment* for additional committee rooms. There is apparently no objection to a candidate using as many committee rooms as his friends are content to *lend* him, subject to a restriction on the kind or description of premises employed to be presently mentioned.

Only payment for committee rooms illegal.

Illegal to pay election expenses except through election agent.   S. 28 of the Act of 1883 creates another illegal practice, which, if committed by any agent, will avoid the election. It declares that no payment and no advance or deposit shall be made, whether by the candidate or any other person, before, during, or after an election, in respect of the expenses incurred on account of the election, except through *the election agent*, acting in person or by a sub-agent. There is

Proviso to this rule.   a proviso to the effect that this section shall not apply to—(1.) any payments made by the returning officer ; or (2.) any sum disbursed by any person out of his own money for any *small* expenses *legally* incurred by himself, if *such sum is not repaid to him*. The design of this section is to secure the payment of all election expenses through the medium of a responsible election agent, who is bound to make a return of every farthing spent. No other person is now allowed to make any payment on account of them, and if any one does his vote is bad. (The *Buckrose Case*, 4 O'M. & H., 116). If any person, other than the election agent, does disburse any sum in promotion of the election it must be for a small expense merely, and he cannot recover it back from the candidate: What is "a small expense" within the meaning of the proviso has yet to be decided. It will probably receive a very strict construction, because the latter portion of s. 28 provides—"All money provided by any person other than the candidate for any expenses incurred on account of or in respect of the conduct and management of the election, whether as gift, loan, advance or deposit, shall be paid to the candidate or his election agent, and not otherwise." Unless, therefore, the permission given in the proviso is strictly limited, it will convert s. 28 into a dead letter. In the *Norwich Case*, 4 O'M. & H., 84, the Court suggested that the proviso might, *perhaps*, excuse the expenditure of half-a-crown.

[marginal note: Parliamentary]

[marginal note: Small sums disbursed by person other than election agent gifts.]

This section effectually prevents the expenditure of any but such a small sum in promoting the election of a candidate by any of the numerous political and trade associations or clubs which have been founded for the purpose of impressing the views of their members upon Parliament, or upon the constituencies. "If any agent of a candidate chooses to expend money illegally in the promotion of that candidate's return, whether the money came from a great political club, or from a subscription of well-wishers, or from an enthusiastic supporter, such expenditure will be fatal to the candidate who succeeds by its help." (Per Denman, J., in the *Ipswich Case*, 4 O'M. & H., 74.)

An important question next arises—to what extent is it possible for a candidate to obtain relief against the consequences of an illegal practice committed by himself or an agent? One penalty of an illegal practice is—and it is the only one with which we are now concerned—the loss of the seat. Can this be averted in any case? It will be

[marginal note: The possibility of relief]

PARLIAMENTARY remembered that the qualified relief given under s. 22 of the
Possibility Act of 1883 applies to illegal practices as well as to treating
of relief. and undue influence, when they are committed by any
person except the candidate personally or his election agent.
Therefore, if any of the illegal practices mentioned in this
chapter be committed by any of the candidate's agents
Under s. 22. (except his election agent), relief against the forfeiture of
the seat *may* be given under s. 22.

But the next section of the Act of 1883—viz., the 23rd
—carries the *possibility* of relief still further, and even
extends it to cases where the illegal practice has been committed by the *candidate* himself *or his election agent*. This
section is in the following terms:—

Under s. 23. "Where, on application made, it is shown to the High
Court or to an election court, by such evidence as seems to
the Court sufficient:

"(*a*.) That any act or omission of a candidate at any
election, or of his election agent, or of any other
agent or person, would, by reason of being a *payment, engagement, employment or contract in contravention of this Act, or being the payment of a sum
or the incurring of expense in excess of any maximum
amount allowed by this Act, or of otherwise being in
Provisions of contravention of any of the provisions of this Act,
s. 23. be, but for this section, an illegal practice, payment,
employment, or hiring ;* and

"(*b*.) That such act or omission arose from inadvertence or
from accidental miscalculation, or from some other
reasonable cause of a like nature, and in any case
did not arise from any want of good faith; and

"(*c*.) That such notice of the application has been given
in the county or borough for which the election
was held as to the Court seems fit :

and under the circumstances it seems to the Court to be
just that the candidate or such election or other agent
or person, or any of them, should not be subject to any of
the consequences under this Act of the said act or omission,
the Court may make an order allowing such act or omission
to be an exception from the provisions of this Act, which

would otherwise make the same an illegal practice, payment, employment or hiring, and thereupon such candidate, agent, or person shall not be subject to any of the consequences under this Act of the said act or omission."

When, in the next section, we treat of illegal practices generally, the majority of the offences pointed at by the above section will appear; but the words "contract in contravention of this Act" seem clearly to embrace the three classes of acts mentioned in s. 7, and the general words of the section are sufficient to cover the offences struck at in s. 28. If this be so, the result is that there is no case of an *illegal* practice (as distinguished from a *corrupt* practice), where the unlawful act of a candidate or a candidate's agent, whether the election agent or any other agent, *necessarily* means the forfeiture of a seat. For an illegal practice committed by the candidate or the election agent there is the possibility of relief under s. 23, if it is shown on application to the High Court or the Election Court that the act or omission arose from inadvertence, or from accident miscalculation, or from other reasonable cause of a like nature, and "not from any want of good faith." On the other hand, for an illegal practice committed by an agent (other than the election agent), there would seem to be the possibility of relief both under s. 22 and under s. 23.

<small>No case of an illegal practice where election necessarily avoided.</small>

In the case of an application for relief made to the High Court under the latter section, the applicant is not, in so many words, required affirmatively to prove the facts which are conditions precedent to relief under the former section, but it is entirely in the discretion of the Court whether it makes an order under s. 23 or not, and it is probable that it would not do so unless the applicant satisfied it that—(*a*.) the offences committed were of "a trivial, unimportant, and limited character;" (*b*.) that the candidate and his election agent took all reasonable means for preventing the commission of corrupt and illegal practices; and (*c*.) that in all other respects the election was free from any corrupt or illegal practice on the part of such candidate and of his agents. The principles on which the Court acts in giving or refusing relief, will be further discussed hereafter.

<small>Terms on which relief under s. 23 will be granted.</small>

SECTION II.—WHEN COMMITTED BY THE CANDIDATE OR THE ELECTION AGENT.

Parliamentary.

The general provision of s. 11 of the Act of 1883 is, that any illegal practice committed by the sitting member or any of his agents, will avoid the election. The four classes of acts dealt with in the last section, come under that rule. But in addition, numerous other offences are created by the Act of 1883, which the Legislature has thought right to say shall only become illegal practices when committed by the candidate or his election agent; or which, through illegal practices, by whomsoever committed, only affect the validity of the election when brought home to the candidate personally, or to his election agent. Those offences are scattered with little method all over the Act. We group them together in this chapter, and for greater clearness it is proposed to divide them, as above indicated, into, first, offences which only become illegal practices when committed by the candidate or his election agent; and secondly, offences which are illegal practices *ab initio*, but which only avoid the election when committed by the candidate or his election agent. In this chapter we would remind the reader we treat exclusively of the law as it relates to parliamentary elections.

Further division of illegal practices.

SUB-SECTION I.—OFFENCES WHICH BECOME ILLEGAL PRACTICES WHEN COMMITTED BY THE CANDIDATE OR THE ELECTION AGENT.

Illegal payment.

(A.) S. 13 of the Act of 1883 enacts that where any person knowingly provides money for any payment which is contrary to the provisions of the Act, or for any expenses incurred in excess of the maximum allowed by the Act, or for replacing any money expended in any such payment or expenses, except where the same may have been previously allowed in pursuance of this Act to be an exception, such person shall be guilty of *illegal payment*. Illegal *payment* is a new offence and generally falls short of *illegal practice;* but by s. 21 (sub-s. 2) a *candidate* or the *election agent* of a candidate who is personally guilty of an offence of *illegal payment, employment,* or *hiring,* shall be guilty of an illegal practice. Therefore, an illegal payment becomes an illegal practice when committed by the candidate or his election agent, and it then avoids the election. The object of s. 13 is in keeping with the main design of the Act of 1883, which is to discourage profusion at elections, and to restrain the cost of a contest within the narrowest limits. As will be shown at greater length hereafter, a sliding scale of maximum expenditure, regulated by the number of electors and the character of the constituency, is contained in the first schedule ; and to enforce compliance with it, and other provisions of the Act directed against prodigality, s. 13 is framed. S. 8, to be presently mentioned, forbids a candidate or his election agent, to pay or incur any expense whatever above the maximum amount allowed. The section under consideration is of somewhat wider scope. It forbids any person to do what the candidate and his election agent have already been prohibited from doing, and it also prohibits any person from providing money for any payment contrary to the provisions of this Act, though it be within the maximum allowed. [Parliamentary illegal payment.]

(B.) The first sub-section of s. 14 makes it an illegal *hiring* for any person to *let, lend* or *employ,* for the purpose of the conveyance of electors to or from the poll, any public stage or hackney carriage, or any horse or other animal kept or used for drawing the same, or any carriage, horse or other animal which he keeps or uses, for the purpose of letting out for hire, where he knows that the same are to be used for the conveyance of voters to or from the poll ; and by the second sub-section any person who hires, borrows or uses, for the purpose of the conveyance of voters to or from the poll, any carriage, horse or other animal which he knows the owner thereof is prohibited by this section to let, lend or employ for that purpose, is also guilty of illegal hiring. If he does not know, no offence is committed. (The *Buckrose Case,* [Illegal hiring. Letting, lending or employing hackney carriages.]

4 O'M. & H. 117.) By s. 21 (sub-s. 2) a candidate, or an election agent of a candidate, who is personally guilty of an offence of illegal payment, employment or *hiring*, shall be guilty of an *illegal practice*.

The prohibitions in s. 14 are threefold. It is an offence either to (1) *let* or *hire*, (2) to *lend* or *borrow*, or (3) to *use* or employ a horse or carriage *which is kept for the purpose of being let out to hire*. So far as regards the prohibition against letting or hiring, it has already been pointed out that s. 7, sub-s. 1, which makes it an illegal practice to make, or contract to make, any payment with or to any person on account of the conveyance of electors to or from the poll, amply provides for the mischief sought to be restrained by this section, unless it be held that the effect of s. 14 (sub-s. 1 and 2) is to take out of the operation of the former section the class of persons mentioned in the latter. It is difficult to think this was intended. On the other hand, why were the words "let" or "hire" introduced into the section? However, this much is certain: It is, *at least*, an illegal hiring, and it may be an illegal practice for jobmasters and others who keep horses and carriages which they let out to hire to let any of them for the purpose of conveying voters to or from the poll, except under the circumstances allowed in sub-s. 3. It is there enacted: "Nothing in this Act shall prevent a carriage, horse or other animal being let to or hired, employed or used by an elector, or several electors at their joint cost, for the purpose of being conveyed to or from the poll." But for this proviso it would hardly have been safe for any jobmaster to have had a single cab on the stand on the polling day, and it would certainly have been an offence for an elector to go to the poll in a hansom at his own expense. The sub-section authorises the latter proceeding, but it is submitted that it will be an illegal act for a person who has hired a cab to pick up another elector on the way and give him a lift to the poll, unless the latter shares the cost of the cab. "Joint cost" is the expression used in the Act. There is no definition of this term given, and it seems open to doubt whether if three electors knowing of the prohibition, drive up to the poll in a hackney cab the failure of any one of them to make up his quota of the fare, though he pay something, will render the whole three electors and the owner of the cab guilty of an illegal hiring. Probably if the Court was of opinion that there was a *bonâ fide* intention to share the cost, and each elector paid a substantial part of it, such a case would be held to be within the protection of the sub-section. On the other hand, if it were shown that a number of electors went together to the poll in a conveyance hired from a livery stableman, and that the fare was really paid by one or two of them, the others contributing a nominal sum, there can be little doubt it would be held that such a case was not protected by sub-s. 3.

Parliamentary "Joint cost."

The same section also prohibits the *lending* of any horse or carriage which is kept for the purpose of being let out to hire. It must be observed that the general use of conveyances in connection with the bringing up of voters to the poll is not forbidden by the Act of 1883; it is the employment of *hired* conveyance which is struck at. As a rule, a candidate or his agent may accept the loan of horses and traps from any quarter where he can get them; but this section introduces an exception to the rule. It expressly prohibits the persons mentioned in it from even lending their horses and carriages. Livery stablemen are certainly within the scope of the section. No matter how keen and disinterested their partizanship may be, they are forbidden to lend the horses and carriages used in the way of their business for the purpose of conveying voters to and from the poll. But the section is not limited to livery stablemen. The prohibition is against lending "any carriage, horse or other animal which any person keeps or uses for the purpose of letting out for hire." Whether these words would cover the case of a person who kept a horse and trap, which he generally used for his own purposes, but which he occasionally let out for hire, may well be doubted; but it would certainly comprehend the case of a publican who, it may be, keeps a single horse and trap for the purpose of letting it out.

Illegal to lend a hackney carriage.

As a rule candidates may use borrowed traps.

Exception to that rule.

80 THE LAW RELATING TO

Parliamentary
Illegal to use a hackney carriage.
Illegal to use any hackney carriage in an election.

The section not merely forbids the lending of a horse or carriage of the description mentioned, it also prohibits its *use* or *employment* in the conveyance of voters to and from the poll. A horse or trap kept for the purpose of being let out for hire, must not, under any circumstances, be used on the polling day to bring up voters, unless in the case excepted by the 3rd sub-section. Thus, a job master cannot himself, or by his servants, convey voters to the booths, nor can he give a friend or acquaintance a lift. S. 48, it should be mentioned here, allows voters to be conveyed by sea to and from the polling place at the candidate's expense under certain circumstances. "Where the nature of a county is such that any electors residing therein are unable at an election for *such county* to reach their polling place without crossing the sea, or a branch or arm thereof, this Act shall not prevent the provision of means for conveying such electors *by sea* to their polling place, and the amount of payment for such means of conveyance may be in addition to the maximum amount of expenses allowed by the Act." The result is, that with regard to the conveyance of voters to or from the poll, it is still legal to carry them in *borrowed* carriages unless the carriages or horses employed are usually let out for hire; but it is in no case lawful to *hire* conveyance or any other means of carrying voters, except some provision of *sea* carriage in the cases within S. 48.

Legal to pay for sea carriage in some cases.

Illegal to corruptly induce a candidate to retire.

(C.) S. 15 provides that any person who corruptly induces or procures any other person to withdraw from being a candidate at an election in consideration of any payment or promise of payment shall be guilty of illegal payment, and any person withdrawing in pursuance of such inducement or procurement shall also be guilty of illegal payment. An illegal payment becomes an illegal practice when committed by a candidate or his election agent. Therefore, if a candidate or his election agent becomes a party to any corrupt arrangement forbidden by the section, his election is liable to be defeated.

Illegal to pay for bands, ribbons, &c.

(D.) By s. 16 all payments, or contracts for payments, on account of bands of music, torches, flags, banners, cockades, ribbons, or other marks of distinction are forbidden, where PARLIAMENTARY they are made for the purpose of promoting the return of a candidate, and all persons concerned in making such payments or in receiving them are declared guilty of an illegal *payment*. It is difficult to say why payments or contracts for payment on account of exhibiting placards, &c., constitute an illegal practice (s. 7) and the class of payments in the section under consideration are only illegal payments; but the distinction is made. In the *Stepney Case* (4 O'M. & H., 39), a flag for which no payment was made was suspended across the street by ropes attached to the roofs of two houses, one of the roofs was injured by the rope, and a voter was paid for repairing the injury. This was held not to be within the section, and the vote stood.

(E.) S. 17 declares that no person shall, for the purpose of promoting or procuring the election of a candidate at any election be engaged or employed for *payment* or *promise of payment* for any purpose or in any capacity whatever except as authorised by the schedule of the Act, and if any person is engaged before, during or after an election in contravention of this section the person engaging or employing him shall be guilty of an illegal *employment*, and the person so engaged or employed shall also be guilty of illegal employment, if he knew that he was engaged or employed contrary to law. It becomes, therefore, material to enquire what persons can be legally employed and *paid* in connection with a parliamentary election, and here care must be taken to distinguish the case of county from the case of borough constituencies.

Illegal to pay agents in excess of the number allowed.

Schedule I. (Part I.) in the case of *counties* allows :— Number of agents allowed.
One election agent.
One sub-agent in each polling district.
One polling agent in each polling station. In counties.
One clerk, and } for the central committee-room when
one messenger }
    the number of electors does not exceed 5,000, and
    where it does exceed 5,000 one additional clerk
    and messenger for each complete 5,000, and if

PARLIAMENTARY there is a number of electors over and above any complete 5,000 or 5,000's, then another clerk and messenger may be employed for such number, although not amounting to a complete 5,000. In addition,

One clerk, and one messenger } for each polling district, and when the number of electors exceed 500 in any polling district one clerk and one messenger for every complete 500 or complete 500's of electors, with this provision, that if there be a number over and above a complete 500, one clerk and one messenger shall be allowed for such number.

Illustration. Suppose a county constituency with 11,000 voters, and polling districts A, B, C, D, and E, having respectively 2,000, 3,000, 300, 700, and 5,000 voters, and twelve polling stations. It is assumed the allowance of paid agents will be as follows: The election agent, five sub-agents, twelve polling agents, three clerks and three messengers for the central committee-room; four clerks and four messengers in polling district A; six clerks and six messengers in B; one clerk and one messenger in C; two clerks and two messengers in D; and ten clerks and ten messengers in E. It may be stated here that there is a proviso in the schedule that the number of clerks and messengers so allowed in any county, may be employed in any polling district where their services may be required.

Number of paid agents allowed. In the case of *boroughs* the number of paid agents allowed is less, viz. :—

One election agent.

In boroughs. One polling agent in each polling station.

One clerk and one messenger for *every* complete 500 electors, and if there is a number over and above any complete 500, or complete 500's of electors, an additional clerk and messenger may be employed.

A regular clerk of the election agent employed without increase of salary or payment to address envelopes and do other work in connection with the election is not a paid clerk, and need not be so returned. (The *Buckrose Case*, 4 O'M. & H., 116.) [PARLIAMENTARY]

The purposes for which and the capacities in which persons may be employed are indicated by the description given in the schedule. Thus, it is illegal to employ persons, for hire, to keep order at a candidate's meetings, although the services of volunteers may lawfully be used for that purpose. (The *Ipswich Case* 4 O'M. & H., 72.)

An illegal employment, by s. 21, is made an illegal practice when committed by the candidate, or his election agent. It must be noted that this section is merely directed against the employment of any *paid* agents in excess of the number allowed. The employment of volunteers is perfectly legal under the new law. But nothing must be given to such volunteers. In the *Barrow Case* (4 O'M. & H.) certain persons gave their services on the polling day gratuitously. But each of them received a meal — a pork pie, a sandwich, and a cup of coffee. It was held that these things constituted "payment," and that, although they did not amount to a corrupt practice, the sitting member must be unseated. [Legal to employ volunteers.]

It has been already stated that it is an illegal practice to *pay for* any committee-rooms in excess of the number allowed in the schedule (s. 7, sub.-s. 3). That section, however, does not place any restrictions upon committee-rooms which are *lent* to the candidate. The section we now proceed to discuss, viz., section 20, does, and it adds to the restrictions upon those hired, by forbidding certain premises being used as committee-rooms, without reference to the question of whether they are lent or hired. Section 20 prohibits the *hire* or *use* as a committee-room for the purposes of an election of (1) any premises on which the sale by wholesale or retail of any intoxicating liquor is authorised by license (whether the license be for consumption on or off the premises), or (2) any premises where any intoxicating liquor is sold, or is supplied to members of a club, society, or association *other than a permanent political club*, or, (3) any premises whereon refreshment of any kind, whether food or drink, is ordinarily sold [Restrictions upon committee rooms Not to be held— (1) On licensed premises, (2) Nor any premises where drink sold except political club, (3) Nor where refreshment sold.]

PARLIAMENTARY for consumption on the premises, or (4) the premises of any
(4) Nor school- public elementary school in receipt of an annual parliamen-
room tary grant; provided that nothing in the section shall apply
to any part of such premises which is ordinarily let for the
purpose of chambers or offices, or the holding of public
meetings, or of arbitrations, *if such part has a separate entrance,
and no direct communication with any part of the premises in
which any intoxicating liquor or refreshment is sold or supplied
as aforesaid*. In the *Buckrose Case* (4 O'M. & H., 113) the
dwellinghouse of a schoolmaster of a public elementary school
in receipt of an annual parliamentary grant had been used
as a committee room, and, although the house was severed
from the school, as it was within the same curtilage, it was
held that the use of the house was illegal. In the same case
the decision was otherwise, where it appeared that the school
house was provided rent free by a subscriber to the school
who was the owner of the premises and paid the rates.
Every member of the committee who uses the prohibited
room commits the offence. (The *Buckrose Case, supra*.)

Any breach of this section, whether on the part of a person
hiring or using any part of the prohibited premises, or on
the part of the person letting, is made an illegal *hiring*. The
main object of the section is to discourage treating by
diminishing the facilities for it. And no doubt those facilities are lessened in view of this rigorous prohibition against
having committee-rooms on licensed premises, or in clubs
other than *permanent political* clubs, or in any place where
refreshments are sold. All hotels, inns, grocers' licensed
premises, temperance hotels, refreshment-rooms, eating-
houses, coffee and cocoa taverns, social, literary, or professional clubs, will come within the prohibition of the
statute. The section contains an absolute prohibition against
the use of any such places as committee-rooms, and one of
the penalties when the candidate or his election agent is a
party to the breach of the law, is the loss of the seat.

SUB-SECTION II.—ILLEGAL PRACTICES WHICH AVOID THE SEAT ONLY WHEN COMMITTED BY THE CANDIDATE OR HIS ELECTION AGENT.

(A.) By s. 8 of the Act of 1883, no sum shall be paid and no expense incurred by a candidate at an election or his election agent in respect of the conduct and management of the election in excess of the maximum amount specified in the schedule and applicable to the particular constituency, and if any candidate or his election agent knowingly acts in contravention of this section he is guilty of an illegal practice. It has been stated already that one of the ways in which the Act strikes at corruption is by prohibiting profusion. This section and s. 13, given before, are auxiliary to this object, and they forbid all persons interested in the election to exceed the maximum sums allowed in the schedule. It will be observed, that by the express words of the section only the candidate or his election agent can be guilty of this particular illegal practice. *Parliamentary Illegal to pay anything in excess of maximum.*

(B.) The first sub-section of s. 9 makes it an illegal practice for any person to vote or to induce or procure any other person to vote at an election, knowing that he or such person is prohibited from voting whether by this Act or any other Act. In view of this provision it becomes important to inquire what persons are prohibited from voting within the meaning of this section. *Illegal to vote where prohibition against voting.*

And first as to persons prohibited by the Act itself. They are as follows:—

(1.) "Every person who, in consequence of *conviction* or of the *report* of any Election Court or Election Commissioners under this Act, or under the Corrupt Practices (Municipal Elections) Act, 1872, or under Part IV. of the Municipal Corporations Act, 1882, or under any other Act for the time being in force relating to corrupt practices at any election for any public office, has become incapable of voting at any election, *Persons prohibited from voting by the Act of 1883.*

THE LAW RELATING TO

PARLIAMENTARY whether a parliamentary election or an election to any
S. 37.   public office, is now prohibited from voting at any such election" (s. 37 of the Act of 1813).

S. 36.   (2.) "Every person guilty of a corrupt or illegal practice, or of illegal employment, payment or hiring at any election is prohibited from voting at *such* election" (s. 36). It will be observed that there is a material difference between the prohibitions enacted in ss. 36 and 37. In the case of a corrupt practice, &c., committed *at* a pending election, the elector committing it comes *at once*—as soon as he is guilty of the act and before he is convicted of it—under the prohibition against voting at *such* election; but where the corrupt practice has been committed at some *other election* the prohibition does not come into operation until he has either been convicted of the offence or reported by an Election Court or Election Commissioner.

Paid agents forbidden to vote   (3.) The election agent, sub-agents, polling-agents, clerks and messengers authorised by the 1st Schedule, *where they are paid*, are forbidden to vote at the election (1st Schedule, Part I.), either in the division in which they are employed, or in any other division of the same borough (s. 15 of the Redistribution of Seats Act, 1885). There is no objection whatever to unpaid agents voting.

Persons prohibited from voting include :—

Persons prohibited from voting by other Acts.   (1.) Any elector who, at or within six months before the election, shall have been retained, hired, or employed for any of the purposes of the election for reward (30 & 31 Vict., c. 102, s. 11 ; 31 & 32 Vict., cc. 48 & 49, s. 8). It should be noted that by the principal Act it is an illegal employment to employ any one for the purpose of promoting or procuring an election, except for the purposes indicated by s. 17 of the Act of 1883.

(2.) Any convict, until his term of punishment has expired, or he has obtained a free pardon. (The 33 & 34 Vict., c. 23, s. 2.)

(3.) Persons under the age of twenty-one years. (7 & 8 Will. III., c. 25, s. 11.)

(4.) A returning officer at a parliamentary election, unless PARLIAMENTARY there is a tie. (35 & 36 Vict., c. 33, s. 2.)

The prohibition against police officers voting at parliamentary elections has been repealed by the Police Disabilities Removal Act, 1887.

Peers of England and Scotland (*Earl of Beauchamp* v. Persons prohibited only *Overseers of the Parish of Madresfield*, 42 L.J. C.P., 32), peers by the common law. of Ireland, when not Members of the House of Commons (*Lord Rendlesham* v. *Haward*, 43 L.J. C.P., 33), women (*Chorlton* v. *Lings*, L.R. 4, C.P. 374 ; 38 L.J. C.P., 25), and aliens are also prohibited from voting ; but the prohibition in these cases arises by *the common law of Parliament* and not by statute, and it is submitted therefore that it is not an illegal practice for any of these persons to vote, nor is it an offence within the meaning of the section we are considering to induce them to do so.

But if anyone who is prohibited by *any statute* votes, or anyone induces anybody else who comes under a *statutory* prohibition to vote, *knowing* that such person falls within any of the above prohibitions, an illegal practice is committed. The knowledge referred to must be, not a knowledge of the statute which creates the disability, because every person is supposed to know the law, but a knowledge of the *facts* in relation to the person's status or past conduct which bring him within the statute. When the illegal practice mentioned in this section is committed by a candidate or his election agent, the election is avoided : but when it is committed by any other person, though he may be an agent of the candidate to bind him by any corrupt act, the election is not defeated (sub-s. 2 of the 9th s.).

(C.) By the 2nd sub-s. of s. 9 it is enacted that any person who, before or during an election, knowingly publishes a false statement of the withdrawal of a candidate at such election, for the purpose of promoting or procuring the election of another candidate, is guilty of an illegal practice, and if the offence is committed by the candidate or his election agent, but not otherwise, the election is avoided. The essence of this offence is—(*a*.) the publication

PARLIAMENTARY of the false intelligence, knowing that it is false; and (b.)
Publishing publishing it with the object stated in the section—viz., to
false state-
ment of with- promote the return of another candidate.
drawal of a
candidate. (D.) " Every bill, placard or poster having reference to an
election shall bear upon the face thereof the name and
Illegal to address of the printer and publisher thereof; and any person
issue bill
without printing, publishing, or posting, or causing to be printed,
printer's published or posted, any such bill, placard, or poster, as
name.
aforesaid, which fails to bear ·upon the face thereof the
name and address of the printer and publisher, shall, if he
is the candidate or the election agent of the candidate, be
guilty of an illegal practice " (s. 18). This section is directed
against anonymous libels, but election agents will require
to take great care that every bill and placard they issue in
connection with the election, no matter how innocent and
businesslike it may be, complies with the provisions of the
law.

"Bill is a very large word indeed "—per Field, J., in the
Barrow Case, 4 O'M. & H. 78—but it is submitted it does
not include election addresses sent by post or distributed
by hand, although, as to this, see *Ex p. Ives*, 5 Times,
L.R., 136. And it has been decided the section does not
include circulars. *Barstow*, 5 Times, L.R. 159.)

The court has no power to relieve the printer of the bill,
placard or poster (*Ex p. Lenanton*, 5 Times L.R., 173),
who is liable to a fine of £100.

(E.) By s. 29, sub-s. 2, it is made an illegal practice for
Illegal to pay an election agent to pay any claim against a candidate
election bills arising out of the election, which is barred by not being sent
except within
specified time. in within the time specified in the Act, and by sub-s. 4 the
election agent is forbidden to pay any claim after the time
specified by the Act for payment, under the penalty of being
guilty of an illegal practice. But, for the protection of an
honest candidate, sub-s. 6 provides that where the election
court reports that· any payment made by an election agent
in contravention of this section was made without the sanction
or connivance of the candidate, the election shall not be void,
and the candidate shall be subjected to no incapacity. The

whole duties and functions of the election agent are treated of in Chapter VIII., and it will be more convenient to leave until then the fuller discussion of the circumstances under which disobedience of s. 29 on the election agent's part will constitute an illegal practice. PARLIAMENTARY

(F.) An election agent is required by s. 33 to make a return of the election expenses within thirty-five days of the declaration of the poll, accompanied by the declaration given in the schedule. By sub-s. 6, failure to comply with any of the requirements of s. 33 is made an *illegal practice*. And by the following sub-s., *knowingly* to make a false return or a false declaration is a *corrupt practice*. Illegal not to make return of expenses within specified time.

It has already been explained in treating in the last section of the illegal practices which avoid the election when committed by any agent, that there is the possibility of relief against the consequences of such acts under s. 22 as well as s. 23 of the Act of 1883. In regard to the illegal practices described in both sub-sections of this section, s. 22 has no application; but in a proper case, the Court may grant relief under s. 23. Candidates and election agents cannot, however, be too emphatically warned against any reckless expenditure or employment in reliance upon the chance of indulgence being extended to them under the terms of this section, because on its plain reading, it is only to apply where the slip has been the result of inadvertance or accidental miscalculation, and where the applicant has not been wanting in good faith. The possibility of relief.

S. 23.

CHAPTER III.

ILLEGAL PRACTICES WHICH AVOID A MUNICIPAL ELECTION.

SECTION 1.—WHEN COMMITTED BY THE CANDIDATE OR ANY AGENT.

MUNICIPAL. THE illegal practices which avoid a municipal election if committed by the candidate or any agent are also four in number. Three are contained in s. 4, and the fourth in s. 5 of the Act of 1884.

Illegal to pay for conveyance of voters, S. 4 of the Act of 1884 corresponds with s. 7 of the Act of 1883, and in identical language it declares that any payment or contract for payment in promotion of the election of a candidate at a municipal election, (1) on account of the conveyance of electors to or from the poll, whether in carriages Or for placards, or by rail, or (2) to an elector for the use of any house, &c., for the exhibition of placards, &c., or (3) on account of any committee-room in excess of the number authorised shall be Or for committee-rooms an illegal practice. All the remarks we have made in the in excess of first section of Chapter II., with reference to the application certain of s. 7 of the Act of 1883 to parliamentary elections, apply number. to the application of s. 4 of the Act of 1884 to municipal elections. The number of committee-rooms allowed in the case of a municipal election is less than the number allowed in any kind of parliamentary election. And so far as is necessary to secure this result the language of the two sections differs. But subject to this their language is exactly the same and a similar interpretation must be given to them.

The number of committee-rooms which may be lawfully paid for is regulated by the size of the borough or ward in which the election is held. "If the election is for a borough one committee-room for the borough, and if the election is for a ward one committee-room for the ward, and if the number of electors in such borough or ward exceeds two thousand, one additional committee-room for every two thousand electors and incomplete part of two thousand electors, over and above the said two thousand." (S. 4, sub-s. 1 (c) of Act of 1884.) It will be noted that while in the case of a borough *parliamentary* election a candidate is permitted to hire one committee-room for each 500 electors, in the case of a municipal election he may only hire one for each 2,000 electors.

<small>MUNICIPAL.

Number of committee-rooms which may be paid for.</small>

The other illegal practice which avoids a municipal election if committed by any agent is created by s. 5 of the Act of 1884, and consists in the candidate or any one of his agents knowingly paying any sum, or incurring any expense in respect of the conduct or management of a municipal election in excess of the maximum amount authorised by the Act. There are also sections of the Act of 1883 rendering payments in excess of the maximum amounts mentioned in the schedule illegal in the case of parliamentary elections, but there is this important difference, that a payment in excess of the maximum is an illegal practice, by *whomsoever* committed, in the case of a municipal election, but in the case of a parliamentary election it is only an illegal practice when committed by the candidate or *the election agent.*

<small>Illegal to pay anything in excess of maximum.</small>

S. 5, sub-s. 1, fixes the maximum sum which may lawfully be spent over a municipal election. " The sum of twenty-five pounds, and, if the number of electors in the borough or ward exceeds five hundred, an additional amount of threepence for each elector above the first five hundred electors." It is also provided that where there are two or more joint candidates at an election, the maximum amount of such expenses shall, for each of such joint candidates be reduced by one-fourth, or if there be more than two joint candidates by one-third (s. 5, sub-s. 3). The next sub-section enacts that where two or more candidates hire or use the same committee-rooms for the election, or employ or use the same clerks, messengers or polling agents, or publish a joint address, or joint circular or notice, these candidates shall be deemed

<small>The maximum.</small>

Municipal. to be joint candidates, subject to this: that the employment or use of the same committee-room, clerk, messenger, or polling agent, if accidental or casual, or of a trivial and unimportant character, shall not be deemed of itself to constitute persons joint candidates (s. 5, sub-s. 4).

Possibility of relief. A candidate at a municipal election may obtain relief against the consequences of an illegal practice committed by him or any one of his agents, under the same conditions as a candidate at a parliamentary election may obtain relief. S. 20 of the Act of 1884 is in substance the same as s. 23 of the Act of 1883, and applying its provisions to the illegal practices under discussion, the result is that upon application to the High Court or an Election Court and after giving such notices in the borough of the application as may be directed, a candidate upon satisfying the Court that the particular act arose from (1) inadvertence or accidental miscalculation, or from some other reasonable cause of a like nature, and (2) did not arise from any want of good faith, may obtain an order allowing such act to be an exception from the provision of the Act, and relieving him from all penal consequences.

SECTION II.—WHEN COMMITTED BY THE CANDIDATE OR WITH HIS KNOWLEDGE AND CONSENT.

The acts which have this effect are very similar to the offences treated of in the second section of Chapter II., which avoid a parliamentary election when committed by the candidate or his election agent.

Illegal payment. (A.) S. 9 of the Act of 1884 is word for word the same as s. 13 of the Act of 1883, and it enacts that where any person knowingly provides money for any payment which is contrary to the provisions of the Act, or for any expense incurred in excess of the maximum allowed by the Act, or for replacing any money expended in any such payment or expenses, except where the same may have been previously allowed in pursuance of this Act to be an exception,

CORRUPT PRACTICES AT ELECTIONS. 93

such person shall be guilty of *illegal payment*; and by the Act of 1884, s. 17 (2)," where an offence of illegal payment . . . . is committed by a candidate or with his knowledge and consent, such candidate shall be guilty of an illegal practice." The remarks we made in the last chapter upon s. 13 of the Act of 1883 apply to the section under consideration, and to avoid repetitions the reader is referred to them.

(B.) The employment of hackney carriages, or of carriage and horses kept for hire at a municipal election is forbidden by s. 10 of the Act of 1884. The prohibition is contained in precisely the same language as is employed in s. 14 of the Act of 1883, and everything we have said with reference to the meaning and interpretation of that important section is strictly applicable to s. 10 of the Act of 1884, with this difference only, that the letting, lending, or employing for the conveyance of electors to or from the poll at a municipal election, of a hackney carriage, &c., only becomes an illegal practice affecting the validity of the election when the candidate himself is a party to it.

(C.) S. 11 of the Act of 1884, following the precise terms of s. 15 of the Act of 1883, makes it an illegal practice in a candidate at a municipal election to corruptly induce or procure any other person to withdraw from being a candidate in consideration of any payment or promise of payment.

(D.) Again, s. 12 of the Act of 1884 is a reproduction of s. 16 of the Act of 1883, and an application of its terms to every municipal election, with the result that if any payment or contract for payment is made by a candidate, or with his knowledge or consent, on account of bands of music, torches flags, banners, cockades, ribbons, or other marks of distinction, the election is liable to be avoided.

(E.) The Act of 1884 contains a similar prohibition against employing and paying agents in excess of the number authorised by the Act to that contained in the Act of 1883. It is an illegal employment to employ and pay more than the number limited (s. 13), and an illegal employment becomes an illegal practice when committed by the candidate or with his knowledge or consent (s. 17). The persons whom a

<small>Municipal.</small>

<small>Illegal hiring.</small>

<small>Corrupt withdrawal.</small>

<small>Bands of music, torches, &c.</small>

candidate is permitted to employ and pay must come under the denomination of clerks, messengers, or polling agents, and their number is regulated, in the case of clerks and messengers, by the size of the constituency as fixed by the burgess roll, and in the case of polling agents by the number of polling stations. It is no objection to the persons employed, that they are electors ; but if they are paid for their services they must not vote (s. 13, sub-s. 3), and in this connection it may be mentioned in anticipation of what will be stated later on, that to induce any person to vote who is forbidden by the Act to vote, is an illegal practice, avoiding the election when committed with the candidate's knowledge or consent. The persons whom a candidate at a municipal election may pay are as follows :—(1.) Two clerks or messengers in any case, *and* if the number of electors in the borough or ward, as the case may be, exceeds two thousand, one additional person may be employed for every thousand electors and incomplete part of a thousand electors over and above the said two thousand. Thus, to illustrate what is meant, if there were 4,001 names upon the burgess roll, five persons might be lawfully employed and paid either as clerks or messengers. (2.) In addition, one polling agent may be employed in each polling station. (S. 13 sub-s. 1.)

(F.) S. 16 of the Act of 1884 is in many respects analogous to s. 20 of the Act of 1883. They both forbid the use of licensed premises for the purposes of a committee-room ; but the section in the Act of 1884 goes beyond the corresponding section in the Act of 1883. The latter only prohibits having committee-rooms upon premises where intoxicating liquors or refreshments are sold, and introduces an important exception in the case of the premises of a permanent political club. S. 16 of the Act of 1884, however, forbids, in connection with a municipal election, the use of any premises on which drink or refreshments are sold, *irrespective of the question of whether they belong to a permanent political club or not*, either as committee-rooms or *for the holding of meetings*. The stringency of this provision must be noted, and a candidate must bear in mind that if he addresses a meeting in the assembly room of an hotel, though that may be the place at which meetings of all kinds are usually held, his election is liable to be upset. There is one minor respect in which this section gives a license to the candidate at a municipal election which is denied to a candidate at a parliamentary election. The latter may not have a committee-room on the premises of any public elementary school in receipt of an annual parliamentary grant. There is no corresponding provision in the Act of 1884, and it is conceived, therefore, that it is lawful for a candidate at a municipal election either to have a committee-room or hold a meeting on the premises of a school in receipt of the Government grant. *Municipal Committee-rooms and meetings on licensed premises.*

(G.) It is an illegal practice for a candidate to vote at a municipal election if he is a person prohibited from voting, and it is equally an illegal practice for him to induce or procure any other person to vote, *knowing* that such person is prohibited, either under the Act of 1884 *or any other Act.* from voting at such election (s. 6 (1) of the Act of 1884), There is a similar enactment in case of parliamentary elections (s. 9 (1) of the Act of 1883). *Prohibited persons voting.*

It is important to inquire who are the persons prohibited, either under the Act of 1884 or any other Act, from voting at a municipal election. As to those prohibited by the Act of 1884, they are exactly the same descriptions of persons as are prohibited by the Act of 1883 in the case of parliamentary elections, viz. :—(1) persons who, by reason of conviction or of the report of any Election Court or Election Commissioners, or the judgment of any Court in an action for penalties, are incapable of voting; (2) persons guilty of any corrupt or illegal practice, or any illegal employment, payment or hiring at the election in question ; and (3) all paid agents.

The persons who are prohibited by other statutes from voting at a municipal election do not seem so considerable in number as in the case of a Parliamentary election. A returning officer at a municipal election may vote, and there is no express statutory prohibition against a minor voting if he is on the burgess roll, nor against an elector who has been employed for reward within six months of the election voting ; but it would seem that police officers are still prohibited, and there is a similar prohibition in the case of convicts. (33 & 34 Vict., c. 23, s. 2.)

False statement of withdrawal of a candidate.

(H.) A candidate who is privy to the publication of a false statement of the withdrawal of a candidate for the purpose of promoting or procuring the election of another candidate, is guilty of an illegal practice, whether at a municipal or a Parliamentary election. (S. 6 (2) of the Act of 1884.)

Placard without printer's name.

(I.) Again, it is provided by s. 14 of the Act of 1884, following the terms of s. 18 of the Act of 1883, that every bill, placard or poster, having reference to an election shall bear on the face thereof the name and address of the printer and publisher thereof; and it is then enacted that if a candidate at a municipal election is a party to the publication of any bill, &c., without the printer's name, he shall be guilty of an illegal practice.

Failing to return election expenses.

(K.) A candidate at a municipal election is required to make a detailed return of his expenses, and such return, accompanied by a declaration according to a form set out in the schedule, must be sent to the Town Clerk of the borough in which the election was held, within twenty-eight days of the election. (S. 21, sub-s. 3.) And by a later sub-section, "If the candidate without such authorised excuse as is mentioned in this Act fails to make the said return and declaration, he shall be guilty of an illegal practice." (Sub-s. 5.)

Paying claims after prohibited time.

(L.) So a candidate at a municipal election is forbidden to pay any expense incurred in connection with the election, unless the claim is sent in within fourteen days after the day of election. (S. 21 (1).) The same section also provides that expenses incurred in connection with a municipal election shall be paid within twenty-one days after the day of election and not otherwise, "and any person who makes a payment in contravention of this section, except where such payment is allowed as provided by this section, shall be guilty of an illegal practice." (*Ibid.*) The section proceeds that if such payment was made without the sanction or connivance of the candidate, the election shall not be void. _{MUNICIPAL.}

A candidate may obtain relief against the consequences of any one of the illegal practices mentioned in this section, by applying to the Court under s. 20 of the Act of 1884. That section has already been referred to, and it is not proposed to repeat its provisions here. It is obvious, however, that where the candidate is personally implicated in the illegal practice in question, the Court will require very clear evidence that the act or omission arose from inadvertence or accidental miscalculation, and not from want of good faith, before it makes an order relieving him. _{Possibility of relief.}

CHAPTER IV.

THE EMPLOYMENT AT A PARLIAMENTARY ELECTION BY THE CANDIDATE OF A CORRUPT AGENT.

<small>PARLIAMENTARY</small> S. 44 of the 31 & 32 Vict., c. 125, provides: "If on the
<small>The enactment on the subject.</small> trial of any election petition under this Act any candidate is proved to have *personally engaged* at the election to which such petition relates, as a canvasser or agent for the management of the election, any person, *knowing that such person has*, within seven years previous to such engagement, been found guilty of any *corrupt* practice by a competent legal tribunal, or been reported guilty of any corrupt practice by a Committee of the House of Commons, or by the report of the judge upon an election under this Act, or by the report of Commissioners appointed in pursuance of the Act of the Session of the fifteenth and sixteenth years of the reign of her present Majesty, chapter 57, *the election of such candidate shall be void*."

The 31 & 32 Vict., c. 125, applies to Parliamentary elections only; and there is no provision similar to that contained in the above section in any Municipal Elections Act. It must be remembered, therefore, that the law laid down in this chapter has no application to municipal elections.

<small>Personal employment of a corrupt agent.</small> The employment of a person as agent who has within seven years of his employment been scheduled for any corrupt practice only avoids the election where the candidate, knowing that he is a scheduled person, employs him personally. That is what the section says; but the authorities
<small>Meaning of "personally" in Act.</small> establish that the word "personally" is not to be taken in a too literal sense, and that a candidate's liability is not limited to the case where he actually appoints the agent by word of mouth or by writing to him. The *North Norfolk Case* (21 L.T., n.s., 265; 1 O'M. & H., 238) was the first

case in which this section came under discussion. There a *Parliamentary* person who had been scheduled in connection with corrupt practices at Yarmouth was proved to have taken a prominent part in the election on behalf of the respondents. He acted as chairman of a district committee; but the respondents denied that they knew he held this position, though it was admitted that one of them asked him to propose him on the nomination, and he did so. Blackburn, J., held that the act of asking another to propose you at the election does not constitute an employment for the purpose of the management of the election, and that though an appointment as chairman of a district would be such an employment, there was no evidence that either of the respondents personally made it. His lordship, in the course of his judgment, laid down (1) that it was not necessary that the appointment should be personal in the sense that the candidate must have an interview with the agent, it was sufficient if it was proved that the appointment was made by another "with the knowledge and consent of the candidate;" (2) that the agent need not be a *paid* agent; (3) that he need not be an agent for the management of the *whole* election, it was enough if he was actually employed to manage a *portion* of it; and (4) that if it were proved that the candidate had reason to believe that a scheduled person would be appointed, and wilfully shut his eyes in order that he should know as little as possible, that would be equivalent to actual knowledge.

North Norfolk Case.

In the *Norwich Case* (2 O'M. & H., 38), Keating, J., fully adopted the construction placed upon the statute in the *North Norfolk Case*. In this case it was proved that a person who had been scheduled for bribery five years before took a public and ostentatious part in forwarding the respondent's candidature. The learned judge said that the circumstances in evidence were such that, but for the fact that the respondent was called and swore that he had no knowledge whatever of the efforts made by the alleged agent on his behalf, and that he never intended to recognise him as an agent, he would have held that the case was made out.

Norwich Case.

In the second *Galway Case* (2 O'M. & H., 196) the facts were that two years before the election the Roman Catholic Bishop of Galway was reported by an election court as guilty of a corrupt practice, viz., undue influence. It was proved that shortly before the election, the return at which was in question, the respondent called upon the bishop, who said that his hands were tied by the report of the election court, and that he would not have act or part in the election; at the same time, he did not conceal his approval of the respondent's candidature. The clergy of the city, who lived in the same house with the bishop, and over whom it was admitted that he had the fullest control, however, met, and, adopting the respondent as their candidate, organised a canvass in his behalf. It was not proved that the canvass was by the direct orders of the bishop, but it was clear that he was aware of and fully approved it. There was evidence likewise that a letter, written by one of the clergy with the view of driving the petitioner out of the field, was revised and corrected by the bishop before it was issued. The learned judge (Lawson, J.), though he was satisfied that the bishop was at the bottom of the whole movement in favour of the respondent, and could have stopped the canvassing of the clergy at any moment, and though affairs were so arranged that the public were led to understand that the bishop approved of everything which was being done in the respondent's interest, did not think there had been such a personal engagement of the bishop by the respondent as brought the case within the section.

It must be noted that a person scheduled for corruption is only under disability for seven years. After the expiry of that time it is no offence for the candidate to employ him in connection with the management of the election. (*Galway Case*, 2 O'M. & H., 51.)

CHAPTER V.

GENERAL CORRUPTION AND GENERAL INTIMIDATION.

AN election, whether Parliamentary or municipal, will be avoided by the existence of general bribery, general treating, general intimidation, or undue influence, although there be no evidence whatever that the candidate returned, or any of his agents, is in any way cognisant of any corrupt practice. An election must be free, and when it takes place amidst general corruption it ceases to be free, and is bad at common law, independent of any statute.

Parliamentary & Municipal.

General corruption.

"If there were general bribery, no matter from what fund, or by what persons, and although the sitting member and his agents had nothing to do with it, it would defeat an election, on the ground that it was not a proceeding pure and free, but that it was corrupted and vitiated by an influence which, coming from no matter what quarter, had defeated it, and shown it to be abortive," per Willes, J. (*Lichfield*, 1 O'M. & H., 22; 20 L.T., 11); and at *Bradford* (1 O'M. & H., 30), Martin, B., said, "If it had been proved that there existed in this town generally bribery to a large extent, and that it came from unknown quarters, but that people were bribed generally and indiscriminately; or if it could be proved that there was treating in all directions on purpose to influence voters—*that houses were thrown open where people could get drink without paying for it;* by the common law such election would be void." And it is no answer that the general corruption took place some time before the election. (*Sligo*, 1 O'M. & H., 300.)

General bribery.

General treating.

In order to avoid an election for general bribery, general treating, or general intimidation, it is not necessary to show that a majority of those who polled, or a majority of the

PARLIAMENTARY & MUNICIPAL.

General treating.

constituency was so corrupted. It is enough to show an organised system of bribery, treating, or intimidation, "spreading over such an extent of ground, and permeating through the constituency to such an extent that freedom of election has ceased to exist in consequence." (*Drogheda*, 1 O'M. & H., 252; 21 L.T., 402.) General drunkenness at or about the time of the election is evidence of general treating. (*Tamworth*, 1 O'M. & H., 75; 20 L.T., 181. *St. Ives*, 3 O'M. & H., 13.) In the *Longford Case* (2 O'M. & H., 7) a considerable sum of money was spent in giving drink to non-voters, related to voters. In some cases the electors participated in these free drinks. As one witness, a publican, put it: "Anybody might have had the drink without distinction." The election was declared void.

In the *Drogheda Case* (21 L.T., 403; 1 O'M. & H., 252), the same principle was enunciated by Keogh, J. "Take, then," he said, "the case of an organised system of treating. I am speaking now of cases in which nothing could be traced to the candidate or his agents, But suppose that at the head of every street, food and drink were provided in large quantities, and places for eating and drinking opened, as to which it was known that every voter who wished to go thither, and seek for food or for drink, would receive it, provided he was on the side of a particular candidate, and that there was an organised system for the purpose of debauching the voters of a particular borough, though all the while not traceable to the member or his agents, so as to disqualify him at future elections, is it to be supposed for a moment that that organised system would not defeat the election?" Such a case could admit of no doubt, but we think that much less bribery or treating than the learned judge there described would be equally fatal. The test must always be, Has the corrupt practice prevailed to such an extent as to affect the result of the election? If it has, it is fatal. It would seem, on principle, that the same test must be applied in cases of alleged general bribery, or treating, as in cases of alleged general intimidation, *i.e.*, Can it be shown that the gross amount of corruption could not have affected the result?

What is the test?

Unless that can be shown, or from the facts inferred, the election ought to be declared void. (*North Durham*, 2 O'M. & H., 152; 31 L.T., 383.) The observations of Willes, J., in the *Tamworth Case* (1 O'M. & H., 75; 20 L.T., 181), do not contravene this proposition. The learned judge did not deny that the same rule applies to general treating as to general bribery. He only insisted that the treating should be shown to be operating upon the minds of the electors at the time of the poll. (See also the *Norwich Case*, 19 L.T., 615; 1 O'M. & H., 8.) If that condition be complied with, lavish treating by publicans themselves, without any reason for expecting payment, would be sufficient to avoid the election. (*Poole*, 31 L.T., 171; 2 O'M. & H., 123.)

In the *Ipswich Case* (4 O'M. & H., 71) Denman, J., suggested, as a limitation to the generality of the proposition, that an election must be declared void where general corruption is found to have prevailed in the constituency at the time of election, that the election should not be declared void " if one found that the bribery which had been committed had not been in favour of the persons who had been elected—there must be that qualification always—for it would be impossible for a person who had been fairly elected to be unseated merely because his opponents had been largely guilty of bribery." It cannot be doubted that this is both good law and good sense.

As to general intimidation, it may possibly, in extreme cases, be allowable to organise a band of stalwart persons to protect voters against the violence of strangers introduced by the other side; but it must always be a dangerous thing to do (*Longford*, 2 O'M. & H., 7), and a thing at almost any cost to be avoided. (*Limerick*, 21 L.T. 567; 1 O'M. & H., 260. *Salisbury*, 4 O'M. & H., 25. *Salford*, 29 L.T., 120.) And they may not be paid. (*Ipswich*, 4 O'M. & H., 72.) It would be an answer to a petition by a defeated candidate, that all the violence and rioting was instigated by the petitioner or his agents, and that the result was not affected. But where not the unsuccessful candidate but an elector complains of general rioting, it is no answer to say that the defeated party were chiefly responsible for it. (*Dudley*, 2 O'M. & H., 115.)

In order to affect the election, the rioting must be serious. It must be such as to deter ordinary men, of ordinary courage from recording their votes. (*Nottingham*, 1 O'M. & H., 245. *Galway*, 2 O'M. & H., 196. *Salford*, 1 O'M. & H., 133; 20 L.T., 120.)

The general rioting and violence in the *Drogheda Case* were too great to allow the case to be profitably discussed. The general intimidation there went far beyond that proved in the *North Durham Case*, *infra*. But the former case establishes the proposition that if voters are deterred from voting by a prevailing terror, but without undue influence being brought to bear upon them individually, the election will be declared void. It was said for the respondent in that case, that he went to voters who were opposed to him and offered to give them his escort to the poll, they being afraid to go, notwithstanding there were military and constabulary in the streets, but the Court considered that this was conclusive evidence out of the respondent's own mouth, that there was not freedom of election in the borough.

As to the amount of the violence and rioting which will vitiate the election, it is very material to observe the state of the poll. If it is a close poll, a less amount of violence will justify an election court in avoiding the election than would be the case if it were quite clear that the rioting and violence had not affected the result. (*North Durham*, 2 O'M. & H., 152; 31 L.T., 383.) If the rioting were local and partial, and the majority large, the election would not be set aside (*ibid.*) "But where it is of such a general character that the result *may have been* affected, it is no part of the duty of a judge to enter into a kind of scrutiny to see whether possibly, *or probably even*, or as a matter of conclusion upon the evidence, if that intimidation had not existed, the result would have been different. What the judge has to do in that case is to say that *the burden of proof is cast upon the constituency* whose conduct is incriminated, and unless it can be shown that the gross amount of intimidation *could not possibly have affected the result* of the election, it ought to be declared void." (Per Bramwell, B., at *North Durham, ibid.*) And it must be declared void if it is *uncertain* whether the result was affected (*ibid.*).

The *Thornbury Case* (4 O'M. & H., 66) is in entire accordance with the *North Durham Case*. It was proved that there was great rioting in three out of the twenty-three polling districts into which the constituency was divided. On the other hand, it was shown that there were 789 persons on the register in these three polling stations, and all but 87 of them voted. In these circumstances the Court came to the conclusion that they could not hold that any such intimidation and violence was used as practically prevented any considerable number of persons from voting, and they declined to avoid the election.

CHAPTER VI.

THE GENERAL PREVALENCE OF ILLEGAL PRACTICES, &c., AT A MUNICIPAL ELECTION.

MUNICIPAL.

Prevalence of illegal practices.

S. 18 of the Act of 1884 enacts :—" Where upon the trial of an election petition respecting a *municipal election* for a borough or ward of a borough it is found by the election court that illegal practices or offences of illegal payment, employment, or hiring, committed in reference to such election for the purpose of promoting the election of a candidate at that election, have so extensively prevailed that they may be reasonably supposed to have affected the result of that election, the election court shall report such finding to the High Court, and the election of such candidate, if he has been elected, shall be void, and he shall not, during the period for which he was elected to serve, or for which, if elected, he might have served, be capable of being elected to or holding any corporate office in the said borough."

Meaning of the enactment

It must be carefully observed that the election is avoided upon the establishment of the facts set out in the above section, though it is not shown that the respondent or any of his agents were in any wise privy to them. The offences, however, must have been committed in the interest of the respondent. They must have been done by persons who, though they had no authority from him, were anxious to secure his return. The Court must be satisfied, to use the language of the sections, that they were committed with reference to the election " for the purpose of promoting the election " of the respondent.

As soon, therefore, as it is established that illegal practices, employments, hirings, and payments have been committed at an election by persons seeking to promote the respondent's election, the next enquiry will be, To what extent did they prevail? Offences of this kind not brought home to the respondent or his agents do not avoid the return, unless they so extensively prevailed that they may be reasonably supposed to have affected the result of the election.

MUNICIPAL

No attempt is made to define what general prevalence of illegal practices will be regarded as fatal. Indeed it would be impossible to do so. Each case must be left to be dealt with by the Election Court with reference to its particular facts. Much will turn upon the size of the borough or ward and the number of the electorate. Illegal practices may be regarded as extensive in a small ward, which would be rightly viewed as insignificant in a large one. But whether the ward is a small or a large one the illegal practices which are fatal must have so generally prevailed that they "may be reasonably supposed to have affected the result" of the election. A question may arise as to the meaning to be given to these words, "the result of the election," and therefore it will be well to set out in this place the interpretation which Grove, J., placed upon similar words in the 13th section of the Ballot Act:—"I am very strongly inclined to think," said his lordship, in the *Hackney Case*, "that the expression, 'the result of the election,' does not necessarily mean the result as to another candidate having been elected at the poll. The result may be of various kinds. The result of the election would, in my judgment, be affected, if instead of a majority of 500, there was a majority of only 10 or even 100. Upon a scrutiny the matter might be very different. Other causes might also produce a very considerable change of relation between the parties, and might have a very important effect upon the ultimate, if not upon the then present representation in Parliament, that effect depending upon the magnitude of the majority. It will also be observed that the words used in the section are not 'did not *alter* the result of the election,' but 'did not *affect* the result of the election.' Does not the word 'affect' mean substantially 'bear upon the result?'" (2 O'M. & H., 84.)

Effect on the poll.

It must be noted that s. 18, of the Act of 1884, applies

MUNICIPAL. only to municipal elections. There is no similar provision in the Act of 1883 or in any other statute relating to corrupt or illegal practices at parliamentary elections; and it is apprehended therefore that the general prevalence of illegal practices, employments, hirings and payments, when not brought home to the candidate or his agents will not affect the validity of a parliamentary election.

CHAPTER VII.

THE CANDIDATE'S AGENTS WITHIN THE MEANING OF THE RULES LAID DOWN IN CHAPTERS I., II. AND III.

It has been the law from the earliest times that no matter how well a member may have conducted his election, so far as regards his personal part in it, no matter how clear his character from any imputation of corrupt practice, yet, if any agent of his has been guilty of a corrupt act, the election cannot be upheld, and the law in this respect applies equally to parliamentary and municipal elections. "The amount of the injury done by the agent is immaterial. If an agent bribes one voter with 2s. 6d., and the voter taking the 2s. 6d. with the purpose, expressed or implied, of voting accordingly, should break his promise and vote for the other side, still the election is void." (Per Willes, J., in the *Blackburn Case*, 1 O'M. & H., 202; 20 L.T., N.S., 826.) *Parliamentary & Municipal. Candidate always liable for act of his agent.*

In these circumstances, the question, what constitutes a person a candidate's agent within the meaning of this rule, is one of the greatest importance. It is, moreover, one of much delicacy and difficulty. Learned judges have again and again stated that it is impossible to give a precise and exhaustive definition of agency which may be safely applied to the infinite variety of cases which arise; and the Legislature itself has designedly refused to attempt anything in the nature of a definition, on the ground, no doubt, that if a hard-and-fast rule were laid down the ingenuity of electioneers would evade it, and so the laws against corruption be frustrated. Parliament, it is true, has by the Act of 1883, defined accurately enough *one class* of the candidate's agents in the case of parliamentary elections and made him liable to the fullest extent for their acts; but it cannot be too clearly stated, that while a candidate at a *Impossible to give precise definition of agent. Responsibility not limited to acts of election agent.*

Parliamentary & Municipal.

The election agent.

Sub-agents.

Extent of their authority in their own district.

parliamentary election, is responsible for the acts of the agents created by and mentioned in the Act of 1883, his liability is not limited to a responsibility for their acts, and he is still liable for the misconduct of a large number of other persons whom the law in certain circumstances will regard as his agents.

It will probably be the more convenient course when, in a later chapter, we proceed to deal in detail with the functions of the election agent, there to set out the full text of the sections creating his office. It is sufficient to say here, that by the 24th and 25th sections of the Act of 1883, a candidate at a parliamentary election is empowered, to appoint, for the purposes of the election, one election agent in each borough constituency, and, in the case of counties, in addition to the election agent, one sub-agent for each polling district. The name and address of the election agent must be declared in writing by the candidate on or before the nomination day, and it is the duty of the returning officer forthwith to give public notice thereof. Where sub-agents may be appointed, the election agent is required, one clear day before the polling day, to declare in writing their names and addresses; and there is this most important provision as to the extent to which sub-agents may bind the candidate in the districts to which they are appointed. S. 25 (sub-s. 2), of the Act of 1883, provides:— "As regards matters in a *polling district*, the election agent may act by the sub-agent for that district, and anything done for the purposes of this Act by or to the sub-agent shall be deemed to be done by or to the election agent, and any act or default of a sub-agent which, if he were the election agent, would be an illegal practice, or other offence against the Act, shall be an illegal practice and offence against this Act committed by the sub-agent, and the sub-agent shall be liable to punishment accordingly; and the candidate shall suffer the like incapacity, as if the said act or default had been the act or default of the election agent." The full significance of this section is realised upon a careful consideration of the long list of illegal practices which avoid the election when committed by the candidate or his election agent, for it is presumed that the effect of the above words is to make every sub-agent, *while acting within his own district*, an election agent within the meaning of the sections creating those offences. PARLIAMENTARY & MUNICIPAL.

There is no provision in the Act of 1884, for the appointment of an election agent in connection with municipal elections. It must be remembered therefore that the above remarks with reference to the election agent and sub-agents have no application to municipal elections.

The first schedule of the Act of 1883 (Part I.) provides that except the election agent, and in the case of counties the sub-agents, and a strictly limited number of polling agents, clerks and messengers, no other persons shall be employed in connection with any parliamentary election *for payment*. And by the 13th section of the Act of 1884, the number of persons who may be employed and paid in connection with municipal elections is strictly limited. It is not, however, the design of either of the Acts to prohibit the employment of *voluntary* agents; and in that respect the law is entirely unaltered. But if a candidate or his authorised agents do appoint persons to take a part in the management of the election and depute authority to them, they make those persons, while performing the particular class of duties entrusted to them, the candidate's agents within the meaning of the rule that a corrupt or illegal practice by a candidate or any one of his agents defeats the election. The fact that the agents are not paid makes no difference whatever, for it has long been settled that a candidate is as much bound by the acts of his agents who give their services for nothing as by the acts of those who are paid. (*Bewdley Case*, 1 O'M. & H., 17; 19 L.T., n.s., 677.) The only question is—Have they, in fact, received authority from the candidate or some undoubted agent of his to do acts of a certain class for the furtherance of his elections? If they have, then the candidate is liable for any corrupt or illegal act which they may be led into committing while engaged in performing the particular duties assigned to them. Thus, in the common Any number of voluntary agents may be appointed.

But if appointed, candidate liable for their acts.

Candidate liable for act of all his agents.

case of an organised canvass in a constituency where a number of persons are selected by the candidate, or, as happens much more frequently, by his principal agents, to canvass each district, there can be no doubt that all those persons are, by express appointment, the candidate's agents while engaged in canvassing the particular districts allotted to them (the *Dublin Case*, 1 O'M. & H., 272), for "authority to canvass constitutes a person an agent while he is canvassing, and authority for the general management of the election involves authority to canvass." (Per Willes, J., in the *Windsor Case*, 19 L.T., n.s., 613 ; 1 O'M. & H., 2 ; also the *Norwich Case*, 19 L.T., n.s., 617.)

In this connection, however, an important limitation of responsibility must be borne in mind. An agent appointed with express powers can only bind the candidate within the scope of his authority—*i.e.*, while he is actually performing (though, it may be, in an improper and unlawful way) the particular work assigned to him. An agent appointed to do work of one kind does not bind the candidate if he officiously assumes duties of an entirely different kind, and, while he is doing the latter, commits a corrupt or illegal act. Thus, a person commissioned to do subordinate work, as a mere messenger (whether paid or not), and having no authority, express or implied, to do anything except act as a messenger, is not an agent for all purposes so as to fix the candidate with liability for acts done by him while carrying on an unauthorised canvass. (*Windsor Case*, 19 L.T., n.s., 613 ; 1 O'M. & H., 2 ; the *Durham Case*, 2 O'M. & H., 137.) " There are many persons who are employed at an election, and who, in one sense, are agents of the candidate, but who are not agents in the sense that the election would be considered void by their misconduct." (Per Willes, J., in *Bodmin Case*, 1 O'M. & H., 119 ; 20 L.T., n.s., 989.) So, when a person is asked to canvass a *particular class* of voters —as a master to canvass his workmen (*Westbury Case*, 1 O'M. & H., 47 ; 20 L.T., n.s., 17 ; *Blackburn Case*, 1 O.M. & H., 199 ; 20 L.T., n.s., 823), or a landlord his tenants (*North Norfolk Case*, 1 O'M. & H., 236 ; 21 L.T., n.s., 264),

he is an agent only while he is engaged in canvassing them Parliamentary & Municipal.
and the candidate is not bound by his unauthorised acts at
other times, and while canvassing other persons. Equally,
where a person is authorised to canvass in a *particular
district*, and there is nothing to show he had authority,
express or implied, to canvass anywhere else, the candidate
is not bound by his acts in other districts. (*Harwich
Case* 3 O'M. & H., 69; 44 L.T., n.s., 185; *Durham Case*,
2 O'M. & H., 136.)

But if it be shown that the agent at the time when he Candidate bound though agent disobeys his instructions.
committed the corrupt act was engaged upon the particular
kind of work assigned to him, the candidate is not exonerated
from the consequences of his agent's act by merely proving
that the latter in doing the corrupt act in question was
acting against his express instructions and in defiance of his
honest wishes. (The *Harwich Case*, 3 O'M. & H., 69; 44
L.T., n.s., 189.) This rigorous rule involves no little hardship to an honest candidate, and in this respect the liability
of a principal for the act of an agent is carried beyond
the ordinary maxims of the common law; but it is founded
on a principle of public policy, that no election which is
tainted by the corrupt act of any agent of the sitting member
can stand.

The distinction made which exonerates a candidate, where Distinction between cases where candidate bound and not bound.
his agent at the time he offends is acting beyond the scope
of his authority, in the sense that he has assumed duties
which do not belong to him, but which binds him, when the
agent, while keeping within the general line of his duty,
disobeys his express instructions to the extent of committing
a corrupt act, as he thinks to further the candidate's interest,
is somewhat fine, but is now well settled. A simple illustration of how it works is this: A is specifically authorised to
canvass street X, and he has no other authority, express or
implied, to act in any other way in connection with the
election. He bribes a voter in street P. The candidate is
not bound. A is authorised to canvass in street X, and
expressly instructed in writing by the candidate, who
honestly wishes his election conducted fairly, not to commit

8

114   THE LAW RELATING TO

Parliamentary & Municipal. any corrupt act. Nevertheless A, in street X, bribes, or treats, or intimidates a voter. The candidate is bound and the seat is forfeited.

When agent actually appointed only question is extent of his authority. So far we have dealt with the comparatively simple case, where it is proved that the persons who are charged with some corrupt act were expressly appointed by the candidate, or his authorised agents, to take some part in the election, and then the only question can be—Was the agent at the time he offended acting within the scope of his authority? But we now come to the much more difficult and more common case in election inquiries, where there is no evidence of any direct appointment by the candidate or his authorised agents, but where the alleged agent is proved to have been more or less openly and actively working in the candidate's *Implied agency.* interest. There the question arises—Are the circumstances such that the Court can *imply* he had authority from the candidate, or has the latter approved and ratified his action on his behalf?

"The difficulty," said Lush, J., in the *Harwich Case* (quoted *supra*), "always is when there is no express appointment, to determine whether the wrongdoer did or not stand in the relation of agent to the candidate in respect of the particular matter of the complaint. An agent is a person employed by another to act for him and on his behalf, either generally or in some particular transaction. The authority may be actual or *it may be implied from circumstances*. It is not necessary, in order to prove agency, to show that the person was actually appointed by the candidate. If a person not appointed were to assume to act in any department of service as election agent, and the candidate accepted *Agent either by employment or recognition.* his services as such, he would thereby ratify the agency. So that a man may become the agent of another in either of two ways by actual employment or by recognition and acceptance. The next question is, if agent, what is he agent for; what is he appointed to do, or what does he profess to do? If a person were appointed or accepted as agent for canvassing generally, and he were to bribe or treat any voter, the candidate would lose his seat. But if he were employed or accepted to canvass a particular class—as if a master were asked to canvass his workman, and he went out of his way and bribed a person who was not his workman, the candidate would not be responsible, because this was not within the scope of his authority. And for the same reason, if a person whom the candidate had not in any way authorised to canvass at all for him were to take upon himself to bribe a voter, the candidate would not be responsible for that wrongful act. No candidate could ever secure a seat if he were made answerable for the acts of unauthorised persons." Parliamentary & Municipal. Candidate not liable for acts of unauthorised persons.

"No one," said Blackburn, J., in the *Bewdley Case* (1 O'M. & H., 17 ; 19 L.T., n.s., 677), "can lay down a precise rule as to what would constitute evidence of being an agent. Every instance in which it is shown that, either with the knowledge of the candidate himself, or to the knowledge of his agents, a person acts at all in furthering his election *is evidence*, tending to show that the person so acting was authorised to act as his agent. It is by no means essential that it should be shown that a person so employed, in order to be an agent for that purpose, is paid in the slightest degree. And I take it that the question for the court sitting to try the case comes ultimately to be, whether upon the *aggregate of all these things taken together*, of which each in itself is little, but is certainly some evidence, the person is shown to have been employed to such an extent as to make him an agent for whom the candidate would be responsible. I take it that in each case the judge must bring common sense to bear upon it, and satisfy himself whether it is sufficient or not." Agent need not be paid.

It will be observed that the question, whether the wrong-doer was the candidate's agent at the time of the offence is treated by the learned judges entirely as a question of fact, to be determined by a reference to the circumstances of each case. Such facts as proof that the alleged agent was canvassing in the candidate's interest, that he had a canvass book with him, that he spoke at the candidate's meetings, that he was seen in the candidate's company in the street, Agency a question of fact.

are *evidence*, but no more than evidence, that he had authority to canvass and bind the candidate.

The *mere fact* that a person is actively working for the candidate does not necessarily make him an agent. "I cannot concur in the opinion that any supporter of a candidate who chooses to ask others for their votes and to make speeches in his favour can force himself upon the candidate as an agent, or that the candidate should be held responsible for the acts of one from whom he actually endeavours to disassociate himself." (*Londonderry Case*, 1 O'M. & H., 278 ; 21 L.T., n.s., 709. *Staleybridge Case*, 1 O'M. & H., 67 ; 20 L.T., n.s., 75.) The circumstance that a person canvassing on behalf of a candidate had a canvass book with him would not be sufficient to make him an agent (the *Bolton Case*, 2 O'M. & H., 141 ; 31 L.T., n.s., 194) ; unless, of course, it could be proved he got it from an authorised agent of the candidate, which would be the strongest evidence of his appointment to canvass.

Nor does the *mere fact* that a person is one of a large committee whose names are published as the General Committee, but which committee is purely ornamental and has no part whatever assigned it in the conduct of the election, make him an agent. This was first decided by Martin, B., in the *Westminster Case* (1 O'M. & H., 89, 20 L.T., n.s., 238), when, at the same time, he took care to point out that if the committee, to which the alleged agent belonged, had been more than a nominal one, had been, in fact a committee within the ordinary meaning of the term, to which some portion of the management of the election had been confided, the decision would have been the other way. In the *Westbury Case* (20 L.T., n.s., 24), Willes, J., acted upon the *Westminster Case*, but he added, "If I see a person's name on the committee from the beginning, if I find that he attended meetings of the committee, that he canvassed and his canvass was recognised so far as it went, I shall require considerable argument to convince me he is not an agent." (See also the *Windsor Case*, 2 O'M. & H., 89).

Again, the *bare act* of accompanying the candidate on his

canvass is not sufficient evidence of agency to make a candidate liable for bribery committed by such person upon an occasion when the candidate was not in his company. (The *first Salisbury Case*, 3 O'M. & H., 131; 44 L.T., n.s., 193; the *second Salisbury Case*, 4 O'M. & H., 21; *Harwich Case*, 3 O'M. & H., 69; 44 L.T., n.s., 189; *Shrewsbury Case*, 2 O'M. & H., 36.) It must be observed, however, that the recognition of a person involved in inviting him to accompany the candidate on his canvass is an important link in the chain of facts which go to make up agency, and combined with very little more would in most cases be held to establish it. It need hardly be said that any corrupt act done by a person accompanying a candidate *and in his presence* is strong evidence against the candidate unless repudiated by him at the time. (*First Salisbury Case, supra; Bewdley Case,* 1 O'M. & H., 17.) Parliamentary & Municipal.
—
accompanying candidate.

But while the law is that if a person, no matter how zealous a partizan he may be, is acting entirely of his own motion, the candidate is not bound by what he does, on the other hand, if he is found carrying on his operations in concert with the candidate's organisation, or if the Court is satisfied that the candidate, or any one of his principal agents, has full knowledge of his efforts and approves and sanctions them—then he is an agent. What is sufficient evidence of agency.

In the *second Taunton Case* (2 O'M. & H. 74), Grove, J., intimated that *mere non-interference* by the candidate with persons who were to his knowledge actively exerting themselves in his interest would not be enough to constitute agency. But this ruling must be considered with reference to the particular facts before his lordship, because the decision of Blackburn, J., in the *first Taunton Case* (1 O'M. & H., 181; 21 L.T., n.s., 169) shows that there are cases where *mere non-interference* with the notorious action of partizans will make the latter the candidate's agents. It is obvious that if a candidate, knowing that certain persons are actively working in his behalf, lies by, and accepting the full benefit of their services, does nothing to repudiate them, it will take a very slight additional Is mere non-interference sufficient?

PARLIAMENTARY & MUNICIPAL.

Suggested law on this point.

Cases where agency held to be proved.

circumstance to lead to the conclusion that he sanctioned their proceedings. Especially is this so where the persons who are so acting are proved to have been working in close concert with him in political matters immediately prior to the election. It is suggested that an intelligible distinction which will reconcile the two Taunton cases (quoted *supra*) and make them accord with the *Harwich Case* (3 O'M. & H., 6, 69; 44 L.T., n.s., 189) is this: Where the alleged agents are found in intimate communication with the candidate prior to the contest, and during its course work in his interest openly but to all appearance independently, and there is no evidence that, knowing of their efforts, he *bonâ fide* repudiated them, they are to be taken as *primâ facie* his agents; but where no privity is established between the candidate and the alleged agents either before or during the election, the mere fact that he does not repudiate them will not *by itself* make them his agents.

In the *Tewkesbury Case* (3 O'M. & H., 99; 44 L.T., n.s. 192) the alleged agent was seen frequently in the candidate's committee room, going out of it in the company of bodies of men who divided themselves and canvassed in different districts. He had a canvass book, and on one or two occasions (though not at the times when the corrupt acts were committed), had canvassed in the candidate's company. It was held in these circumstances that his agency was established.

In the *Hereford Case* (1 O'M. & H., 195) it was proved that the person who was charged with bribery had, at the request of an agent, canvassed two voters, that on one occasion he canvassed in the respondent's company, and that after the election was over he *received a letter of thanks for his exertions from the respondent*. It was held that the agency was established.

In the *Stroud Case* (3 O'M. & H., 11), the alleged agent was proved to have canvassed three times a week, though he did not have a regular canvass book, he was attending continually at the committee room, and was bringing up voters on the polling day, and after the election he was employed in connection with the petition. It was proved that the respondent's principal agent had told the alleged agent that he would not employ him in connection with the election, but inasmuch as the learned judge, Piggott, B., was satisfied on the facts that other agents of the respondent, working side by side with the principal agent, had countenanced and employed him, the decision was that he was an agent for whose acts the candidate was responsible. His lordship laid down the law of agency in the terms in which it has generally been expressed. "It is clear that a person is not to be made an agent by his merely acting, that is not enough; he must act in promotion of the election, and he must have authority, *or there must be circumstances from which we can infer authority.*" There he held there were such circumstances.

<small>PARLIAMENTARY & MUNICIPAL.</small>

A person who is an agent may have implied authority to appoint sub-agents necessary to carry out the work assigned to him, and in that case the candidate is bound by the acts of those sub-agents, though he may never have seen them or had any communication with them. (The *Bewdley Case*, 1 O'M. & H., 17; 19 L.T., n.s., 677.) On this principle, when the wife of an agent bribed, it was held that inasmuch as an agent may use the instrumentality of another, the candidate was bound. (The *Cashel Case*, 1 O'M. & H, 288). In the *Westminster Case* (1 O'M. & H., 89; 20 L.T., n.s., 238) the son of an agent bribed, and it was held the candidate was not bound. These two cases have been quoted in at least one work of authority as sustaining the proposition that a candidate is bound by the acts of his agent's wife, but not of his agent's son. It is submitted they give no support to such a distinction. The wife as well as the son can only bind on the principle of delegated authority; and all that the two cases quoted show is that on the facts the Court was satisfied that in one case authority had been delegated by the agent to a sub-agent, and in the other it had not.

<small>Agent may act by sub-agency.</small>

A very important question next arises, as to what extent is a candidate liable for the acts of political and other associations in sympathy with his candidature, and exerting themselves to promote it. It need not be said that this is a

<small>Liability of candidate for acts of political associations.</small>

PARLIAMENTARY & MUNICIPAL.

The Blackburn Case.

Liable when he adopts committee of association as his election committee.

subject of increasing interest; and its practical importance warrants some examination of the authorities. When the candidate adopts the committee of the association as his committee, avails himself openly of its organisation, and carries on the work of the election in concert with it, no question can arise. In such a case the authorised agents of the association are to the fullest extent his agents. This was what happened in the *Blackburn Case* (20 L.T., n.s., 823; 1 O'M. & H., 198). There, a month before the election a circular was issued by the Conservative Association, addressed to every millowner, manager and overlooker, calling upon them to use personal efforts to secure the return of the respondents. This circular was afterwards adopted by the respondents, and the association which had issued it was accepted by them in place of a committee for the management of the election. Willes, J., held that the circular must be taken to be the act of the respondents just as much as if each of them had written a letter to the same purport to the persons mentioned in it. And as to its effect he said: "It appears to me that the effect of this circular was to make an agent of every person having authority, down to the last grade, that of overlookers over the hands, and to request, and therefore authorise each such to influence the hands who were under him for the purpose of inducing them to vote for the candidates upon whose behalf this document was issued; and any overlooker, and consequently anybody in that or any higher grade, who *bonâ fide* took up the Tory side, and who acted upon this circular, and did canvass for the sitting members, became their agent, and his acts did bind them to the extent and under the circumstances which I have already explained."

But in the *Norwich Case* (4 O'M. & H., 87), where a somewhat similar circular was sent to a very large number of persons who had joined in a requisition to the respondent asking him to stand, the *Blackburn Case (supra)* was distinguished. It was pointed out that in the latter case the circular was sent to certain selected persons, who were known to have exceptional influence, and the Court (Denman and Cave, JJ.), came to the conclusion that the mere fact of sending this circular did not make every person who received it the agent of the respondent.

Parliamentary & Municipal.

In the great majority of cases, however, the operations of the association are carried on independently of the candidate's organization; and then the material points to be considered in determining the question of agency would seem to be the previous relations of the candidate with the association, the source whence it derives its funds, and the extent or character of the connection between it and the candidate during the course of the contest.

Liability of candidate for political associations.

The *Westminster Case* (1 O'M. & H., 89; 20 L.T., n.s., 238) is a somewhat curious case, and, opposed as it seems to be to the current of authority, it is respectfully doubted whether it is now law. There it was proved that the alleged agent was an official of an association which had actively exerted itself in the respondent's interest. The latter had been its president, and he and his partners supplied a very large portion of its funds. During the progress of the contest the canvass books of the association (*which had been supplied by the respondent's election agent*) were compared with the canvass books kept at the respondent's committee-rooms, and there was an interchange of information in relation to the election between the two organizations. On these facts Martin, B., held that the officials of the association engaged in the election were *not* the respondent's agents. It is obvious that if this case were a governing authority on the subject there would be an open door to the most flagrant evasions of the law against corruption.

Westminster Case.

Submitted it is not law.

In the *Westbury Case* (3 O'M. & H., 78) bribery was suggested on the part of the responsible agents of a political association in sympathy with the respondent, but inasmuch as though he was invited to stand by this association, no communication whatever was established between him and it during the election, it was held that its acts did not bind him.

Westbury Case.

In the *Wigan Case* (1 O'M. & H., 188; 21 L.T., n.s., 122) it was proved that *some months before the election* a

Wigan Case.

PARLIAMENTARY & MUNICIPAL. sub-agent of a political association of which the respondent was a member, and to the funds of which he subscribed, was guilty of a corrupt act. It was held that there was no such privity between the respondent and the association as would avoid the election.

Harwich Case. The *Harwich Case* (3 O'M. & H., 69; 44 L.T., n.s., 189) is an instructive one. There it was proved that a political association (1) invited the respondent to contest the seat; (2) its committee considered and revised his election address; (3) it met during the election from time to time at rooms for which the respondent paid; and (4) several of its leading members attended him in his canvass. It was suggested that one of the latter had been guilty of bribery, and the question of the relation established between the respondent and the association became material. The Court When candidate takes conduct of election himself, not bound. held that the facts above stated afforded *primâ facie* evidence of the agency of the association, but upon the respondent proving that at the outset of the contest he *bonâ fide* declared his determination to canvass the constituency personally without the aid of any committee, and publicly announced that determination, the ultimate decision was that the proof of agency failed. This case is an authority for the proposition that a candidate may protect himself against the misdeeds of persons whom the law would otherwise construe to be his agents by taking the whole burden of the management of the election upon himself, and expressly forbidding all other persons to take any part in it upon his behalf.

Turning to the cases where a candidate has been fixed with responsibility for the acts of a political association, the first case in order of time carries the liability a long way. In the Taunton Case. *first Taunton Case* (1 O'M. & H., 181; 21 L.T., n.s., 169) it was proved that there had been formed in the borough a body called "The Conservative Association," for the purpose of conducting the registration in September, and the election in the following November; that during the election people met at the rooms of the association, and that papers and circulars were sent out from it; that the association canvassed actively and did all those things which would be commonly done by a committee for promoting an election, and that they were done openly and over a considable time; that at the time of the registration the agents of the respondent were aware of the association and acted in concert with it, and that both the respondent and his agents knew that the association was actively canvassing on his behalf. The acts of bribery suggested were, that about the first week in November and on the eve of the election, the association gave 5s. a-piece to a number of voters who attended the registration in September, as a day's pay for their loss of time in so doing, and that these sums were practically paid to everyone who came forward and asked for them without precautions being taken that those who got the money had done anything to earn it. In these circumstances, Blackburn, J., held that the association was the agent of the respondent. "When things," said his lordship, "are thus openly done, which would not be done in the ordinary course of things, except with the cognizance of a candidate, *who sanctioned them*, the natural inference in the absence of proof to the contrary would be, that they were done by a person acting as agent for the candidate. The respondent and his agents might have shown that they *had had no communication* with that body, that they repudiated it, and if that repudiation was *bonâ fide* they would not have been responsible for its acts. The respondent might have shown that a body, acting in such a way as this body acted, was acting officiously for him, as I may call it, that it was not with his consent and against his will; but the presumption does arise, I think, that it was done in his favour, done for him, unless there be something to show the contrary. I think, in this case, such a degree of benefit was derived from their assistance, that their assistance was so important to the candidate that it fairly establishes this, that if he took their assistance and did not hold them off, or repudiate them, he must abide the consequences and be responsible for their malpractice." Blackburn, J., must not be understood as laying down as a matter of law, that when an association is acting openly on behalf of a candidate he is necessarily liable, unless he

Parliamentary & Municipal.

Where *bonâ fide* repudiation, candidate not liable.

publicly repudiates its action. All he held was, that having regard to the facts of the case before him, and the very intimate connection which subsisted between the candidate and the association immediately prior to the election, there was, in the absence of evidence of repudiation, in fact, a presumption that he sanctioned what was being done. So regarded, the decision is in conformity with the more recent *Harwich Case* already quoted.

In the *Wakefield Case* (2 O'M. & H., 102) the facts were that the respondent was a vice-president of a political association, that he spoke at meetings of the association, that many of the members of the association were to his knowledge actively canvassing on his behalf, and that the committee rooms of the association were placarded with his election bills, *and used for the purpose of promoting his election*. Grove, J., held that these facts *primâ facie* brought the case within the law of agency and were (in the absence of evidence of *bonâ fide* repudiation) sufficient to satisfy the Court that the respondent "had put himself, or allowed himself to be in the hands of certain persons, or had made common cause with them."

In the *Londonderry Case* (21 L.T., n.s., 709) the alleged briber was a principal official of the Liberal Registration Association. It was proved that the respondent was the adopted candidate of the association, and had subscribed largely to its funds. The work of registration, with the respondent's approval, had been conducted by the association, and when the revision was completed, the funds and staff of the society, with Peacock (the alleged briber) as the principal of the staff were, with the respondent's assent, used for the purpose of promoting the election. The learned judge held upon these facts, that the respondent was clearly liable for the acts of the association.

In the *Gravesend Case* (44 L.T., n.s., 64), where it was proved that the respondent gave a political association a sum of money, large in proportion to its normal funds, and this money was spent by the association in treating Denman, J., intimated that the agency of the association was established.

The *Bewdley Case* (3 O'M. & H., 145; 44 L.T., n.s., 283) is an important case on this subject. There it was proved: (1.) that an association had been formed before the election to promote the candidature of the respondent; (2) that it was in constant communication with the respondent's chief election agent; (3) that the chief election agent supplied it with minute books and communicated with its secretary as to its progress, and reported the progress of the respondent's candidature to it; and (4) that during the progress of the contest he used in common with it a marked register containing an account of the favourable, adverse, and doubtful voters. The Court (Denman and Lopes, JJ.) held that the agency of the association had been established, and in giving judgment the latter learned judge made the following pertinent remarks. "I desire shortly to allude to the position of political associations and the liability of candidates. There appear to be persons who think that a candidate may escape the responsibility attaching to the acts of an agent by the employment of the active members of a political association, instead of an individual or individual agents; if this could be done the Corrupt Practices Act would become a dead letter. There may be, doubtless, in a borough a political association existing for the purpose of a political party, advocating the cause of a particular candidate and largely contributing to his success, yet in no privity with the candidate or his agents—an independent agency, and acting in its own behalf. To say that the candidate should be responsible for the corrupt acts of any member of that association, however active, would be unjust, against common sense, and opposed to law. There may on the other hand be a political association in the borough advocating the views of a candidate, of which that candidate is not a member, to the funds of which he does not subscribe, and with which he personally is not ostensibly connected, but at the same time *in intimate relationship with his agents, utilised by them for the purpose of carrying out his election, interchanging communication and information with his agents respecting the canvassing of voters and the conduct of the election*, and largely contributing to the result.

PARLIAMENTARY & MUNICIPAL.

Bewdley Case.

Judgment of Lopes, J.

PARLIAMENTARY & MUNICIPAL. To say that the candidate is not responsible for any corrupt acts done by an active member of such an association would be repealing the Corrupt Practices Act, and sanctioning a most effective system of corruption."

Result of the authorities. The result of the authorities would seem to be this: The mere fact that a political association in sympathy with the respondent is actively working in his favour does not, *taken by itself*, establish agency; but, though there is no original request to the association to give its services, if the respondent or his principal agents, knowing what it is doing, approves and sanctions its proceedings, then agency is made out. It is not necessary to show that the approval or sanction was ever given in so many words. The Court will generally infer it from the fact that communications in relation to the election have during the contest passed between the respondent and the association; and where the connection between the two was very intimate immediately before the election, and the services rendered at the latter are real and public, it may even infer it without proof of actual communication after the contest began. On the other hand, it is open to the respondent to exonerate himself by showing that he never had any connection with the association, and that it was acting officiously, or that he *bonâ fide* repudiated its action at the time.

An organization of the clergy may be agents. The principles which have been laid down with reference to the responsibility, under certain conditions, of a candidate for the acts of a political association in sympathy with him, apply equally to every other kind of association or combination which may espouse the cause of a candidate and render him active assistance, which he accepts and adopts. In this connection the *Limerick Case* (21 L.T., n.s. 567; 1 O'M. & H., 262) is worth consulting. There Fitzgerald, B., intimated a strong opinion that if the clergy in a given constituency make the cause of a candidate their own, and if the latter represents that his cause is identical with that of the clergy, and publicly gives out that the question between him and his adversaries is whether the clergy shall be put down or raised up, and if he is accompanied in his canvass by certain of the clergy—in such a case the organisation of [margin: Parliamentary & Municipal.] the clergy in the various districts of the constituency becomes an agency of the candidate.

Another question that presents itself is the extent to which, [margin: Agency in case of joint candidature.] where two or more candidates coalesce and stand together, as it is called, the agents of the one candidate bind the other. The law on this point was laid down in the clearest terms by Blackburn, J., in the *North Norfolk Case* (1 O'M. & H., 240 ; 21 L.T., n.s. 264). "It happens that in this case the respondents have stood jointly. They have chosen to what we commonly call coalesce. They united in a canvass, and, in fact, have made each an agent for the other, and they have chosen to stand or fall together ; consequently if any corrupt act is shown to be done by an agent appointed by one member it will affect both Such are the consequences of a coalition. If, therefore, a corrupt act is brought home to one, both are unable to hold their seats." In a later case, the *Norwich Case* (2 O'M. & H., 39), it was suggested that in giving a particular bribe the agent of one of two candidates who had coalesced, gave the bribe exclusively in the interest of his immediate principal. Upon this contention Keating, J., observed : "I think if it were clearly established that Ray (the agent) had gone to a voter and, wishing to exclude the respondent, had said, 'I give you this bribe to vote for Sir W. R., but not to vote for T., because my object is that you should not vote for T.,' it might be successfully argued that he was thereby determining the joint agency and no longer acting in the bribery as the respondent's agent. But that has not been proved." It may be taken, [margin: Agency where joint candidature.] therefore, that during the continuance of a joint candidature each candidate is liable to the fullest extent for the misdeeds of the duly-authorised agent of the other.

It is otherwise, however, with respect to acts committed by agents prior to the commencement of the coalition. In the *Tamworth Case* (1 O'M. & H., 82; 20 L.T., n.s., 181), it was decided that joint attention to the registration by two persons, who subsequently became candidates, did not necessarily imply joint action at the election ; and in *Malcolm*

PARLIAMENTARY & MUNICIPAL. v. *Parry* (L.R. 10, C.P. 168; 44 L.J., C.P. 121; 31 L.T., n.s., 845; 23 W.R., 322) the full Court of Common Pleas decided that where a candidate has been guilty of bribery by his agent, and *subsequently* to such acts of bribery another candidate coalesces with him, in ignorance of any previous corruption, and having no reason to suspect its existence, the latter is not liable by reason of the joint candidature to be unseated in respect of such prior acts of bribery. As to what will and will not constitute evidence of a joint candidature, where it is denied, see the *Bridgwater Case* (1 O'M. & H., 113), and also consider the Act of 1883, first schedule (Part V.), and the Act of 1884, s. 5, sub-s. 4).

Candidate not liable for a treacherous agent. It has been stated already that a candidate is liable for the acts of those persons whom the law construes to be his agents, although he has expressly forbidden them to commit any corrupt act, and though in committing it they are flying in the teeth of his honest wishes in the matter. But while this is so, it has been decided, for the necessary protection of candidates against treachery, that the candidate is not liable where the corrupt act was done by the agent with *Stafford Case.* the view of betraying his principal. This is the effect of the judgment in the *Stafford Case* (1 O'M. & H., 231; 21 L.T., n.s., 210), where Blackburn, J. said, " I wish to point out the distinction which I make, that according as the law stands at present, if a member employs an agent, and that agent, contrary to his wish and contrary to his direction, commits a corrupt act, the sitting member is responsible for it; but where he employs an agent and the agent treacherously or traitorously agrees with the other side, then if he does a corrupt act it would not vacate the seat unless it is proved that the corrupt act was at the special request of the member himself or some untainted and authorised agent of the member, who directed the act to be done. I say if Machin was a treacherous agent he loses the power of upsetting the seat by reason of his unauthorised acts of corruption, as it would require actual proof of authority. It is a very different affair if a man, being an agent, has been tricked by the other party into committing a corrupt act, he himself honestly still intending to act as agent."

Parliamentary & Municipal.
—

The last point we need consider is this: When does the authority of an agent to bind the candidate begin and when does it cease? Where the agent has been expressly appointed, in the great majority of cases the appointment will itself fix the time over which the authority extends. But with regard to the agency which the law will infer from active service in promotion of a candidature sanctioned by the candidate, it would seem that it begins with the rendering of the services which afford the evidence of the agency, and this whether at the time the election contest has actually begun or not (the *Youghal Case*, 1 O'M. & H., 294.) Just as a candidate may himself be guilty of a corrupt act before the occurrence of the vacancy in respect of which the election is held, so is he responsible at the like time for the corrupt act of any person who in fact is his agent. (*Ibid.*) And if a person is guilty of bribery, or any corrupt act, before he is expressly or implied appointed an agent, and afterwards the candidate, *with knowledge of his misconduct*, appoints him, his appointment relates back to the corrupt act or acts so as to make the candidate responsible for them.

Commencement of agency.

Agency may be terminated in various ways, chief among which are the following: (1) express repudiation and withdrawal of authority (*Harwich Case* and *first Taunton Case*); (2) an act of deliberate treachery on the part of the agent (*Stafford Case*, quoted *supra*); (3) in the case of a joint candidature, where it is shown the agent of one candidate has acted solely in the interest of his principal and *against the interest* of the other candidate (*Norwich Case*, 1 O'M. & H., 10); and (4) the termination of the election. Martin, B., decided in the *Salford Case* (1 O'M. & H., 133; 19 L.T., n.s. 120) that the authority of an agent came to an end with the termination of the election, and that a corrupt act committed the day after the polling, did not affect the sitting member; and this decision was acted upon by Willes, J., in the *Southampton Case* (1 O'M. & H. 222)

When agency ceases.

9

"The agency at the election," said Blackburn, J., giving his decision to the same effect in the *North Norfolk Case* (21 L T., n.s., 270; 1 O'M. & H., 243), "which was solely from the canvassing before the election, expires with the election."

It must be borne in mind, however, that if the bribe was given after the election, in pursuance of a promise made or an understanding arrived at *during the election*, then the act of bribery is committed at the latter period, and while the candidate is bound by the misdeeds of the agent: and, of course, if the act of bribery is committed even after the election by *the express direction* of the candidate, that would confer a fresh authority upon the agent, independent of his previous employment.

CHAPTER VIII.

THE OFFICE AND DUTIES OF THE ELECTION AGENT AT A PARLIAMENTARY ELECTION.

SECTION I.—HIS APPOINTMENT.

THE Act of 1883 creates in cases of Parliamentary elections a new officer, the election agent, with difficult and important duties, upon the due fulfilment of which the validity of the election largely depends. This officer bears no resemblance to any other agent known to the law, except the agent for election expenses, created by the statute 26 & 27 Vict., c. 29, s. 2, whose duties and many other duties he will have to discharge. He is not to be confounded with the person who has hitherto borne the name of the election agent, meaning thereby the person to whose experience and intelligence the management and conduct of the election have hitherto been confided. In future, "the election agent," using the phrase in its statutory sense, may or may not be the person who plans and directs the operations of the campaign. As the election agent is to make all contracts and payments relating to the conduct of the election, and as the measure of the candidate's responsibility for his acts is greater than that for the acts of any other agent, it will be found safer, though perhaps inconvenient, to dissever these offices in future. A candidate will be at some disadvantage who imposes on his chief counsellor and manager the very anxious and difficult duties which the Act of 1883 thrusts upon "the election agent." If the offices should be dissevered, the person who manages the election for the candidate must do so gratuitously. He cannot be legally employed for payment. (Schedule I., Part I, and s. 17 of the Act of 1883). It is proper to add that the "election agent" need not be a solicitor, but, in view of the direct and immediate responsibility of the candidate for his acts and omissions, it can

PARLIAMENTARY
The election agent.

Should be a person of business habits and conversant with the law.

hardly be doubted that any candidate will do well to avail himself of the professional caution and legal training of a solicitor, if he can induce a solicitor to accept the office. If the candidate choose he may be his own election agent. In that event he will have only himself to blame for any slip on the part of the election agent. But, whether he choose to be his own election agent or to appoint some other person, it is of urgent necessity that the election agent should be a person of business habits, of experience in the conduct of elections, and intimately conversant with the provisions of the election law.

The object of the legislature. The object aimed at by the legislature in requiring the appointment of an election agent, through whose hands all money shall pass, and by whose hands all accounts shall be paid, is the regulation and diminution of election expenses. The evil of excessive expenditure at elections has been struck at by many statutes, beginning with the 7 & 8 Will. III., c. 4, which was directed against " the excessive and exorbitant expenses, contrary to the laws and in violation of the freedom due to the election of representatives for the Commons of England in Parliament, to the great scandal of the kingdom, dishonourable, and may be destructive to the constitution of Parliament." The statute 17 & 18 Vict., c. 102, with the same view, provided for the appointment of election auditors; but the fruit being no sweeter than the tree, these were found useless; and the Act of 1883 would imply a similar condemnation upon the agents for election expenses who were called into existence by the Act 26 & 27 Vict., c. 29, and through whom all payments for election expenses, other than the candidate's personal expenses, were to be made, under pain of fine and imprisonment.

When and how election agent to be named. The appointment of the election agent is regulated by s. 24 of the Act of 1883. The section does not prescribe any particular form of appointment, which should, however, be in writing; but it provides that on or before the nomination day the election agent shall be *named* by or on behalf of the candidate. As contracts relating to the election are to be made, and polling agents and clerks appointed by the election agent (s. 27), it is obviously desirable that the PARLIAMENTARY election agent should be appointed and named as soon as the candidate takes the field. What will happen if the candidate should not name himself or some other person as election agent on or before the nomination day is not very clear; but an inquiry on the subject is idle, for so flagrant a violation of the Act of Parliament would involve the candidate in many difficulties and considerable danger, any payments made by him, except through an election agent, being illegal practices avoiding the election. If a candidate prefers to be his own election agent he must name himself as such, and thereupon he will be subject to the liabilities imposed by the Act on election agents, as well as to those imposed upon candidates. If a candidate be nominated in his absence, or without his consent, the election agent is to be named "on his behalf." One of the nominators or seconders had better name the election agent in such a case.

In regard to naming the election agent, it is provided by s. 24 (sub-s. 3) of the Act of 1883, that on or before the day of nomination the name and address and the office of the election agent of each candidate shall be declared *in writing* by the candidate, or some other person on his behalf to the returning officer, and the returning officer shall *forthwith* give public notice of the name and address of every election agent so declared. [Notice of his appointment.]

The "public notice" to be given by the returning officer is regulated by s. 62 of the Act of 1883, and the Ballot Act, 1872, Schedule 1., Rule 46. He may give the notice "by advertisements, placards, handbills, or such other means as he thinks best calculated to afford information to the electors."

A candidate can only appoint one person to be his election agent; but any appointment, whether of the candidate himself or of any other person, can be revoked. If any appointment is revoked, or the election agent die before, during, or after the election, but before the requirements of the Act have been fully complied with, the candidate must *forthwith* appoint a new election agent, and *in writing* [Changing the election agent.]

THE LAW RELATING TO

PARLIAMENTARY declare his name and address and office to the returning officer, who will immediately give public notice of the fact. (Sub-s. 4 of s. 24.)

Sub-agents in counties and certain boroughs
In counties, but not in boroughs (Schedule I., Part I.), the election agent may and apparently nobody else may, appoint a deputy or sub-agent to act within each polling district. (S. 25 of the Act of 1883.) The number of these sub-agents is regulated by the first schedule of the Act.

Risks of appointing sub-agents.
But the wisdom of appointing sub-agents where it is practicable to do without them seems extremely doubtful, for by s. 25 (sub-s. 2) of the Act of 1883 the candidate is made responsible, and the return may be avoided for many acts done by the sub-agent which, if committed by any other agents except the election agent, would not affect the seat. At all events it would be safer to delay the formal appointment of sub-agents until one clear day before the polling. Before that time the zeal of some friend may have outrun his discretion, in which case the injury to the candidate would not be so great as if he had been previously appointed a sub-agent. For the purpose of avoiding the seat every sub-agent, *acting in his own district*, is placed in the position of the election agent. If a remote sub-agent should employ and pay an assistant in excess of the number allowed, or issue a bill without the printer's name appended, the candidate's seat might not be worth an hour's purchase. In such a case the better opinion would seem to be that the candidate could have no relief under s. 22 of the Act of 1883; but in some instances he might have relief under s. 23

The candidate's liability for sub-agent's acts.
of the same Act. S. 25, sub-s. 2, enacts: "As regards matters in a polling district, the election agent may act by the sub-agent for that district, and anything done for the purposes of this Act by or to the sub-agent *in his district* shall be deemed to be done by or to the election agent, and any act or default of a sub-agent which, if he were the election agent, would be an illegal practice or other offence against this Act, shall be an illegal practice and offence against this Act committed by the sub-agent, and the sub-agent shall be liable to punishment accordingly; and the

candidate shall suffer the like incapacity as if the said act or default had been the act or default of the election agent." If, notwithstanding these dangers, the candidate should direct the election agent to appoint sub-agents, he should satisfy himself of the caution and ability of the persons to be appointed, and their knowledge of the law, and the election agent *must* at least one clear day before the polling declare *in writing* to the returning officer the name and address of each sub-agent and his office within his district, just as the candidate must in the case of the election agent have previously done. The returning officer will then give public notice of the appointments in the usual way.

It would seem from the language of s. 34, sub-s. 2, of the Act of 1883, that the authority of the sub-agent does not come to an end with the poll or with the return. This view is strengthened by s. 25, sub-s. 2, which places him in the position of the election agent, so far as the candidate's liability for his acts is concerned. But it would be prudent on the part of the election agent to revoke the appointment of the sub-agents as soon as the poll has closed. By s. 25, sub-s. 4, it is provided : "The appointment of a sub-agent shall not be vacated by the election agent who appointed him ceasing to be election agent, but may be revoked by the election agent for the time being of the candidate, and in the event of such revocation or of the death of a sub-agent, another sub-agent may be appointed, and his name and address shall be forthwith declared in writing to the returning officer, who shall forthwith give public notice of the same."

<small>Revocation of sub-agent's appointment.</small>

Although there is no express provision on the point, it would be well to give the returning officer immediate notice in writing of the revocation.

The election agent and sub-agents must have offices. By s. 26, sub-s. 1, it is provided that an election agent at an election for a county or borough shall have within the county or borough, or within any county of a city or town adjoining thereto, and a sub-agent shall have within his district, or

<small>Offices of the election agent and sub-agent.</small>

PARLIAMENTARY within a county of a city or town adjoining thereto, an office or place to which all claims, notices, writs, summonses, and documents may be sent, and the address of such office shall be declared at the same time as the appointment of the said agent to the returning officer, and shall be stated in the public notice of the name of the agent.

Service of notices.
Service of any claim or document or notice by delivery at the office, and addressed to the election agent or sub-agent, will be equivalent to personal service on the election agent or sub-agent, as the case may be, and if the agent should make himself personally liable to be sued by any person in respect of any matter connected with the election, then (s. 26) he may be sued in any Court having jurisdiction in the county or borough in which the office is.

Polling agents, clerks and messengers to be appointed by election agent
Every polling agent, clerk and messenger employed for payment on behalf of the candidate is to be appointed, and every committee room hired in his behalf is to be hired by the election agent, acting by himself or his sub-agent. It would not be a corrupt practice, nor apparently, notwithstanding s. 27 of the Act of 1883, would it necessarily be an illegal practice, although improper, for some other person *to appoint* a polling agent, clerk or messenger, or to hire a committee room, provided the statutory number was not exceeded; but *to pay* the person appointed or the lessor of a committee room, except through the election agent, would be an illegal practice. And no such contract could be enforced against the candidate. Persons asked to give credit in connection with an election have public notice of the

and to be paid by him.
names of the persons who can pledge the credit of the candidate, and they give credit to other persons at their peril. By s. 28, sub-s. 2, it is provided that a contract whereby any expenses are incurred on account of or in respect of the conduct or management of an election shall not be enforceable against a candidate at such election, unless made by the candidate himself or by his election agent, either by himself or by his sub-agent; provided that the inability under this section to enforce such contract against the candidates shall not relieve the candidate from the consequences of any

corrupt or illegal practice having been committed by his **Parliamentary agent.** The word agent in the last line means any agent, constructive or otherwise.

No election agent is provided for by the Act of 1884 in the case of municipal elections and therefore, none need be appointed.

SECTION II.—THE NATURE AND AMOUNT OF THE ELECTION EXPENSES AT A PARLIAMENTARY ELECTION.

The statute insists on all payments for election expenses being made by or through the election agent. The candidate may himself pay his personal expenses up to £100, and any person authorised *in writing* by the election agent may pay "any necessary expenses for stationery, postage, telegrams and other petty expenses," but only to the amount named in the authority (s. 31 of the Act of 1883). Subject to these exceptions, neither the candidate nor any agent (except the election agent acting personally or through a sub-agent in the district of the latter) may pay any election expenses, under pain of the consequences of an illegal practice, affecting the seat as well as the individual. S. 28 of the Act of 1883 provides: (1). "Except as permitted by or in pursuance of this Act, no payment and no advance or deposit shall be made by a candidate at an election, or by any agent on behalf of the candidate, or by any other person at any time, whether before, during or after such election, in respect of any expenses incurred on account of or in respect of the conduct or management of such election, otherwise than by or through the election agent of the candidate, *whether acting in person or by a sub-agent;* and all money provided by any person other than the candidate for any expenses incurred on account of or in respect of the conduct or management of the election, whether as gift, loan, advance or deposit, shall be paid to the candidate or his election agent, and not otherwise;" Provided that this section shall not be deemed to apply to a tender of security to or any payment by the

All payments to be made by the election agent.

Exceptions.

Money provided to pay expenses.

PARLIAMENTARY returning officer, or to any sum disbursed by any person out of his own money for any small expenses legally incurred by himself, if such sum is not repaid to him. (2.) A person who makes any payment, advance or deposit in contravention of this section, or pays in contravention of this section any money so provided as aforesaid, shall be guilty of an illegal practice."

The question, what are and what are not " election expenses " within the meaning of the Act, bristles with difficulties. Doubts may arise whether a given item of expense is an " election expense," because of the time at which it is incurred, of the purpose with which it was incurred, or of the character of the service rendered for it. By s. 63 of the Act of 1883, the expression " candidate " means " unless the context otherwise requires " —an expression which at once introduces uncertainty—a candidate returned and " any person who is nominated as a candidate . . . . or is declared by himself or by others to be a candidate on or after the day of the issue of the writ for such election, or after the dissolution or vacancy in consequence of which such writ has been issued." That section cannot be read as relieving candidates of an obligation to return expenses incurred before the issue of the writ, or before the dissolution or vacancy. It defines a candidate. It does not define an election or an election expense.

In the *Stepney Case* (4 O'M. & H., 38), it was held that the expense of employing a voter before the candidate was actually selected, was an election expense.

In other words, a candidate must return election expenses incurred before that date. (Per Denman, J., in the *Norwich Case*, 4 O'M. & H., 85.) How long before cannot be exactly stated in the form of a rule. It is submitted that it must depend in each case upon the purpose with which a given item of expense was incurred, and the character of the service rendered for it, and if this is the test there is probably nothing irreconcileable in the *Norwich Case* (4 O'M. & H., 84, and the *Stepney Case*, 4 O'M. & H., 38).

If a candidate should issue his election address a year

before the dissolution of Parliament, it could hardly be contended that the expense thereby incurred was not an election expense. We think that the time is only important as affording an "argument that a given item of expense is or is not incurred on account of or in respect of the conduct or management" of an election. If a candidate should address the electors after the dissolution of Parliament, no one could doubt that the expense thereby incurred was an election expense. But if he did the same thing years or months before the election, different considerations might arise, and much would, we think, depend on the answers to such questions as the following :—(*a*) Was he then declared by himself or others to be a candidate? (*b*) Was the election generally supposed to be near at hand? (*c*) Was the object of the meeting to recommend him to the electors, or merely to persuade them that the Government had earned the confidence or the disapprobation of the electors?

In the *Norwich Case* (4 O'M. & H., 84), the question was whether the expenses of a meeting at which it was resolved to invite the respondent to stand, and of a meeting at which he consented to become a candidate, were election expenses. Cave, J., said : "This is a new point, which arises under the Act of 1883 (46 & 47 Vict., c. 51), and if the petitioners were successful in their contention, it would, to my mind, in some cases seriously interfere with the power of a candidate to carry on the campaign. If he is to take into account expenses incurred before he ever started as a candidate at all, he may find himself beginning a campaign, which must cost some money, with all the money which under ordinary circumstances he would use in carrying on the campaign already exhausted by preliminary expenses before he was in the field at all. In this particular case it was clearly established that in the first instance the respondent was unwilling to stand. On September 21st a meeting was called, and it was agreed to get up a requisition for signature. Now I myself am unable to see why that should not be done. It is most important to each party in a constituency that they should bring forward a candidate likely to be successful. I do not see any reason why they should not hold meetings among themselves for the purpose of selecting their candidate, and I cannot see how it can properly be said that expenses which are so incurred are the expenses of the candidate in procuring his election. To my mind there is a great distinction between the expenses of getting a candidate, and the expenses of promoting his election after you have got him. If the primary and direct and real object is to get a candidate, I think that the expenses incurred in so doing are not within the Act, although indirectly they may promote the interests of the party. If the nominal object is to get a candidate, but the real object is to promote the election of the individual candidate, then, I should say, it would be within the Act."

Then, as to the kind of expenditure permitted to be returned. Sections 16 and 17 make certain kinds of expenditure at all times illegal if incurred "for the purpose of promoting or procuring" the election of a candidate. But the expenses which are to be returned are not those incurred "for the purpose of promoting or procuring" the election of the candidate. They are those "incurred on account of or in respect of the conduct or management" of the election. We think that these words are narrower than the others, and that there may be cases in which expenses incurred "for the purpose of promoting or procuring" the election of a candidate are not incurred "on account of or in respect of the conduct or management" of an election. For example—A, a candidate intending to stand for the borough of B, buys or runs a party newspaper, with the intention that it should recommend his principles to the electors, or, to gain popularity, subscribes liberally to local charities, or pays the registration expenses of his party in the borough. These expenses are incurred for the purpose of promoting or procuring A's election, but they are not, we think, generally incurred "on account of or in respect of the conduct or management" of his election. (*Kennington*, 4 O'M. & H., 94.) Still, every case must depend upon its own circumstances. A newspaper might, for example, be nothing but a succession of A's election addresses and speeches, and exhortations to vote for him.

<small>PARLIAMENTARY</small>

Part III. of the First Schedule to the Act of 1883 permits not more than £200 to be spent upon "miscellaneous matters," other than those mentioned in Parts I. and II. of the schedule. "Miscellaneous matters" have not been defined.

The candidate and the election agent ought, at the beginning of the election, to estimate their election expenditure, and regulate the expenditure by the estimate, otherwise there will be some danger of the maximum expenditure allowed by the Act of 1883 being exceeded. But as we have already indicated it is not to be assumed that only such expenses as are incurred after the dissolution or after the creation of a vacancy in the representation are election expenses within the meaning of the Act. The provisions of the Act limiting expenditure would be a nullity if contracts could be entered into and expenses incurred for the purpose of promoting the return of an intending candidate before the dissolution or creation of a vacancy, and no account taken of them in the return of election expenses.

<small>Candidate should estimate his election expenditure.</small>

<small>What are election expenses.</small>

It has been supposed that the stringent provisions of the new legislation as to the amount and mode of payment of election expenses may be evaded by making payments to agents, nominally, for registration work between elections, upon an understanding that at the election time these agents shall work gratuitously for the candidate. But the arm of the law is long enough to overreach such transactions. Nor can these provisions be evaded by the work of the election being undertaken by a political association or the members of it. They may, indeed, work gratuitously for the candidate of their choice, but payments made by them for expenses incurred by them in working the election, unless these expenses were their own personal expenses, or any small expense legally incurred by them and not repaid, would constitute an illegal practice. Thus, for a political club to engage and pay a canvasser would be clearly illegal.

<small>Standing salaries to agents.</small>

PARLIAMENTARY — What need not be included in the estimate.
(a) Costs of taking voters by sea.
(b) Returning officer's expenses.

In estimating the expenses of the election, no account need be taken of the personal expenses of the candidate, nor of the charges of the returning officer, nor yet of the cost of the conveyance of voters by sea, where, under s. 48, that is allowed. They must be included in the returns made by the election agent, but they are not included in the maximum sums allowed by the Act (Schedule 1., Part IV.). But it would be illegal to pay to the returning officer any larger sum than is allowed by the earlier statute (38 & 39 Vict. c. 84). And in the *Cambridgeshire Case* (*ex rel. edit.*), since the Act of 1883 came into force, Mathew, J., at chambers, refused an application on behalf of the sitting member, made with the concurrence of the unsuccessful candidate, for leave to pay to the returning officer sums in excess of those allowed by the statute, but which had, in fact, been *bonâ fide* spent upon the proper conduct of the polling.

(c) Personal expenses.

The expression "personal expenses," as used with respect to the expenditure of a candidate in relation to an election includes (s. 64 of the Act of 1883) his *reasonable* travelling expenses, and the *reasonable* expenses of his living at hotels or elsewhere for the purposes of and in relation to the election. We think that it should not be held to include the travelling or hotel expenses of his family or the hotel expenses of any guest invited by the candidate to stay with him during the whole or part of the election.

Heads of election expenses.

The chief heads of expense to be taken account of and kept within the maximum allowed by the Act of 1883 are those indicated and limited by Schedule I. to that Act, Parts I. and II. They are :—

(1.) The remuneration of persons legally employed for payment ; only one election agent may be employed, but in counties one sub-agent to act within each polling district may be also employed. The number of clerks and messengers who may be employed has already been discussed.

(2.) The expenses of printing, the expenses of advertising

and the expenses of publishing, issuing, and distributing addresses and notices.

(3.) The expenses of stationery, messages, postage, and telegrams.

(4.) The expenses of holding public meetings.

(5.) In a borough the expenses of one committee-room, and if the number of electors in the borough exceeds 500, then of a number of committee-rooms not exceeding the number of one committee-room for every complete 500 electors in the borough; and if there is a number of electors over and above any complete 500 or complete 500's of electors, then of one committee-room for such number, although not amounting to a complete 500.

(6.) In a county the expenses of a central committee-room and in addition of a number of committee-rooms, not exceeding in number one committee-room for each polling district in the county, and where the number of electors in a polling district exceeds 500, one additional committee-room may be hired for every complete 500 electors in such polling district over and above the first 500.

The number of committee-rooms allowed has already been discussed. It may be said here that in a borough an extra committee-room is allowed for any fraction of 500 electors, but in a county an extra committee-room is not allowed in any polling district for any fraction of 500 electors, but only for each complete number of 500 electors after the first 500.

(7.) Miscellaneous expenses (not exceeding £200 in all, or less in case of a joint candidature), and not incurred in respect of anything prohibited by any Act of Parliament. As to the limitations upon miscellaneous expenses, see the first schedule to the Act of 1883, Part III. and Part V., paragraph (3.)

Parliamentary Prohibited payments. For instance (s. 16), payments for bands, torches, flags, banners, cavalcades or ribbons are prohibited. Payments for chairing the candidate, or for horses and carriages for conveying voters, or for railway or steamboat passes, or for a right to exhibit placards, made to any elector, except to an ordinary advertising agent, or to persons to hold up their hands for the candidate at the nomination, when the show of hands was taken, have also been prohibited.

The candidate and the election agent, in mapping out their expenditure, will do well to leave a margin for contingencies, otherwise they may find they have exceeded the maximum expenditure allowed by the Act, and so come within the perils of s. 8 of the Act of 1883.

The maximum expenditure. The maximum expenditure allowed is stated in the first schedule, Part IV., to the Act of 1883. It is to be remembered that, in all cases, the candidate's personal expenses and the returning officer's charges, and the costs of conveying voters by sea, where allowed, under s. 48 are payable in addition. The scale is regulated by the number of electors on the register, and no deductions are to be made for dead men, double entries, or the like.

In boroughs. The words of the Act (Schedule I., Part IV.), limiting the maximum expenditure as to boroughs are these:—

If the number of electors on the register—
Does not exceed 2,000 . . The maximum amount shall be—£350.
Exceeds 2,000 . . £380, and an additional £30 for every complete 1,000 electors above 2,000.

Provided that in Ireland, if the number of electors on the register—
Does not exceed 500 . . The maximum amount shall be—£200.
Exceeds 500, but does not exceed 1,000 . . . £250.
Exceeds 1,000, but does not exceed 1,500 . . . £275.

Since the Redistribution Act of 1885 the special provision for constituencies containing less than 1,500 electors is of little moment. There are at present no constituencies with so few electors.

CORRUPT PRACTICES AT ELECTIONS.

The words of the same schedule in regard to the maximum Parliamentary expenditure in counties are these :—

If the number of electors on the register—	The maximum amount shall be— In counties.
Does not exceed 2,000	£650 in England and Scotland and £500 in Ireland.
Exceeds 2,000	£710 in England and Scotland, and £540 in Ireland ; and an additional £60 in England, and Scotland, and £40 in Ireland, for every complete 1,000 electors above 2,000.

The following is the scale in boroughs where the candidate stands alone, and *not jointly with another candidate* :— Scale in all English and Scotch boroughs and in Irish boroughs with over 1,500 electors.

Number of Electors on the Register.	Maximum amount allowed.	Number of Electors on the Register.	Maximum amount allowed.
2,000 or under	. £350	13,000 to 13,999 inclusive	. £710
2,001 to 2,999 inclusive	£380	14,000 to 14,999 ,,	. £740
3,000 to 3,999 ,,	. £410	15,000 to 15,999 ,,	. £770
4,000 to 4,999 ,,	. £440	16,000 to 16,999 ,,	. £800
5,000 to 5,999 ,,	. £470	17,000 to 17,999 ,,	. £830
6,000 to 6,999 ,,	. £500	18,000 to 18,999 ,,	. £860
7,000 to 7,999 ,,	. £530	19,000 to 19,999 ,,	. £890
8,000 to 8,999 ,,	. £560	20,000 to 20,999 ,,	. £920
9,000 to 9,999 ,,	. £590	21,000 to 21,999 ,,	. £950
10,000 to 10,999 ,,	. £620	22,000 to 22,999 ,,	. £980
11,000 to 11,999 ,,	. £650	23,000 to 23,999 ,,	£1,010
12,000 to 12,999 ,,	. £680	24,000 to 24,999 ,,	£1,040

and so on, adding to £380 an additional £30 for every complete 1,000 electors above 2,000 enumerated on the register.

This scale applies to all boroughs except to Irish boroughs having less than 1,500 electors.

The following is the scale in counties where the

PARLIAMENTARY candidate stands alone, and *not jointly with another candidate*:—

Scale in counties.

Number of Electors on Register.	Maximum amount allowed in England and Scotland.	Maximum amount allowed in Ireland.
2,000 or under	£650	£500
2,001 to 2,999 inclusive	£710	£540
3,000 to 3,999	£770	£580
4,000 to 4,999	£830	£620
5,000 to 5,999	£890	£660
6,000 to 6,999	£950	£700
7,000 to 7,999	£1,010	£740
8,000 to 8,999	£1,070	£780
9,000 to 9,999	£1,130	£820
10,000 to 10,999	£1,190	£860
11,000 to 11,999	£1,250	£900
12,000 to 12,999	£1,310	£940
13,000 to 13,999	£1,370	£980
14,000 to 14,999	£1,430	£1,020
15,000 to 15,999	£1,490	£1,060
16,000 to 16,999	£1,550	£1,100
17,000 to 17,999	£1,610	£1,140
18,000 to 18,999	£1,670	£1,180
19,000 to 19,999	£1,730	£1,220
20,000 to 20,999	£1,790	£1,260
21,000 to 21,999	£1,850	£1,300
22,000 to 22,999	£1,910	£1,340
23,000 to 23,999	£1,970	£1,380
24,000 to 24,999	£2,030	£1,420

and so on, adding, in England or Scotland, to £710, an additional £60 for every 1,000 electors over 2,000, and adding, in Ireland, to £540 an additional £40 for every 1,000 electors above 2,000.

Further restrictions on expenditure in case of joint candidature.

It will frequently happen that candidates will stand jointly. In that case (Schedule I., Part V., 3) the maximum expenditure allowed *to each* is to be reduced, if there are two joint candidates, by *one-fourth*, and if there are more than two joint candidates by *one-third*. The maximum expenditure allowed to two joint candidates is therefore one and a half times that which would be allowed *to each* if he stood separately, and the maximum allowed to three joint candidates is just twice as much as that allowed *to each* if he stood separated.

Having regard to that enactment, it is important to notice PARLIAMENTARY what constitutes a joint candidature for this purpose.

A case of joint candidature arises (Schedule I., Part V., 4) What is a joint when *any one* of the following events happen:— candidature.

(*a*.) Two or more candidates appoint the same election agent.

(*b*.) Two or more candidates by themselves *or any agent* hire *or use* the same committee room or rooms for the election.

(*c*.) Two or more candidates by themselves *or any agent* employ *or use* the services of the same sub-agents, clerks, messengers, or polling agents at the election. It would seem that for both candidates *by any agent* to use, *e.g., one* committee-room or *one* messenger in common, although in all other respect the rooms used and persons employed by each candidate were different and separate, would constitute a joint candidature for the purposes of this section.

(*d*.) Two or more candidates by themselves *or any agent* publish a joint address, or joint circular, or joint notice at the election.

The severity of this enactment is modified by a provision which, however, affects (*b*) and (*c*) only. If the employment or use of the same committee-room, sub-agent, clerk, messenger, or polling agent is (1) accidental or casual or (2) of a trivial and unimportant character, a case of joint candidature will not be thereby created. (Schedule I., Part V., 4 (*a*).)

Candidates may at any time cease to be joint candidates, Severance of a joint in which case they had better give public notice of the fact. candidature. In the event of a candidate ceasing to be a joint candidate or becoming a joint candidate after having begun to conduct his election as a separate candidate, he will occupy an anomalous position in regard to the maximum amount of expenditure allowed to him. It would seem that his election expenditure is to be regulated as if he had been a joint candidate throughout the election. But he may

PARLIAMENTARY
Case of candidature partly joint and partly several.

under certain circumstances get relief under the provisions of the Act of 1883, s. 23, and Schedule I., Part V., 4 (c), for any excess of expenditure above the amount allowed to a joint candidate if his total expenses do not amount to what the Act would have allowed him as a separate candidate. That clause, 4 (c), provides: "Where any excess of the expenses above the maximum allowed for one of two or more joint candidates has arisen owing to his having ceased to be a joint candidate, or to his having become a joint candidate after having begun to conduct his election as a separate candidate, and such ceasing or beginning was in good faith and such excess is not more than under the circumstances is reasonable, and the total expenses of such candidate do not exceed the maximum amount allowed for a separate candidate, such excess shall be deemed to have arisen from a reasonable cause within the meaning of the enactments respecting the allowance by the High Court or election court of an exception from the provisions of this Act which would otherwise make an act an illegal practice, and the candidate and his election agent may be relieved accordingly from the consequences of having incurred such excess of expenses."

Evidence on application for relief.

The candidate who applies for relief under this clause must therefore prove to the Court the following things:—

(1.) That the excess of expenditure has arisen from the candidate having ceased to be a joint candidate or from his becoming a joint candidate after having been a separate candidate, and

(2.) That he began or ceased to be a joint candidate in good faith and without any intention to evade the provisions of the Act, and

(3.) That the excess is not more than under the circumstances is reasonable, and

(4.) That his expenses do not exceed the maximum amount allowed to a separate candidate.

If the application is made to the High Court, it must be by motion or by a judge's summons at chambers before judge on the rota for the trial of election petitions.

Such previous notice of the application as the Court may *Parliamentary* direct must be given in the constituency.

Under s. 28, requiring all moneys provided for the election expenses to be paid to the candidate or his election agent, it would seem to be necessary that a fund raised by subscription to defray A's election expenses be paid to A himself or to his election agent. *Subscriptions to pay candidate's expenses.*

The proviso in the same section only amounts to this, that if any person, not intending to corrupt an elector, disburses any trifling sum for any small expense incurred *by himself* without thinking of repayment, and without the fact of repayment, no harm is done. Thus, if B, a partisan of A's, hires and himself pays for a carriage to enable him to canvass for votes for A, that is unobjectionable. But still the amount disbursed must be small, otherwise the first subsection of s. 28 would be nullified. By sub-s. 2 of s. 28, contravention of the section by any agent, constructive or otherwise, would avoid the seat. *Petty expenditure by partisans not repaid.*

Section III.—The Payment of Parliamentary Election Expenses.

Subject to the trifling exceptions mentioned in s. 28, it is the business of the election agent to make all payments. He will do well to postpone the making of these payments, except in the rare cases in which credit is refused, until 14 days after the declaration of the result of the election, when he will know what is the total amount of the claims upon his candidate. There is nothing in the Act to make it obligatory on the election agent to advertise for creditors to send in their claims. Creditors have public notice of the election agent's appointment, and they must be presumed to know the law that their bills must be sent in to the election agent within 14 days next after the declaration of the result of the election. But it may sometimes be convenient to advertise for claims, and there is nothing in the Act to forbid an advertisement. *By the election agent. Advertising for claims.*

150   THE LAW RELATING TO

Parliamentary Every claim against a candidate at an election, *or* his
When claims election agent (which in counties includes sub-agents acting
to be sent in. in their own districts), in respect of any expenses incurred
on account of or in respect of the conduct or management of
the election, must be sent in to the election agent by a bill,
stating the particulars of the claim within fourteen days
next after the day on which the candidates returned are
declared elected (s. 29 of the Act of 1883). The time will
run from the nomination day if there is no poll, and if there
is a poll, from the day on which the returning officer declares
the result of the poll. In the case of petitions against the
return for corrupt practices, the time runs from the day on
which the return comes to the hands of the clerk of the
Crown so that he can act upon it. As the Act speaks of the
claims being " sent in," and not of the time of their receipt,
it would seem that if the returning officer declares the result
on the 1st of a month, the claims may be posted or otherwise " sent " at any time, so that in the ordinary course of
the post or other usual means of transmission adopted they
will be delivered at the office of the election agent on or
before the 15th of the month, *i.e.*, within the fourteen days.

Account of candidate's personal expenses to be sent in. It is to be remembered, that although a candidate is allowed (s. 31) himself to *pay* his personal expenses not exceeding £100 in connection with the election (which by s. 64 includes " the reasonable travelling expenses of such candidate and the reasonable expenses of his living at hotels or elsewhere for the purposes of and in relation to such election "), yet the candidate *must*, within fourteen days after the returning officer has declared the result of the election, send to the election agent a written statement of the *amount* of the personal expenses paid by him. Seemingly, the par-
ticulars of the amount need not be stated. Any excess on
Personal expenses over £100 to be paid by the election agent. account of personal expenses over £100 *must* be paid by the election agent (s. 31), and any person authorised under s. 31, sub-s. 2, to make petty disbursements for stationery, postage, telegrams, and other expenses, *must* within the same
Particulars of petty disbursements. time, send to the election agent a statement of the *particulars* of the payments made by him, and he must also send in a

receipted bill vouching the payment (sub-s. 3). The Act <small>PARLIAMENTARY</small>
applies, so far as circumstances will admit, to the claims by
the election agent for his remuneration and payment. He
can hardly be bound to send his claim in to himself, but he <small>Remuneration</small>
would do well to give notice of his claim within the fourteen <small>of election agent.</small>
days next after the declaration of the result to his candidate.
His claim must then be satisfied by the candidate within the
next fourteen days (s. 32), otherwise it will become a "disputed claim," and be dealt with accordingly. (Compare
s. 29, sub-s. 5, 7 and 8, and s. 30.)

The returning officer *must* transmit to the election agent, <small>Returning officer's charges.</small>
within *twenty-one* days after the return, an account of the
charges claimed by him (s. 32, sub-s. 2). The account need
not be sent to the candidate or anybody else. (*Cf.* the
statute, 38 & 39 Vict., c. 84.) As to the power of the
returning officer to require security for the payment of his
charges and the amount of the security which can be
required, and the amount of the charges, see the statutes
38 & 39 Vict., c. 84, and 48 & 49 Vict., c. 62.

If a claim be not "sent in" within the proper time, the <small>Late claims barred.</small>
creditor will be barred of all right of action against the
candidate or the election agent. They are prohibited from
paying any late claim, and if the election agent should pay
any such claim he would be guilty of an illegal practice.
But certain relief against this somewhat severe enactment
may be obtained upon conditions, under sub-ss. 6 and 9 of
s. 29 of the Act of 1883, which will be dealt with presently.

The election agent having received the claims against his <small>Examination and payment of claims.</small>
candidate will examine them, and separate those which are
in respect of contracts made or expenses incurred by the
candidate or the election agent acting by himself or by a
sub-agent. These, except in cases in which the candidate's
liability is admitted, but the amount claimed is disputed,
must be paid within a second period of 14 days, *i.e.*, within
28 days of the day on which the candidates returned were
declared duly elected. To pay them afterwards would be
an illegal practice. By sub-s. 4 of s. 29 of the Act of 1883,
it is enacted: "All expenses incurred by or on behalf of a

THE LAW RELATING TO

Parliamentary candidate at an election, which are incurred on account of or in respect of the conduct or management of such election, shall be paid within the time limited by this Act and not otherwise; and subject to such exception as may be allowed in pursuance of this Act an election agent who makes a payment in contravention of this provision shall be guilty of an illegal practice."

Time of payment. Probably it would be held that a payment was made in good time if the money or cheque were posted or despatched to the creditor in such time that in the ordinary course of the post or other means of transmission it would be delivered at his address within the 28 days. It would not matter, we think, that the payment was by a crossed cheque, which could not be cleared until after the 28 days had expired.

All claims sent in within the proper time, *disputed* by the election agent, or which the election agent *refuses or fails* to pay within the 28 days, become " disputed " claims within the Act, and are to be dealt with as such. (S. 29, sub-ss. 7 and 8.)

Relief against payments out of time. The election agent may, by inadvertence or otherwise, commit the illegal practice of paying a claim after the 28 days, or of paying a claim sent in after the 14 days. In that case he may be relieved under the provisions of s. 23 of the Act of 1883. The candidate may also be relieved. The High Court, under the powers of s. 23, and upon compliance with the somewhat stringent conditions of that section, might excuse him from the consequences of the Act, and thereupon it might possibly stay a petition presented against his return, and based on the election agent's illegal practice in so paying, and (sub-s. 6 of s. 29) the judges *at the trial* of the petition *may* report, in a proper case, that the payment made by the election agent in contravention of the section was made *without the sanction or connivance* of the candidate. If they do so report, the election will not be void on account of that payment, nor will the candidate be subject to any incapacity, but he may have to pay the costs of the petition.

Action in disputed claims. As to all disputed claims, the election agent should await the action of the persons making the disputed claims.

If the claimant has made a slip by sending in his claim too late, or sending it to the candidate personally, he should apply to the High Court, by a notice of motion served on the candidate, for an order giving leave for the payment of the claim (s. 29, sub-s. 9). The application should be supported by an affidavit of the facts. Leave may then be given to make payment. As the claimant's slip occasions the application, it seems reasonable that he should pay the candidate's costs of appearing upon it. The candidate or the election agent may himself make the application if he think fit to do so. When the order has been made, the sum specified in the order of leave may be paid *either* by the candidate or his election agent, and when paid in pursuance of the order of leave is to be deemed to have been paid within the time limited by the Act. PARLIAMENTARY Order of leave to pay irregular claim.

Any claimant whose claim is disputed, or left unpaid, may, if he thinks fit, bring an action against the candidate, or the election agent, if the latter has made himself personally liable (s. 29, sub-s. 8). If the candidate is the defendant, the action may be brought in any Court having jurisdiction, which will generally be the High Court or where the amount claimed does not exceed £50, the County Court holden in the district. If the election agent is the defendant, he may be sued in any Court having jurisdiction in the county or borough in which his appointed office is (s. 26, sub-s. 2), or in the High Court. Action for a disputed claim.

When the action is brought it will proceed like any other action. It will be no defence to it that if the candidate were to allow or pay the claim he would thereby exceed the maximum amount of expenditure allowed him by the Act of 1883 (s. 19), unless when the contract was made the plaintiff was aware that it contravened the Act. If, therefore, a judgment or order goes against the defendant, ordering him to pay a sum of money to the plaintiff, although any sum paid in pursuance of the judgment or order is to be deemed (s. 29, sub-s. 8) to be paid within the time limited by the Act of 1883 (28 days after the declaration of the return), and to be an exception from the provisions of the Act requiring all claims to be paid by the election agent, yet

154 THE LAW RELATING TO

PARLIAMENTARY any excess thereby caused over the maximum expenditure allowed is nevertheless an illegal practice. If the candidate or the election agent should before judgment discover that the plaintiff's claim was erroneously disputed, leave to pay the amount may be obtained on a motion in the High Court under s. 29, sub-s. 9.

If amount only disputed may be referred to taxation.

On the other hand, if in the action the plaintiff's right of action is not disputed, but only the amount of his claim, the question is to be referred to taxation, unless the Court on a summons taken out by the plaintiff or on the plaintiff's motion, otherwise directs. S. 30 of the Act of 1883 directs: "If any action is brought in any competent Court to recover a disputed claim against any candidate at an election, or his election agent, in respect of any expenses incurred on account or in respect of the conduct or management of such election, and the defendant admits his liability, but disputes the amount of the claim, the said amount shall, unless the Court, on the application of the plaintiff in the action, otherwise directs, be forthwith referred for taxation to the master, official referee, registrar or other proper officer of the Court, and the amount found due on such taxation shall be the amount to be recovered in such action in respect of such claim."

SECTION IV.—THE RETURN AND DECLARATION OF PARLIAMENTARY ELECTION EXPENSES.

The return of expenses.

The duties of the election agent do not end with the examination and payment of the claims sent in. Within seven days after the last day allowed for payment of the claims— that is to say, within 35 days after the declaration of the result of the election—he *must* transmit to the returning officer a return of his candidate's election expenses.

The return and declaration must be made and transmitted even though the candidate should have incurred no election expenses at all. (*Ex p. Robson*, 18 Q.B.D., 336.)

The return must contain (s. 33, sub-s. 1)— *Parliamentary*

(*a*) A statement of all payments made by the election agent, together with all the bills and receipts (which bills and receipts are included in the expression " return respecting election expenses "). *Contents of the return.*
(*b*) A statement of the amount of personal expenses, if any, paid by the candidate.
(*c*) A statement of the sums paid to the returning officer for his charges, or, if the amount is in dispute, of the sum claimed and the amount disputed.
(*d*) A statement of all other disputed claims of which the election agent is aware.
(*e*) A statement of all the unpaid claims, if any, of which the election agent is aware, in respect of which application has been or is about to be made to the High Court.
(*f*) A statement of all money, securities, and equivalent of money received by the election agent from the candidate or any other person for the purpose of expenses incurred or to be incurred on account of or in respect of the conduct or management of the election, with a statement of the name of every person from whom the same may have been received.

The words of the section do not give a complete idea of the particularity and exactness required in the return. These will be appreciated by a perusal of the form of return contained in the second schedule to the Act given in the Appendix. In each case the name, address and business (the *Norwich Case*, 4 O'M. & H., 91, the *Buckrose Case*, 4 O'M. & H., 117) of the person paid, and the nature of the goods, work, labour or services in respect of which he is paid, must be set out, and any room hired must be described so as to identify it. (The *Buckrose Case*, 4 O'M. & H. 118.) *Particulars required.*

At the same time, the election agent *must* send to the returning officer, accompanying the return, a declaration to *Declaration verifying return.*

PARLIAMENTARY be made by him *before a justice of the peace*, verifying the return. The declaration *must* be in the form set out in the second schedule to the Act. But if the candidate has had no election agent, and has been his own election agent, the declaration provided in the schedule for an election agent is not to be used. But, instead of it, the candidate *must* make and transmit the declaration by the candidate respecting election expenses, as specified in the second schedule to the Act. (S. 33, sub-s. 3) In any case the candidate, whether he has had an election agent or not, *must*, at the time when the return of election expenses is transmitted to the returning officer, *or within seven days afterwards*, transmit

Declaration by candidate. to the returning officer a declaration, made *before a justice of the peace*, respecting election expenses, and of general purity (s. 33, sub-s. 4). For the form see Schedule II. in the Appendix.

Where candidate abroad. It may happen that the candidate is out of the United Kingdom when the election agent sends in his return and declaration. In such a case, the time for the candidate to make his declaration will be extended until the expiry of 14 days after he returns to the United Kingdom, within which time it *must* be made. If the candidate were cruising in a yacht and touched at a port in the United Kingdom, that would probably be held to be a " return " to the United Kingdom within the meaning of the section (s. 33, sub-s. 8). The candidate's absence confers no right on the election agent to delay the transmission of his return and declaration for an hour, and when the candidate on his return has made the required declaration, the latter *must* be *forthwith* transmitted to the returning officer. (*Ibid.*)

If the candidate has been declared a candidate or nominated in his absence, and has taken no part in the election, he must send to the returning officer a special form of declaration as to expenses, in effect declaring that he has incurred no expenses, nor paid any money, with stated exceptions, and that he will not pay any expenses afterwards. (For the form see Schedule II., Part II. to the Act of 1883).

By s. 33, sub-s. 9, it is provided that when after the date at which the return respecting election expenses is transmitted, leave is given by the High Court for any claims to be sent in or paid (as to which see s. 29, sub-s. 9) *the candidate or his election agent shall, within seven days* after the payment thereof, transmit to the returning officer, a return of the sums paid in pursuance of such leave, *accompanied* by a copy of the order of the Court giving the leave, and in default he shall be deemed to have failed to comply with the requirements of the section without authorised excuse, *i.e.*, he will thereby become guilty of an illegal practice, avoiding the election. We think that if the returning officer has ceased to be such since the election, and before a return or declaration is sent in, the proper person to whom to send the return or declaration will be the late returning officer, and not his successor. The latter would seem to be a stranger to the election. The safest course would be to transmit the return and declaration to both, and if the late returning officer has died, then to transmit them to his successor. If a *bonâ fide* mistake were made in this respect relief might be obtained under s. 23 of the Act of 1883.

PARLIAMENTARY Return concerning irregular claims paid.

The penalties for any omission or failure to comply with the requirements of the law regarding the making and transmission of a proper return and declarations are very severe. In the first place, the omission or failure is an illegal practice, which, on a petition, avoids the seat, or, if the candidate has been unsuccessful at the election, renders him liable to the ordinary penalties imposed for an illegal practice. In the second place, even though no petition be presented, if the return and declarations be not transmitted within the proper time, the candidate shall not (s. 33, sub-s. 5), after the expiration of that time, sit or vote in the House of Commons for the constituency until (*a*) the returns and declaration have been transmitted, *or* (*b*) until the date of the allowance by the Court of an "authorised excuse" for the failure to transmit them (*cf.* s. 34, sub-s. 4). If the candidate do sit or vote, he is to forfeit the sum of £100 for every day he so sits or votes, to any person who cares to sue

Penalties.

PARLIAMENTARY for it. The action might be maintained by a common
informer. (*Bradlaugh* v. *Clarke*, 8 App. Cas., 354.)

Wilful false declaration. If the candidate *or* the election agent should *knowingly* make the declaration falsely, he would commit a corrupt practice. (S. 33, sub-s. 7.) For such an offence the candidate could have no relief under s. 23, or otherwise, because, for a corrupt practice, other than treating or undue influence, there can be no relief under any section. In addition, the person, whether candidate or election agent, who actually made the false declarations would be liable, on conviction, to the punishment of wilful and corrupt perjury, which may be *seven years' penal servitude*.

Relief on innocent mistake. The Court has power to relieve a candidate or an election agent from the consequences of an *innocent* mistake, either when the returns and declarations have not been transmitted as required by the Act, or when, being transmitted, they contain some error or misstatement. (S. 34 of the Act of 1883.) The way to obtain the relief, in the Act called an "authorised excuse," and the conditions on which it is granted, are treated of hereafter under the title of "Procedure." S. 34 also indicates the course to be adopted when the candidate and election agent cannot make the requisite
Or default of sub-agent. return and declarations, owing to the default of some sub-agent.

No sub-agent is required to send any return or declaration to the returning officer.

Publication and inspection of returns and declarations. Within ten days after receiving the returns respecting election expenses the returning officer (s. 35) must publish a summary of the returns in two or more newspapers in circulation in the constituency. For two years the returning officer must keep the returns and declarations open to inspection, on payment of the fee of one shilling, by any person; after that time he may destroy them, or, if required by the candidate or his election agent, he shall return them to the candidate.

CHAPTER IX.

ELECTION EXPENSES AT MUNICIPAL ELECTIONS.

THE expenditure at elections to corporate offices in England has been for the first time regulated and limited by the Act of 1884, s. 5. No limitation has been placed upon the expenditure permitted at elections of members of local boards, school boards, improvement commissioners or poor law guardians (s. 27 of the Act of 1884), possibly because the object of the Legislature has lately been to strike at the cost of elections fought on political grounds and that the excepted elections have seldom partaken of that character. But it seems to be the result of ss. 5 and 34 of the Act of 1884, the definition of the word "candidate" contained in s. 77 of the Municipal Corporations Act, 1882 (45 & 46 Vict., c. 50), and the definition of the term "corporate office" contained in s. 7 of the same Act, that no sum may be paid and no expense may be incurred by or on behalf of any candidate for the office of mayor, alderman, elective auditor, or revising assessor in any borough, before, during or after an election, on account of the conduct or management of such election. An election of a town councillor and an election of a county councillor are, among elections to corporate offices (except in the City of London), the only elections at which any expenditure at all is legal, and in the case of an election of a councillor the maximum expenditure now permitted is the sum of £25 if the number of electors in the borough or ward for which the election is held is 500 or less, but if the number exceeds 500, there is also permitted the expenditure of an *additional* sum of three-pence for each elector on the roll above 500. (S. 5 of the Act of 1884). Sub-s. 3 of s. 5 is ill-expressed, but the effect of that sub-section and of the following sub-sections is to apply to

_{MUNICIPAL.}
_{Regulated by Act of 1884.}

_{No expenditure allowed except in elections of councillors.}

160   THE LAW RELATING TO

MUNICIPAL. elections of councillors the same provisions (excepting all references to the parliamentary election agent) as already exist in regard to parliamentary elections in regard to
Joint candidature. (1) the reduction of the maximum expenditure in cases of joint candidature; (2) the definition of a joint candidature; and (3) the conditions on which a candidate who has incurred an excess of expenses through his having ceased to be a joint candidate, or through his having become a joint candidate after having begun to conduct his election as a separate candidate, may be relieved from the consequences of such excess.

Penalty for unauthorised expenditure. Anyone, whether candidate, agent, or other person, who at an election of a councillor knowingly pays or incurs any expenses in excess of the maximum, is guilty of an illegal practice, as is anyone who at any election to any other corporate office knowingly pays any expense on account of the conduct or management of the election (s. 5, sub-s. 2 of the Act of 1884). The word "knowingly" in that sub-section is not to be found in the corresponding section (s. 28) of the Act of 1883.

No election agent in municipal elections. With the view of cutting down the expenses of elections of councillors, the Legislature has made no provision in the Act of 1884 for the appointment or creation of the "election agent" and his "sub-agents," upon whom so large a portion of the work of parliamentary elections will in future devolve. Generally speaking, the candidate at an election of councillors must be his own election agent. He may be assisted by voluntary and, to a limited extent, by paid agents, so long as he keeps within the limits of the maximum expenditure permitted to him, and he is not restricted, like a parliamentary candidate, to certain heads of expenses under which alone he can spend the permitted sum. But the small sum allowed for election expenses to the candidate will nearly always forbid the luxury of a paid agent. It will generally, therefore, be the business of the candidate himself to map out his expenditure when he enters upon the contest.

Payment of expenses of When the contest is over the candidate will have to receive the returns of his expenses from his agents, and the accounts of his creditors, to pay them and to make the return and declaration respecting election expenses required by the new law—duties which, in the case of a parliamentary election, are cast upon the election agent. By s. 21, sub-s. 1, of the Act of 1884, it is provided that every claim against any person in respect of any expenses by or on behalf of a candidate at an election of a councillor on account of or in respect of the conduct or management of such election shall be sent in within 14 days after the day of election, and if not so sent in shall be barred and not paid. This seems to mean that the claims are to be sent in to the person to whom the claimant gave credit, not necessarily to the candidate. Then it is provided that all such expenses are to be paid within 21 days after the day of election, and that payment after the expiration of the 21 days, except by leave of the Court, shall be an illegal practice. But in order to provide for accidental and innocent omissions, the High Court or an Election Court or the County Court for the district in which the election was held may (sub-s. 6 of s. 21), on the application of either the candidate or the creditor, *give leave* for any claim to be sent in or expense paid after the proper time, but a return of any sum so paid is immediately to be sent to the town clerk. Except that in elections of councillors, jurisdiction in this respect is given to the County Court, the effect of this section seems to be similar to that of s. 29, sub-s. 9, of the Act of 1883. By sub-s. 2 of the same section every agent is required to send to his candidate a return in writing "of all expenses incurred by such agent" in respect of the conduct or management of the election, under the penalty of a fine of £50, but somewhat strangely, an agent may do this at any time within 28 days after the election, although the candidate must pay all expenses within 21 days.

In regard to the making of payments after the 21 days, Parliament has provided by s. 21 of the Act of 1884, that if any such payment was made "without the sanction or connivance of the candidate," his election shall not be void, nor shall the payment subject him to any incapacity under the Act.

<small>MUNICIPAL. candidate for town council.</small>

<small>When claims to be sent in.</small>

<small>Leave to pay after proper time.</small>

MUNICIPAL.
Return and declaration of expenses.

Having paid the election expenses, the candidate must, within 28 days after the election, send to the town clerk (s. 21, sub-s. 3, of the Act of 1884) a return of all his expenses, vouched by bills, stating the *particulars* and receipts, except in the case of sums under 20s. In parliamentary elections the exception is of sums under 40s. The candidate must also send to the town clerk, accompanying the return, a declaration respecting the election expenses, made before a justice of the peace, and in the form given in the fourth schedule to the Act of 1884, or to the like effect. The words "and my agents" in the third line of the form make the declaration incomprehensible and should be omitted.

After the expiration of the 28 days, the candidate elected a councillor, must not, until he has made the return and declaration or until the date of the allowance of an authorised

Penalties for sitting in council without complying with Act.

excuse, under s. 21, sub-s. 7, of the Act of 1884, sit or vote in the council, under a penalty of £50 per day, to be recoverable by any person minded to sue for the same (sub-s. 4) ; and it is further provided that failure to make the return and

Wilfully false declaration.

declaration, without an authorised excuse, shall be an illegal practice, avoiding the election, and that any candidate knowingly making the declaration falsely, shall be guilty of a corrupt practice and liable to the same punishment as if he had committed perjury, *i.e.*, seven years' penal servitude.

Allowance of authorised excuse.

By s. 21, sub-s. 7, of the Act of 1883 provision is made for the allowance of an authorised excuse for failure to make the return and declaration correctly, in cases in which the indulgence is allowed, but these provisions are more properly treated in the next chapter, under the title of "Applications for Relief."

Inspection and destruction of return and declaration.

The town clerk is to keep the return and declaration at his office for 12 months, open to inspection by anyone on payment of a fee of one shilling, and he is to furnish copies at the price of 2d. a folio. After the expiration of that time he may destroy the return and declaration, unless the candidate require them to be returned to him (s. 21, sub-s. 11). In cases of parliamentary elections, as already stated, the like documents are to be preserved for two years.

The Act of 1884, and Part IV. of the Municipal Corporations Act, 1882 (45 & 46 Vict., c. 50), apply to municipal elections in the City of London, subject to certain exceptions which may be summarised as follows:—In the City of London municipal elections are elections to the office of mayor, aldermen, common councilmen or sheriffs, and include the election of any officer elected by the mayor, aldermen and liverymen in common hall.

<small>MUNICIPAL.

Election expenses in the City of London.</small>

In the case of an election of aldermen or common councilmen, the maximum election expenditure is the same as in the case of an election of town councillor, *i.e.*, £25 for the first 500 electors, and an additional sum of 3d. for each elector beyond the first 500.

In the case of an election by liverymen in common hall, the maximum election expenditure is £40 if no poll be demanded, and £250 if a poll be demanded.

As to the time and mode of holding such elections see s. 35 of the Act of 1884.

CHAPTER X.

PRACTICE AND PROCEDURE.

SECTION I.—ON APPLICATIONS FOR RELIEF.

SUB-SECTION I.—PARLIAMENTARY ELECTIONS.

Parliamentary MANY candidates will probably discover, during or after the election, that more or less by inadvertence, illegal practices, payments, employments, or hirings, have been done, made or entered into by themselves or their agents. "Inadvertence" means negligence or carelessness when the circumstances show an absence of bad faith. (*E.c. p.* Applications *Lenanton*, 53 J.P. 263, 5 Times L.R. 173.) As soon as the to the Court discovery is made, application should be made to the High against Court (or, if the election court is sitting, to that court), illegal acts. under the proper section of the Act of 1883, to be relieved against the consequences and penalties incurred, as well in How made. regard to the election as to the individuals. The procedure is to apply by motion to a Divisional Court in the Queen's Bench Division, but it may be made upon the appointed day by summons at chambers, or by motion in Court, before a judge on the rota for the trial of election petitions, or in cases in which a master has jurisdiction before a master at chambers. (S. 56 of the Act of 1883.) It should be made Upon what promptly. The application, if under s. 23, must be supevidence. ported by evidence that the act or omission in question arose from inadvertence, or from accidental miscalculation, or from some other reasonable cause of a like nature, and not from any want of good faith. (S. 23, sub-s. (*b*).) The provision in the section as to notice implies that, upon the application, any candidate or elector may be heard. Certainly, if a Parties to be petition has been presented, it would seem highly conheard. venient to adjourn the application generally, or to refer it to the election court, which will hear all the witnesses. Any intending petitioner should oppose the application for relief.

In *Ex p. (Wilks* 16 Q.B.D. 114), where it appeared that a PARLIAMENTARY petition against the applicant's return was pending, the Court ordered the application for relief to stand over until after the trial of the petition. (*Cf. Ex p. Hempson*, 5 Times L.R. 290.) But in *Ex p. Clark* (52 L.T. 260) relief was granted by the Court, although a prosecution against the applicant was pending. In *Ex p. Stevens* (5 Times L.R. 203), where a petition was only threatened, the Court, under special circumstances, granted relief.

If the illegal practice, payment, employment, or hiring amount to bribery, no relief can be given to the candidate or other applicant.

S. 22 of the Act of 1883, protecting innocent candidates, in certain cases, from the consequences of the commission of the offences of treating, and undue influence, and illegal practices by agents, can only be invoked at the trial of an election petition, and not upon any preliminary application for relief.

By s. 33, sub-s. 6, of the Act of 1883, if a candidate, or his election agent, fails to comply with the requirements of s. 33, as to the making and transmitting of the return and declarations concerning the election expenses, he shall be guilty of an illegal practice, and the candidate's election will be avoided; and if the return and declarations are not made and transmitted within the time provided by the statute, the candidate returned may not sit or vote in the House until they have been transmitted. (S. 33, sub-s. 5.) Default concerning the return of expenses and declarations.

As soon as any such failure or delay is discovered, the candidate affected should apply to the High Court to be allowed an "authorised excuse" for the failure to transmit the return and declaration, or for any error or false statements. (S. 34 of the Act of 1883.) The order allowing an "authorised excuse" will prevent the omission or error being an illegal practice, and save the election in that respect, and protect the candidate (whether returned or not) and his agent against penalties. An election court has jurisdiction to make the order; but if a candidate applies to an election court for this relief, he will probably have to pay the costs Applications should be made without delay.

PARLIAMENTARY of the petition in any event. On the other hand, by an immediate application to the High Court, he may stall off a petition; at all events, he may take a powerful weapon out of the hand of any petitioner, and save a great deal in the costs of litigation.

Notice of the application.
The notices of the intended application usually required by the Court are advertisements in the local papers and placards, published in such a way as to ensure a reasonable certainty that all persons interested in the matter will have notice, and written notices to the opposing candidates and the returning officer. (*Ex p. Perry*, 48 J.P. 824; *Ex p. Lenanton*, 53 J.P. 263, 5 Times L.R. 173.) The Attorney-General need not be served with notice.

The application must be supported before the Court or a judge at chambers by evidence (1) that due notice has been given; (2) of the applicant's good faith; and, if the applicant

Evidence in support.
was a candidate (3) that the failure to transmit the return and declarations, or any of them, or any error or false statement in them, has arisen by reason of his illness, or of the absence, death, illness, or misconduct of some agent or agent's clerk or officer, or by reason of inadvertence, or of some reasonable cause of a like nature—*e.g.*, by a slip—and not by reason of any want of good faith on the part of the candidate. The affidavit must show a reasonable cause for the alleged inadvertence. (*Ex p. Perry, supra.*)

If the application for relief is made to an election court, no notice of the application is required. (The *Buckrose Case*, 4 O'M. & H., 89.)

If the applicant be an election agent anxious to be relieved from the consequences of an illegal practice, he must give evidence in support of his application to the effect that his failure or error was caused by his own illness, or the death or illness of some prior election agent of the candidate, or the absence, death, illness, or misconduct of some sub-agent, clerk, or officer of the election agent, or by inadvertence or other reasonable cause, and not from want of good faith on the part of the applicant. (S. 34 of the Act of 1883.)

If the evidence satisfy the Court or the judge, the order

will then be made allowing an authorised excuse for the failure to transmit the return and declaration, or for the error or false statement in question. *[Parliamentary]*

If the return and declaration cannot be made and transmitted, owing to the refusal or failure of the election agent or a sub-agent, the Court, before making an order allowing an authorised excuse, will order the defaulter to attend before the Court, and unless he successfully show cause to the contrary, will, on his attendance, order him to do his duty by making the return and declaration, or by giving the necessary particulars, or may order him to be examined on oath. In default of compliance, the defaulter might be fined £500, and probably imprisoned for contempt of court. (S. 34, sub-s. 2, of the Act of 1883.) *[Procedure where agent in default.]*

In any case, if the candidate proves that the act or omission of the election agent regarding the return or declaration was without the candidate's connivance, and that he took all reasonable means to prevent it, the Court *must* relieve the candidate from the consequences of the election agent's act or omission. (S. 34, sub.-s. 3, of the Act of 1883.) In such cases the candidate may obtain relief without satisfying the stringent conditions which are precedent to the granting of relief against treating and undue influence, and other illegal practices by agents, under s. 22; but the Court, before exercising its discretion in other cases, may require similar evidence to that necessary under s. 22. *[When Court must relieve.]*

Any order made under s. 34 may make the allowance of an authorised excuse conditional upon the making of the return and declaration in a modified form, or within an extended term, or upon other terms being complied with. (Sub-s. 3.)

As to the practice, when relief is sought by a candidate against the consequences of an excess of expenditure caused by the candidate having been a joint candidate, see p. 148, *supra*.

Applications to the High Court, under the jurisdiction conferred by the Act of 1883, may be made (s. 56)— *[To whom applications to be made.]*

"(*a*) In criminal proceedings, to any judge of the Queen's Bench Division;

PARLIAMENTARY

Limits of master's jurisdiction.

"(b) In other matters, (1) to any judge on the rota for the trial of election petitions, and either in Court or at chambers; or (2) to a master, subject to appeal;" except that a master has no jurisdiction at all on applications under s. 23 or s. 34; that is, in regard to applications for (1) orders declaring any act or omission to be an exception from the provisions of the Act with respect to illegal practices, payments, employments or hiring; or (2) orders allowing an "authorised excuse" in regard to the return or declaration of expenses. Yet a master may make orders allowing the withdrawal of election petitions.

The general practice is to move in a Divisional Court.

In the case of municipal elections an appeal lies to the Court of Appeal from the refusal of the Divisional Court to grant relief. (*Ex p. Walker*, 22 Q.B.D. 384; 58 L.J., Q.B., 190; 37 W.R., 293; 53 J.P., 260.) It has not yet been decided whether an appeal lies in the case of Parliamentary elections, but we assume that it does.

The Court has granted relief where the illegal act was due to the applicant's ignorance of the law—(*Ex p. Hutchinson*, 5 Times L.R. 136)—where a meeting had been held at a public-house. But the Courts will be stricter than they have been. It will be very difficult to excuse any one from penalties on the ground of ignorance of the law. (*Ex p. Walker*, supra, per Lord Esher, M.R.) People who seek election to such offices ought to study the provisions of the Acts regulating these elections.

It is an element to be considered in the granting of relief that the act was not one which was likely to influence the election. (Per Wills, J., in 5 Times L.R. 221.) And the Courts will be less inclined to grant relief if the act was one morally reprehensible, as that the placard in respect of which relief was sought was libellous. (Per Wills, J., in *Ex p. Lenanton*, 5 Times L.R. 174.)

Relief was granted in a case where the applicant's error was due to his studying a law book which did not accurately or sufficiently state the law (5 Times L.R. 221); where an address was issued without bearing the printer's name (*Ex p. Ives*, 5 Times L.R., 136); where too many messengers (twelve, instead of two) were employed (*Ex p. Darlington*, J.P., 71; 5 Times L.R., 183), although Stephen, J., said the case was very near the line. The Court has no power to relieve the printer of a bill which ought to bear his name. (*Ex p. Lenanton*, *supra*.)

PARLIAMENTARY

Sub-Section II.—Upon Municipal Elections.

The law relating to applications for relief against the consequences of infractions of the election law in cases of municipal elections is almost the same as that applicable in parliamentary cases, except in so far as the fact that in municipal cases there is no election agent makes a difference.

MUNICIPAL. Similar to practice relating to parliamentary elections.

The provisions of the Act of 1884, s. 5, for the allowance by the High Court, or an election court, of relief to a candidate at an election of councillor, or, in the City of London, of an alderman, common councilman, or officer elected by the livery in common hall, in case there has been an excess of expenditure over the amount allowed by law, owing to the candidate having been in part a joint candidate, have already been adverted to.

S. 19 of the Act of 1884 (which is in nearly the same terms as s. 22 of the Act of 1883, relating to parliamentary elections), makes provision for a report, *by the election court*, exonerating the candidate in certain cases in which his agents have, without his consent, been, guilty of (*a*) treating, (*b*) undue influence, and (*c*) illegal practices, but as relief under this section can only be obtained upon the trial of the petition, it will be more properly referred to when the proceedings upon the trial are discussed.

Report by election court exonerating candidate.

Apart from these sections, there are two sections of the Act of 1884 under which relief can be given to a candidate. S. 21, sub-s. 7 (which, *mutatis mutandis*, is nearly in the same words as s. 34 of the Act of 1883), is the narrower of the two in its scope and application, for it relates only to the

Failure to make return or declaration of expenses.

MUNICIPAL. obtaining of relief against the failure of the candidate to make his return or declaration of expenses, or against any error or false statement in the return or declaration. It only applies, therefore (s. 37 of the Act of 1884), to candidates for the office of councillor (whether town councillor or county councillor), or, in the City of London, for the office of alderman or common councilman, or any office to which election is made by the liverymen in common hall. Such a candidate may at any time, although, of course, the courts would discourage anything in the nature of delay (*re Pembroke*, 5 Times L.R., 272), apply to the High Court (*i.e.*, by motion or summons) or to the election court, at the trial of the petition, for an order allowing an "authorised excuse" for his failure to make the return and declaration of election expenses in the proper manner and within the proper time, or for an error or false statement in
Evidence on application for relief. the return or declaration. The application must be supported by evidence, oral or by affidavit, showing that the failure or mis-statement for which an authorised excuse is sought, arose by reason of his illness or absence, or of the absence, death, illness, or misconduct of any agent, clerk, or officer, *or* by reason of inadvertence, *or* of any reasonable cause of a like nature, *and* showing that it did not arise by reason of any want of good faith on the part of the applicant, *and* showing what notice of the application has been given in the constituency. The grounds of the application should be stated in the notice of motion or summons. (S. 21, sub-s. 7.) Thereupon the Court may make the order sought, either unconditionally or upon compliance with such terms as the Court may think calculated to carry the objects of the Act of
Operation of order allowing excuse. 1884 into effect. When made, the order will relieve the applicant from any liability or consequences under the Act in respect of the matters excused by the order. But if the order is conditional on certain terms being complied with, there will be no "allowance of the excuse" until those terms have been fully complied with, and the date of full compliance will be reckoned the date of the allowance of the excuse.

S. 20 of the Act of 1884 is of wider application both with regard to the applicants and the subject matter of the application. Under it relief may be granted to any candidate for the office of mayor, alderman, councillor, elective auditor, or revising assessor in a borough or ward, or member of a local board, member of improvement commissioners, poor law guardian, or member of a school board, or, in the City of London, mayor, alderman, common councilman, or sheriff or for any office to which election is made by the mayor, aldermen and liverymen in common hall. (See ss. 35 and 36 of the Act of 1884.) Any such candidate who finds that he has or any of his agents have done or omitted anything which would be an illegal practice, or an illegal payment, employment or hiring may apply to the High Court, by motion or summons, or to the election court at the trial of the petition for " an order allowing such act or omission to be an exception from the provisions of the Act (1884), which would otherwise make the same an illegal practice, payment, employment, or hiring." The application should be made as soon as the act or omission in question is discovered. The application must be supported by evidence (*a*) that the act or omission in question arose from inadvertence or from accidental miscalculation or from some other reasonable cause of a like nature, and in any case did not arise from any want of good faith, and (*b*) that such notice of the application has been given in the borough as to the Court seems fit. The notices required have already been mentioned. (See p. 166, *supra*.) Otherwise the practice will be similar to that upon application for relief under the corresponding section (23) of the Act of 1883, as to which see the last sub-section. Upon application the Court may make the order relieving the candidate, agent, or other person, or all of them, from the consequences of the act or omission in question. If the application fail, the candidate may still possibly escape at the trial under the provisions of s. 19 of the Act of 1884, upon compliance with certain stringent conditions.

MUNICIPAL. Relief against illegal practices, hirings, &c.

How obtained

Evidence in support.

Section II.—On Election Petitions.

Sub-Section I.—Parliamentary Elections.

Election petitions. The practice upon Parliamentary election petitions is now regulated by the Parliamentary Elections Act, 1868, and the rules thereunder of Michaelmas term, 1868, March, 1869, and January, 1875, and the Act of 1883, all of which are contained in the Appendix hereto.

To what Courts presented. An election petition, which lies in England to the Queen's Bench Division of the High Court of Justice, in Scotland to the Court of Session, and in Ireland to the Court of Common Pleas, may be presented by any one or more of the following persons:—

Who may petition.
(1.) Some person who voted, *or* who had a right to vote at the election to which the petition relates; *or*
(2.) Some person claiming to have had a right to be returned or elected at such election; *or*
(3.) Some person alleging himself to have been a candidate at such election, *i.e.*, one who has been nominated as, or has declared himself a candidate at such election.

Several persons should join. It is safer to join several petitioners, lest there should turn out to be some objection to one petitioner. The question has been raised, but not decided, whether a person who has been guilty of bribery at the election can himself petition. (*Youghal*, 1 O'M. & H. 291.)

The respondent or respondents will be the person or persons whose return is impeached, and the returning officer if he is charged with misconduct; but a person who claims to have been elected and acts as such may also be made a respondent. (*Yates* v. *Leach*, L.R., 9 C.P., 605; 43 L.J., C.P., 337; 30 L.T., 790.)

How petition abated. An election petition abates by the death of the petitioner or of the survivor of several petitioners, but not by the death of the respondent. Upon the respondent's death

another person may be substituted as respondent. (*Morton* Parliamentary
v. *Mitchel*, 9 Ir. R. C.P., 173 ; 3 O'M. & H., 20.)

A petition may be presented, although the candidate returned die after the return and before presentation of the petition. (*Ibid.*)

A dissolution of Parliament brings a petition to an end. (*Carter* v. *Mills*, 9 L.R., C.P., 117; 43 L.J., C.P., 111; 22 W.R., 318.) But the successful party was declared entitled to his costs where the dissolution took place after the decision of the petition, but before the judge's certificate reached the speaker. (*Marshall* v. *James*, 9 L.R., C.P., 702 ; 43 L.J., C.P., 281 ; 30 L.T., 559, 22 W.R., 738.)

The petition must be signed by all the petitioners.

If the petition question the return on the ground of corrupt practices, or on any other ground than an allegation of "illegal practices" under the Act of 1883, it must be presented within 21 days after the return has been made to the Clerk of the Crown, "unless it question the return or election upon an allegation of corrupt practices, and specifically alleges a payment of money or other reward to have been made by any member or on his account, or with his privity, since the date of such return, in pursuance or in furtherance of such corrupt practices, in which case the petition may be presented at any time within 28 days after the date of such payment." (Parliamentary Elections Act, 1868, s. 6, sub-s. 2. As to subsequent illegal practices, see s. 40 of the Act of 1883.) The 21 days begin to run when the return has come to the hands of the Clerk of the Crown so that he can act on it. Where, therefore, it was left at his office with a housekeeper, on the evening of February 4, and was received by the Clerk of the Crown from the housekeeper on the morning of the 5th, the time began to run from the 5th. (*Hindle* v. *Waring*, L.R., 9 C.P., 435 ; 43 L.J., C.P., 209 ; 30 L.T., 329 ; 22 W.R., 735.)

Within what time to be presented.

When the time begins to run.

Sundays do not count in any of the periods allowed for filing Parliamentary petitions. (*Pease* v. *Norwood*, L.R., 4 C.P., 235 ; 38 L.J., C.P., 161. S. 40, sub-s. 5, of the Act of 1883.)

PARLIAMENTARY — The provision that a petition may be presented within 28
When the days of a corrupt payment made *after* the return, seems to
corrupt act apply only where the corrupt payment is made by the mem-
is after the
election. ber, or with his privity. (*Salford*, 20 L.T., 120 ; 1 O'M & H.,
133.) Whether on such a petition the petitioner would be
confined to evidence of such corrupt payments made after the
return, or would be allowed to charge and prove corrupt
practices at or before the return, is doubtful. (*Galway*,
1 O'M. & H., 303 ; *Kidderminster*, 2 O'M & H., 170.)

These rules as to the limit of time for the presentation of
a petition for corrupt practices, irregularities at the poll, mis-
counting or improper return, are untouched by the Act of
1883. By s. 40 of that Act it is declared that that section
shall apply where the illegal practice amounts to a corrupt
practice. But as sub-s. 2 shows that the 21 days' rule is
preserved in regard to petitions under the Act of 1868, it
would seem that the limit fixed by s. 40 applies not in cases
of corrupt practices generally, but applies when the illegal
practice charged—as, for instance, paying for the exhibition
of election addresses—turns out to have been done with
the intent to corrupt the payee or some elector.

Time for If this view is correct, a petition which might have been
presenting
petition for presented had the Act of 1883 not been passed, must still be
an offence
against the presented within the 21 days. But if a petition is presented
Act of 1883. for an "illegal practice" done under the new Act, it will be
in time if presented before the expiration of 14 days after the
day on which the returning officer receives the return and
declarations respecting election expenses by the member to
whose election the petition relates.

What such a If the 21 days from the return be allowed to slip by, a
petition may
charge. petition subsequently and duly presented, complaining of an
"illegal practice," may not charge any of the common
corrupt practices chargeable under the Act of 1868. A
petition should generally therefore be presented within 21
days after the return, and if any illegal practice be discovered
within the 14 days after the returning officer receives the
returns and declarations, the High Court may within these
14 days amend the petition. (S. 40.) The application for

leave to amend should be by motion or by summons at chambers to a judge on the rota (s. 56) or a master, upon notice to the other side and an affidavit speaking generally to the facts. Just as in regard to corrupt practices, so in regard to illegal practices, if (s. 40) the election petition specifically alleges a payment of money or some other act to have been made or done since the day when the returning officer received the returns and declarations, by the member or *any agent* of the member, or with the privity of the member or his election agent in pursuance or in furtherance of the illegal practice alleged in the petition, the petition may be presented at any time within 28 days after such payment or other act. PARLIAMENTARY
Time for petition in respect of acts done after the return of expenses.

The time for presenting a petition for illegal practices counts, when the returns and declarations are received on different days, from the last of these days, or where there is "an authorised excuse" or excuses for failing to send in the returns and declarations, from the date of the "allowance of the excuse" or the date of the allowance of the last excuse (s. 40, sub-s. 4.) By s. 34, sub-s. 4, of the Act of 1883, the date of the allowance of the excuse is the date of the order allowing it, or if conditions are to be complied with the date at which they are fully complied with; and by sub-s. 5, for the purposes of s. 40, time is to be reckoned just as it is reckoned for the purposes of the Parliamentary Elections Act, 1868, that is to say, the first day does not count, nor any Sunday, but the last day does count. How the time is reckoned under Act of 1883.

If circumstances likely to invalidate an election transpire, and it is decided to present a petition, get the petition settled by counsel, fair copied, and signed by all the petitioners. Draw the recognizance (Gen. Rules, Parl., 1868, R. 19, contains the form, *post*, Appendix), *and get it acknowledged by all the sureties. Within the 21 days (or 14 or 28 days, as the case may be) leave the original petition and a fair copy thereof, and the recognizance, and an affidavit by each of the sureties that he is possessed of property above what will satisfy his debts of the clear value of the sum for which he is bound, at the office of the master (the election petition office in the Royal Courts of* Practice on filing petition,

PARLIAMENTARY *Justice), and take the receipt of himself or his clerk for the petition; at the same time leave a notice in writing of the name and address (within three miles of the General Post Office) of the petitioner's agent.*

Filing petition during holidays.
Note that if the last day for filing a petition (or anything else required to be filed in a given time) fall on a holiday, the petition must be put into the letter box at the Master's office *on that day* (or earlier), and an affidavit, stating when it was so delivered, must be filed *on* the first day after the expiration of the holidays. (Rule 4, 1875.)

The recognizance must be acknowledged before a judge at chambers or the Master in town, or a justice of the peace in the country. A London magistrate in town will not do. (*Shrewsbury*, 19 L.T. 499).

Service of petition.
Within five days after presentation of the petition, serve a copy of it personally on the respondent or on his town agent if he has appointed one. If service cannot be effected, then within such five days apply to the judge at chambers for an order for substituted service. As to the necessary affidavit, see *General Rules (Parliament)*, 1868, R. 14. *A notice of the nature of the proposed security is to be served in like manner.*

Immediately after service of the petition and notice of the nature of the security given, *file with the Master an affidavit of the time and manner thereof* (Rule 2, 1875).

The respondent does not enter an appearance, but before service of a petition or at any time within a week after service, he or his agent must leave at the Master's office a similar notice in writing of the name and address of his town agent.

Demurrable petition.
If the petition is what may be called demurrable, the respondent should move the Court, or apply by summons at chambers, that it may be taken off the file or all proceedings under it stayed.

Security for costs.
Although the petition be against two or more respondents *one* surety for £1,000 will suffice (*Hereford*, 49 L.J., Q.B., 686). Under no circumstances can security for more than £1,000 be required. (*Pease v. Norwood*, L.R., 4 C.P. 235, 38 L.T., C.P. 161, 19 L.T., 648; *Thomas v. Wylie*, 19 L.T., 498.)

If the respondent has any objection to the recognizance, *Parliamentary Objections to the recognizance.* notice in writing of the objection, stating the grounds of it, must within five days after service of the petition be served on the petitioner's agent and left at the Master's office. At the same time, take out a Master's summons to declare the security insufficient, and support the summons by affidavits or witnesses. (*General Rules of* 1868, 21 & 22). Give the petitioner's agent notice to produce the sureties for cross-examination.

If the Master's decision is adverse, within five days appeal to the judge at chambers by summons, and support the appeal in the same way. (*General Rules of* 1868, *rule* 23.) An appeal will lie from the judge to the Court. (*Kingston-upon-Hull*, 19 L.T., 648; 38 L.J., C.P. 161.)

If the security be declared insufficient, the order will declare the amount of the insufficiency. Within five days from the date of the order, not including the day of the date, the petitioner's agent must pay that amount into the Bank of England, to the account of "The Parliamentary Elections Act, 1868, Security Fund," otherwise the petition will drop. *If successful, payment into Court to be made.*

If this is duly done the petition will then be at issue.

The Master will give all parties 15 days' notice of trial.

It is provided by General Rules (Parliament), 1868, R. 60, that no proceeding under the Act shall be defeated by any formal objection, but it would be very unwise for any party to rely upon this provision. However, where the petition complained of the conduct of the returning officer, but no notice of the petition was given to him, nor did the petitioner name any town agent at all, the Court refused to strike the petition off the file. (*Shrewsbury*, 19 L.T., 499.) *Formal objections.*

In the course of the proceedings new facts may come to the knowledge of the petitioner, making it desirable to amend the petition. The Court, or a judge at chambers, may allow the amendment, where it relates to a matter discovered upon the inspection of the ballot papers, or to a corrupt payment by the respondent or with his privity after his return. (*Pickering* v. *Startin*, 28 L.T., 111.) But it seems that in *Amendment of the petition*

12

178   THE LAW RELATING TO

PARLIAMENTARY other cases, except as provided by s. 40 of the Act of 1883, the Court has no jurisdiction to allow new charges to be made, for that would be in effect to allow a new petition to be presented after the expiration of the proper time. (*Maude* v. *Lowley*, L.R. 9, C.P. 165, 43 L.J., C.P. 105, 30 L.T., 168 ; *Clark* v. *Wallond*, 52 L.J., Q.B. 321, 31 W.R., 551.) The Court has power to allow an amendment alleging an illegal payment, employment, or hiring, as well as an amendment alleging an illegal hiring. (The *Buckrose Case*, 4 O'M. & H., 116.) It is competent to the Court to amend an election petition at any time by striking out allegations therein where it is satisfied that no injurious result, or a beneficial one, will follow, but the Court will not amend by striking out, after the lapse of the time limited by the Act for presenting it, that part of the prayer which claims the seat for the petitioner and the allegations applying to a scrutiny which would be dependent thereon, for that would affect the rights of the constituency. (*Aldridge* v. *Hurst*, 1 C.P.D., 410 ; 45 L.J., C.P. 431 ; 35 L.T., 156 ; 24 W.R., 708.)

In any case in which it is sought to amend, the procedure is by motion before a judge on the rota, or by summons before such a judge or a Master at Chambers, in either case with affidavits in support.

Withdrawal of petition.   If it should become desirable to withdraw the petition, *the petitioner's agent must leave a signed notice of the application for leave to withdraw at the Master's office and serve a copy upon the respondent, the returning officer and the Director of Public Prosecutions.*

How application for withdrawal to be made.   The notice must state the grounds of the application. (General Rules (Parliament) 1868, R. 45.) Not less than a week after the notice has been left with the Master, the Court will hear the application. The application must be supported by the affidavits of all the parties to the petition, and all their solicitors, that the withdrawal has not been brought about by any corrupt bargain (s. 41 of the Act of 1883). The Court may on special grounds dispense with any affidavit. In practice it never does.

CORRUPT PRACTICES AT ELECTIONS. 179

As to what the affidavits must state, see s. 41 of the Act of 1883, sub-ss. 2 and 3. Copies of the affidavits must be delivered to the Director of Public Prosecutions a reasonable time before the application for leave to withdraw is heard, and he will be heard upon the application in opposition, and the Court may receive the evidence of anybody whose evidence the Director of Public Prosecutions may consider material (sub-s. 5). *Parliamentary*
Copy
affidavits to
be left with
Director of
Public
Prosecutions.

For the penalties for any corrupt bargain to withdraw a petition, see sub-s. 4. In addition, if the withdrawal be the result of any arrangement prohibited by the Act, the Court may direct the £1,000 security given by the petitioner to remain as security for any costs that may be incurred by any substituted petitioner, and to the extent of the sum named in the security the original petitioner will be liable to pay the costs of the substituted petitioner (Parliamentary Elections Act, 1868, s. 35). The Court reports to the Speaker whether the withdrawal is the result of any improper arrangement (sub-s. 7 of s. 41 of the Act of 1883). On principle, although not expressly named, an agreement to withdraw one petition in consideration of another petition not being presented, would be an illegal agreement. Penalties
for corrupt
bargains for
withdrawal.

It would seem that the new enactment as to the withdrawal of petitions does not apply to an Election Court. If such an application be made to an Election Court, it may either adjourn in order that the High Court may be moved under s. 41, or, finding no evidence offered, declare the respondent duly elected. (*North Durham*, 3, O'M. & H. 2.)

Where there are more petitioners than one, no application to withdraw a petition can be made except with the consent of all the petitioners (Parliamentary Elections Act, 1868, s. 35.)

The notice of intention to apply for leave to withdraw is of statutory obligation, and essential. Therefore, where at the trial the petitioner informed the Court that he intended to withdraw the petition, it was held there must be an adjournment of the trial in order that the statutory notice of withdrawal might be given, and other persons substituted Notice of
application
essential.

Withdrawal
at the trial.

PARLIAMENTARY for the petitioners if they so desired. (*Hartlepool*, 19 L.T., 821) In the *Brecon Case* (2 O'M. & H. 33), where notice was given three days before the trial, the judge, when the case was called on and no evidence was offered in support of the petition, decided that the withdrawal must be in open Court, and in the *Gloucester Case* (3 O'M & H., 72), no adjournment was required, the petitioner simply saying that he offered no evidence. " There might possibly be cases in which a judge would not allow a petition to be withdrawn, and would, as far as he could, use his power to prevent it. He might, for instance, exercise the power which is given him of recommending the Court not to allow the deposit to be withdrawn without considerable explanation. The task, no doubt, would be an extremely difficult one, and the mode in which a judge is to compel parties to go on with a petition which they have determined to withdraw remains to be discovered." (Per Grove, J., *North Durham*, 3 O'M. & H., 3, 4.)

If the respondent cannot defend his return he should give notice that he does not intend to oppose the petition, by leaving notice thereof in writing at the Master's office six clear days before the day appointed for trial. The notice must be signed by the respondent (R. 52).

The practice upon the withdrawal of a part of the petition (*e.g.*, a claim to the seat) is similar to that upon the withdrawal of a whole petition. (*Aldridge* v. *Hurst*, L.R., 1 C.P., D. 410, 45 L.J., C.P., 431, 35 L.T., 156, 24 W.R., 708.)

A copy of every order and of all particulars must be filled with the Master (Rule 1, 1875).

Stating a special case.
If the petition raises a question of law, and the facts are not in dispute, the Court, upon motion, or a judge at chambers, upon summons (Rule 37, 1875), will order a special case to be stated for the opinion of the Court, whose decision shall be final Or, if the questions of law can be conveniently severed from the questions of fact, the questions of law may be decided upon a special case, and the questions of fact left for trial in the usual way. (Parliamentary

Elections Act, 1868, s. 11, sub-s. 16; *Hereford*, 19 L.T., Parliamentary 702; *Salisbury*, 19 L.T., 528).

In a municipal case (*Mallam* v. *Bear*, 51 J.P., 231) the petitioner having claimed the seat, the parties agreed to refer their dispute to arbitration. The arbitrator made his award in favour of the respondent, and on application the Court allowed the petitioner to withdraw the petition.

If the petition does not come to an end in any of these ways, either party may find it desirable to procure inspection of the ballot papers and counterfoils. But in proceedings under an election petition, interrogatories cannot be administered (*Wells* v. *Wren*, 5 C.P.D., 546; 49 L.J., Q.B., 681), nor can any order be made for inspection or discovery of documents (*Moore* v. *Kennard*, 10 Q.B.D., 290; 48 L.T., 236; 31 W.R., 610). {Discovery and interrogatories}

Evidence is not to be stated in the petition, but the Court will order the petitioner to give particulars (Rule 6, 1868). These should be applied for by a judge's summons at chambers, that the petitioner may be ordered to deliver to the respondent seven clear days before the day appointed for trial, particulars in writing of the names, addresses and numbers on the register of the persons alleged to have bribed or to have been bribed, or to have treated or to have been treated, or to have intimidated or to have been intimidated, or to have been guilty of undue influence, or to have incited any and what other person to personate any and what elector, or to have personated any and what elector, or to have practised, done, made or had any illegal practice, payment, employment or hiring, stating in each case by whom and where and when and with what consideration, thing, threat, promise or incitement, or by what other act, each person alleged to have been bribed, treated, intimidated, unduly influenced or incited to personate, was so bribed, treated, intimidated or incited, and particulars with dates and items of such illegal practices, payments, employments and hirings and the names, addresses, and numbers on the register of the persons in, to, upon, or with whom such illegal practices, {Delivery of particulars. Summons for delivery of particulars.}

PARLIAMENTARY payments, employments and hirings were respectively practised, done, made or had and that the petitioner may be precluded at the trial from giving in evidence any act, omission, matter or thing not comprised in such particulars so to be delivered. The words "so far as known" ought not to be inserted in the order for particulars. (*Lenham* v. *Barber*, *infra*.)

Time for delivery of particulars. It is now the practice, in the absence of exceptional circumstances, to order particulars to be delivered seven clear days before the hearing. (*Lenham* v. *Barber*, 10 Q.B. Div., 293, 52 L.J., Q B., 312, 31 W.R., 428; *Clark* v. *Wallond*, 52 L.J., Q.B., 321.) But as little as three days before trial has been ordered for the delivery of the particulars (*Beal* v. *Smith*, L.R., 4, C.P., 145; 38 L.J., C.P. 145); on the other hand in the *Bewdley Case* (1880), as much as fourteen days was allowed. Sundays, Christmas Day and Good Friday do not count in the "so many days before the day appointed for trial." (Rule 3 of 1875.)

Settling the particulars. In framing the particulars, two dangers are to be avoided. If they are made too voluminous and cases are introduced which fail of proof, the petitioner, although successful in the result, may have to bear the cost occasioned by the unsuccessful charges, or even the whole of his costs. (*Berwick*, 3 O'M. & H., 178, 44 L.T., 289; *Hereford*, 1 O'M. & H., 194, 21 L.T., 117; *Norwich*, 2 O'M. & H., 38.) On the other hand, the petitioner should mention in the particulars every case on which he means to rely at the trial, otherwise he may be precluded from giving evidence of any case omitted. Where it is sought at the trial to give evidence of cases not in the particulars, the judges usually require an **Amendment of particulars.** affidavit, before allowing the amendment, that the facts have come to the knowledge of the petitioner's agent since the delivery of the particulars, and that all due and reasonable inquiry was made before the delivery of the particulars (*Longford*, 2 O'M. & H., 7.) But the object of particulars is to prevent an unfair surprise upon the respondent, and therefore the judge's order precluding the petitioner from going into cases not in the particulars, may be disregarded at the trial, if the Court be satisfied that no Parliamentary injustice is thereby done to the respondent. (*Wigan*, 4 O'M. & H., 1, per Bowen, J.) We think that if the petitioner's agent discovers a corrupt or illegal practice not included in the particulars, he should immediately after the discovery notify to the respondent's agent that application will be made at the trial for leave to go into the matter so discovered, giving particulars of the charge intended to be made.

The Court is loth to allow an amendment where the respondent having had no previous notice has not had an opportunity before the trial of inquiring into the charge. (Per O'Brien, J., in the *West Belfast Case*, 4 O'M. & H., 107.) The leave to amend may be more readily granted if the new charge is one of general corruption and not one of corruption by an agent (*ibid*).

Where the particulars were not delivered within the time limited by the order, Martin, B., would neither permit the cases not mentioned in them to be gone into, nor an amendment. (*Yorkshire, S. W. Riding*, 1 O'M. & H., 213.) But it is doubtful if this would be followed. It would seem to be more correct to adjourn the trial at the petitioner's expense if the omission has really damnified the respondent. (*Bristol*, 2 O'M. & H., 27, per Bramwell, B.)

The tendency of the later cases is to let in evidence of cases not in the particulars, unless the omission be wilful, or the consequence of admitting the evidence be a surprise to the respondent. (*Evesham*, 3 O'M. & H., 95; *Tewkesbury*, 3 O'M. & H., 97; *Wigan*, 4 O'M. & H., 1; *West Belfast*, 4 O'M. & H., 106.)

It is submitted that where the seat is claimed and the Particulars respondent delivers a list of objections to the petitioner's of objections. election (under Rule 8 of 1868), the petitioner is entitled to similar particulars of such objections. Rule 6 & 7 are to be read together. (*Salford*, 19 L.T., 502.)

The Court has jurisdiction to order the Post Office autho- Production rities to produce specified telegrams. (*Bolton*, 31 L.T., 194; of telegrams. 1 O'M. and H., 139; *Harwich*, 3 O'M. & H., 61, 44 L.T., 188; *Coventry*, 19 L.T., 742.)

Parliamentary Notice to admit and produce.

Before the trial, the usual notices to produce and admit should be given. The notice to produce should specify the documents intended to be referred to. It may be insufficient to refer to them in general terms. (*Westminster*, 1 O'M. & H., 89, 20 L.T., 238.)

Commission to examine witness.

An order may be made for a commission to examine a witness alleged to be ill and unable to attend the trial on an affidavit that he is ill and unable to attend and that he is a material witness. (*Staleybridge*, 19 L.T., 702.)

Procuring and compelling attendance of witnesses.

The witnesses should be subpœnaed in the usual way. Sometimes they require to be watched. Everyone who is familiar with election petitions is aware that important witnesses will mysteriously disappear shortly before the trial and fail to re-appear until after the trial. In such a case, Lush, J., declared he would adjourn, if need be, for six months. (*Stroud*, 2 O'M. & H., 107.)

If a witness is in another part of the kingdom, he may be subpœnaed on the special order of the Court or a judge (17 & 18 Vict. c. 34, s. 1).

On proof of fruitless efforts to serve a subpœna the Court will issue an order for the attendance of a witness at the trial. (*Waterford*, 2 O'M. & H., 3.) To disobey such an order would be a contempt of Court (see Rules 41 and 42 of 1868).

But where it was stated that some persons had evaded service, Lush, J., said the Court had no power to issue a warrant for their apprehension. (*Chester*, 44 L.T., 286.) In the same case, evidence that the clerk of the respondent's solicitor had offered an inducement to one of the petitioners to leave the city, was rejected.

Taking proofs of witnesses.

In conducting election petitions, it has been usual for the solicitors engaged to interview persons able to throw light upon the matter in dispute, to take down their statements, and to obtain the signature of such persons to the statements. The practice is a very useful one, but in all cases evidence should be preserved that the witness was not threatened or unduly influenced when he signed the statement and was not ignorant of what he signed. In the *Wigan Case*

(4 O'M. & H., 1), the Court disapproved of such statements being obtained after it was known that the witnesses were about to be called on the other side or *during the trial*. (See also *Chester*, 44 L.T., 268.)

It would seem to be legal to offer rewards for evidence. (*Mallow*, 2 O'M. & H. 19.)

Parliamentary

Rewards for evidence.

Where the allegations of fact in a parliamentary election petition are not in dispute, but are specifically admitted by the respondent so as to render it unnecessary at the trial to call witnesses from the district in which the election took place, the Court may order the petition to be tried in London on the ground that "special circumstances" exist within the meaning of s. 11, sub-s 11, of the Parliamentary Elections Act, 1868 (31 & 32 Vict., c. 125), which render it desirable that the petition be tried elsewhere than in the county or division where the election took place. (*Arch* v. *Bentinck*, 18 Q.B. Div. 548.)

So far as practicable, the trial of an election petition proceeds *de die in diem*, and the jurisdiction of the judges trying the case is not affected by the expiration of the term of the judges on the rota (s. 43 of the Act of 1883).

Trial de die in diem.

Where the seat is claimed the scrutiny of votes may be taken before the recriminatory case. (*Stepney*, 4 O'M. & H. 35.)

The Act of 1883 has done something to lengthen the trial of election petitions, by directing new inquiries to be made upon the trial. But it is probable that so far as these inquiries may not concern the parties to the petition, they will not go to the expense of attending the Election Court while issues which may be indifferent to them are being considered.

By s. 38 of the Act of 1883 before any person, not being a party to the petition or a candidate for whom the seat is claimed, is reported by an Election Court to have been guilty of any corrupt or illegal practice, he is to be summoned by the Court and heard by himself in his defence, and any evidence he may call, heard. In *R.* v. *Mansel-Jones* (23 Q.B. Div. 29), the Court held that this section excluded the right of a person charged with any corrupt or illegal practice to be heard

New inquiries at the trial.

by his counsel or solicitor. The interest of the petitioner in such an inquiry will generally be remote. As to appeals from the report and special punishments, see s. 38 and Part II. *infra.*

By s. 43, the Director of Public Prosecutions, or his representative, is to attend at the trial of the petition, in order to summon and there examine such witnesses as the Court may direct, and of his own motion to summon witnesses and to examine them with the leave of the Court. But he will not be allowed to cross-examine witnesses called by other parties. (*Stepney*, 4 O'M. & H. 35) He is also to prosecute any person who appears to him to have been guilty of any corrupt or illegal practice, whereupon the Election Court may proceed to try any person so prosecuted, unless a trial before some other Court be ordered in the interests of justice. Except that the Court (s. 34, sub-s. 8) may order the costs of the Director of Public Prosecutions to be paid by any of the parties to the petition or may report any of the parties to the petition to the Speaker of the House of Commons, their interest in the action of the Director will generally be remote. The Court will not as a rule order the costs of the Public Prosecutor to be paid by the petitioner unless the petition is a groundless one (*Kennington*, 4 O'M. & H.), or unless the countercharges against the petitioner are successful (*Stepney*, 4 O'M. & H. 58, *cf. West Belfast*, 4 O'M. & H. 109.)

No inquiry into past elections.

The Act of 1883 makes a complete amnesty in respect of the past. In future, no witness can be asked, or will be bound to answer, on the trial of an election petition or before Election Commissioners, any questions for the purpose of proving the commission of any corrupt practice at or in relation to any election prior to the passing of the Act, (s. 49). But if at an election, after the passing of the Act, A should pay B a sovereign, there can be no doubt that evidence tending to show a bargain made before the passing of the Act, that A should pay a sovereign to B for his vote hereafter, would be admissible as showing what the transaction really was.

Upon nearly every petition based upon allegations of corrupt or illegal practices, the parties should be prepared with evidence at the trial upon the issues raised by s. 22 of the Act of 1883. By that section the Court trying the petition is enabled to uphold the election, although the agents of the respondent may be proved to have been guilty of (*a*) treating, (*b*) undue influence, or (*c*) illegal practices, or all of these offences. The Court has no power to relieve where these offences, or any of them, have been committed by the candidate himself or his election agent, or where the agents, or any of them, are or is proved guilty of bribery or of personation, or of instigating personation. *[Parliamentary Procedure upon the relief sections of the Act of 1883.]*

It is exceedingly likely that in cases in which relief is granted to a respondent under s. 22 of the Act of 1883, he will be ordered, unless it appears that the petition was frivolous and vexatious, or that other special circumstances exist, to pay the petitioner's costs of the petition.

It is important to observe how stringent are the conditions to be complied with by the party seeking relief before he can be assisted. *[Conditions precedent to relief under s. 22.]*

He must satisfy the Court—for the burden is upon him to prove affirmatively—

(1.) That the offences were of a trivial, unimportant, and limited character; *and*

(2.) That they were committed contrary to the orders, *and* without the sanction *or* connivance of the candidate, or the election agent.

(3.) That no corrupt or illegal practice was committed at the election by the candidate *or* his election agent.

(4.) That both the candidate and his election agent took all reasonable means to prevent the commission of corrupt and illegal practices.

(5.) That in all other respects the election was free from *any* corrupt or illegal practice by the candidate *or any* of his agents.

It would seem that the candidate is not required to prove that he and his election agent took any means to prevent

PARLIAMENTARY the commission of the offences of illegal employment, payments, and hirings by other agents of the candidate.

Proof that the election was actually free from illegal employment, payment, and hiring, is not required.

It will be difficult for a respondent to satisfy these stringent conditions, but it would seem that when he does satisfy them, the Court has no discretion—the election is saved.

The petitioner, on his side, should be prepared with evidence to prove that the respondent cannot satisfy the statutory conditions.

Respondent's declaration of personal innocence.
When the respondent, finding the return cannot be supported, has surrendered, and the election is declared void for corrupt practices, it has been usual for him to go into the box and declare on oath his personal innocence of any corrupt practice. In one case the Court allowed the respondent's legal agents to declare their innocence on oath. (*Wigan*, 4 O'M. & H., 1.) But in the *Boston Case*, 44 L.T., the Court held that the rule must be adhered to, that the sitting members only could be called after the seat had been vacated.

Difference of opinion between the judges.
If on the trial of the election petition the two judges trying the petition should differ in opinion as to whether the respondent was duly elected, the respondent will retain his seat (42 & 43 Vict., c. 75). On the same principle, if the judges differ as to the subject of a report to the Speaker, they are to certify the difference, and make no report on the subject in difference (*ibid*).

The judges upon the trial of the petition may reserve any point of law for the consideration and discussion of the High Court (s. 12 of the Parliamentary Elections Act, 1868). The usual manner of doing this is by the judges stating a special case for the opinion of the High Court. (The *Bristol Case*, 2 O'M. & H., 29).

It has been held that the application for a case to be stated should be made before the decision of the Election Court has been given. (*West Belfast*, 4 O'M. & H., 103. *Sed quaere*).

When the trial is concluded, the registrar will ascertain and certify the amount to be paid to any witness whose expenses may be allowed by the Court (Rule 5 of 1875). The registrar's certificate is not conclusive as between the petitioner and the respondent. The registrar only taxes as between the witness and the party who subpœnaed him. (*M'Laren* v. *Home*, 7 Q.B.D., 477; 50 L.J., Q.B., 658.) *Parliamentary Witnesses' expenses to be taxed by Registrar.*

SUB-SECTION II.—UPON MUNICIPAL ELECTIONS.

By the combined effect of ss. 7 & 87 of the Municipal Corporations Act, 1882 (45 & 46 Vict., c. 50), ss. 25, 35 & 36 of the Act of 1884, and s. 7 of the Local Government Act, 1888, an election to any of the following offices on any of the grounds hereinafter mentioned can be questioned only by an election petition, *i.e.*— *Municipal. What elections questioned by petition.*

(1.) The office of mayor, alderman, councillor, elective auditor, or revising assessor in any borough;

(2.) In the city of London, the office of mayor, alderman, common councilman, and sheriff, and any office to which election is made by the mayor, alderman and liverymen in common hall;

(3.) The office of member of a local board, or of member of improvement commissioners, as defined by the Public Health Act, 1875;

(4.) The office of member of a school board;

(5.) The office of poor law guardian elected under the Poor Law Amendment Act, 1834, subject as in section 36, par. (*h*) of the Act of 1884 mentioned.

(6.) The office of county councillor.

The grounds on which the petition may be presented are (s. 87 of the Municipal Corporations Act, 1882):—

(*a.*) That the election was avoided by general bribery treating, undue influence, or personation; *And on what grounds.*

(*b.*) That the election was avoided by a corrupt practice committed by the person elected, or some of his agents;

190 THE LAW RELATING TO

MUNICIPAL.
(c.) That the person whose election is questioned was at the time of the election disqualified;

(d.) That he was not duly elected by a majority of lawful votes;
and (ss. 18 & 8 of the Act of 1884)

(e.) That the election was avoided by the extensive prevalence of illegal practices, illegal employments, hirings, or payments, and

(f.) That the election was avoided by an illegal practice committed by the person elected or some of his agents.

The law relating to the practice and procedure upon municipal petitions is contained in ss. 87 to 104 inclusive of the Municipal Corporations Act, 1882, ss. 2, 3, 8, 13, 25 to 29 inclusive, 32, 33 & 38 of the Act of 1884, and the General Municipal Election Petition Rules of 1883 (April 17), all of which are set out in the Appendix hereto.

Practice on parliamentary petitions followed.
By s. 100 sub-s. 3 of the Municipal Corporations Act, 1882, it is enacted that subject to the provisions of that Act and of the rules made under it (*i.e.*, those of 1883) the principles, practice and rules for the time being observed in the case of parliamentary election petitions, and in particular the principles and rules with regard to agency and evidence and to a scrutiny, and to the declaring any person elected in the room of any other person declared to have been not duly elected, shall be observed, as far as may be, in the case of a municipal election petition. The practice and procedure upon parliamentary election petitions have been already stated, *supra*, pp. 172–189, but there are certain differences which remain to be observed.

By whom petitions may be presented.
One elector cannot present a municipal election petition. It must be signed by at least four persons who voted or had a right to vote at the election, or by a person alleging himself to have been a candidate at the election (s. 88 of the Municipal Corporations Act, 1882). The petition must be presented within 21 days after the day on which the election was held, but a petition on the ground of a payment of money received, made, or promised, or an illegal practice committed, after the election, with the privity of the

person elected, may be presented within 28 days after the date of the payment or promise or act (*ibid.* and s. 25 of the Act of 1884). A petition complaining of *illegal* practices must be presented within 14 days after the day on which the return and declaration respecting election expenses is received from the candidate whose return is questioned.   *Municipal.* *And within what time.*

In the computation of the 21 days within which a parliamentary petition is to be presented, Sundays are excluded, but in computing the number of days within which a municipal election may be presented *Sundays and every other day are to be counted.* But if the last of the days limited for presentation be a Sunday, Christmas Day, Good Friday, or Monday or Tuesday in Easter week, or a day appointed for public fast, humiliation or thanksgiving, the petition may be presented on the next day. (See s. 230 of the Municipal Corporations Act, 1882. *Archer* v. *McGirr*, Pearson, J., at chambers, 2nd January, 1884.)   *How time reckoned.*

An election petition may be presented against some only of the persons returned at a municipal election, although the ground of the petition is one affecting the validity of the petition as a whole; and the court can on the petition declare the persons petitioned against not to have been duly elected. (*Line* v. *Warren*, 14 Q.B.D. 548.)

The security to be given by the petitioner for payment of costs and witnesses' expenses is to be not less than £300; on the application of the respondent the High Court or a judge may order the amount to be increased to £500 (s. 89 of the Municipal Corporations Act, 1882, and General Rules (Municipal) of 1883, *rule* 26).   *Security for costs.*

The petition is heard by a barrister of at least 15 years' standing. He may reserve any question of law for the Court, but otherwise his decision cannot be appealed from, except that any fine inflicted or order of committal made by him may be discharged by the High Court on motion (s. 92 of the Municipal Corporations Act, 1882). But orders made under s. 28 of the Act of 1884, cannot be discharged.   *The trial.*

Should he state a case for the opinion of the High Court, the decision of the High Court is final. No appeal lies to the Court of Appeal (*Unwin* v *Macmullen*, 55 J.P., 582) unless leave to appeal be given by the High Court. (*Line* v. *Warren*, 14 Q.B.D. 548.)

Witnesses' expenses. If the petitioner neglects or refuses for three months after demand to pay any costs or the expenses of any of his witnesses, which he is bound to pay, every recognizance given by way of security for costs and witnesses' expenses is forfeited (s. 98 of the Municipal Corporations Act, 1882.)

General provisions. S. 26 of the Act of 1884 makes the same stringent provisions regarding the withdrawal of municipal petitions as were enacted by s. 41 of the Act of 1883, in regard to the withdrawal of parliamentary petitions, and the provisions of the Act of 1883 (ss. 28 & 29) for the attendance of the director of public prosecutions on the trial of election petitions and for the prosecution by him of offenders, and enabling the Election Court to order payment by a peccant borough or individual of the costs of an election petition in whole or in part, are by ss. 28 & 29 of the Act of 1884, extended to municipal election cases.

General rules. The General Rules of 1883 (Municipal) are, with the necessary verbal alterations, to the same effect as the General Rules relating to parliamentary election petitions, which have been already discussed, *supra* pp. 172–189. The Municipal Rules are set out at length in the Appendix hereto.

By s. 19 of the Act of 1884, the Election Court is enabled to make a report exonerating the candidate in certain cases of corrupt and illegal practices by his agents. The similar section of the Act of 1883 is s. 22. On comparing the two sections it will be noticed that there are certain differences.

Relief at trial against corrupt and illegal practices. The section of the Act of 1884 necessarily omits all reference to "the election agent." Under that section, too, the candidate will not have to prove that the corrupt or illegal practices from which he seeks to be exonerated were committed contrary to his orders; but he must prove that no corrupt or illegal practice was committed with his knowledge or consent, and that all reasonable means for preventing the commission of corrupt and illegal practices were taken by and *on behalf of* the candidate.

SECTION III.—ON A SCRUTINY.—PARLIAMENTARY
AND MUNICIPAL.

A scrutiny takes place when the petition claims the seat for one or more of the defeated candidates as having been duly elected. The seat is not often claimed by a petition because of the difficulty in wiping off any but the most inconsiderable majority upon a scrutiny, the cost of a scrutiny, and the fact that when the seat is claimed by the petition, it becomes permissible for the respondent to give recriminatory evidence against the candidate for whom the petition claims the seat (31 & 32 Vict., c. 53, and the Municipal Corporations Act, 1882, s. 93 sub-s. 10.) The practice and procedure upon a scrutiny in case of a municipal election are, except where otherwise specially provided, the same as upon a scrutiny following a parliamentary election (Municipal Corporations Act, 1882, s. 100, sub-s. 3.) Any person entitled to petition is entitled to claim a scrutiny of the votes given, upon an allegation that a candidate other than the person returned was duly elected. But after such a petition has been presented, the claim of the seat may be withdrawn with the leave of the Court on motion or by a judge at chambers on summons (*Stroud*, 3 O'M. & H., 7). But, ordinarily, the Court will not allow the claim of the seat to be withdrawn (*Aldridge* v. *Hurst*. 1 C.P.D., 410; 45 L.J., C.P. 431; 35 L.T. 156; 24 W.R. 708.) *[margin: PARLIAMENTARY & MUNICIPAL. When a scrutiny is made. Who entitled to claim. Withdrawal of claim]*

If the petitioner, at the trial, having established that the respondent's election was void for corrupt practices, should then abandon the claim of the seat, recriminatory evidence cannot be gone into (*Gravesend*, 44 L.T., 64; 3 O'M. & H. 81.) Indeed, if once it be ascertained that there is no claim laid to the seat, even the account of the election expenses of the unsuccessful candidate sent to the returning officer could not be called for (*Thirsk*, 3 O'M. & H., 113). *[margin: Recriminatory case when excluded.]*

For forms of petitions in cases in which the seat is claimed see the General Rules (Parliamentary), 1868, r. 5; *Stroud* 3 O'M. & H., 7; and *Berwick*, 3 O'M. & H., 178; 44 L.T., 289. *[margin: Forms of petitions for scrutiny]*

PARLIAMENTARY
& MUNICIPAL.
———
Inspection
of ballot
papers, &c.

In cases of scrutiny and whenever questions of the improper rejection or reception of voting papers arise, it is generally desirable, before trial, to obtain inspection of the rejected ballot papers, the counted ballot papers, and sometimes of the sealed packet of counterfoils. A judge at chambers may order inspection of the rejected ballot papers to be had, but only the Court can order inspection of the counted ballot papers and counterfoils. (The Ballot Act, 1872, s. 1. rr. 40 & 41.) The procedure is by summons or motion.

In municipal cases an order of the county court, having jurisdiction in the borough or of any tribunal in which a municipal election is questioned (*e.g.* the High Court), will entitle the applicant to inspection. An appeal lies from the decision of the county court. (The Ballot Act, 1872, s. 1, c. 64.) In municipal cases the ballot papers and election documents are sent to the town clerk.

Any application for inspection must be supported by affidavit. The Court will jealously preserve the secrecy of the ballot In the *Tyrone Case* (21 W.R., 627 ; 7 I.R.,C.L., 190), the Court would not allow either party to see the counterfoils or the backs of the ballot papers, but only their faces. This was followed in *Stowe* v. *Jolliffe*, (L.R. 9, C.P., 447 ; 43 L.J., C.P., 173 ; 30 L.T., 299 ; 22 W.R., 946), but, in neither of these cases was it alleged that votes improperly marked had been received. In the *Berwick Case* (1880), the judge at chambers, by consent of both parties, ordered inspection of the counterfoils and all the ballot papers

Whether, upon a parliamentary petition, the Court can order inspection of the ballot papers used at a municipal election is doubtful. (See *Gloucester*, 2 O'M. & H., 60.

All the other documents forwarded by the returning officer to the clerk of the Crown (or in municipal cases, to the town clerk), including the marked register, are open to public inspection ; Ballot Act, 1872, s. 1, r. 42 (*James* v. *Henderson*, 43 L.J., C.P., 238 ; 30 L.T., 527). It is immaterial that a scrutiny is not prayed (*ibid.*).

Delivery of
scrutiny lists

The practice up to trial in scrutiny cases is similar to that in cases of ordinary petitions, except that the petitioner is bound, in addition to particulars, to deliver scrutiny lists, and the respondent must deliver scrutiny lists and a list of his objections to the election of the candidate for whom the seat is claimed.

Parliamentary & Municipal. and list of objections.

The rules are as follows :—

RULE VII. (1868).—" When a petitioner claims the seat for an unsuccessful candidate, alleging that he had a majority of lawful votes, the party complaining of or defending the election or return, shall, six days before the day appointed for trial, deliver to the master and also to the address, if any, given by the petitioners and respondent, as the case may be, a list of the *votes intended to be objected to and of the heads of objection to each such vote*, and the master shall allow inspection and office copies of such lists to all parties concerned ; and no evidence shall be given against the validity of any vote nor upon any head of objection not specified in the list, except by the leave of the Court or judge upon such terms as to amendment of the list, postponement of the inquiry and payment of costs as may be ordered "

RULE VIII. (1868).—" When the respondent in a petition under the Act, complaining of an undue return and claiming the seat for some person, intends to give evidence to prove that the election of such person was undue, pursuant to the fifty-third section of the Act, such respondent shall six days before the day appointed for trial, deliver to the master and also at the address, if any, given by the petitioner, a list of objections *to the election* upon which he intends to rely, and the master shall allow inspection and office copies of such lists to all parties concerned ; and no evidence shall be given by a respondent of any objection to the election not specified in the list, except by leave of the Court or judge upon such terms as to amendments of the list, postponement of the inquiry and payment of costs as may be ordered."

The rules in municipal cases are almost in the same words. See the Municipal Election Petition Rules of 1883, rr. 7 & 8, set out in the Appendix.

If the respondent's list of objections is vague and general, *Application* the petitioner should apply at chambers for an order for particulars. The Court has probably jurisdiction to make such an order under Gen. Reg. (Parl.), 1868, r. 6, or in municipal cases under the Municipal Rules of 1883, r 6.

The scrutiny lists and list of objections must be delivered six clear days before the trial, exclusive of Sunday, and of the day of trial and of the day of service (*Joyce* v. *O'Donnel*, 22 W.R., 655); and if the lists are not delivered within the time the Court cannot allow evidence to be given against the validity of votes or allow a list to be subsequently delivered (*Nield* v. *Batty*, L.R. 9, C.P., 104; 43 L.J., C.P., 73; 29 L.T., 747; 22 W.R., 407). But if an imperfect list were delivered in proper time the Court could afterwards allow amendments in, or additions to it, to be made (*ibid.* per Denman, J.)

Under "special circumstances" the venue may be changed. In *Arch* v. *Bentinck* (18 Q.B.D. 548), the trial was ordered to be had in London.

At the trial it has been usual for the petitioner to open his general case against the respondent (without going into a scrutiny) with the view of disqualifying the respondent, whether he be in a majority or no. Then the respondent answers the case made against him, and proceeds to open his general case against the unsuccessful candidate, which is then answered. Afterwards the scrutiny will, if necessary, be gone into. The reason for postponing the scrutiny is, that if both parties be disqualified (*e.g.*, for bribery by an agent) a scrutiny becomes useless. If the petitioner be so disqualified, his claim to the seat is gone, but the scrutiny may proceed for the purpose of unseating the other, by placing him in a minority, in which case there would be a new election. (*York, South-West Riding*, 1 O'M. & H., 213; *Southampton* 1 O'M. & H., 222.) If the respondent be so disqualified, he may continue his resistance to the petitioner's efforts upon a scrutiny to place himself in a majority, and if the resistance be successful, there must of course be a new election (*Norwich*, 19 L.T., 619, 1 O'M. & H., 8.)

The practice is not, however, invariable. In one case the

petitioner, having withdrawn his general charges, proceeded *Parliamentary & Municipal.* with the scrutiny, and placed himself in a majority. Then the respondent proceeded with his general recriminatory charges and the scrutiny, and finally placed himself in a majority. (*Berwick*, 3 O'M. & H., 178; 44 L.T., 289.) In another case the recriminatory case was postponed until after the scrutiny. (*Stepney*, 4 O'M. & H., 35.)

When the scrutiny is opened it is for the petitioner to put himself (or the persons whom he alleges to have been duly elected) in a majority. For this purpose he may begin with any class of objections he likes, but it is usual to require him (and the respondent in his turn) to finish all his objections of the class he begins with before proceeding to any objection of another class. Thus, if the petitioner begins with a case of bribery, he finishes all the cases of bribery before opening any case of intimidation.

In the *Oldham Case* (20 L.T., 302; 1 O'M. & H., 151), there were four candidates standing on the poll in the following order, H. P, C and S. The scrutiny proceeded in the first instance as between C and P, on the understanding that when C had been placed in a majority over P, the scrutiny should then be proceeded with as between S and H.

Upon a scrutiny a voter, whose vote is attacked, has no *locus standi* as a party, and is not entitled to be heard by his counsel. (*Malcolm* v. *Parry*, L.R 9, C.P., 614; 43 L.J., C.P., 331; 31 L.T., 331.) *Elector has no locus standi.*

The decision of the returning officer as to any question arising in respect of any ballot paper is final, subject to reversal on petition questioning the return. (The Ballot Act, 1872, s. 2).

A petition may be presented on the sole ground that the returning officer has miscounted the votes, in which case the ballot papers will be re-counted in the presence of the Court. (*Renfrew*, 2 O'M. & H., 213.) A petitioner is not entitled to a re-count as a matter of right, but a re-count will be ordered if the evidence tends to show that the counting of the returning officer cannot be relied upon. (*Stepney*,

4 O'M. & H., 51, in which case Denman, J., himself recounted the votes.)

Parliamentary & Municipal.

Equality of votes. If the returning officer at a parliamentary election finds the votes equal, and *he is a registered elector*, he may, but he is not bound to, give a casting vote. (Ballot Act, 1872, s. 2.) If he gives no casting vote he will make a double return. On the other hand, in the case of a municipal election the returning officer can give a casting vote *whether he is an elector or not*. (Municipal Corporations Act, 1882, s. 58 (5).) He is not bound to give a casting vote, but if he fails to do so the Queen's Bench will, by mandamus, direct him to hold a fresh election (*North Maryport*.)

On a scrutiny register generally conclusive. Upon a scrutiny only those persons whose names are on the register for the time being in force can be admitted as having been entitled to vote, and the register is conclusive of the right of any person upon it to vote, although such person ought to have been struck off by the revising barrister. The Court, upon a scrutiny, will only strike off the votes of persons who ought not to be upon the register if from some inherent, or, for the time, irremovable quality in themselves, they have not the status of parliamentary electors —for instance, peers, women, persons holding certain offices or employments, and persons convicted of crimes which disqualify them from voting. (The Ballot Act, 1872, s. 7 ; *Stowe v. Jolliffe*, No. 2, 43 L.J., C.P., 265 ; L.R. 9, C.P., 734.)

Votes given after notice for a candidate incapable of being elected. As votes perversely given for a candidate who is incapable of being elected after notice of his incapacity, are thrown away, they will be struck off upon a scrutiny, and so the candidate apparently in a minority may be returned. But if a candidate has been guilty of bribery he is not so incapacitated that votes given for him after notice of the bribery will be thrown away. It would be otherwise if notice were given that he had been found guilty of bribery. In order that votes given after notice may be struck off, there must be something wanting in the candidate himself which cannot be supplied, the existence or non-existence of which is not dependent on argument or decision, but which the law insists shall exist in every one who puts himself forward as a candidate. (*Drinkwater* v. *Deakin*, L.R., 9, C.P. 626; 43 Parliamentary & Municipal. L.J., C P., 355; 30 L T., 832; not following *Trench* v. *Nolan*, Ir. L. Rep. 6, C.L. 464; or the *Norwich Case*, 19 L.T., n.s, 619; the *Clitheroe Case*, 2 P.R. & D., 276, 285; and *Moore* v. *Scully*, 9 R.I. Rep. C.L, 217.)

If a case arises for giving notice of the disqualification of a candidate, the notice should be express and positive, and it should be served personally upon as many electors as possible, and advertised generally. (*Yates* v. *Leach*, L.R., 9, C.P., 608, 609; 43 L.J., C.P., 377, 30 L.T., 790.) Notice of candidate's incapacity.

Another class of votes which will be struck off upon a scrutiny is those given by ballot papers open to any of the following objections: (1) want of official mark; (2) voting for more candidates than entitled to; (3) writing or mark by which the voter can be identified; (4) unmarked or void for uncertainty. (Ballot Act, 1872, Schedule 1, r. 36.) On the other hand, ballot papers improperly rejected on any of these grounds may be added to the poll on a scrutiny. Generally it the Court can infer that the voter intended to vote, and gather for whom he intended to vote, the vote will be admitted. As to what marks on the ballot paper will render it good or bad, see *Wigtown*, 2 O'M. & H., 215; *Woodward* v. *Sarsons*, L.R., 10, C.P., 738; 44 L.J., C.P., 293; 32 L.T., 867; *Berwick*, 3 O'M. & H., 178; 44 L.T., 289; *Stepney*, 4 O'M. & H., 34. If the returning officer marked the paper with the voter's number on the register, as that might lead to identification of the voter the vote would be bad. (*Woodward* v. *Sarsons*, *supra*.) Ballot papers ill marked or defective.

The votes of the following classes of persons are also bad upon a scrutiny: (1) bribers; (2) persons bribed; (3) treaters; (4) persons treated; (5) persons guilty of using undue influence; (6) persons unduly influenced; (7) persons procuring personation; (8) personators; (9) persons guilty of any illegal practice; (10) persons guilty of illegal employment; (11) persons guilty of illegal payment; (12) persons guilty of illegal hiring; (13) paid agents employed for any of the purposes of the election; (14) returning officer (unless but for his votes there would be an equality of votes; (15) Votes struck off on a scrutiny.

PARLIAMENTARY & MUNICIPAL. persons convicted of corrupt practices; (16) infants, (17) women; (18) imbeciles and lunatics; (19) peers; (20) aliens (see *Berwick*, 44 L.T., 289, 3 O'M. & H., 178; *Oldham*, 1 O'M. & H., 151; 20 L.T., 302; and *Stepney*, 4 O'M. & H., 45); (21) policemen at municipal but not parliamentary elections; (22) traitors; (23) convicted felons; (24) the holders of certain offices the subject of statutory prohibitions; and (25) a person who has already voted in another division of the borough, it being a divided borough. (48 & 49 Vict., c. 23, s. 8, and *Stepney*, 4 O'M. & H., 45.) The vote of a person who has merely *offered* his vote for sale is not to be struck off (*Mallow*, 2 O'M. & H., 22).

Rule as to striking off votes for persons corrupted.

By the Ballot Act, 1872. s. 25, "where a candidate, on the trial of an election petition claiming the seat for any person, is proved to have been guilty, by himself or by any person on his behalf, of bribery, treating or undue influence, in respect of any person who voted at such election, or where any person retained or employed for reward by or on behalf of such candidate for all or any of the purposes of such election, as agent, clerk, messenger, or in any other employment, is proved on such trial to have voted at such election, there shall, on a scrutiny, be struck off from the number of votes appearing to have been given to such candidate, one vote for every person who voted at such election and is proved to have been so bribed, treated or unduly influenced, or so retained or employed for reward as aforesaid." Rule 41 in the first schedule of the same Act seems to contemplate that the Court shall ascertain how the voter bribed did vote, and that his vote shall be struck off the poll of the candidate for whom he voted. The question becomes important where a voter bribed to vote for A votes against him. The section and the rule have been construed in the case of *Malcolm* v. *Parry* (L.R., 9, C.P., 610; 43 L.J., C.P., 331; 31 L.T. 331) with this result,

When the ballot paper of the corrupted voter will be examined.

that if a corrupt practice by a candidate, or his agent, is proved in regard to a voter, and that voter voted, then, upon a scrutiny, one vote in respect of such voter will be struck off the poll of such candidate *without regard to the* question *whether the voter so corrupted voted for such candidate or for his opponent.* If the corrupt practice was neither by a candidate nor his agent, the Court must look at the counterfoils to see how the voter voted, and strike a vote off the poll of the candidate for whom he voted. *In each case proof that the voter acted corruptly is necessary.*

Where on a scrutiny, one person (who voted) claims to be the person on the register, and it is alleged that another person, who does not himself claim the vote, is the person on the register, the nature of the qualification may be inquired into for the purpose of deciding who is the elector. (*Berwick*, 44 L.T., 289.)

<small>PARLIAMENTARY & MUNICIPAL.</small>

<small>Two persons of the same name—one only on the register.</small>

When a marked register shows that a voter has already voted, it is *prima facie* sufficient for adding his subsequently tendered vote to the poll that he swears that he did not previously vote, and that the marked register is wrong; and when the marked register shows that a voter did not vote, it is not conclusive on a scrutiny, but it may be proved that the voter did vote, and his vote, on a paper bearing the number of another elector, will be valid (*ibid.*).

<small>Tendered votes.</small>

If the judges differ in opinion on the question whether a voter ought to be *struck off* the poll, it remains on. If they differ on the question whether a vote ought to be put on, it is not put on. *Omnia presumantur pro negante.* (See *Berwick*, 3 O'M. & H., 178; 44 L.T., 287.)

<small>Difference of opinion between the judges.</small>

As to when a recount of the ballot papers will be ordered, see the *Stepney Case*, 4 O'M. & H., 49.

Section IV.—The Evidence upon Election Petitions.

Sub-section I.—Parliamentary.

With some few exceptions, the rules of evidence on the trial of election petitions are the same as those in force on the trial of actions at *nisi prius*. But the nature of the subject has caused the introduction of some special rules of evidence, and there are certain other exceptions to the general law derived from the practice of the House

<small>PARLIAMENTARY. Generally the rules of the common law apply.</small>

PARLIAMENTARY of Commons Committees which, until 1869, tried petitions against the return of members. It is enacted by section 26 of the Parliamentary Elections Act, 1868, "Until rules of Court have been made in pursuance of this Act, and so far as such rules do not extend, the principles, practice, and rules on which committees of the House of Commons have heretofore acted in dealing with election petitions, shall be observed so far as may be by the Court and judge in the case of election petitions under this Act." The rules (of 1868, 1869 and 1875) which are set out in the Appendix hereto, do not deal with the subject of evidence generally. The Courts have faithfully followed the instructions contained in s. 26. One result, and that not a very happy result, of the section, has been the refusal of the High Courts to allow discovery of documents to be had or interrogatories administered on election petitions, following the practice of the committees of the House. The Act of 1883 makes no change in this respect, and indeed does not affect the rules of evidence heretofore observed by the Court.

As in other kinds of litigation, subject to the powers in the Court of amending the particulars, the petitioner must succeed *secundum allegata et probata*. Therefore, at *Greenock* (1 O'M. & H., 247), Lord Barcaple rejected altogether evidence of the polling booth having been placed in an illegal position, there being no specific allegation of that fact in the petition.

Witnesses ordered out of Court.

The witnesses in the cause will be ordered out of Court on the application of either side, but the agent of neither party will be ordered out of Court, although he may be charged with personal bribery. (*Knaresborough*, 3 O'M. & H., 141.)

If charges of personal misconduct are made against a candidate, the Court finds it "startling" if he is not called to deny them, and draws its own inference. (*Evesham*, 3 O'M. & H., 19.)

Formal proof of election.

It is not usual to require formal proof of the holding of the election and of the return. At *Coventry* (20 L.T., 406,

1 O'M. & H., 97), Willes, J.. said, "I shall not require the election to be proved in any of the cases. I know, as a matter of public notoriety, that there has been a general election, and therefore an election for the town of Coventry. There was a return for this borough. If the respondents were not returned at that election I ought to reject them. The poll books are here, and they tell me that an election was held." *Parliamentary*

Perhaps no more important deviation from the common law, so far as regards the law of evidence, exists, than is to be found in the fact that if the Election Court should erroneously admit or reject evidence, no appeal or new trial could be had (although the improper admission or rejection of evidence should have caused a miscarriage of justice) unless the judges should agree to reserve a case for the High Court under section 12 of the Parliamentary Elections Act, 1868. *Improper admission or rejection of evidence.*

At common law evidence cannot be given against a party of an act done or thing said by some other person until that other person has been proved to be an agent of the party sought to be affected But by the Parliamentary Elections Act, 1868, (31 & 32 Vict., c. 125), s. 17, it is provided that "on the trial of an election petition under this Act, unless the judge otherwise directs, any charge of a corrupt practice may be gone into, and evidence in relation thereto received before any proof has been given of agency on the part of any candidate in respect of such corrupt practice." The judges are somewhat reluctant to avail themselves of the powers conferred by this section unless there is a reasonable prospect of proving agency afterwards. (*Bristol*, 2 O'M. & H., 29 ; *Guildford*, 1 O'M. & H., 14.) But in the *West Belfast Case* (4 O'M. & H., 107) evidence of conversations was admitted before evidence of the agency of the persons who conversed was given, even where the conversation was held after the declaration of the poll. The judges thought there might possibly have been general personation.

Again, as the trial of a petition is something more than a contest between the parties, and as the duties of the Court, especially under the Act of 1883, are in some sort inquisitorial, the rule at *nisi prius* that evidence tendered to *Discrediting and contradicting a witness.*

PARLIAMENTARY contradict a witness upon some matter collateral to the issue is inadmissible, has not been very strictly adhered to in the trial of election petitions. In the *North Norfolk Case* (1 O'M. & H., 239), Blackburn, J., admitted such evidence.

Witnesses called by a petitioner are in some cases unfriendly and often hostile. Therefore, where a witness is put into the witness-box to admit that he was bribed, has denied the fact, the party calling him has been allowed to put into his hands his previous written statement admitting the bribery, not for the purpose of discrediting him as a witness become hostile, under the Common Law Procedure Act, 1854, but — and the effect is much the same — for the purpose of testing and probing his memory. (*Chester*, 44 L.T., 285.)

Hostile witness.

But generally, the provisions of the Common Law Procedure Act, 1854, section 22, are to be complied with. The circumstances connected with the making of the statement must be recalled to the witness's recollection, and he must, in the first instance, be proved to be hostile. (*Cheltenham*, 1 O'M. & H., 62; *Bradford*, 1 O'M. & H., 30.) That done, he may be cross-examined as to previous statements made by him, and inconsistent with his evidence in the box. The attempt to read a previous written statement to one's own witness, and to put questions to him to show that the statement is true, has been discouraged.

Previous statement of witness.

And it was laid down in the *Wigan Case* (4 O'M. & H., 1) that these written statements, which it has been common to procure from witnesses before the trial, are of little value. If a witness's signed statement is in direct conflict with his sworn testimony, the latter is not thereby invalidated. It is weakened, no doubt, but the judges must decide for themselves from the probabilities of the case, the demeanour of the witness, and the other circumstances proved, on which side the truth lies. In the same case, Grove, J., severely reprehended the practice of getting persons who were known to be witnesses on the other side, to sign statements at all. He made the same objections to the obtaining of such statements during the trial.

Upon the principle of the *North Norfolk Case* (*supra*), where a man denied that he had been bribed, the Court allowed another person to be called to prove that the first had admitted the bribery in his hearing. (*Lichfield*, 1 O'M. & H. 22.) But in the *King's Lynn Case* (2 O'M. & H., 208), such evidence was rejected. It is quite clear that the declarations of the petitioner against the character of his own witness are admissible against him (*Londonderry*, P. & K., 277; C. & R., 253; *Berwick*, June 30th, 1820); and as each voter is in a sense a party to the case when the seat is claimed, what the voter admits about his vote, showing that it was an invalid vote, is admissible upon a scrutiny. (*Tipperary*, 2 O'M. & H., 31.) There is all the difference in the world between a scrutiny and an ordinary petition. Yet in the *Windsor Case* (1 O'M. & H., 5), the question of the seat and of the scrutiny were considered to be, to a certain extent, one, so as to make evidence admissible if applicable to either issue, but only, we think, for the purposes of affecting the issue to which it should be applicable.

Parliamentary Admissions by witness.

Effect of the vote being claimed.

Where it is sought to prove that a voter has made a statement of his having been bribed to a third person, and it is intended to fix the consequences of the bribery upon a person other than the voter himself, *e.g.*, the sitting member, the evidence of the person to whom the statement is alleged to have been made cannot be received until the voter himself has been called as a witness. (*Guildford*, 19 L.T., 733.)

In the *Worcester Case* (3 O'M. & H., 185), in support of an allegation that the poll was improperly closed before four o'clock, a witness was called to prove that he was refused a ballot paper by the returning officer. He was asked in cross-examination "Were you not bribed to vote?" but that question was disallowed. The Court considered his right to vote was concluded by the register, except where the seat was claimed. (Acc. *King's Lynn*, 1 O'M. & H., 206.) Indeed, when the seat is not claimed, a witness may be put into the box to say: "A B gave me a sovereign to vote for C D," subject to this, that the Court may, in its discretion, require the agency of A B to be proved first.

Discrediting a witness.

Parliamentary Agency to be first proved. (*cf. King's Lynn*, 1 O'M. & H., 208; *Lichfield*, 1 O'M. & H., 22; cf. *West Belfast*, 4 O'M. & H. 107.) In the peculiar case of the death of the respondent before the trial of the petition and on the substitution of another respondent by the Court in his stead, it has been held that the admissions of the former respondent may be given in evidence against substituted respondent. The latter steps into the shoes of the former. (*Tipperary*, 3 O'M. & H., 34.)

Result of canvass. In order to support a suggestion that the verdict of the constituency has been changed by bribery, the petitioner's election agent was called and asked what result was shown by the canvass books sent in to him by his sub-agents. The question has often been allowed without objection, but in this case it was objected to, and the objection was sustained. The evidence would clearly have been hearsay. The proper course was to call the sub-agents to verify their canvass books and then to ask the chief agent, as an accountant, what the general result was. (*King's Lynn*, 1 O'M. & H., 206.) In the *Westminster Case* (1 O'M. & H., 95; 20 L.T., 238), a canvasser was allowed to be asked how many promises he had received, it being argued that his information on this point was, according to its character, likely or unlikely to discourage bribery by him.

But where general intimidation was alleged, the general question was allowed to be asked whether the witness found any particular difficulty in getting promises in a particular district, and if so whether he could attribute it to any cause. (*North Durham*, 2 O'M. & H., 152, 153.)

A married woman cannot be asked whether her husband told her that he had promised to vote for A (*Lichfield*, 1 O'M. & H., 22), but Blackburn, J., admitted the evidence of a married woman that her husband handed her money and told her that B had given it to him to vote for A. (*Bridgwater*, 1 O'M. & H., 113.)

Bribery by a gift of a postal order may be proved without putting in the postal order. (*Londonderry*, 4 O'M. & H., 103.)

Secrecy of the ballot. The question how a witness voted cannot be put, for it tends to violate the secrecy of the ballot. On a somewhat similar ground a witness who did not vote cannot be asked, even in cross-examination, to what party he belongs. But there is some authority for saying that a voter who has openly avowed his opinions may be asked to what party he holds himself out as belonging. (*North Durham*, 3 O'M. & H., 1; *Harwich*, 3 O'M. & H., 63.)

There has already been occasion to observe that the Act of 1883 proclaims an amnesty for past offences, and that a witness may not be asked as to any corrupt practices at an election before the passing of the Act. But evidence that the respondent had employed an agent convicted of bribery at a previous election would seem to be undoubtedly admissible still. Evidence that the respondent had employed persons whom on a previous petition he had charged with bribery is irrelevant. (*Taunton*, 2 O'M. & H., 68.) Even under the old law the Court was very reluctant to connect the pending inquiry with what occurred at a previous election, and especially so where the respondent was not a candidate at that election. (*Windsor*, 1 O'M. & H. 95; 19 L.T., 615; *Westminster*, 20 L.T., 238.)

Acts done at previous elections.

Here, it seems, a distinction is to be taken. If the conduct of the respondent at the previous election has already been enquired into and adjudicated upon, the matter is closed and no evidence in regard to it can be admitted. Thus in the *Taunton Case* (L.R. 4, C.P. 361), there were three candidates at an election, B, C, and J. The returning officer returned B and C. Two electors presented a petition against C and claimed the seat for J. At the trial, C cross-examined the petitioner's witnesses with a view to prove bribery by J's agents, but the judge negatived that contention and declared J duly elected *and so certified*. A petition alleging bribery, &c., was then presented against J's return, but the Court of Common Pleas held that the judge's previous decision was final and that the second petition must be taken off the file. Brett, J., suggested that if a fraud were practised upon the Court, so that the inquiry into the conduct of J's agents upon the first petition had been a

Distinction where charges previously adjudicated upon.

PARLIAMENTARY sham and collusive inquiry, the judgment might not have been final. (And see *Goodwin's Case*, 2 State Trials, 91.) In the *Taunton Case*, it will be observed, the case against J was persisted in and the judge certified the result to the Speaker. It was otherwise in the *Norwich Case* (L.R., 6 C.P., 147.) There, A was a candidate at an election at which B was returned. A having petitioned against his return and claimed the seat, recriminatory charges were made. At the trial of the petition, B was proved guilty of corrupt practices by his agents, and decided by the judge not to have been duly elected, and after some of the matters contained in the recriminatory charges were gone into and not proved, B *withdrew* the charge by permission of the judge, and A then abandoned his claim to the seat, and the judge certified to the House of Commons that B was not

Distinction between judge's report and certificate

duly elected, and reported, amongst other things, that he believed the election on the part of A to have been perfectly pure. At the election which ensued, A was returned, and a petition was presented against his return, alleging that he had been guilty of corrupt practices by himself and his agents at the previous election at which B had been returned, the matters intended to be relied on having been discovered since the former trial. On a rule to strike out these allegations from the petition on the ground that the matters alleged might have been given in evidence in support of the recriminatory charges at the previous trial, it was held that the report of the judge at an election trial is not final and conclusive like his certificate as to the matters contained in it, and that the present petitioner was entitled to give evidence of the alleged corrupt practice.

Corruption at municipal election.

But where it is suggested that bribery was committed at a municipal election in order to influence the voting at the parliamentary election, evidence of the bribery at the municipal election is of course admissible. (*Beverley*, 20 L.T., 792, *Blackburn*, 20 L T., 823; *Hastings*, 21 L.T., 234.)

It would seem that the proper court and time to try an objection to the *status* of the petitioner is not the Election Court, but the High Court, some convenient time before the day appointed for trial of the petition, yet in the *Youghal* Parliamentary *Case* (21 L.T., 307), the Election Court admitted evidence to show that the petitioner had no *status*, rather than imperil the legality and regularity of the trial by rejecting it.

In a case of intimidation the respondent himself gave evidence that on the polling day he went to voters who were opposed to him and offered to give them his escort to protect them to the poll, they being afraid to go, although there were military and constabulary in the streets. This evidence had the contrary effect to what was intended, for the Court treated it as conclusive evidence out of the respondent's own mouth to prove that there was not freedom of election in the borough. (*Drogheda*, 21 L.T., 402.) Evidence of intimidation.

An unstamped document may be given in evidence upon an election petition without paying the penalty. (*Windsor*, 21 O'M. & H., 6.) The stamp law.

Documents in the possession of the other side, particular notice to produce which has been given, may be called for, and when produced will generally be evidence. If not produced, secondary evidence of them may be given. (*Bradford*, 1 O'M. & H., 30.) If a party refuse to produce a document when called for, after due notice, the Court may refuse to allow him to put it in afterwards for the purpose of explanation. (*Windsor*, 1 O'M. & H., 5.) A notice to produce "all documents relating to the matters in question" will not entitle the party giving the notice to production of returns made by each or any canvasser to the candidate's committee. A general notice of that kind only covers documents which ought to be filed and returned. (*Westminster*, 1 O'M. & H., 193. Production of documents.

When the bank pass-book of the respondent and that of his agent were called for, it was held they must first be shown to be material to the issue. (*Tamworth*, 1 O'M. & H., 76.) Strictly, a bank account is not evidence but only a means of refreshing the memory of the witness. (*Salford*, 1 O'M. & H., 136.) When the respondent's canvass book was called for, Willes, J., said that any particular entry in it might be asked for. (*Northallerton*, 1 O'M. & H., 167.)

The practice as to the production of telegrams, and of ballot papers, marked register and counterfoils, has already been discussed.

A candidate is not responsible for the acts of his election agents (other than the election agent appointed under the Act of 1883) done after the polling. (*North Norfolk*, 1 O'M. & H., 243; 21 L.T., 264. *Salford*, 1 O'M. & H., 133; 19 L.T., 120.) It would be otherwise if it were previously shown that the agent's act was done with the privity of the candidate. The relation of principal and agent, unless expressly continued, ends with the election; evidence of an act of bribery committed after the election may be admitted, but only for the purpose of shedding light on what took place before the election. (*Southampton*, 1 O'M. & H., 222.) On the general principle that the agency is terminated by the election, the declarations and admissions made by an agent after the election are not admissible in evidence against the candidate. (*Harwich*, 3 O'M. & H., 61; *Cheltenham*, 3 O'M. & H., 86.) In the *Dover Case* (1 O'M. & H., 210), it was ruled that a witness might be asked what directions an agent gave him during the election, but not what statements the agent made. But query as to this. " The act of an agent is evidence against a respondent, but, speaking generally, it is confined to that, although it is possible he may be such an agent as to make his statements evidence also. But clearly you cannot make use of a statement made by an agent upon a matter with which the agency is not connected, which is really nothing more than hearsay. (*King's Lynn*, 1 O'M. & H., 207, 208.) Probably the rule is no more than this, that statements made during the election by a person proved to be an agent are admissible if made at the time of the commission of the corrupt or illegal act, for then they are a part of the *resgestæ*, or if made at any time during the election, in relation to the particular portion of the work of the election deputed to him.

As to the proof of statements by persons deceased, the ordinary rule applies, that they are admissible if made against interest or in the course of business by persons

having a duty to make them, but a statement made by A <small>PARLIAMENTARY</small>
deceased to B, and tending to show how he came by a sum
of money, with the view of proving that A was an agent of
the respondent, would appear to be inadmissible. (*Londonderry*, 1 O'M. & H., 276.)

Where a respondent was asked in cross-examination what
a previous election cost him, and whether he had not committed bribery at a previous election, both questions were
disallowed, apparently on the ground of irrelevancy. (*Cashel*,
1 O'M. & H., 287.)

If it is charged that the respondent or his agents have
kept "open house" at public houses, the most convenient
way of proving it is to call the publicans. (*Tamworth*, 1
O'M. & H, 83, 84.)

Any account sent in to the respondent may be called
for, and when produced and put in it becomes evidence,
whether the liability upon it be disputed or not. The
weight of it is another matter. (*Bradford*, 1 O'M. &
H., 31.)

Unless the seat is claimed recriminatory evidence is
quite inadmissible. (*Thirsk*, 3 O'M. & H., 113.)

Evidence of an intention by the respondent to pay
bribes after the hearing of the election petition is also
inadmissible, because in that case a fresh petition might
be presented. (*Galway*, 1 O'M. & H., 303; Parliamentary
Elections Act, 1868, s. 6.)

Evidence that certain persons have been corrupted may <small>Evidence of intention to</small>
be given in order to make out a case of general corruption, <small>pay bribes.</small>
although the names of such persons are not in the particulars. (*Wigan*, 4 O'M. & H., 182.)

By Parliamentary Elections Act, 1868, s. 2, it is enacted:
"On the trial of an election petition under this Act, the judge
may, by order under his hand, compel the attendance of any
person as a witness who appears to him to have been con- <small>Witnesses</small>
cerned in the election to which the petition refers, and any <small>may be called by the Court.</small>
person refusing to obey such order, shall be guilty of contempt
of Court. The judge may examine any witness so compelled
to attend, or any person in Court, although such witness is

PARLIAMENTARY. not called and examined by any party to the petition. After the examination of a witness as aforesaid by a judge, such witness may be cross-examined by or on behalf of the petitioner and respondent, or either of them." Under this section witnesses were called by the Court in the *Salisbury Case* (3 O'M. & H., 134), but the prevailing opinion has been that the duties of the judges are judicial and not inquisitorial. (*Chester*, 44 L.T., 287; *Stroud*, 2 O'M. & H., 107.)

And by leave by the Public Prosecutor. Now by the Act of 1883, s. 43, it is provided: "On every trial of an election petition, the Director of Public Prosecutions shall, by himself or by his assistant, or by such representative as hereinafter mentioned, attend at the trial, and it shall be the duty of such director to obey any directions given to him by the Election Court with respect to the summoning and examination of any witness to give evidence on such trial, and with respect to the prosecution by him of offenders, and with respect to any person to whom notice is given to attend with a view to report him as guilty of any corrupt or illegal practice. It shall also be the duty of such director, without any direction from the Election Court, if it appears to him that any person is able to give material evidence as to the subject of the trial, to cause such person to attend the trial, and with the leave of the Court to examine such person as a witness." As the Director of Public Prosecutions will have little knowledge of the constituency, will be regarded with disfavour by the class of persons who can give evidence of corrupt practices, and will not be allowed to see the inside of counsel's briefs, it may be doubted whether this section will be found to be very efficacious or far-reaching in its operation.

SUB-SECTION II.—MUNICIPAL.

MUNICIPAL.
Evidence in municipal election petitions. The law relating to evidence upon parliamentary and municipal election petitions is the same. (See the Municipal Corporations Act, 1882, s. 100, sub-s. 3.) We think that in the case of a municipal petition it would be convenient that

the Commissioner, by analogy to the *Coventry Case* (1 O'M. & H., 97; 20 L.T., 406), should take judicial notice of the holding of the election in question. But until this rule is established it may be well for the petitioner's agent to ask the respondent's agent in writing to admit the fact of the election being held. If the admission be refused, the petitioner should subpœna the town clerk or other holder of them, to produce all the papers relating to the election, and the returning officer to prove the holding of the election. Probably a vexatious refusal to admit that fact would induce the Commissioner to order the respondent to pay all the costs necessarily incurred by reason of such refusal, whatever the event. If inspection of the ballot papers, marked register or counterfoils, which are committed to the custody of the town clerk, should at a municipal election be required, the application for leave must be made to the County Court having jurisdiction in the borough. (Ballot Act, 1872, 1st Sch., rule 64. (The decision of the County Court is subject to appeal in the usual way. (*Ibid.*)

MUNICIPAL.

Proof of the holding of the election.

SECTION V.—THE AWARDING AND TAXATION OF COSTS.

SUB-SECTION I.—PARLIAMENTARY.

The costs of election proceedings are in the discretion of the Court, which will disallow any costs occasioned by "vexatious conduct, unfounded allegations, or unfounded objections," by either party, and have regard to the "discouragement of any needless expense" by throwing the same on the author of it. (Parliamentary Elections Act, 1868, s. 41.) The general rule is that the costs follow the event, but "the event" may be distributive when the seat is claimed. Thus, where the petitioner succeeded in unseating the respondent and then withdrew his claim to the seat, he got no costs occasioned by the latter claim. (*Gravesend*, 44 L.T., 64, 3 O'M. & H., 81.) And in the *Petersfield Case* (2 O'M. & H., 94), where the charges of corrupt practices by agents failed, the petitioner had to

PARLIAMENTARY

Costs in the discretion of the Court.

Usually follow the event.

pay the costs of those charges, irrespective of the result of the scrutiny.

Exceptions to the rule, where petitioner succeeds. The petitioner, though successful, may be left to bear his own costs where (1) the petitioner is a man of straw, put up by others in order to avoid liability for costs (*Poole*, 2 O'M. & H., 123; 31 L.T., 171), but not where the petition is a *bonâ fide* petition by the petitioner, however poor he may be (*Wigan*, 4 O'M. & H., 1) ; (2) where the particulars are exceedingly voluminous, and make many charges which fail (*Westbury* 1 O'M. & H., 50; 20 L.T., 17 ; *Norwich*, 2 O'M. & H., 42 ; *Norwich*, 4 O'M. & H., 91), where Denman, J., described the petitioner's case as " a most terribly overloaded case; it has been an oppressive case on the part of the petitioner"; (3) where the petitioner has himself acted illegally or improperly (*Wallingford*, 1 O'M. & H., 57; *Longford*, 2 O'M. & H., 7) ; (4) where much time is wasted in consequence of the petitioner's solicitor not getting up his case properly (*Wallingford*, 1 O'M. & H., 60). If the petitioner's particulars are insufficient he may be deprived of his costs or ordered to pay the costs of an adjournment necessitated by their insufficiency (*Penrhyn*, 1 O'M. & H., 128).

Or a successful petitioner may be ordered to pay a part of the costs. At *Bewdley* (44 L.T., 283, 3 O'M. & H., 145), he was ordered to pay the costs of unfounded charges of treating. (And see *Londonderry*, 1 O'M. & H., 279). At *Boston* (2) (44 L.T., 289, 3 O'M. & H., 150), he was ordered to pay the costs of charges which he withdrew, and no costs were allowed on either side in respect of charges not proven. And the costs incurred through calling useless witnesses may have to be paid by a successful petitioner (*Salisbury*, 3 O'M. & H., 130, 131), who will also be ordered to pay the costs of charges of personal bribery which break down. (*Ibid.*)

At *Gravesend* (44 L.T., 64, 3 O'M. & H., 81), where the seat was claimed, and the election was avoided, and the claim to the seat abandoned, whereupon, by a mistake, the recriminatory charges were proceeded with, no **costs** of the recriminatory charges, or of the scrutiny, or of charges not proven, were allowed on either side.

Parliamentary

A successful respondent has been deprived of his costs altogether, where there was reasonable and probable cause for presenting the petition; (*Westminster*, 1 O'M. & H., 89; 20 L.T., 228; *Guildford*, 1 O'M. & H., 15; *Coventry*, 1 O'M. & H., 97, 20 L.T., 405; *Salisbury*, 4 O'M. & H., 30; *Stepney*, 4 O'M. & H., 58), or where the respondent or his agents had committed illegal acts not vitiating the election (*Bolton*, 2 O'M. & H., 138, 31 L.T., 194; *Longford*, 2 O'M. & H., 17); or improper acts, (*Windsor*, 2 O'M. & H., 92.)

Where respondent succeeds.

Where the respondent failed to prove some of his countercharges, but was successful on the whole, the petitioner was ordered to pay two-thirds of his costs. (*Berwick*, 44 L.T., 289; 3 O'M. and H., 178.)

In the *Buckrose Case* (4 O'M. & H.) the petitioner succeeded in obtaining the seat on a scrutiny. He was allowed the costs of the scrutiny. On the other hand, he was ordered to pay the whole costs of a recriminatory case made by the respondent, which failed; but the feature of this case was that it only failed because the Court had, under s. 34, excused an irregularity in the return of election expenses, which, but for such excuse would have been an illegal practice which would have avoided the election.

Where the petition is caused by the errors of the returning officer, he is not, in the absence of wilful misconduct, ordered to pay costs. (*Hackney*, 2 O'M. & H., 77. *Wigtown*, 2 O'M. & H., 232. *Woodward* v. *Sarsons*, L.R., 10 C.P., 738; 44 L.J., C.P., 293; 32 L.T., 867. *Mayo*, 2 O'M. & H., 192. *Drogheda*, 2 O'M. and H., 211.) But where the conduct of the returning officer is unsuccessfully impeached, the losing party will generally be ordered to pay his costs. (*Worcester*, 3 O'M. & H., 186.)

Where returning officer in fault.

Effect has been given to an agreement between the parties that, whatever the result, neither shall ask for costs. (*Nottingham*, 1 O'M. & H., 245.)

Agreement that no costs shall be asked for.

The old rules relating to the incidence of costs were found

to bear hardly upon innocent candidates, and the Legislature has introduced a new rule, which will, in many cases, go some way to relieve innocent parties of the burden of costs, and impose that burden on persons on whom it should in justice be placed.

By s. 44 of the Act of 1883, it is enacted:—

Guilty persons and constituencies may be ordered to pay costs.

"(1.) Where upon the trial of an election petition respecting an election for a county or borough, it appears to the Election Court that a corrupt practice has not been proved to have been committed in reference to such election, by or with the knowledge and consent of the respondent to the petition, and that such respondent took all reasonable means to prevent corrupt practices being committed on his behalf, the Court may make one or more orders with respect to the payment either of the whole or such part of the cost of the petition as the Court may think right, as follows:—

When corruption general.

"(a) If it appears to the Court that corrupt practices extensively prevailed in reference to the said election, the Court may order the whole or part of the costs to be paid by the county or borough; and

When individuals largely engaged in corruption.

"(b) If it appears to the Court that any person or persons is, or are proved, whether by providing money, or otherwise, to have been extensively engaged in corrupt practices, or to have encouraged or promoted extensive corrupt practices in reference to such election, the Court may, after giving such person or persons an opportunity of being heard by counsel or solicitor, and examining and cross-examining witnesses to show cause why the order should not be made, order the whole or part of the costs to be paid by that person or those persons, or any of them, and may order that if the costs cannot be recovered from one or more of such persons, they shall be paid by some other of such persons, or by either of the parties to the petition, and

In solitary

"(2.) Where any person appears to the Court to have been

guilty of the offence of a corrupt or illegal practice, the Court may, after giving such person an opportunity of making a statement to show why the order should not be made, order the whole or any part of the costs of, or incidental to any proceeding before the Court in relation to the said offence, or to the said person, to be paid by the said person." PARLIAMENTARY case of corrupt or illegal practice.

The order under this section may be made only by the judges who try the election petition, or by the High Court, if the matter comes before the High Court.—(S. 64 of the Act of 1883.) But there is no jurisdiction to make an order under s. 44 at all, unless two events concur, namely that no corrupt practice, "by or with the knowledge of the respondent," is proved, *and* it is shown that the respondent took all reasonable means to prevent corrupt practices. Apparently the jurisdiction would not be destroyed if the respondent had committed or encouraged illegal practices or illegal payments or the like, although in that event the Court would have little disposition to relieve an unsuccessful respondent of the liability to pay costs. By what Court. When jurisdiction arises.

The jurisdiction conferred by the section is not large. If corrupt practices extensively prevailed, the Court may throw the costs of the petition on the constituency. Having regard to the language of sub-s. 3 of s. 44, probably "costs of the petition" will be held to include the costs of both parties.

If the author of extensive corruption can be ascertained, the Court may order him to pay the costs of the petition, but only after the propriety of making the order has been tried out with all the machinery of counsel, solicitors, examination and cross-examination. In fact, after the petition has been heard there may be another trial to decide whether a third party is to pay the whole or any part of the costs, and as the petitioner and respondent will be deeply interested in the result of this latter trial, they will remain and see it out. In fact, being interested parties, they ought to be heard on it. Inquiries precedent to order.

The last case is that in which it shall appear to the Court

PARLIAMENTARY that some stranger to the petition has been guilty of a corrupt or *illegal* practice, in which case he may be ordered to pay, not the costs of the petition, but only the costs of the proceedings before the Court in relation to those offences, *e.g.*, of his prosecution before the Court. Such a person cannot be heard by his counsel as of right, or examine or cross-examine witnesses with a view of preventing the making of the order. He is only entitled to make a statement.

It is probable that in every case in which a respondent would have been ordered to pay the costs of a successful petition, he will still be ordered to do so in the event of a stranger to the petition ordered to pay them failing to comply with the order.

Expenses of witnesses.

As between a witness whose expenses were allowed by the judge and the party who subpœnaed him, the registrar, or if he is incapacitated, the judge of the Election Court will ascertain and certify the amount to be paid to the witness. Gen. Rules (Parl.), 1875, r. 5.

Enactments regarding the taxation of costs.

The taxation of costs is regulated by s. 41 of the Parl. Elections Act, 1868, and by s. 44, sub-s. 3, of the Act of 1883. The former section enacts, "That all costs, charges, and expenses of and incidental to the presentation of a petition under this Act and to the proceedings consequent thereon, with the exception of such costs, charges and expenses as are by this Act otherwise provided for, shall be defrayed by the parties to the petition in such manner and in such proportions as the Court or judge may determine, regard being had to the disallowance of any costs, charges, or expenses, which may, in the opinion of the Court, or judge, have been caused by vexatious conduct, unfounded allegations, or unfounded objections on the part either of the petitioner or the respondent, and regard being had to the discouragement of any needless expense by throwing the burden of defraying the same on the parties by whom it has been caused, whether such parties are or are not on the whole successful. The costs may be taxed in the prescribed manner, but according to the same principle as costs between attorney and client are taxed in a suit in the High

Court of Chancery, and such costs may be recovered in the same manner as the costs of an action at law or in such other manner as may be prescribed." By s. 44, sub-s. 3, of the Act of 1883 it is enacted:—" The rules and regulations of the Supreme Court of Judicature with respect to costs to be allowed in actions, causes and matters in the High Court shall in principle and so far as practicable apply to the costs of petitions and other proceedings under the Parliamentary Elections Act, 1868, and under this Act, and the taxing officer shall not allow any costs, charges or expenses on a higher scale than would be allowed in any action, cause or matter in the High Court on the higher scale as between solicitor and client." Parliamentary

It would seem that s. 44, sub-s. 3, has not materially altered the principle on which the costs are to be taxed. "Charges and expenses" are still to be allowed, and the taxation is still to be as between solicitor and client. The only difference is that the costs are now expressly directed to be taxed on the higher scale, allowing, however, no more than would be allowed in an action of such importance, difficulty and complexity as the petition. Effect of the Act of 1883.

What is included in the expression, "Costs as between solicitor and client?" "Costs as between solicitor and client, payable by one party to another, will not include all costs to which the solicitor would be entitled as against his client. It is impossible to lay down with exactness any rule upon this subject, but generally it would seem that all such costs would be allowed as a solicitor would ordinarily incur in the conduct of his client's business, excluding those extraordinary costs which may have been occasioned, either by the default of the client, as by his incurring a contempt, or by his express instructions, as to employ an unusual number of counsel" (*Morgan and Davey on Costs*, p. 4.) Costs as between solicitor and client. What are?

Even as between party and party, a liberal scale of costs is to be allowed on taxation, when the action is one to which the higher scale is applicable, and, as between solicitor and client, there must be an extension of this allowance. This was the intention of the Legislature. In a recent case the Costs to be taxed liberally.

Court said—"It appears to us that the parties entitled to their costs under the orders were entitled to an indemnity for all costs that were reasonably incurred by them in the ordinary course of matters of this nature, but not to any extraordinary or unusual expenses incurred in consequence of over caution or over anxiety as to any particular case, or from considerations of any special importance arising from the rank, position, wealth or character of either of the parties, or any special desire on his part to insure success. We think, also, that such extraordinary costs as an attorney would not be justified in incurring without distinct and special instructions from his client, ought not to be allowed, nor the costs of purely collateral proceedings upon which a party has failed, nor those which may have been occasioned by his default, negligence, or mistake." (*Hill* v. *Peel*, L.R., 5 C.P., 180; 39 L.J. C.P., 89; 22 L.T., 98.)

And in the *Kennington Case* (4 O'M. & H. 95), where the petition in the opinion of the Court was wholly unfounded, Field, J., said: "I think in this case there should be a full indemnity," and an order was made directing taxation as between solicitor and client. In *Pascoe* v. *Puleston* (54 L.T., n.s., 733; 50 J.P. 134) it was laid down that under s. 44 costs of a petition will usually be allowed in the higher scale.

When Court will review taxation.
If the taxing master, in taxing, proceeds upon a wrong principle, the Court will review his decision, but if he has not erred in principle, and has exercised his discretion so that it is only as to the amount to be allowed, the Court is generally unwilling to interfere. (*Hill* v. *Peel*, *supra*.)

Number of counsel allowed.
As to the number of counsel to be allowed. In cases of unusual difficulty, complexity, or importance, three counsel may be allowed on taxation (*Wentworth* v. *Lloyd*, L.R., 2 Eq. 607, *Kirkwood* v. *Webster*, 9 Ch. Div. 239; 47 L.J., Ch. 880; 26 W.R., 812.) But in petitions in which the evidence is not voluminous, and the trial is not likely to consume more than two or three days, it is usual to allow only two counsel. The costs of two counsel are always allowed. (*Tillet* v. *Stracey*, L.R. 5, C.P., 185; 39 L.J., C.P., 93; 22 L.T., 101; 18 W.R., 631.)

As to the amount of counsel's fees. In the *Southampton Case* (L.R., 5, C.P., 174; 39 L.J., C.P., 89; 22 L.T., 98) the leading counsel received 200 guineas on his brief, and 50 guineas a day for refreshers, besides consultation fees. The junior received 150 guineas on his brief, and 30 guineas a day for refreshers, besides consultations. The master allowed just half of each of these fees, and disallowed the consultations. Looking at the difficulty and length of the case, the Court directed the taxation to be reviewed. Fees for consultations from day to day are to be allowed (*Tillet* v. *Stracey*, *supra*.) Amount of counsel's fees.

In the *Tamworth Case* (L.R. 5, C.P., 173; 39 L.J., C.P., 89; 22 L.T., 98) the leading counsel received 250 guineas with his brief, and 50 guineas a day for refreshers; and the junior 100 guineas with his brief, and 25 guineas a day for refreshers. The master allowed 100 guineas and 25 guineas a day refresher, and 75 guineas and 15 guineas a day refresher respectively. The case being one of an ordinary description, the Court declined to send the taxation back to the master to be reconsidered. In the *Penrhyn Case*, reported with the *Tamworth Case*, the master allowed each of the counsel 25 guineas extra on the brief, on account of the distance from town, and the Court declined to interfere. (*Cf. Tillet* v. *Stracey*, L.R. 5, C.P., 185; 39 L.J., C.P., 93; 22 L.T., 101; 18 W.R., 631; *Hargreaves* v. *Scott*, 4 C.P.D. 21; 40 L.T., 35; 27 W.R., 323, a case of a municipal election.)

The taxing master, in exercising his discretion as to the number of counsel, the amount of their fees, the number of consultations, the amount of consultation fees and refreshers, and the expenses of subpoenas to witnesses, telegrams and messages, ought to have regard to the difficulty, magnitude and importance of the particular case. (*Trench* v. *Nolan* (*the Galway Case*) 7 Ir. R., C.L., 445; 21 W.R., 640.) In that case the Court held that the successful petitioner on taxation was entitled to—(1) The sums actually paid by him for copies of the shorthand writer's notes; (2) the expenses of witnesses *bonâ fide* summoned but not called (but compare Regard to be had to circumstances of each case.

Tillett v. *Stracey*, L.R. 5, C.P., 185; 39 L.J., C.P., 93; 22 L.T., 101; 18 W.R., 631); (3) the cost of an illustrated map of the county; (4) a retainer of 10 guineas paid to each of the two leading counsel; (5) the fees paid to the junior counsel on the hearing of a case reserved, as well as the fees of the leading counsel; and (6) the cost of proceedings to draw the fund deposited as security out of Court.

Instructions for brief and preliminary expenses. As to instructions for brief and preliminary inquiries. In practice it will be found necessary, between the filing of the particulars and the delivery of the briefs, to make inquiries as to the evidence likely to be given, and generally to get up the case. In the *Tamworth Case*, *supra*, £105 were claimed for "instructions of brief," and £90 for money paid to a solicitor to prosecute the preliminary inquiries. The master disallowed the £90, and, the items making up the £90 not being before the Court, the Court refused to interfere. In the *Penrhyn Case*, *supra*, £105 were charged for "instructions for brief," and all the preliminary expenses in detail in addition. The master allowed £150 to include the preliminary expenses, and the Court would not interfere. In the *Southampton Case* £1,000 was charged for preliminary expenses, and the master allowed £105; but having regard to the circumstances of the case, the Court thought £105 insufficient, and sent it back to the master.

Master must examine the items. The parties are entitled to have the master's judgment upon the particular items in the preliminary expenses, if they think fit, instead of their being included in the allowance of one sum in gross to cover the whole of what the master may think right to be allowed (*Hill* v. *Peel*, L.R. 5, C.P., 183; 39 L.J., C.P., 89; 22 L.T., 98). But the master may allow a lump sum for instructions for brief, provided the items making up the lump sum have been brought before him, so as to enable him to judge whether it represents reasonable and proper charges (*Barnstaple Case*, 44 L.J., C.P., 200).

Number of witnesses allowed. If an excessive number of witnesses be subpœnaed, and the master disallows the costs of some of them, the Court will not interfere (*Tillett* v. *Stracey*, *supra*). The same course will

be taken if the successful party have all his witnesses *Parliamentary*
in attendance day by day, and not merely a sufficient
number to occupy the Court for the day (*M'Laren* v. *Home*,
7 Q.B.D., 447; 50 L.J., Q.B. 658). The certificate of the
registrar of the amount for witnesses is not conclusive of
the amount as between petitioner and respondent. The
master must still tax the witnesses' costs (*ibid.*). On an
application to review the taxation, it is wise to have the
briefs in Court (*Tillett* v. *Stracey, supra*).

As to the time at which costs should be incurred, the time
appointed for the delivery of particulars is not analogous to
notice of trial in an action. Before the particulars are
delivered the respondent may reasonably incur costs in
preparing the defence (*Hughes* v. *Meyrick*, L.R. 5, C.P., 407;
39 L.J., C.P., 219. In that case the trial was appointed for *At what time costs to be incurred.*
April 1. On March 22 an order for particulars was obtained.
On March 23 and 27 briefs were delivered and witnesses subpoenaed; on March 29 notice of withdrawal of the petition
was given. The master taxed the costs from £920 down to
£63. He disallowed the subpoenas and fees to counsel, and
substantially the costs of drawing and copying briefs and all
the expenses of preliminary inquiries. The Court decided
that he was wrong, and sent the case back to him. The costs
were then re-taxed at £700, including £288 for instructions
for brief, £85 for drawing and copying briefs, and 100
guineas and 75 guineas on the briefs. In point of fact, £210
and £105 were paid on the briefs.

As to the scale of fees to be allowed for witnesses, see *Scale of fees to witnesses.*
Turnbull v. *Janson*, 3 C.P.D., 264; 48 L.J., C.P., 384;
26 W.R., 815; *Mackley* v. *Chillingworth*, 2 C.P.D., 273;
46 L.J., C.P., 484; 36 L.T., 514; 25 W.R., 650; and
M'Laren v. *Home*, 7 Q.B.D., 477; 50 L.J., Q.B., 658.)

With regard to the costs of the Public Prosecutor, whose
representative must now attend the trial of every election petition, s. 43, sub-s. 8, provides that in the first instance they shall
be paid by the Treasury; "but if for any reasonable cause
it seems just to the Court so to do, the Court shall order all
or part of the said costs to be repaid to the Commissioners

of Her Majesty's Treasury by the parties to the petition, or such of them as the Court may direct." This power of ordering one of the parties to pay the costs of the Public Prosecutor is one which the Court has been very chary in exercising. In the *Norwich Case* (4 O'M. & H., 92) it was said it ought to be a strong case of misconduct to warrant an order being made. In the *Kennington Case* (4 O'M. & H. 95) it is to be assumed there was such a case, for there the order was made, Day, J., saying: "If this had been a well-grounded petition, I should have felt it unreasonable to put upon the petitioner these costs, but I think that it has been unfounded and that the public should be protected. In *Pascoe* v. *Puleston* (54 L.T., n.s. 733), it was held that where a petition was withdrawn before trial there was no power to allow as against the parties the Public Prosecutor's preliminary costs, *i.e.*, of inquiries made by them with a view to the hearing.

Recovery of costs.

In regard to the recovery of costs, it is provided by s. 58 of the Act of 1883 : (1) " Where any costs or other sums (not being costs of a prosecution on indictment) are, under an order of an Election Court, or otherwise under this Act, to be paid by a county or borough, the Commissioners of Her Majesty's Treasury shall pay those costs or sums, and obtain repayment of the amount so paid in like manner as if such costs and sums were expenses of Election Commissioners paid by them, and the Election Commissioners Expenses Acts, 1869 and 1871, shall apply accordingly as if they were herein re-enacted, and in terms made applicable to the above-mentioned costs and sums. (2) Where any costs or other sums are, under the order of an Election Court or otherwise under this Act, to be paid by any person, those costs shall be a simple contract debt due from such person to the person or persons to whom they are to be paid, and if payable to the Commissioners of Her Majesty's Treasury, shall be a debt to Her Majesty, and in either case may be recovered accordingly."

Payment of security fund out of Court.

As regards the money (if any) deposited by the petitioner in Court, by way of security for costs and claims of witnesses, all claims to it will be adjudicated upon by the Court or a PARLIAMENTARY judge. The person claiming to be entitled to it should give notice to the other side that he is about to apply for payment out, and should so apply by judge's summons at chambers. The application must be supported by affidavits, proving that due notice of intention to apply has been given, and that all proper claims upon the fund have been satisfied or provided for. The judge, by his order, may direct payment either to the party in whose name the money was deposited, or to any person entitled to receive it. When the order has been made, drawn up and signed, it should be taken to the Clerk of the Lord Chief Justice of England, who will endorse on the order a draft on the Bank of England for the payment of the money. The bank will pay the amount on the presentation of the draft in the usual way. (Gen. Rules (Parl.), March, 1869).

Sub-section II.—Municipal.

The law relating to the taxation and awarding of costs incidental to municipal election petitions, is similar to that relating to the same matter in parliamentary election petitions. (See s. 98 of the Municipal Corporations Act, 1882.) Upon municipal petitions the costs are taxed on the higher scale as between solicitor and client. (See s. 29 of the Act of 1884.) The taxing master generally has regard to the distance of the place of trial from London and other circumstances. The scale, however, is less liberal than in the case of parliamentary election petitions and in practice is nearly assimilated to that in use in ordinary common law actions of an important class. By s. 29 of the Act of 1884 power is given to the Election Court upon a municipal election petition to saddle the borough or any person guilty of corrupt practices, with the costs of the petition or a part of them, just as is provided in reference to parliamentary petitions by s. 44 of the Act of 1883. It should be noted that under s. 29 of the Act of 1884 the power, upon proof

Law similar in cases of municipal elections.

In practice scale allowed generally less liberal.

of the extensive prevalence of corrupt practices, is to throw the costs upon the whole borough—not upon the guilty ward.

S. 58 of the Act of 1883, in regard to the payment and recovery of costs, is not re-enacted in the Act of 1884, but, instead, it is provided by the latter Act, s. 32, "(1) Where any costs of a petition are, under an order of a Municipal Election Court, to be paid by a borough, such costs shall be paid out of the borough fund or borough rate. (2) Where any costs or other sums are, under the order of an Election Court or otherwise under this Act, to be paid by any person, those costs shall be a simple contract debt due from such person to the person or persons to whom they are to be paid, and if payable to the Treasury shall be a debt due to Her Majesty, and in either case may be recovered accordingly."

The amount to be paid to any witness whose expenses may be allowed by the commissioner trying the petition is to be ascertained and certified by the registrar, or if he becomes incapacitated by the commissioner. (R. 53 of the General Rules of April, 1883, under the Municipal Corporations Act, 1882, Part 4.)

The Court has power, "if for any reasonable cause it seems just," to order either of the parties to pay the costs of the Public Prosecutor attending the trial. (S. 28 (9).)

Marginal notes: Municipal. No power to saddle guilty ward with costs. Payment and recovery of costs. Expenses of witnesses to be certified.

PART II.

THE PUNISHMENT OF OFFENDERS.

THE Acts of 1883 and 1884, with a view to the more effectual repression of offences against the election laws, provide increased facilities for detecting offenders, a new machinery for their prosecution, and augmented penalties for their punishment. <small>PARLIAMENTARY & MUNICIPAL.</small>

CHAPTER I.

THEIR DETECTION AND PROSECUTION.

ONE of the most efficacious means of unearthing corruption in a constituency has been found to be the appointment of Election Commissioners, who visited the particular county or borough, and, armed with the largest powers, held an exhaustive inquiry on the spot. This procedure, however, is limited to the case of parliamentary elections and has no application as a means of detecting corrupt and illegal practices at a municipal election. Election Commissioners are appointed by the Crown under the 15th & 16th Vict., c. 57, and the 31st & 32nd Vict., c. 125, upon the joint address of both Houses of Parliament, representing that an Election Court has reported to the Speaker that corrupt practices have, or that there is reason to believe that corrupt practices have, extensively prevailed at an election for the particular county or borough in question. Under the old statutes the Commissioners when appointed were restricted to an inquiry into the existence of corrupt practices only; but now by s. 12 of the Act of 1883 they are directed to inquire into the prevalence of *illegal practices* as well as *corrupt practices*, and report to the House accordingly. <small>Inquisitorial powers of commissioners.</small>

PARLIAMENTARY & MUNICIPAL.

Having regard to the fact that the Act of 1883 creates some fifteen or sixteen new offences, which are called illegal practices, it is obvious that there is here a considerable extension of the jurisdiction of the Commissioners. The latter have the largest powers of examining witnesses on oath, compelling their attendance, and the production of books and documents; and witnesses examined before them are not entitled to the common law right of refusing to answer questions which may tend to criminate them. They are bound to answer, though, if they answer truly, they become entitled to certificates of indemnity, which will protect them against any criminal prosecution (except a prosecution for perjury). A witness's right to a certificate of indemnity is, however, entirely dependent upon his truly answering all the questions put to him, and the Commissioners are the sole judges whether or no he has done so. The Queen's Bench, upon an application for a mandamus, will not review the discretion of the Commissioners when they have refused a certificate on the ground that the witness has not given full and truthful answers. (*R.* v. *Holl*, 7 Q.B.D., 575; 50 L.J., Q.B., 45, throwing doubt upon *R.* v. *Price*, L.R. 6, Q.B. 411.) But even though a certificate has been granted, the persons who have received it may still be scheduled by the Commissioners as guilty of corrupt or illegal practices, as the case may be, and thereupon they come under the disabilities and incapacities to be presently mentioned. It is the duty of Election Commissioners to report the names of all persons who they are satisfied have been guilty of corrupt or illegal practices, and to state whether certificates of indemnity have been given to them. And by s. 60 of the Act of 1883, the reports of all Election Courts and of Election Commissioners shall be laid before the Attorney-General, "with a view to his instituting and directing a prosecution against such persons as have not received certificates of indemnity, if the evidence shall, in his opinion, be sufficient to support a prosecution."

Witnesses may be compelled to criminate themselves.

But while there is this extension of the jurisdiction of Election Commissioners as to the *class of offences* into which they may inquire, the Act of 1883 provides a remarkable limitation as to the *time* over which their inquiries may range. By the 15th & 16th Vict., c. 57, the Commissioners were directed, if they found corrupt practices at the last election, to inquire if there were any at the election before, and if they found there were, they were to investigate the election before that, and so on; but now, by s. 49 of the Act of 1883, it is provided: "Notwithstanding the provisions of the Act 15th & 16th Vict., c. 57, or any amendment thereof, in any case where after the passing of this Act any Commissioners have been appointed on a joint address of both Houses of Parliament for the purpose of making inquiry into the existence of corrupt practices at any election, the said Commissioners shall not make inquiries concerning any election that shall have taken place prior to the passing of this Act, and no witness called before such Commissioners, or at any election petition after the passing of this Act, shall be liable to be asked or bound to answer any question for the purpose of proving the commission of any corrupt practice at or in relation to any election prior to the passing of this Act, provided that nothing herein contained shall affect any proceedings that shall be pending at the time of such passing." <small>PARLIAMENTARY & MUNICIPAL. An amnesty for the past.</small>

The extended jurisdiction of Election Commissioners is, so far as parliamentary elections are concerned, one fresh means of detecting offences. Another, which is applicable alike to parliamentary and municipal elections, is the compulsory attendance at the trial of every election petition of a representative of the Director of Public Prosecutions. He attends there with two-fold functions. The one is, in proper cases, to prosecute offenders before the Election Court. The other is to protect the public interest and prevent, as the result of an arrangement between the parties or otherwise, any evidence being suppressed or withheld which may cast further light on the proceedings at the election under investigation. <small>The Director of Public Prosecutions. His functions.</small>

But, first, it should be observed that no election petition once presented can be withdrawn without the consent of <small>Withdrawal of petitions prohibited.</small>

PARLIAMENTARY & MUNICIPAL. the Court, and until the Director of Public Prosecutions has been heard in opposition to its withdrawal. Very stringent conditions in regard to this matter are contained in s. 41 of the Act of 1883, and s. 26 of the Act of 1884.

S. 43 of the Act of 1883, defines the duties of the Director of Public Prosecutions in aid of the detection of offences: "On every trial of an election petition the Director of Public Prosecutions shall by himself or by his assistant, or by such representative as hereinafter mentioned, attend at the trial, and it shall be the duty of such director to obey any directions given to him by the Election Court with respect to the summoning and examination of any witnesses to give evidence on such trial, and with respect to the prosecution by him of offenders, and with respect to any person to whom notice is given to attend with a view to reporting him as guilty of any corrupt or illegal practice." And by sub-s. 2: "It shall also be the duty of such director, without any direction from the Election Court, if it appears to him that any person is able to give material evidence as to the subject of the trial, to cause such person to attend the trial, and with the leave of the Court, to examine such person as a witness." There are exactly similar provisions in the Act of 1884, with regard to the trial of a municipal election petition (s. 28). The hearing of an election petition is, therefore, no longer a proceeding merely between the two parties, which can be brought to a conclusion when it suits their interest or convenience, but is a public investigation which can, to the extent of calling new witnesses and prosecuting offenders, be prolonged at the instance of the official attending in the public interest until either such disclosures have been made as justify the Election Court in reporting that there is reason to believe that corrupt or illegal practices extensively prevailed, or until information to found criminal proceedings has been obtained or until the Court in the exercise of its summary powers has itself administered adequate punishment.

Attendance of Director at trial of every petition.

He has power to call witnesses.

But counsel for the Public Prosecutor has in general no right to cross-examine witnesses; *Stepney Case* (4 O'M. & H., 37), where Denman, J., said: "It would be extremely inconvenient and unfair to the parties by prolonging the inquiry, if the Public Prosecutor were allowed to interfere on his own mere motion with every witness. We shall expect to have no application for leave to examine a witness made to us by the Public Prosecutor unless it is founded upon something substantial." And in the *Buckrose Case* (4 O'M. & H.), it was held that the Public Prosecutor was not entitled to address the Court upon the question whether a witness had been guilty of an illegal practice unless he was in a position to actually prosecute such witness before the Court. [Parliamentary & Municipal.]

Coming next to the machinery for the prosecution of offenders, it must be observed that the right of a private prosecutor to institute proceedings is in no way interfered with. Indeed ss. 10, 12 & 13 of the 17 & 18 Vict., c. 102—which in the case of private prosecutions for corrupt practices give the Court power: (1) when the prosecutor has duly entered into the recognizances mentioned in the s. 13 to order the defendant, if convicted, to pay him the costs and expenses to which he has been put, and which (2) direct that the defendant shall have his costs from the prosecutor when he is acquitted—are expressly extended to any private prosecution for the offence of a *corrupt practice* within the meaning of the new Acts (s. 53 of the Act of 1883, and s. 30 of the Act of 1884.) [Private prosecutions still permissible.]

It is, however, contemplated that, as a rule, prosecutions will be instituted by the order of the Attorney-General, or by the Director of Public Prosecutions. S. 60 of the Act of 1883, which directs that all reports of Election Courts and Election Commissioners shall be submitted to the Attorney-General, with a view to his directing prosecutions, has already been mentioned. The duties cast upon the Director as Director of Public Prosecutions are, however, more specific and onerous. And first, by s. 45 of the Act of 1883 (made applicable to municipal elections by s. 30 of the Act of 1884), "When information is given to the Director of Public Prosecutions that any corrupt or illegal practices have prevailed in reference to any election, it shall be his duty, [Prosecutions generally by order of (a) Attorney-General, or (b) Director of Public Prosecutions.]

subject to the regulations under the Prosecution of Offences Act, 1879, to make such inquiries and institute such prosecutions as the circumstances of the case appear to him to require," and later sections provide that the costs and charges to which the Director of Public Prosecutions is put in connection with the prosecution of offenders against the election laws shall be provided in the same manner as the funds for the prosecution of felonies are provided.

But he should not wait for information. He has to seek it, and as we have seen already, his duty is to attend in person, or by his deputy, every Election Court. He is bound to obey any instructions given him by the Election Court with respect to the prosecution by him of offenders (s. 43 of the Act of 1838, and s. 28 of the Act of 1844), and not only so but by sub-s. 3 of the same sections it is enacted in almost identical words " It shall also be the duty of the said Director, *without any direction from the Election Court*, if it appears to him that any person who has not received a certificate of indemnity has been guilty of a corrupt or illegal practice, to prosecute such person for the offence before the said Court, or if he thinks it expedient in the interests of justice before any other competent Court." (See the *Ipswich Case*, 4 O'M. & H. 75).

CHAPTER II.

THEIR PUNISHMENT.

THE tribunals which have jurisdiction to inquire into corrupt and illegal practices, and to inflict penalties of a varying character upon offenders, are as follows :— PARLIAMENTARY
& MUNICIPAL.

1. Election Commissioners.
2. The Election Court.
3. A Court of Summary Jurisdiction.
4. The Court of Assize, or where the indictment is removed by *certiorari*, the Central Criminal Court, or the Queen's Bench Division of the High Court of Justice; and
5. The High Court of Justice or the County Court, in suits for penalties.

Courts which
may punish.

It is proposed to consider what offences fall under the cognizance of each of these tribunals and the extent and kind of punishment which may be inflicted.

SECTION I.—ELECTION COMMISSIONERS.

An Election Commission, which, as before explained, is only issued to inquire into corrupt or illegal practices at a *Parliamentary* election, is constituted of three members. The Commissioners must be barristers of at least seven years' standing, "not being members of Parliament, or holding any office or place of profit under the Crown, other than that of a recorder of any city or borough." (15 & 16 Vict., c. 57, s. 1.) PARLIAMENTARY

Election Commissioners have no power to impose either fine or imprisonment upon any person who is shown to them to have committed an offence at an election. Their power is confined to reporting that he has been guilty of the particular The effect of
the report of
Commis-
sioners.

corrupt or illegal practice in question, and *then by virtue of their report*, certain disabilities attach to him. S. 38 (5) of the Act of 1883, says:—" Every person who, after the commencement of this Act is reported by any Election Court, or *Election Commissioners* to have been guilty of any corrupt or illegal practice, shall, whether he obtain a certificate of indemnity or not, be subject to the same *incapacity* as he would under the Act be subject to, if he had at the date of the report been convicted of the offence of which he is reported to have been guilty." This section at once raises the question —What are the incapacities imposed upon a person by a conviction of either a corrupt or an illegal practice?

<small>PARLIAMENTARY</small>

<small>The incapacities imposed by it.</small>

First, in the case of *corrupt practices*, by s. 6 (3) a person convicted on indictment of any *corrupt practice* is incapacitated for a period of *seven years* from

<small>(1.) May not vote at any election.</small>

(*a.*) Being registered as an elector, or voting at any election in the United Kingdom, whether it be a parliamentary election or an election for any public office.

<small>(2.) Nor hold office.</small>

(*b.*) Holding any public or judicial office, and if he holds any such office the office shall be vacated.

<small>(3.) Nor sit in House of Commons for seven years.</small>

(*c.*) Being elected to or of sitting in the House of Commons during the seven years next after his conviction: and if at that date he has been elected, his election shall be vacated from the time of such conviction.

In addition to these incapacities, which result from the *mere report* of Election Commissioners, s. 38, sub-ss. 6, 7, 8 and 9, provide for other measures of severity against the particular classes of persons mentioned in them when they are reported for any *corrupt practice*. (1.) If the person reported is a justice of the peace, " whether he has obtained a certificate of indemnity or not," it is the duty of the Director of Public Prosecutions to report the case to the Lord Chancellor, with such evidence as may have been given of his guilt, and the Lord Chancellor, if he thinks fit, may remove him from the bench. (2.) If the person reported is a barrister or a solicitor, or belongs to any profession the admission

<small>(4.) Special severities against—</small>

<small>(1.) Justices of the peace.</small>

<small>(2.) Barristers and solicitors.</small>

to which is regulated by law, "whether such person has obtained a certificate of indemnity or not," the Director of Public Prosecutions must bring the matter before the Inn of Court, High Court or tribunal having power to take cognizance of any misconduct of such person in his profession, and "such Inn of Court, High Court, or tribunal may deal with such person in like manner as if such corrupt practice were misconduct by such person in his profession." It would seem that the words "who belongs to any profession the admission to which is regulated by law," bring medical practitioners (the 21 & 22 Vict., c. 56), dentists (the 41 & 42 Vict., c. 33) and persons in the army, navy, and civil service, within the operation of the section. It is probable, also, that it applies to the case of clergymen of the Churches of England and of Scotland, the admission to whose respective professions is regulated by the ecclesiastical law. (3.) If the person reported holds a license or certificate under the Licensing Acts, and the particular corrupt practice for which he is reported is having "knowingly suffered any bribery or treating in reference to any election to take place upon his licensed premises," then, whether such person obtains a certificate of indemnity or not, it shall be the duty of the Director of Public Prosecutions to bring the report of the Commissioners before the licensing justices. The justices are bound to enter the report in the proper register of licenses, and they may, if they like, refuse to renew his license in consequence.

{PARLIAMENTARY}

{(3.) It is submitted also against doctors, dentists and clergymen.}

{Severities against licensed persons.}

{May lose their licenses.}

Secondly, in the case of *illegal practices*, the consequences which result from being reported by Election Commissioners are not so serious, though they are serious enough. Section 10 provides that "a person guilty of an illegal practice shall, on summary conviction, be liable to a fine not exceeding one hundred pounds, and be incapable during a *period of five years from the date of his conviction*, of being registered as an elector or voting at any election (whether it be a parliamentary election or an election for a public office within the meaning of the Act), held for or within the county or borough in which the illegal practice has been

PARLIAMENTARY committed." Therefore, the effect upon a person of being scheduled for illegal practices is that for the next *five years* he is disqualified from being registered or voting—not generally, but *in the county or borough in which he has offended*.

Effect of being reported for illegal practices.

It has been said that all these incapacities result from the mere report of Election Commissioners or of the Election Court. They are in every case of a stringent, and in some cases of a ruinous character; and, therefore, it is important to see what precautions are taken to prevent the great injustice of the Commissioners reporting innocent persons.

Person heard in his defence before reported.

S. 38 (1) of the Act of 1883, so far as it is material to the action of Election Commissioners, provides—"Before any person is reported by Election Commissioners to have been guilty at an election of any corrupt or illegal practice . . . . the Commissioners . . . shall cause notice to be given to such person, and, if he appears in pursuance of the notice, shall give him an opportunity of being heard *by himself*, and of calling evidence in his defence to show why he should not be so reported." In *R*. v. *Mansel-Jones* (23 Q.B. Div. 29), the Court held that these words must be taken strictly, and that a person charged must make his defence in person, and cannot appear either by counsel or solicitor.

An appeal given.

The decision of the Commissioners is not final, for by sub-s. 2 of s. 38, every person reported by *Election Commissioners* to have been guilty at an election of any corrupt or illegal practice, may appeal against such report to the next court of oyer and terminer, or gaol delivery, that is, to the next assizes, in and for the county or place in which the offence is alleged to have been committed. The section contemplates the framing of rules to regulate the procedure incident to such appeals. But subject to such rules the section proceeds: Such appeal may be brought, heard and determined in like manner as if the Court were a court of quarter sessions, and the said commissioners were a court of summary jurisdiction, and the person so reported had been convicted by a court of summary jurisdiction for an offence under this Act." Notice of the appeal, which must be in writing, is to be given to the Director of Public Prosecutions within a time to be directed by rules of court, and subject to such rules then within three days after the appeal is brought. There is a provision that if the trial of appeals under s. 38 appears to the Lord Chancellor to be likely to interfere with the ordinary business of the assizes, he may direct that they shall be heard by the judges on the rota for the trial of election petitions, and one of such judges shall then proceed to the place in which the offences are alleged to have been committed, and hear and determine the appeals. It is presumed that the appeals will be heard by a single judge without a jury, that counsel representing the Director of Public Prosecutions will support the report, and that the appellant will appear in person, or by counsel. The appeal will be in the nature of a re-hearing, and the Court will decide whether the report of the Commissioners is to be affirmed, or varied, or disallowed. Parliamentary

Appeal against report of Commissioners.

Section II.—The Election Court.

Sub-Section I.—In the case of a Parliamentary Election.

The Election Court consists of two judges of the Queen's Bench Division, selected from the rota of judges appointed every year to try election petitions. The primary object with which the Election Court sits, is to try a petition; but in addition to this duty, it is now bound to report to the Speaker (*a*) whether any corrupt practice or illegal practice has or has not been proved to have been committed by or with the knowledge and consent of any candidate at such election, and the nature of such corrupt or illegal practice; (*b*) the names of all persons, if any, who have been proved at the trial to have been guilty of any corrupt or illegal practice; and (*c*) whether corrupt or illegal practices have, or whether there is reason to believe, corrupt or illegal What the Election Court must report to the Speaker.

Parliamentary practices have extensively prevailed at the election to which the petition relates. (S. 11 of the Act of 1883.)

That is one duty cast upon the Election Court, in addition to the trial of the petition. Another duty is, subject to the important limitation on this jurisdiction to be presently stated, summarily to try all such persons as may be charged before it by the Director of Public Prosecutions with any corrupt or illegal practice committed at the election.

The effect of the report.

The effect of the report of the Election Court must be considered first, as it affects the candidate, and secondly, as it affects other persons. The incapacities imposed upon a candidate by the report differ materially, according as he is declared to have committed a corrupt practice personally, or by his agent, or an illegal practice personally or by his agent. These must be carefully distinguished.

(a) When candidate guilty of corrupt practice.

(A.) If the Election Court report that any *corrupt* practice (other than treating or undue influence) has been committed with reference to such election *by* or *with the knowledge* and *consent of any* candidate (whether the successful or the unsuccessful candidate at such election, or that the offence of treating or undue influence has been committed *by* any candidate, then such candidate, in addition to being unseated, is declared incapable (*a*) of *ever* sitting in the House of Commons for the said county or borough; (*b*) of sitting in the House of Commons for *any constituency* for the next seven years; (*c*) of being registered as an elector or voting at *any election* in the United Kingdom (whether a parliamentary election or any election for any public office) during a period of seven years; (*d*) of holding any public or judicial office for seven years; and (*e*) if he happens to be a justice of the peace, or a licensed person, or belongs to any one of the professions mentioned in s. 38, his misconduct is ordered to be brought by the Director of Public Prosecutions under the cognizance of the Lord Chancellor, or the licensing justices, or any tribunal connected with his profession that takes notice of professional misconduct.

(b) When candidate by

(B.) On the other hand, the Election Court may merely

report that a candidate has been guilty, by *his agents*, of a corrupt practice. In that case, in addition to losing his seat, if he has been elected, he is incapable for the next *seven years* of sitting in the House of Commons for *the county or borough in which the offence was committed.* {*Parliamentary his agent guilty of corrupt practice.*}

(C.) The third possible report which the Election Court may make, is that some *illegal practice* has been committed *by* or *with* the knowledge and consent of the candidate. In that case the candidate, besides losing his seat, if he has been elected, is (*a*) incapacitated from sitting in the House of Commons for the county or borough in which the offence was committed for the next *seven* years; and (*b*) is rendered incapable for the next five years of being registered as an elector, and voting at any election (whether a parliamentary election or an election to any public office) held for the county or borough in which the offence was committed. {*(c) When candidate guilty of illegal practice.*}

(D.) If, as the fourth alternative, the report is that the candidate *by any agent* has been guilty of an illegal practice, the seat is avoided if he fills it, and he is declared incapable of being elected for the same place during *the Parliament for which the election was held.* {*(d) When candidate guilty by agent of illegal practice.*}

The Election Court also reports the names of all other persons who have been guilty of corrupt or illegal practices. The disabilities which such report imposes upon those persons are exactly the same as those imposed by the report of Election Commissioners. They have been set out in detail at page 234, and it is unnecessary to repeat them here. {*Effect of report of Election Court upon other persons.*}

Before an Election Court reports any person as guilty of a corrupt or illegal practice, it is bound by s. 38 of the Act of 1883, to cause notice to be given to such person, and if he appears in pursuance of such notice, he shall have an opportunity of being heard by himself, and of calling evidence in his defence to show why he should not be reported. {*Persons to be heard before reported.*}

In the *Ipswich Case* (referrred to in the argument in *R.* v. *Mansel-Jones,* 23 Q.B. Div., 30), the Court allowed a

PARLIAMENTARY person charged with bribery to appear by counsel; but *quære*, since the judgment of the Queen's Bench in *R.* v. *Mansel-Jones* (*supra*), whether that was right. In the latter case Lord Coleridge, C.J., said, "With great deference to the opinion of the judges who tried the Ipswich election petition, I doubt whether there is any reason for construing the words ' by himself,' occurring in the Act of 1883, with any greater laxity than I construe them in the Act of 1884. The Act of 1883 expressly gives a person reported by Election Commissioners a right of appeal to the next Court of oyer and terminer or gaol delivery held for the county or place in which the offence is alleged to have been committed. Where summary proceedings are taken, the person accused may appear in any way he pleases. It seems to me tolerably clear that, in the case of parliamentary election petitions, the proceedings before the Commissioners is merely initiatory to doing something further, and that the Legislature meant in the Act of 1883 what it has said, namely, that the person accused, and the person accused only, shall be heard on such a proceeding. Parliament must be taken to have had in view the extreme inconvenience, in the initiatory process of determining whether three or four hundred people should be scheduled, of hearing counsel or solicitor for each person."

Power of the Election Court to try offenders.
The other jurisdiction which the Election Court has, is the summary trial of persons charged with corrupt or illegal practices. (S. 43 (4).) The Director of Public Prosecutions, or his representative, has a discretion whether a person charged with corrupt or illegal practices shall be tried before the Election Court, or by some other competent Court. And the Election Court itself has a discretion whether it will deal with the case summarily, or commit the accused for trial. Where illegal practices, illegal hirings, employments or payments merely are charged, the defendant has no right of trial by jury, and if the prosecution elects to proceed before the Election Court, and the latter determines to hear the case he has no means of preventing its being disposed of summarily. On the other hand where the

charge is one of corrupt practices he is entitled to a trial {Parliamentary} by a jury, and if he insists upon his right the Court can only commit him for trial. (S. 43 (4).) In determining whether he will prefer a charge of corrupt practices before an Election Court, the Director of Public Prosecutions will take this right of the defendant into consideration, and also bear in mind that in the event of the defendant consenting to the case proceeding and a conviction following, the Election Court cannot impose so heavy a sentence as the Court upon the trial of an indictment or information.

If, however, the charge is preferred before the Election Court, "the Summary Jurisdiction Acts shall, so far as is consistent with the tenor thereof, apply to the prosecution of an offence summarily before an Election Court in like manner as if it were an offence punishable only on summary conviction, and accordingly the attendance of any person may be enforced, the case heard and determined, and any summary conviction by such Court be carried into effect and enforced, and the costs thereof paid, and the record thereof dealt with under those Acts in like manner as if the Court were a petty sessional court for the county or place in which such conviction took place" (s. 55 of the Act of 1883). The effect of this is that the procedure on the trial of an offence before the Election Court is assimilated to the procedure in petty sessions. The accused is present, and is entitled to call, examine, or cross-examine witnesses either by himself or his counsel or solicitor, and to address the Court by himself or by his counsel or solicitor. {Application of Summary Jurisdiction Acts.}

There is no jury upon a trial before an Election Court. The Court is the judge of the law and facts, and if it finds the charge proven it will proceed to pass sentence. Its powers, however, in this respect are strictly limited.

Upon conviction for a *corrupt practice* it may impose a sentence of fine or imprisonment—the fine not to exceed £200, and the imprisonment not to be for a longer term than six months, *with* or without hard labour. There is no power to imprison for an *illegal practice*, but a fine of £100 may be inflicted. In addition, the effect of the conviction {Punishments by the Election Court.}

PARLIAMENTARY is to impose upon the person convicted all those incapacities and disabilities which result from the report of Election Commissioners, which have already been stated.

The Election Court, as well as the High Court, has power under s. 34 (2) to impose a fine not exceeding £500 upon any election agent who makes default in complying with an order directing him to deliver a statement of the particulars required to be contained in the returns and declarations of election expenses, or otherwise to do his duty in regard to the return of expenses.

Saddling guilty constituency or individual with costs.

Another punitive jurisdiction vested in the Election Court consists in its power of saddling a constituency or an individual, other than the parties to the petition, with the costs occasioned by it. S. 44 (1) enacts that when it appears to the Court that no corrupt practice has been committed by or with the knowledge and consent of the respondent to the petition, and that he took reasonable means to prevent corrupt practices being committed on his behalf, and if it further appears that *corrupt practices* extensively prevailed in reference to the election, the Court may order the whole or part of the costs to be paid by the county or borough, or if it appears that any person or persons extensively engaged in or encouraged *corrupt practices*, the Court may order such person or persons to pay the whole or part of the costs. By sub-s. 2 of the same section, if it appears that any person has been guilty of the offence of a *corrupt* or *illegal practice*, the Court may order " the whole or any part of the costs of or incidental to any proceedings before the Court in relation to the said offence, or to the said person, to be paid by the said person." Before any order is made under the last sub-s., the person against whom the order is made must have an opportunity of making a statement ; but before an order is made under the 1st sub-s. the Court must " give the inculpated person " an opportunity of being heard by counsel or solicitor, and examining and cross-examining witnesses, to show cause why the order should not be made." (S. 44 (1).)

The Election Court may

But, though the Election Court has absolute jurisdiction

to summarily try any person charged with illegal practices and a qualified jurisdiction to try persons charged with corrupt practices, we have already stated it is not bound to summarily determine any case brought before it. It may direct that the accused shall be prosecuted on indictment, or before a court of summary jurisdiction, and it may commit him for trial. Accordingly (s. 43, sub-s. 5), in such a case, the Court makes an order, naming the tribunal before which the accused is to be tried; and steps must forthwith be taken to bring him before such tribunal. If the offence is an indictable one, and the accused is present before the Election Court, the latter may at once commit him into custody to await his trial, or hold him to bail. If it is only an offence punishable on summary conviction, the Court may hold him to bail, or order him to be taken before the Court of Summary Jurisdiction before which he is to be tried. On the other hand, if the accused is not present, the Election Court may issue a warrant for his apprehension, or, in its discretion, a summons directing him to appear before a Court of Summary Jurisdiction. PARLIAMENTARY commit for trial.

Sub-section II.—In the Case of a Municipal Election.

The Election Court consists of a Commissioner selected from the rota of barristers appointed by the Election Judges to try municipal election petitions, sitting without a jury. (S. 36 of the Act of 1884.) He must be of fifteen years' standing at the Bar, and must not be a member of the House of Commons, or hold any office or place of profit under the Crown other than that of recorder. Further, he is incapable of constituting an Election Court in any borough of which he is recorder, or in which he resides, or which is included in the circuit upon which he practises. (S. 92 of the Municipal Corporations Act, 1882.) Municipal. Election Court, how constituted.

The primary object with which the Municipal Election Court sits is to determine the validity of the election; but, in addition, it is bound to report to the High Court all those particulars with regard to the existence of corrupt and Duties of the Court.

MUNICIPAL. illegal practices at the election in question, their nature, and the persons guilty of them, which a Court for the trial of a parliamentary petition must report to the Speaker of the House of Commons, and in the next place, it has the same power of trying persons charged with corrupt and illegal practices and offences against the election laws.

Effect of report by the Court.
The effect of the report of the election Court differs according to the position of the person reported, and the offence for which he is reported.

(A.) If the Election Court reports that any corrupt practice (other than treating or undue influence) has been committed with reference to such election by or with the knowledge and consent of any candidate, or that the offence of treating or undue influence has been proved to have been committed in reference to such election by any candidate at such election, then such candidate is declared (1) incapable of ever holding a corporate office in the said borough, and (2) he becomes subject to the same incapacities as if at the date of the report he had been convicted of a corrupt practice. (S. 3 (1) of Act of 1884.) By s. 2 (2) of the same Act "a person who commits any corrupt practice in reference to a municipal election shall be guilty of the like offence, and shall, on conviction, be liable to the like punishment, and *subject to the like incapacities*, as if the corrupt practice had been committed in reference to a parliamentary election." The effect of this section is to impose upon a candidate at a municipal election as the result of the report of an Election Court all the incapacities and disabilities set out.

(B.) If the report of the Court is that the candidate *by his agent* has been guilty of a corrupt practice, in addition to losing his seat, if he has been elected, he becomes incapable of being elected to or holding any corporate office in the said borough for *three years*. (S. 3 (2) of the Act of 1884.)

(C.) If the report of the Court is that the candidate has himself been guilty of any illegal practice at the election, he becomes (1) incapable of being elected to or holding any corporate office in the said borough during the period for which he was elected to serve, or for which, if elected, he

CORRUPT PRACTICES AT ELECTIONS. 245

might have served, and (2) incapable during a period of five years of being registered as an elector or voting at any election (whether it be a parliamentary election or an election for a public office within the meaning of the Act) held for or within the borough in which the illegal practice was committed. (Ss. 8 (2) and 7 of the Act of 1884.)

Municipal.

(D.) If the report is that the candidate by any agent has been guilty of any illegal practice, he becomes incapable of being elected to or holding any corporate office in the said borough, during the period for which he was elected to serve, or for which, if elected, he might have served.

Effect of report by the Court.

(E.) If, finally, the report is that illegal practices, or the offences of illegal payment, employment, or hiring have so extensively prevailed that they may be reasonably supposed to have affected the result of the election, he becomes incapable of being elected to or holding any corporate office in the said borough during the period for which he was elected to serve, or for which, if elected, he might have served. (S. 18 of the Act of 1884.)

The Election Court also reports the names of all persons other than the candidates guilty of corrupt or illegal practices, and by virtue of such report they come under the incapacities mentioned already. But before any person is reported he is entitled to an opportunity of being heard and of calling witnesses in his defence—(S. 23 of the Act of 1884, and s. 38 of the Act of 1883); though in *Preece* v. *Harding* (24 Q.B. Div., 110; 59 L.J., Q.B., 82) it was held that where, after the trial of a petition, the commissioner has reported persons as guilty of corrupt practices the Queen's Bench has no power to set aside or amend his report on the ground that the notices provided by the Act had not been given to the person so reported. And generally it must be taken that there is no appeal to the Queen's Bench from the Commissioner except upon any point of law which he may in his discretion state for the opinion of the Court. (*Ex.p. Ayres*, 54 L.T., n.s., 296.)

The jurisdiction of a Municipal Election Court to summarily try persons charged before it with corrupt and

Jurisdiction of the Court.

MUNICIPAL. illegal practices at the election under inquiry, and the punishments which may be imposed, are exactly the same as in the case of a Parliamentary Election Court. The Director of Public Prosecutions or his representative attends the Court, and it is in his discretion whether to proceed against offenders forthwith or upon indictment. The Court has to exercise a further discretion as to whether it will summarily dispose of each or any of the cases or commit for trial, and where a corrupt practice is charged the accused is entitled to a trial by jury. (S. 28 of the Act of 1884. And see *R.* v. *Shellard*, 23 Q.B. Div. 273, where it was held that the Commissioner before committing or issuing a summons was not required to hear all the evidence relating to the particular offender over again.)

A Commissioner may commit to the Assizes of an adjoining county, and his order is sufficient without describing the particular corrupt practice. (*R.* v. *Riley*, 59 L.J., M.C. 122.)

Generally with regard to the summary trial, punishment, commitment for trial or apprehension of offenders, the powers of a Municipal Election Court are, by the Act of 1884, assimilated to those of a Parliamentary Election Court, and by s. 29 of that Act, following s. 44 of the Act of 1883, the Court can order the borough, or individuals, other than the parties to petition, to pay the costs of the petition, or some part thereof.

SECTION III.—THE COURT OF SUMMARY JURISDICTION.

PARLIAMENTARY & MUNICIPAL.

Powers of a Court of Summary Jurisdiction.

A Court of Summary Jurisdiction within the meaning of the Acts of 1883 and 1884 is constituted of any two justices of the peace sitting in Petty Sessions, or in the Metropolitan district, or in districts to which stipendiary magistrates have been appointed, of a stipendiary magistrate. Its functions in regard to offences against the election laws are twofold, viz., to commit accused persons to take their trial where the offence is an indictable one, or, where it is an offence punishable on summary conviction, to hear and dispose of it.

CORRUPT PRACTICES AT ELECTIONS.   247

With regard to *indictable* offences, where the Election Court has issued its warrant or summons directing the accused to be taken before a Court of Summary Jurisdiction, the proceedings before the latter are purely formal. "That Court (*i.e.*, Court of Summary Jurisdiction), if the offence is an indictable offence, shall, on proof only of the summons or warrant and the identity of the accused, commit him to take his trial, or cause him to give bail to appear and take his trial" (S. 43, sub-s. 6 (*c*), of the Act of 1883, and s. 28, sub-s. 6 (*c*), of the Act of 1884; *R.* v. *Shellard*, 23 Q.B. Div. 273.) In other cases, where an indictable offence is charged against any person, and he is brought before a Court of Summary Jurisdiction in order that he may be committed for trial, it is presumed the procedure will be the same as in the common case of a charge made of an indictable offence before justices in petty sessions, with a view to the commitment of the prisoner. A summons or warrant will be issued by the justices in the first instance, the depositions of witnesses will be taken and signed, the prisoner by himself, his counsel or solicitor, will have the usual facilities for cross-examining, calling evidence, and addressing the Court, and if the justices are of opinion that there is a *primâ facie* case, they will commit him for trial, either remanding him into custody or admitting him to bail.

The Acts of 1883 and 1884, however, contemplate that a Court of Summary Jurisdiction will itself hear and finally dispose of a considerable number of the offences created by them. Before we mention the classes of offences over which this Court has complete jurisdiction, it should be observed that all charges under any of the Corrupt Practices Prevention Acts must be made within a certain limit of time. If that time is allowed to go by and no prosecution instituted, it is too late after that to prefer a charge; and this rule applies as much to any proceeding on indictment as to a summary proceeding before the Election Court or Justices. The limitation of time is given in s. 51 of the Act of 1883 (incorporated into the Act of 1884 by s. 30 of the latter). It enacts "A proceeding against a person in respect

PARLIAMENTARY & MUNICIPAL. of the offence of a corrupt or illegal practice or any other offence, under the Corrupt Practices Prevention Acts, or this Act, shall be commenced within *one year* after the offence was committed, or if it was committed in reference to an election, with respect to which an inquiry is held by election commissioners it shall be commenced within one year after the offence was committed, or *within three months after the report of such commissioners* is made, whichever last happens, so that it shall be commenced *within two years after the offence was committed.*" The *issue* of a summons, warrant, writ, or other process, shall be deemed to be the commencement of a proceeding within the meaning of the above section, where service or execution of the same on or against the alleged offender is prevented by his absconding or concealing himself, or by any other act on his part, and in other cases the *service* of the writ, &c., is the commencement of the proceedings.

Offences with which Court of Summary Jurisdiction must deal.
(1.) Illegal practices.

The offences at parliamentary or municipal elections with which a Court of Summary Jurisdiction must deal, are:—

I. All *illegal practices*, whether committed by the candidate, his election agent, or any other person. There is no power of imprisonment upon conviction of any illegal practice, but a fine not exceeding £100 can be imposed, and there results from the fact of conviction, or from the fact of being reported by an Election Court or Election Commissioners, an incapacity to be registered as an elector, or of voting for the next five years in the county or borough in which the offence was committed. (S. 10 of the Act of 1883, and s. 7 of the Act of 1884.)

(2.) Illegal payments, &c.

II. All illegal payments, hirings and employments. These offences, it has already been explained, become illegal practices when committed by the candidate or his election agent, and they must be dealt with by the Court accordingly; but committed by other persons they are something less than illegal practices, and subject those guilty of them to a somewhat less punishment. There is no power of imprisonment, but a fine of £100 may be imposed. (S. 21 (1) of the Act of 1883, and s. 17 of the Act of 1884.) No incapacity, however, results from conviction of an illegal payment, hiring or employment. <small>Parliamentary & Municipal.</small>

III. By s. 18 of the Act of 1883, and s. 14 of the Act of 1884, it is provided that every bill, placard or poster issued in reference to the election shall bear upon the face thereof the name and address of the printer and publisher thereof. If a candidate, or his election agent, is guilty of a breach of this enactment he commits an illegal practice. Any other person infringing it is not guilty of an illegal practice, nor does the offence which he commits receive any particular denomination, but he "shall be liable on summary conviction to a fine not exceeding £100." (See *Bettesworth* v. *Allingham*, 16 Q.B. Div., 44.) <small>(3.) Publishing bills, &c., without printer's name.</small>

In order to get rid as much as possible of technical objection to the form of the charge, and to the necessary evidence of the holding of the election at which the offence was committed, it is provided by s. 53 (3) of the Act of 1883 (applied to municipal elections by s. 30 of the Act of 1884) that it shall be sufficient to allege that the person charged was guilty of an illegal practice, payment, employment or hiring, as the case may be, and the certificate of the returning officer at an election that the election mentioned in the certificate was duly held, and that the person named in the certificate was a candidate at such election shall be sufficient evidence of the facts therein stated. The accused or the husband or wife of such person, may give evidence in the case. (S. 53 (2).) And there is a provision that if, upon hearing the evidence, the Court is satisfied that, though an illegal practice merely is charged, in fact a corrupt practice has been committed, the accused may still be convicted of the former; and so where an illegal payment, hiring or employment is charged, and a corrupt or illegal practice is proved, there may still be a conviction for the offence charged. <small>Rules as to procedure.</small>

Before a Court of Summary Jurisdiction the defendant has, of course, no right to a trial by jury. If, however, a person is *convicted*, a right of appeal to Quarter Sessions is given him. "A person aggrieved by a conviction by a <small>Appeal to Quarter Sessions.</small>

Court of Summary Jurisdiction for an offence under this Act may appeal to Quarter Sessions against such conviction." (S. 54 (2) of the Act of 1883, and s. 30 of the Act of 1884.) Where the summary conviction has been made in a city or borough which has an independent Court of Quarter Sessions, the appeal will go there and be heard by the recorder; when it is made anywhere else it will go to the County Quarter Sessions.

It is presumed that the procedure as to the time within which the appeal must be brought, the notices to be given and so forth, will be the same as in the case of an ordinary appeal to sessions from a summary conviction. The appeal will be in the nature of a re-hearing, and the Quarter Sessions will have power to quash the conviction or affirm or vary it. There is no appeal beyond the Quarter Sessions, but the latter has power, in the exercise of its discretion, when any difficult question of law arises, to state a case for the opinion of the Queen's Bench Division.

Parliamentary & Municipal.

SECTION IV.—THE COURT OF ASSIZE.

All offences whatever committed at a parliamentary or municipal election, punishable by indictment, will, in the ordinary course, be tried at the next Assizes for the county in which they were committed (but see *R.* v. *Riley*, 59, L.J., M.C., 112, as to the power to order a prosecution elsewhere) unless the Election Court deals with them summarily, or unless, in the case of misdemeanours, the Attorney-General files an information in the Queen's Bench Division of the High Court of Justice. The Quarter Sessions has no jurisdiction at all in regard to *indictable* offences. There is, however, power of changing the venue and removing the trial either to the Central Criminal Court, or, when a special jury is ordered, into the Queen's Bench Division. (S. 50 of the Act of 1883.)

Where indictable offences tried.

Venue may be changed.

The limitation with regard to the time within which

proceedings must be taken, the provisions as to the form of the charge, the proof of the holding of the election, and the right of a defendant, or his wife or her husband to give evidence, apply to a trial on indictment or on information as much as to trial before a Court of Summary Jurisdiction, and it is also provided that if, on an indictment for a corrupt practice, it is proved that an illegal practice only was committed, the defendant shall be acquitted of the former, but may be convicted of the latter. (S. 52 of the Act of 1883.) In *R.* v. *Stroulger* (17 Q.B. Div. 327; 53 L.J., M.C., 137) upon an indictment for corrupt practices, it was held necessary to specify the particular corrupt practice with which the accused was charged. Parliamentary & Municipal.

All corrupt practices within the meaning of the Acts of 1883 and 1884, are indictable offences. The punishment is the same in the case of parliamentary and municipal elections, though it varies with reference to the offence charged. All corrupt practices indictable.

I. Any candidate or his election agent who makes a false declaration as to the election expenses is by s. 33 of the Act of 1883 and s. 21 of the Act of 1884, declared guilty of a corrupt practice, and upon indictment, is liable to the same penalty as if he were convicted of *wilful and corrupt perjury*. The maximum penalty for perjury is *seven years' penal servitude*. Therefore, the Court has power to sentence a candidate or his election agent, who knowingly makes a false declaration, to such a term of penal servitude. False declaration

II. "A person who commits the offence of personation or of aiding, abetting, counselling, or procuring the commission of that offence, shall be guilty of *felony*, and any person convicted thereof, on indictment, shall be punished by imprisonment for a term not exceeding two years, *together with hard labour.*" (S. 6 (2) of the Act of 1883 and 2 (2) of the Act of 1884.) The Court has no power to impose a fine for this offence. Upon conviction the punishment is imprisonment, and such imprisonment *must* be accompanied by hard labour. Personation.

III. "A person who commits any corrupt practice other Bribery, than personation, or aiding, abetting, counselling or procuring the commission of the offence of personation, shall be guilty of a misdemeanour, and on conviction, or indictment, shall be liable to be imprisoned, *with or without hard labour*, for a term not exceeding one year, or to be fined any sum not exceeding £200." (S. 6 (1) of the Act of 1883 and s. 2 (2) of the Act of 1884.) The corrupt practices which come under this sub-section are bribery, treating and undue influence. It will be observed, that the penalty is appreciably less stringent than in the case of the other corrupt practices, viz., personation and a false declaration. There is a power to impose a fine instead of imprisonment, and where imprisonment is inflicted it is in the discretion of the Court whether it shall be with or without hard labour.

IV. By s. 41 (4) of the Act of 1883 and s. 26 (4) of the Act of 1884, if any person makes any agreement or terms, or enters into any undertaking in relation to the withdrawal of an election petition and such agreement, terms or undertaking is, or are, for the withdrawal of an election petition in consideration of any payment, or in consideration that the seat shall at any time be vacated or in consideration of the withdrawal of any other election petition, he shall be guilty of a misdemeanour and shall be liable on conviction on indictment to imprisonment for a term not exceeding 12 months and to a fine not exceeding £200.

V. By the 30 & 31 Vict., c. 102, s. 50, "No returning officer for any borough or county, nor his deputy nor any partner or clerk of either of them, shall act as agent for any candidate in the management or conduct of his election as a member to serve in Parliament for such county or borough; and if any returning officer, his deputy, the partner or clerk of either of them, shall so act, he shall be guilty of a misdemeanour," and as a misdemeanant he will be liable upon indictment to fine or imprisonment.

It should be added, that in addition to suffering a term of imprisonment or a fine, any person convicted of a corrupt practice comes under all the incapacities and disabilities, which have been already set out, and it may be repeated here, that though a person who has obtained a certificate of indemnity may not be proceeded against criminally in any court in respect of any corrupt or illegal practice, he is still liable to all the disabilities mentioned.

There is no appeal against a conviction upon indictment tried at the Assizes or the Central Criminal Court, though the judge may reserve any question of law for the opinion of the Court for Crown Cases Reserved. On the other hand, if the case has been tried in the Queen's Bench Division, and the offence charged is only a *misdemeanour*, a new trial may be granted on the ground of misdirection, or improper admission, or rejection of evidence, or verdict against the weight of evidence, or, indeed, on any of the grounds upon which in a civil cause a new trial can be obtained. (See *Archbold's Criminal Evidence and Pleading*.)

In the common case, however, of a trial at the Assizes or the Central Criminal Court, the verdict of the jury is final, and, should the innocence of a person convicted be afterwards established, the only appeal is to the clemency of the Crown which may pardon the offence and remit any portion of the punishment still to be endured.

With respect, however, to the incapacities which are nominally no part of the punishment of the offence, but result from the fact of the conviction, a person may apply to the High Court to have them removed. S. 46 of the Act of 1883 is as follows:—" Where a person has either before or after the commencement of this Act become subject to any incapacity under the Corrupt Practices Prevention Acts or this Act, by reason of a conviction or of a report of any election court or election commissioners, and any witness who gave evidence against such incapacitated person upon the proceeding for such conviction or report is convicted of perjury in respect of that evidence, the incapacitated person may apply to the High Court, and the Court, if satisfied that the conviction or report, so far as respects such person, was based upon perjury, may order that such incapacity shall thenceforth

PARLIAMENTARY & MUNICIPAL.

cease and the same shall cease accordingly." (See also s. 30 of the Act of 1884.) This section contemplates an independent application to the High Court by any person under incapacity who desires to be relieved from it. A condition precedent to such application is the conviction for perjury of the person who gave evidence against him in respect of the evidence he so gave, and the Court, if satisfied that the conviction of the applicant or the report against him was based upon such perjured testimony, "may order that such incapacity shall thenceforth cease and the same shall cease accordingly."

Ex-officio information.

It has been mentioned that instead of a proceeding by indictment the Attorney-General may file an information against any person accused of an indictable misdemeanour against the election laws, and then the trial may be had either in London or the information may be sent down to the assizes for trial. In all material regards the procedure on the trial of an information is the same as on the trial of an indictment. (For the law and practice with reference to *ex officio* informations see *Archbold's Criminal Evidence and Pleadings*, 19th ed., p. 116.)

SECTION V.—CIVIL SUIT FOR PENALTIES.

Pecuniary penalties.

Under the old Acts directed against electoral corruption a common mode of punishing offenders was by exposing them to actions for penalties at the instance of any persons who chose to bring them. In practice it was found that this was a weak deterrent, and, in consequence, most of the enactments which gave suits for penalties have been repealed and more stringent punishments substituted. In a few cases, however, the liability to pecuniary penalties is still preserved.

40s. for *giving* cockades.

1. By s. 7 of the Act of 1854, applicable to *Parliamentary* elections only, it is provided, "No candidate before, during or after any election shall in regard to such election, by

himself or his agent, directly or indirectly, *give* or *provide* to or for any person having a vote at such election, or to or for *any inhabitant* of the county, city, borough, or place for which such election is held, any cockade, ribbon, or other mark of distinction; and every person so giving or providing shall for every such offence forfeit the sum of two pounds to such person as shall sue for the same, *together with full costs of suit.*" It will be remembered that by s. 16 (1) of the Act of 1883, any *payment* or *contract for payment* made on account of, among other things, " banners, cockades, ribbons or other marks of distinction," is declared an illegal payment, imperilling the seat when committed by a candidate or his election agent. S. 7 of the Act of 1854 strikes at the mere *giving* of cockades to voters or inhabitants of the constituency in question, and though the seat is not affected by any violation of this enactment, any candidate or agent of a candidate who, at a Parliamentary election, gives a bit of ribbon or a cockade exposes himself to an action to recover the penalty of two pounds given by the statute.

2. Another case in which a person may be sued for an infringing of the election laws is under s. 33 (5) of the Act of 1883, which provides that if the return and declaration of election expenses for a county or borough required by the Act are not transmitted within the time limited for that purpose, the candidate shall not sit or vote in the House of Commons as member for such county or borough "until either such return and declaration have been transmitted, or until the date of the allowance of such an authorised excuse for the failure to transmit the same, as in this Act mentioned, and if he sits or votes in contravention of this enactment *he shall forfeit one hundred pounds for every day on which he so sits or votes to any person who sues for the same.*"

[Margin: £100 a day for sitting in Commons before expenses returned.]

3. The Act of 1884 contains a similar provision with reference to the failure to transmit the return and declaration of expenses in the case of a municipal election: but under this Act the penalty is only £50 a day, though it may be recovered by any person who sues for it.

4. S. 61 (1) of the Act of 1883 is as follows: "S. 11 of the Ballot Act, 1872, shall apply to a returning officer or presiding officer or clerk who is guilty of any wilful misfeasance or wilful act or omission in contravention of this Act in like manner as if the same were in contravention of the Ballot Act of 1872." A reference to s. 11 of the Ballot Act shows that if any returning officer, presiding officer, or clerk is guilty of any wilful misfeasance, wilful act or omission, he *forfeits to the person aggrieved a sum not exceeding one hundred pounds.*

5. S. 61 (2) of the Act of 1883 provides that s. 97 of the Registration Act, 1843, shall apply to every registration officer who is guilty of any wilful misfeasance or any wilful act of commission or omission contrary to this Act in the same manner as if the same were contrary to the Act of 1843. The section in question of the Act of 1843 exposes the persons mentioned in it (viz., every sheriff, under-sheriff, clerk of the peace, town clerk, secondary, returning officer, clerk of the crown, postmaster, overseer or other person or public officer required by the Act to do any matter or thing) to a penalty not exceeding one hundred pounds, to be recovered by any person aggrieved, when it is proved that any one of such persons has been guilty of a wilful act of commission or omission contray to this Act.

6. S. 24 of the Act of 1884 directs the town clerk of every municipal borough to make out a list of persons who, though otherwise entitled to be on the burgess roll, have become incapacitated by reason of being convicted or scheduled for some corrupt or illegal practice, and the parish overseers are commanded to publish this list. The last sub-section then provides: "Any town clerk or overseer who fails to comply with the provisions of this section shall be liable to the like fine as he is liable to under s. 75 of the Municipal Corporations Act, 1882, for any neglect or refusal in relation to a parish burgess list as therein mentioned." The fine given by the section named does not exceed £50, and a moiety of it, after payment of the costs of the action, is to be paid to the plaintiff. The action must be brought within three

months of the occurring of the cause of action. (S. 75 of the Municipal Corporations Act, 1882.)

Actions brought under any of these Acts must be commenced by writ in the Queen's Bench Division, where the penalty claimed exceeds £50, but where a penalty of £50 or less is sought to be recovered, it is apprehended they may also be brought by plaint in the County Court. (*Hargreaves* v. *Simpson*, 4 Q.B. Div., 403), and they will proceed in the way in which actions of contract or tort ordinarily proceed, down to and including judgment and execution.

PART III.

THE APPLICATION OF THE ACT OF 1884 TO CERTAIN OTHER ELECTIONS IN ENGLAND AND WALES.

CHAPTER I.

ELECTIONS OF MAYOR, ALDERMAN, ELECTIVE AUDITOR OR REVISING ASSESSOR IN ANY BOROUGH.

Municipal. Application of Act of 1884. THE Act of 1884 applies to elections to the office of mayor, alderman, elective auditor, or revising assessor in any borough (s. 34 of the Act of 1884). But the different modes in which these officers and town councillors are elected (as to which see Part III. of the Municipal Corporations Act, 1882), and other reasons, render certain modifications in the application of the Act necessary.

No election expenditure allowed. The law allows certain expenditure at an election of a councillor, but "no sum shall be paid and no expense shall be incurred by or on behalf of a candidate at an election" to the office of mayor, alderman, elective auditor, or revising assessor, "whether before, during or after an election on account of or in respect of the conduct or management of such election" (s. 5 of the Act of 1884). No candidate at any such election may incur any election expense at all, and if he do, he will commit an illegal practice, which, on petition (s. 8), will avoid his election. The incurring of any election expense by any agent of the candidate would equally avoid the election, subject, of course, to the possibility of relief under ss. 19 and 20 of the Act of 1884. It *Consequential inapplicability of certain sections.* follows from what has been said that in the elections under consideration the provisions of the Act of 1884 relating to the time for sending in and paying claims, and those which relate to the maximum amount of election expenses or the return or declaration respecting election expenses have no application. <small>MUNICIPAL.</small>

As an election to the office of mayor or alderman is made by the members of the town council assembled together and voting otherwise than by ballot papers, the provisions of the Act of 1884, the Ballot Act, 1872, and the Municipal Corporations Act, 1882, relating to personation, polling agents, and disclosure of votes cannot apply to such an election.

An election to the office of mayor, alderman, elective auditor or revising assessor can only be questioned by an election petition, when the objection to the election is— <small>Petitions against return</small>

(*a*) That the election was avoided by general bribery, treating, undue influence or personation; or

(*b*) That the election was avoided by corrupt practices; or

(*c*) That the election was avoided by any illegal practice, or by the general prevalence of illegal practices; or

(*d*) That the person whose election is questioned was at the time of election disqualified; or

(*e*) That he was not duly elected by a majority of lawful votes. (Municipal Corporations Act, 1882, s. 87; the Act of 1884, s. 8, and *Summers* v. *Moorhouse*, 9 Q.B. Div., 388).

In other cases, *Quo Warranto* will still be the remedy. <small>*Quo Warranto*</small>

CHAPTER II.

ELECTIONS OF MEMBERS OF LOCAL BOARDS, IMPROVEMENT COMMISSIONERS, GUARDIANS, MEMBERS OF SCHOOL BOARDS AND MEMBERS OF COUNTY COUNCILS.

SECTION I.—LOCAL BOARD AND IMPROVEMENT COMMISSIONERS ELECTIONS.

MUNICIPAL. How elections conducted. Local Boards and Improvement Commissioners are elected in their respective districts by the resident ratepayers and the registered owners of property. The voting is by means of voting papers, which are delivered at the place of residence of the voter and collected within the ensuing two or three days. The voter is required to place his initials opposite the names of the persons for whom he votes and to sign the paper. After the papers have been collected the votes are counted by the returning officer in the presence of the candidates, if they choose to attend, and the result is declared.

Prior to the Act of 1884 the only way in which the validity of the return could on any ground be impeached was by a *quo warranto* proceeding in the Queen's Bench; but that remedy was costly, dilatory and altogether inadequate.

How elections questioned; Now the election may be questioned by election petition filed within the same time and subject to the same conditions as to signature of the petition and security for costs and so forth as in the case of a municipal election petition, and the proceedings subsequently had upon the petition up to and including trial are exactly the same in both cases. (S. 36 (1) and the first schedule of the Act of 1884.)

And on what grounds. The grounds upon which an election to a Local Board or a Board of Improvement Commissioners can be challenged are largely, though not entirely, the same as those upon which a municipal election can be upset. Thus in both cases an election will be invalidated where any act of bribery, treating, undue influence or personation is brought home to the respondent, or any one of his agents; or for the general prevalence of corruption; or for the general prevalence of illegal practices, illegal employments, hirings or payments which may be reasonably supposed to have affected the result; or where the illegal practices of paying for committee-rooms in excess of the authorised number, or paying electors on account of the exhibition of placards, addresses, &c., are proved against the respondent or his agents; or where it is shown that he personally induced persons to vote who are prohibited by statute from voting, or published a false declaration of the withdrawal of another candidate, or entered into any corrupt arrangement to secure his withdrawal, or made any payments or contracts for payment on account of bands of music, torches, &c., or published bills, placards, &c., without the printer's name appended thereto, or used as a committee-room licensed premises or premises on which refreshments are sold, or in the metropolis or within the area of any urban sanitary district, held a meeting upon any licensed premises. Upon proof of the commission of any one of the above enumerated offences, a local board election will, upon petition, be declared void, or if the petitioner claims the seat for the unsuccessful candidate the latter may be seated if the result of a scrutiny is to show that he has a majority of legal votes.

MUNICIPAL.

On what grounds elections questioned.

It must be carefully noticed, however, that there are several grounds of objection to a municipal election, which have no application to a local board election. (1.) It is expressly provided that the provisions of the Act of 1884, which prohibit the payment of any sum and the incurring of any expense by and on behalf of a candidate at an election, on account of, or in respect of, the conduct or management of the election, and those which relate to the time for sending in and paying claims, and those which relate to the maximum amount of election expenses shall not apply to the case of Local Board or Improvement Commissioners elections (s. 37 of the Act

Provisions as to election expenses, &c.

of 1884). It follows therefore that a candidate at a local board election cannot be guilty of the corrupt practice of making a false return and declaration of election expenses, or of the illegal practices of failing to make a return within the specified time, or failing to pay all bills within the specified term, or expending any sum in excess of an authorised maximum. But though there is no limitation upon the *mere amount* which a candidate may spend over a local board election, if he spends any sum, however trifling, for any corrupt or illegal purpose, his election is avoided, subject to the possibility of relief under ss. 19 and 20. (2.) In the case of local board elections the poll is, so to speak, brought to the door of every elector. There is therefore no temptation to a candidate to expend money in the conveyance of voters to or from the poll, and it is accordingly provided that the provisions of the Act of 1884, which relate to the conveyance of voters, shall not apply to local board elections. (S. 36, sub-s. 1 (*g*) of the Act of 1884.) The return cannot therefore be questioned either on the ground of the illegal practice of paying or contracting to pay for the conveyance of voters to or from the poll, or the illegal practice of using carriages or horses commonly let out for hire in the conveyance of voters. (3.) It is further provided by s. 36, sub-s. 1 (*f*) that it shall not be unlawful to hold a *meeting* for the purpose of promoting the election of any person to a Local Board or Board of Improvement Commissioners, on any licensed or other premises, *not situate in an urban sanitary district or in the metropolis.*

The Director of Public Prosecutions, or his representative, will attend the trial of a local board election petition. He can prosecute offenders before it or before any other competent court, and the court has, with an exception to be mentioned immediately, the same power of inflicting punishment, followed by the same incapacities, as in the case of a municipal election. The one exception to the rule that the punishment for offences in relation to a local board election are the same as the punishment for offences at municipal elections is in the case of personation. The full offence of personation is only committed when a ballot paper is applied for; and local board elections are conducted by voting papers. The punishment prescribed by the Public Health Act of 1875 for personation was a fine of £20, or threee months' imprisonment with or without hard labour. (Rule 69, 2nd schedule of the Act of 1875.) That penalty is still in force, but in addition, personation in the case of any election which is taken by means of voting papers is now declared to be an *illegal practice* (s. 36 (1) *g* of the Act of 1884), subjecting the offender upon summary conviction to a fine of £100, and certain disabilities which have been already set out.

<small>Municipal</small>

Section II.—Board of Guardians Elections.

Guardians of the Poor are elected by means of voting papers, which are sent out to the electors and collected in the same manner as in the case of local board elections. The return could formerly only be questioned by *quo warranto* information or by application to the Local Government Board, which might send down one of its officials to enquire, and upon his report make such order as it thought right. The latter power is still preserved to the Local Government Board, but its exercise is much curtailed. S. 36, sub-s. 1 (*h*) of the Act of 1884, provides: "The Local Government Board shall have the same power as heretofore under s. 8 of the Poor Law Amendment Act, 1842, to determine any question arising as to the rights of a person to act as guardian, except that the board shall not have power (*a*) to determine, until after the expiration of 21 days after the election of a person as guardian, any question which can be determined upon an election petition under this section: nor (*b*) to determine any question which is raised by an election petition under this section, and is either awaiting decision or has been decided by an election court; nor (*c*) to determine any question of general corruption, or of any corrupt or illegal practice."

<small>How elected.</small>

<small>Power of Local Government Board.</small>

Therefore the ordinary, and in most instances, the only method of challenging the election of a guardian is by

<small>How return questioned.</small>

264   THE LAW RELATING TO

MUNICIPAL. election petition, as in the case of a local board election, and the return may be questioned on exactly the same grounds It is unnecessary to repeat them here. The reader is referred to the last section.

Procedure. The procedure up to and upon the trial of the petition is identical in both cases, and there is no difference in the nature and amount of the punishments for corrupt and illegal practices at guardian and local board elections.

SECTION III.—SCHOOL BOARD ELECTIONS.

How conducted. A school board, where a contest takes place, is elected by ballot. (36 & 37 Vict., c. 86, s. 26.) But prior to the Act of 1884, the return could not be questioned by petition. (*In re the West Bromwich School Board*, 5 C.P.D., 191.) The only remedies were by *quo warranto* information, or by an application to the Education Department, under s. 33 of the Education Act, 1870.

How questioned. Now the proper method is by election petition under the Act of 1884, and Part IV. of the Municipal Corporations Act, 1882, and the election can be questioned upon all the grounds set out in the first and second sections of this chapter as applicable to local board and guardian elections, *with the addition of the following:*—

Special grounds. (1.) It is an illegal practice avoiding the election, if committed by the respondent or any agent, to make any payment or contract for payment on account of the conveyance of voters to or from the poll. (Ss. 4 (1) & 36 (1) *g* of the Act of 1884.)

(2.) It is an illegal hiring invalidating the election if done with the consent of the respondent, to let, lend or employ any horse or vehicle commonly let out for hire in the conveyance of voters to or from the poll. (Ss. 10 & 36 (1) *g* of the Act of 1884.)

(3.) Personation is a *corrupt* practice when committed in connection with a school board election, and must be charged as such in the petition.

There is, however, no limitation upon the amount of a

candidate's expenditure, and no provisions requiring the sending in and payment of bills by a certain time and directing a return of election expenses. Therefore, the various offences which may arise out of infractions of the scale of expenditure, or failure to comply with the requisitions as to election expenses cannot be committed at a school board election. It should also be mentioned that while it is illegal to have *committee-rooms* upon licensed premises, *meetings* may be held there, provided the election in question is not within the metropolis or any urban sanitary district.

<small>MUNICIPAL. Inapplicability of certain provisions.</small>

The punishments and incapacities which result from conviction before an election court, or any other competent tribunal, or from the report of an election court, are the same as in the case of a municipal election, and only differ from those applicable to the elections dealt with in the former sections of this chapter in this, that personation is punishable as a corrupt practice, with a maximum penalty of two years' imprisonment with hard labour.

Section IV.—County Council Elections.

County councillors, whether in the country or in the metropolis, are the creation of the Local Government Act, 1888 (51 & 52 Vict., c. 41); s. 2 of the latter Act provides that the council of a county shall be elected in like manner as the council of a borough, divided into wards, with certain exceptions of which it is, in this place, only necessary to mention the exception which provides that the divisions of the county shall be called electoral divisions and not wards, and that one county councillor only shall be elected for each electoral division. S. 40 (sub-s. 4) provides for the special case of the metropolis, and enacts in substance that two county councillors shall be elected for each parliamentary division in the metropolis.

S. 75 further enacts as follows: "For the purpose of the provisions of this Act with respect to county councils,

MUNICIPAL. and to the chairmen, members, committees, and officers of such councils, and otherwise for the purpose of carrying this Act into effect, the following portions of the Municipal Corporations Act, 1882, namely, Part Two, Part Three, Part Four (as amended by the Municipal Elections (Corrupt Practices) Act, 1884), section one hundred and twenty-four in Part Five, Part Twelve, Part Thirteen, the Second Schedule, Part Two and Part Three of the Third Schedule, and Part One of the Eighth Schedule shall, so far as the same are unrepealed and are consistent with the Provisions of this Act, apply as if they were herein re-enacted with the enactments amending the same in such terms and with such modifications as are necessary to make them applicable to the said councils and their chairmen, members, committees, and officers, and to the other provisions of this Act."

In *Ex p. Walker* (22 Q.B. Div. 384) the Court of Appeal held that the effect of the above section was to incorporate with the Act of 1888 the general provisions of the Municipal Elections (Corrupt and Illegal Practices) Act, 1884, and to make candidates at county council elections generally amenable to the provisions of the Act of 1884. This is now the undoubted law, and candidates for election to the County Councils of England and Wales are referred for a statement of their responsibilities to the law generally applicable to elections in municipal boroughs.

CHAPTER III.

MUNICIPAL ELECTIONS IN THE CITY OF LONDON.

WITH certain modifications which will be found noticed below, the Act of 1884 and the unrepealed portion of Part IV. of the Municipal Corporations Act, 1882, apply to certain municipal elections in the City of London, as distinguished from the Administrative County of London. (S. 35 of the Act of 1884.) {Municipal. Application of the Act of 1884, and the Municipal Corporations Act, 1882.}

These elections are those to the offices of
(1.) Lord mayor.
(2.) Alderman.
(3.) Common councilman.
(4.) Sheriff, and
(5.) Any officer elected by the mayor, aldermen and liverymen in common hall.

In the case of the election of lord mayor or sheriff of the City of London, no election expense at all may be incurred or paid by or on behalf of a candidate under the penalty (*inter alia*) of avoiding the election.

In the case of the election of an alderman or common councilman, the same maximum is allowed for election expenses as is allowed in the case of the election of a town councillor in a borough. (Ss. 5 & 35, sub-s. 6 of the Act of 1884. {Maximum election expenditure.}

In the case of an election by liverymen in common hall, a distinction is taken. If a poll be not demanded, a candidate is limited to an election expenditure of £40. But if a poll be demanded the maximum is raised to £250. With the view of keeping down expenditure, it is enacted (s. 35, sub-s. 7 of the Act of 1884), that the poll, if demanded, be held on the third day after the demand for a poll, or if the third day be a Sunday, on the fourth day, and the poll shall last for one day only, commencing at 8 a.m. and closing at 6 p.m.

MUNICIPAL.
Certain sections do not apply.

As none of the city elections to which the Act of 1884 applies is made by ballot, the enactments relating to personation, polling agents and disclosure of votes do not apply, but it is provided (s. 35, sub-s. 4 of the Act of 1884) that any offences under the City of London Municipal Elections Amendment Act, 1867 (30 Vict., c. 1, local and personal), relating to the declaration required to be made at the poll shall be deemed a corrupt practice, avoiding the election if committed by the candidate returned or any of his agents.

Payment of costs of petition.

It has already been observed that an election court is empowered in certain cases where corrupt practices have extensively prevailed at a municipal election (ss. 29 & 32 of the Act of 1884), to order the whole or a part of the costs of the petition to be paid by the borough out of the borough fund or borough rate. This principle has been partly applied to the City of London (s. 35, sub-s. 3 of the Act of 1884), power being given to the election court in the case of the election of an alderman or common councilman for any ward to order payment of the costs of the petition out of the ward rate for that ward, and in any other case by the City Chamberlain out of the city cash. Provision is also made (s. 35, sub-s. 8) for the omission from the ward list of persons entitled to vote, of all persons mentioned in the corrupt and illegal practices list, which is to be sent by the town clerk to the ward clerk at least 14 days before the day appointed for making out the ward list of persons entitled to vote.

APPENDIX.

CORRUPT PRACTICES PREVENTION ACT, 1854.

17 & 18 Vict. c. 102.

An Act to consolidate and amend the Laws relating to Bribery, Treating, and Undue Influence at Elections of Members of Parliament. [10th August, 1854.]

WHEREAS the laws now in force for preventing corrupt practices in the election of members to serve in Parliament have been found insufficient: And whereas it is expedient to consolidate and amend such laws, and to make further provision for securing the freedom of such elections:

Be it enacted by the Queen's most Excellent Majesty, by and with the advice and consent of the Lords Spiritual and Temporal and Commons, in this present Parliament assembled, and by the authority of the same, as follows:—

2. The following persons shall be deemed guilty of bribery, and shall be punishable accordingly: *Bribery defined.*
   1. Every person who shall, directly or indirectly, by himself, or by any other person on his behalf, give, lend, or agree to give or lend, or shall offer, promise, or promise to procure or to endeavour to procure, any money or valuable consideration, to or for any voter, or to or for any person on behalf of any voter, or to or for any other person in order to induce any voter to vote, or refrain from voting, or shall corruptly do any such act, as aforesaid, on account of such voter having voted or refrained from voting at any election:
   2. Every person who shall, directly or indirectly, by himself or by any other person on his behalf, give or procure, or agree to give or procure, or offer, promise, or promise to procure or to endeavour to procure, any office, place, or employment to or for any voter, or to or for any person on behalf of any voter, or to or for any other person, in order to induce such voter to vote or refrain from voting, or shall corruptly do any such act as aforesaid, on account of any voter having voted or refrained from voting at any election:

3. Every person who shall, directly or indirectly, by himself or by any other person on his behalf, make any such gift, loan, offer, promise, procurement, or agreement as aforesaid to or for any person, in order to induce such person to procure or endeavour to procure the return of any person to serve in Parliament, or the vote of any voter at any election:

4. Every person who shall, upon or in consequence of any such gift, loan, offer, promise, procurement, or agreement, procure or engage, promise, or endeavour to procure the return of any person to serve in Parliament, or the vote of any voter at any election:

5. Every person who shall advance or pay, or cause to be paid, any money to or to the use of any other person with the intent that such money or any part thereof shall be expended in bribery at any election, or who shall knowingly pay or cause to be paid, any money to any person in discharge or repayment of any money wholly or in part expended in bribery at any election: Provided always that the aforesaid enactment shall not extend or be construed to extend to any money paid or agreed to be paid for or on account of any legal expenses *bonâ fide* incurred at or concerning any election.

Bribery further defined.

3. The following persons shall also be deemed guilty of bribery, and shall be punishable accordingly:—
1. Every voter who shall, before or during any election, directly or indirectly, by himself or by any other person on his behalf, receive, agree, or contract for any money, gift, loan, or valuable consideration, office, place, or employment, for himself or for any other person, for voting or agreeing to vote, or for refraining or agreeing to refrain from voting at any election:
2. Every person who shall, after any election, directly or indirectly, by himself or by any other person on his behalf, receive any money or valuable consideration on account of any person having voted or refrained from voting, or having induced any other person to vote or refrain from voting at any election.

No cockades, &c., to be given at elections.

7. No candidate before, during, or after any election shall in regard to such election, by himself or agent, directly or indirectly, give or provide to or for any person having a vote at such election, or to or for any inhabitant of the county, city, borough, or place for which such election is had, any cockade, ribbon, or other mark of distinction; and every

Penalty.

person so giving or providing shall for every such offence forfeit the sum of two pounds to such person as shall sue for the same, together with full costs of suit.

Voters not to serve as special constables during elections.

8. No person having a right to vote at the election for any county, city, borough, or other place, shall be liable or compelled to serve as a special constable at or during any election for a member or members to serve in Parliament for such county, city, borough, or other place, unless he shall consent so to act; and he shall not be liable to any fine, penalty, or punishment whatever for refusing so to act, any statute, law, or usage to the contrary notwithstanding.

APPENDIX. 271

10. It shall be lawful for any criminal court, before which any prosecution shall be instituted for any offence against the provisions of this Act, to order payment to the prosecutor of such costs and expenses as to the said court shall appear to have been reasonably incurred in and about the conduct of such prosecution: Provided always, that no indictment for bribery or undue influence shall be triable before any court of quarter sessions.

Costs and expenses of prosecutions.

12. In case of any indictment or information by a private prosecutor for any offence against the provisions of this Act, if judgment shall be given for the defendant, he shall be entitled to recover from the prosecutor the costs sustained by the defendant by reason of such indictment or information, such costs to be taxed by the proper officer of the court in which such judgment shall be given.

In cases of private prosecutions, if judgment be given for the defendant.

13. It shall not be lawful for any court to order payment of the costs of a prosecution for any offence against the provisions of this Act, unless the prosecutor shall, before or upon the finding of the indictment or the granting of the information, enter into a recognisance, with two sufficient sureties, in the sum of two hundred pounds (to be acknowledged in like manner as is now required in cases of writs of *certiorari* awarded at the instance of a defendant in an indictment), with the conditions following—that is to say, that the prosecutor shall conduct the prosecution with effect, and shall pay to the defendant or the defendants, in case he or they shall be acquitted, his or their costs.

35. On the trial of any action for recovery of any pecuniary penalty under this Act the parties to such action, and the husbands and wives of such parties respectively, shall be competent and compellable to give evidence in the same manner as parties, and their husbands and wives are competent and compellable to give evidence in actions and suits under the Act of the fourteenth and fifteenth Victoria, chapter ninety-nine, and "The Evidence Amendment Act, 1853," but subject to and with the exceptions contained in such several Acts: Provided always, that any such evidence shall not thereafter be used in any indictment or criminal proceeding under this Act against the party giving it.

In actions for penalties, parties, &c., to be competent witnesses.

PARLIAMENTARY ELECTIONS ACT, 1868.

31 & 32 Vict. c. 125.

31 & 32 Vict. c. 125.

An Act for amending the Laws relating to Election Petitions, and providing more effectually for the Prevention of Corrupt Practices at Parliamentary Elections. [31st July 1868.]

WHEREAS it is expedient to amend the laws relating to election petitions, and to provide more effectually for the prevention of corrupt practices at Parliamentary Elections:

Be it enacted by the Queen's most excellent Majesty, by and with the advice and consent of the Lords Spiritual and Temporal, and Commons, in this present Parliament assembled, and by the authority of the same, as follows :—

Preliminary.

Short title of Act.

1. This Act may be cited for all purposes as "The Parliamentary Elections Act, 1868."

Definition and jurisdiction of court.

2. The expression "the court" shall, for the purposes of this Act, in its application to England, mean the Court of Common Pleas at Westminster, and in its application to Ireland the Court of Common Pleas at Dublin, and such court shall, subject to the provisions of this Act, have the same power, jurisdiction and authority with reference to an election petition, and the proceedings thereon as it would have if such petition were an ordinary cause within their jurisdiction.

Interpretation of terms.

3. The following terms shall in this Act have the meanings hereinafter assigned to them, unless there is something in the context repugnant to such construction (that is to say):

"Metropolitan district:"

"Metropolitan district" shall mean the City of London and the liberties thereof, and any parish or place subject to the jurisdiction of the Metropolitan Board of Works:

"Election:"

"Election" shall mean an election of a member or members to serve in Parliament:

"County:"

"County" shall not include a county of a city or county of a town, but shall mean any county, riding, parts or division of a county returning a member or members to serve in Parliament:

"Borough:"

"Borough" shall mean any borough, university, city, place or combination of places, not being a county as hereinbefore defined, returning a member or members to serve in Parliament:

"Corrupt practices:"

"Corrupt practices," or "corrupt practice," shall mean bribery, treating, and undue influence, or any of such offences, as defined by Act of Parliament, or recognised by the common law of Parliament:

"Rules of Court:"

"Rules of Court" shall mean rules to be made as hereinafter mentioned:

"Prescribed:"

"Prescribed" shall mean "prescribed by the rules of court."

APPENDIX.

4. For the purposes of this Act "Speaker" shall be deemed to include Deputy Speaker; and when the office of Speaker is vacant, the Clerk of the House of Commons, or any other officer for the time being performing the duties of the Clerk of the House of Commons, shall be deemed to be substituted for and to be included in the expression "the Speaker." Provisions as to speaker.

Presentation and Service of Petition.

5. From and after the next dissolution of Parliament a petition complaining of an undue return or undue election of a member to serve in Parliament for a county or borough may be presented to the Court of Common Pleas at Westminster, if such county or borough is situate in England, or to the Court of Common Pleas at Dublin, if such county or borough is situate in Ireland, by any one or more of the following persons: To whom and by whom election petition may be presented.

1. Some person who voted or who had a right to vote at the election to which the petition relates; or,
2. Some person claiming to have had a right to be returned or elected at such election; or,
3. Some person alleging himself to have been a candidate at such election:

And such petition is hereinafter referred to as an election petition.

6. The following enactments shall be made with respect to the presentation of an election petition under this Act:— Regulations as to presentation of election petition.
   1. The petition shall be signed by the petitioner, or all the petitioners if more than one:
   2. The petition shall be presented within 21 days after the return has been made to the Clerk of the Crown in Chancery in England, or to the Clerk of the Crown and Hanaper in Ireland, as the case may be, of the member to whose election the petition relates, unless it question the return or election upon an allegation of corrupt practices, and specifically alleges a payment of money or other reward to have been made by any member, or on his account, or with his privity, since the time of such return, in pursuance or in furtherance of such corrupt practices, in which case the petition may be presented at any time within 28 days after the date of such payment:
   3. Presentation of a petition shall be made by delivering it to the prescribed officer or otherwise dealing with the same in manner prescribed:
   4. At the time of the presentation of the petition, or within three days afterwards, security for the payment of all costs, charges and expenses that may become payable by the petitioner—
      (a) To any person summoned as a witness on his behalf; or,
      (b) To the member whose election or return is complained of (who is hereinafter referred to as the respondent) shall be given on behalf of the petitioner:
   5. The security shall be to the amount of £1,000; it shall be given either by recognisance to be entered into by any number of sureties not exceeding four, or by a deposit of money in manner prescribed, or partly in one way and partly in the other.

18

274 APPENDIX.

Copy of petition after presentation to be sent to returning officer.

7. On presentation of the petition the prescribed officer shall send a copy thereof to the returning officer of the county or borough to which the petition relates, who shall forthwith publish the same in the county or borough, as the case may be.

Recognisance may be objected to.

8. Notice of the presentation of a petition under this Act, and of the nature of the proposed security, accompanied with a copy of the petition, shall, within the prescribed time, not exceeding five days after the presentation of the petition, be served by the petitioner on the respondent; and it shall be lawful for the respondent, where the security is given wholly or partially by recognisance, within a further prescribed time, not exceeding five days from the date of the service on him of the notice, to object in writing to such recognisance, on the ground that the sureties, or any of them, are insufficient, or that a surety is dead, or that he cannot be found or ascertained from the want of a sufficient description in the recognisance, or that a person named in the recognisance has not duly acknowledged the same.

Determination of objection to recognisance.

9. Any objection made to the security given shall be heard and decided on in the prescribed manner. If an objection to the security is allowed it shall be lawful for the petitioner, within a further prescribed time, not exceeding five days, to remove such objection, by a deposit in the prescribed manner of such sum of money as may be deemed by the court or officer having cognisance of the matter to make the security sufficient.

If on objection made the security is decided to be insufficient, and such objection is not removed in manner hereinbefore mentioned, no further proceedings shall be had on the petition; otherwise, on the expiration of the time limited for making objections, or, after objection made, on the sufficiency of the security being established, the petition shall be deemed to be at issue.

List of petitions at issue to be made.

10. The prescribed officer shall, as soon as may be, make out a list of all petitions under this Act presented to the court of which he is such officer, and which are at issue, placing them in the order in which they were presented, and shall keep at his office a copy of such list, hereinafter referred to as the election list, open to the inspection in the prescribed manner of any person making application.

Such petitions, as far as conveniently may be, shall be tried in the order in which they stand in such list.

Trial of a Petition.

Mode of trial of election petitions.

11.* The following enactments shall be made with respect to the trial of election petitions under this Act:—

   1. The trial of every election petition shall be conducted before a *puisne* judge of one of Her Majesty's superior courts of common law at Westminster or Dublin, according as the same shall have been presented to the court at Westminster or Dublin, to be selected from a rota to be formed as hereinafter mentioned:

   2. The members of each of the courts of Queen's Bench, Common

---

* See changes in practice made by 42 & 43 Vict. c. 75, and the Act of 1883.

Pleas and Exchequer in England and Ireland shall respectively, on or before the third day of Michaelmas term in every year, select, by a majority of votes, one of the *puisne* judges of such court, not being a member of the House of Lords, to be placed on the rota for the trial of election petitions during the ensuing year :

3. If in any case the members of the said court are equally divided in their choice of a *puisne* judge to be placed on the rota, the Chief Justice of such court (including under that expression the Chief Baron of the Exchequer) shall have a second or casting vote :

4. Any judge placed on the rota shall be re-eligible in the succeeding or any subsequent year :

5. In the event of the death or the illness of any judge for the time being on the rota, or his inability to act for any reasonable cause, the court to which he belongs shall fill up the vacancy by placing on the rota another *puisne* judge of the same court :

6. The judges for the time being on the rota shall, according to their seniority, respectively try the election petitions standing for trial under this Act, unless they otherwise agree among themselves, in which case the trial of each election petition shall be taken in manner provided by such agreement :

7. When it appears to the judges on the rota, after due consideration of the list of petitions under this Act for the time being at issue, that the trial of such election petitions will be inconveniently delayed unless an additional judge or judges be appointed to assist the judges on the rota, each of the said courts (that is to say), the Court of Exchequer, the Court of Common Pleas, and Court of Queen's Bench, in the order named, shall, on and according to the requisition of such judges on the rota, select, in manner hereinbefore provided, one of the *puisne* judges of the court to try election petitions for the ensuing year ; and any judge so selected shall, during that year, be deemed to be on the rota for the trial of election petitions :

8. Her Majesty may, in manner heretofore in use, appoint an additional *puisne* judge to each of the courts of Queen's Bench, the Common Pleas, and the Exchequer in England :

9. Every election petition shall, except where it raises a question of law for the determination of the court, as hereinafter mentioned, be tried by one of the judges hereinbefore in that behalf mentioned, hereinafter referred to as the judge sitting in open court without a jury :

10. Notice of the time and place at which an election petition will be tried shall be given, not less than fourteen days before the day on which the trial is held, in the prescribed manner :

11. The trial of an election petition, in the case of a petition relating to a borough election, shall take place in the borough, and in the case of a petition relating to a county election, in the county : Provided always, that if it shall appear to the court that special circumstances exist which render it desirable that the petition should be tried elsewhere than in the borough or county, it shall be lawful for the court to appoint such other place for the trial as shall appear most convenient : Provided

also, that in the case of a petition relating to any of the boroughs within the metropolitan district, the petition may be heard at such place within the district as the court may appoint :

12. The judge presiding at the trial may adjourn the same from time to time, and from any one place to any other place within the county or borough, as to him may seem expedient :

13. At the conclusion of the trial the judge who tried the petition shall determine whether the member whose return or election is complained of, or any and what other person, was duly returned or elected, or whether the election was void, and shall forthwith certify in writing such determination to the speaker, and upon such certificate being given such determination shall be final to all intents and purposes :

14. Where any charge is made in an election petition of any corrupt practice having been committed at the election to which the petition refers, the judge shall, in addition to such certificate, and at the same time, report in writing to the speaker as follows :

(a.) Whether any corrupt practice has or has not been proved to have been committed by or with the knowledge and consent of any candidate at such election, and the nature of such corrupt practice :

(b.) The names of all persons (if any) who have been proved at the trial to have been guilty of any corrupt practice :

(c.) Whether corrupt practices have, or whether there is reason to believe that corrupt practices have extensively prevailed at the election to which the petition relates :

15. The judge may at the same time make a special report to the speaker as to any matters arising in the course of the trial an account of which in his judgment ought to be submitted to the House of Commons :

16. Where, upon the application of any party to a petition made in the prescribed manner to the Court, it appears to the Court that the case raised by the petition can be conveniently stated as a special case, the Court may direct the same to be stated accordingly, and any such special case shall, as far as may be, be heard before the Court, and the decision of the Court shall be final ; and the Court shall certify to the speaker its determination in reference to such special case.

Applications to the court respecting trials.

12. Provided always, that if it shall appear to the judge on the trial of the said petition that any question or questions of law as to the admissibility of evidence or otherwise require further consideration by the Court of Common Pleas, then it shall be lawful for the said judge to postpone the granting of the said certificate until the determination of such question or questions by the Court, and for this purpose to reserve any such question or questions in like manner as questions are usually reserved by a judge on a trial at *nisi prius*.

House of Commons to carry out report.

13. The House of Commons on being informed by the speaker of such certificate and report or reports, if any, shall order the same to be entered in their journals, and shall give the necessary directions for confirming or altering the return, or for issuing a writ for a new election, or

APPENDIX. 277

for carrying the determination into execution, as circumstances may require.

14. Where the judge makes a special report the House of Commons may make such order in respect of such special report as they think proper. *House of Commons may make order on special report.*

15. If the judge states in his report on the trial of an election petition under this Act that corrupt practices have, or that there is reason to believe that corrupt practices have extensively prevailed in any county or borough at the election to which the petition relates, such statement shall for all the purposes of the Act of the Session of the fifteenth and sixteenth years of the reign of Her present Majesty, chapter fifty-seven, intituled "An Act to provide for more effectual Inquiry into the existence of Corrupt Practices at Elections of Members to serve in Parliament," have the same effect, and may be dealt with in the same manner as if it were a report of a committee of the House of Commons appointed to try an election petition, and the expenses of any commission of inquiry which may be issued in accordance with the provisions of the said Act shall be defrayed as if they were expenses incurred in the registration of voters for such county or borough. *Report of the judge as to corrupt practices.*

17. On the trial of an election petition under this Act, unless the judge otherwise directs, any charge of a corrupt practice may be gone into and evidence in relation thereto received before any proof has been given of agency on the part of any candidate in respect of such corrupt practice. *Evidence of corrupt practices how received.*

18. The trial of an election petition under this Act shall be proceeded with notwithstanding the acceptance by the respondent of an office of profit under the Crown. *Acceptance of office not to stop petition.*

Proceedings.

20. An election petition under this Act shall be in such form and state such matters as may be prescribed. *Form of petition.*

21. An election petition under this Act shall be served as nearly as may be in the manner in which a writ or summons is served, or in such other manner as may be prescribed. *Service of petition.*

22. Two or more candidates may be made respondents to the same petition, and their case may for the sake of convenience be tried at the same time, but for all the purposes of this Act such petition shall be deemed to be a separate petition against each respondent. *Joint respondents to petition.*

23. Where, under this Act, more petitions than one are presented relating to the same election or return, all such petitions shall in the election list be bracketed together, and shall be dealt with as one petition, but such petitions shall stand in the election list in the place where the last of such petitions would have stood if it had been the only petition presented, unless the court shall otherwise direct. *Provision in cases where more than one petition is presented.*

APPENDIX.

Shorthand writer to attend trial of election petition.

24. On the trial of an election petition under this Act the shorthand writer of the House of Commons or his deputy shall attend and shall be sworn by the judge faithfully and truly to take down the evidence given at the trial, and from time to time as occasion requires to write or cause the same to be written in words at length; and it shall be the duty of such shorthand writer to take down such evidence, and from time to time to write or cause the same to be written at length, and a copy of such evidence shall accompany the certificate made by the judge to the speaker; and the expenses of the shorthand writer shall be deemed to be part of the expenses incurred in receiving the judge.

Jurisdiction and Rules of Court.

Rules to be made by court.

25. The judges for the time being on the rota for the trial of election petitions in England and Ireland may respectively from time to time make, and may from time to time revoke and alter, general rules and orders (in this Act referred to as the rules of court) for the effectual execution of this Act, and of the intention and object thereof, and the regulation of the practice, procedure and costs of election petitions and the trial thereof, and the certifying and reporting thereon.

Any general rules and orders made as aforesaid shall be deemed to be within the powers conferred by this Act, and shall be of the same force as if they were enacted in the body of this Act.

Any general rules and orders made in pursuance of this section shall be laid before Parliament within three weeks after they are made, if Parliament be then sitting, and if Parliament be not then sitting, within three weeks after the beginning of the then next session of Parliament.

Practice of House of Commons to be observed.

26. Until rules of court have been made in pursuance of this Act, and so far as such rules do not extend, the principles, practice and rules on which committees of the House of Commons have heretofore acted in dealing with election petitions shall be observed so far as may be by the court and judge in the case of election petitions under this Act.

Performance of duties by prescribed officer.

27. The duties to be performed by the prescribed officer under this Act shall be performed by such one or more of the masters of the Court of Common Pleas at Westminster as may be determined by the Chief Justice of the said Court of Common Pleas, and by the Master of the Court of Common Pleas at Dublin, and there shall be awarded to such Masters respectively, in addition to their existing salaries, such remuneration for the performance of the duties imposed on them in pursuance of this Act as the Chief Justices of the said Courts of Common Pleas in Westminster and Dublin may respectively, with the consent of the Commissioners of the Treasury, determine.

Reception, Expenses and Jurisdiction of Judge.

Reception of judge.

28. The judge shall be received at the place where he is about to try an election petition under this Act with the same state, so far as circumstances admit, as a judge of assize is received at an assize town; he shall be received by the sheriff in the case of a petition relating to a county election, and in any other case by the mayor, in the case of a borough having a mayor, and in the case of a borough not having a

APPENDIX. 279

mayor, by the sheriff of the county in which the borough is situate, or by some person named by such sheriff.

The travelling and other expenses of the judge, and all expenses properly incurred by the sheriff or by such mayor or person named as aforesaid in receiving the judge and providing him with necessary accommodation and with a proper court, shall be defrayed by the Commissioners of the Treasury out of money to be provided by Parliament.

29. On the trial of an election petition under this Act the judge shall, subject to the provisions of this Act, have the same powers, jurisdiction and authority as a judge of one of the superior courts and as a judge of assize and *nisi prius* and the court held by him shall be a court of record. Power of judge.

30. The judge shall be attended on the trial of an election petition under this Act in the same manner as if he were a judge sitting at *nisi prius*, and the expenses of such attendance shall be deemed to be part of the expenses of providing a court. Attendance on judge.

Witnesses.

31. Witnesses shall be subpœnaed and sworn in the same manner, as nearly as circumstances admit, as in a trial at *nisi prius* and shall be subject to the same penalties for perjury. Summons of witnesses.

32. On the trial of an election petition under this Act the judge may, by order under his hand, compel the attendance of any person as a witness who appears to him to have been concerned in the election to which the petition refers, and any person refusing to obey such order shall be guilty of contempt of court. The judge may examine any witness so compelled to attend, or any person in court, although such witness is not called and examined by any party to the petition. After the examination of a witness as aforesaid by a judge, such witness may be cross-examined by or on behalf of the petitioner and respondent, or either of them. Judge may summon and examine witnesses.

34. The reasonable expenses incurred by any person in appearing to give evidence at the trial of an election petition under this Act, according to the scale allowed to witnesses on the trial of civil actions at the assizes, may be allowed to such person by a certificate under the hand of the judge or of the prescribed officer, and such expenses, if the witness was called and examined by the judge, shall be deemed part of the expenses of providing a court, and in other cases shall be deemed to be costs of the petition. Expenses of witnesses.

Withdrawal and abatement of Election Petitions.

35. An election petition under this Act shall not be withdrawn without the leave of the court or judge upon special application, to be made in and at the prescribed manner, time and place. Withdrawal of petition and substitution of new petitioners.

No such application shall be made for the withdrawal of a petition until the prescribed notice has been given in the county or borough to which the petition relates of the intention of the petitioner to make an application for the withdrawal of his petition.

On the hearing of the application for withdrawal, any person who might have been a petitioner in respect of the election to which the petition relates may apply to the court or judge to be substituted as a petitioner for the petitioner so desirous of withdrawing the petition.

The court or judge may, if it or he thinks fit, substitute as a petitioner any such applicant as aforesaid ; and may further, if the proposed withdrawal is in the opinion of the court or judge induced by any corrupt bargain or consideration, by order direct that the security given on behalf of the original petitioner shall remain as security for any costs that may be incurred by the substituted petitioner, and that to the extent of the sum named in such security the original petitioner shall be liable to pay the costs of the substituted petitioner.

If no such order is made with respect to the security given on behalf of the original petitioner, security to the same amount as would be required in the case of a new petition, and subject to the like conditions, shall be given on behalf of the substituted petitioner before he proceeds with his petition, and within the prescribed time after the order of substitution.

Subject as aforesaid a substituted petitioner shall stand in the same position as nearly as may be, and be subject to the same liabilities as the original petitioner.

If a petition is withdrawn, the petitioner shall be liable to pay the costs of the respondent.

Where there are more petitioners than one, no application to withdraw a petition shall be made except with the consent of all the petitioners.

Abatement of petition.

37. An election petition under this Act shall be abated by the death of a sole petitioner or of the survivor of several petitioners.

The abatement of a petition shall not affect the liability of the petitioner to the payment of costs previously incurred.

On the abatement of a petition the prescribed notice of such abatement having taken place shall be given in the county or borough to which the petition relates, and within the prescribed time after the notice is given, any person who might have been a petitioner in respect of the election to which the petition relates may apply to the court or judge, in and at the prescribed manner, time and place to be substituted as a petitioner.

The court or judge may, if it or he thinks fit, substitute as a petitioner any such applicant who is desirous of being substituted, and on whose behalf security to the same amount is given as is required in the case of a new petition.

Admission in certain cases of voters to be respondents.

38. If before the trial of any election petition under this Act any of the following events happen in the case of the respondent (that is to say)—

(1.) If he dies ;

(2.) If he is summoned to Parliament as a peer of Great Britain by a writ issued under the Great Seal of Great Britain ;

(3.) If the House of Commons have resolved that his seat is vacant ;

(4.) If he gives in and at the prescribed manner and time notice to the court that he does not intend to oppose the petition ;

notice of such an event having taken place shall be given in the county or borough to which the petition relates, and within the prescribed time after the notice is given any person who might have been a petitioner in respect of the election to which the petition relates may apply to the court or judge to be admitted as a respondent to oppose the petition, and such person shall on such application be admitted accordingly, either with the respondent, if there be a respondent, or in place of the respondent; and any number of persons not exceeding three may be so admitted.

39. A respondent who has given the prescribed notice that he does not intend to oppose the petition shall not be allowed to appear or act as a party against such petition in any proceedings thereon, and shall not sit or vote in the House of Commons until the House of Commons has been informed of the report on the petition: and the court or judge shall in all cases in which such notice has been given in the prescribed time and manner report the same to the speaker of the House of Commons. *Respondent not opposing not to appear as party or to sit.*

40. Where an election petition under this Act complains of a double return and the respondent has given notice to the prescribed officer that it is not his intention to oppose the petition, and no party has been admitted in pursuance of this Act to defend such return, then the petitioner, if there be no petition complaining of the other member returned on such double return, may withdraw his petition by notice addressed to the prescribed officer, and upon the receipt of such notice the prescribed officer shall report the fact of the withdrawal of such petition to the speaker, and the House of Commons shall thereupon give the necessary directions for amending the said double return by taking off the file the indenture by which the respondent so declining to oppose the petition was returned. or otherwise as the case may require: *Provisions for cases of double return where the member complained of declines to defend his return.*

Costs.

41. All costs, charges and expenses of and incidental to the presentation of a petition under this Act, and to the proceedings consequent thereupon, with the exception of such costs, charges and expenses as are by this Act otherwise provided for, shall be defrayed by the parties to the petition in such manner and in such proportions as the court or judge may determine, regard being had to the disallowance of any costs, charges or expenses which may, in the opinion of the court or judge, have been caused by vexatious conduct, unfounded allegations or unfounded objections on the part either of the petitioner or the respondent, and regard being had to the discouragement of any needless expense by throwing the burden of defraying the same on the parties by whom it has been caused, whether such parties are or are not on the whole successful. *General costs of petition.*

The costs may be taxed in the prescribed manner, and such costs may be recovered in the same manner as the costs of an action at law, or in such other manner as may be prescribed.

42. If any petitioner in an election petition presented under this Act neglect or refuse for the space of six months after demand to pay to any person summoned as a witness on his behalf, or to the *Recognisances, when to be estreated, &c.*

respondent, any sum certified to be due to him for his costs, charges and expenses, and if such neglect or refusal be, within one year after such demand, proved to the satisfaction of the court of elections, in every such case every person who has entered into a recognisance relating to such petition under the provisions of this Act shall be held to have made default in his said recognisance, and the prescribed officer shall thereupon certify such recognisance to be forfeited. and the same shall be dealt with in England in manner provided by the Act of the third year of the reign of King George the Fourth, chapter forty-six, and in Ireland in manner provided by "The Fines Act (Ireland), 1851."

Punishment of Corrupt Practices.

Penalty for employing corrupt agent.

44. If on the trial of any election petition under this Act any candidate is proved to have personally engaged at the election to which such petition relates as a canvasser or agent for the management of the election any person, knowing that such person has within seven years previous to such engagement been found guilty of any corrupt practice by any competent legal tribunal, or been reported guilty of any corrupt practice by a committee of the House of Commons, or by the report of the judge upon an election petition under this Act, or by the report of commissioners appointed in pursuance of the Act of the session of the fifteenth and sixteenth years of the reign of her present Majesty, chapter fifty-seven, the election of such candidate shall be void.

Miscellaneous.

Returning officer may be sued for neglecting to return any person duly elected.

48. If any returning officer wilfully delays, neglects, or refuses duly to return any person who ought to be returned to serve in Parliament for any county or borough, such person may, in case it has been determined on the hearing of an election petition under this Act that such person was entitled to have been returned, sue the officer having so wilfully delayed, neglected, or refused duly to make such return at his election in any of Her Majesty's courts of record at Westminster, and shall recover double the damages he has sustained by reason thereof, together with full costs of suit, provided such action be commenced within one year after the commission of the act on which it is grounded, or within six months after the conclusion of the trial relating to such election.

Calculation of time.

49. In reckoning time for the purposes of this Act, Sunday, Christmas Day, Good Friday, and any day set apart for a public fast or public thanksgiving, shall be excluded.

Controverted elections to be tried under Act.

50. From and after the next dissolution of Parliament no election or return to Parliament shall be questioned, except in accordance with the provisions of this Act.

Returning officer if complained of to be respondent.

51. Where an election petition under this Act complains of the conduct of a returning officer, such returning officer shall, for all the purposes of this Act, except the admission of respondents in his place, be deemed to be a respondent.

APPENDIX. 283

52. A petition under this Act complaining of no return may be presented to the court, and shall be deemed to be an election petition within the meaning of this Act, and the court may make such order thereon as they think expedient for compelling a return to be made, or may allow such petition to be heard by the judge in manner hereinbefore provided with respect to ordinary election petitions. Petition complaining of no return.

53. On the trial of a petition under this Act complaining of an undue return, and claiming the seat for some person, the respondent may give evidence to prove that the election of such person was undue in the same manner as if he had presented a petition complaining of such election. Recrimination when petition for undue return.

54. From and after the next dissolution of Parliament, the Acts contained in the schedule hereto are repealed so far as relates to elections and petitions to the extent therein mentioned. Repeal of Acts.

55. The additional *puisne* judge appointed under this Act to each of the courts of Queen's Bench, the Common Pleas, and the Exchequer in England, shall, as to rank, salary, pension, attendant officers, jurisdiction, and all other privileges and duties of a judge, stand in the same position as the other *puisne* judges of the court to which he is attached. Provision as to payment of additional judges and remuneration of judges for duties to be performed under this Act.

Any *puisne* judge of the said courts appointed in pursuance of or after the passing of this Act, shall be authorised to sit, and shall, when requested by the Lord Chancellor, sit as judge of the Court of Probate and Court of Marriage and Divorce, or of the Admiralty Court.

56. If, upon a petition to the House of Commons, presented within 21 days after the return to the Clerk of the Crown in Chancery in England, or to the Clerk of the Crown and Hanaper in Ireland, of a member to serve in Parliament for any borough or county, or within 14 days after the meeting of Parliament, and signed by two or more electors of such borough or county, and alleging that corrupt practices have extensively prevailed at the then last election for such borough or county, or that there is reason to believe that corrupt practices have there so prevailed, an address be presented by both Houses of Parliament, praying that such allegation may be inquired into, the Crown may appoint commissioners to inquire into the same, and if such commissioners in such case be appointed, they shall inquire in the same manner, and with the same powers, and subject to all the provisions of the statute of the 15th & 16th of Vict. c. 57. Commissions of inquiry into corrupt practices.

57. Any person who at the time of the passing of this Act was entitled to practise as agent, according to the principles, practice, and rules of the House of Commons in cases of election petitions and matters relating to election of members of the House of Commons, shall be entitled to practise as an attorney or agent in cases of election petitions and all matters relating to elections before the court and judges prescribed by this Act : Provided that every such person so practising as aforesaid shall, in respect of such practice and everything relating thereto, be subject to the jurisdiction and orders of the court as if he were an attorney of the said court : and further, provided that no such person shall practise as aforesaid until his name shall have been entered Rules as to agents practising in cases of election petitions.

on a roll to be made and kept, and which is hereby authorised to be made and kept, by the prescribed officer in the prescribed manner.

Application of Act to Scotland

58. The provisions of this Act shall apply to Scotland, subject to the following modifications:—
1. The expression "the court" shall mean either division of the inner house of the court of session, and either of such divisions shall have the same powers, jurisdiction and authority with reference to an election petition in Scotland, and the proceedings thereon, which by this Act are conferred on the Court of Common Pleas at Westminster with respect to election petitions in England:
2. The expression "county" shall not include a county of a city, but shall mean any county or division of a county, or any combination of counties, or of counties and portions of counties, returning a member to serve in Parliament:
3. The expression "borough" shall mean any university or universities, or any city, town, burgh, or district of cities, towns, or burghs, returning a member or members to serve in Parliament:
4. "Recognisance" shall mean a bond of caution with usual and necessary clauses:
5. The trial of every election petition in Scotland shall be conducted before a judge of the court of session, to be selected from a rota to be formed as hereinafter mentioned:
6. The judges of the court of session shall, on or before the first day of the winter session in every year, select, by a majority of votes, two of the judges of such court, not being members of the House of Lords, to be placed on the rota for the trial of election petitions during the ensuing year:
7. If in any case the judges of the said court are equally divided in their choice of a judge to be placed on the rota, the lord president shall have a second or casting vote:
8. Any judge placed on the rota shall be re-eligible in the succeeding or any subsequent year:
9. In the event of the death or illness of any judge for the time being on the rota, or his inability to act for any reasonable cause, the judges shall fill up the vacancy by placing on the rota another judge:
10. The judges for the time being on the rota shall, according to their seniority, respectively try the election petitions standing for trial under this Act, unless they otherwise agree among themselves, in which case the trial of each election petition shall be taken in manner provided by such agreement:
11. Where it appears to the judges on the rota, after due consideration of the list of petitions under this Act for the time being at issue, that the trial of such election petitions will be inconveniently delayed unless an additional judge or judges be appointed to assist the judges on the rota, the judges of the court of session shall, on and according to the requisition of such judges on the rota, select in manner hereinbefore provided, a judge to try election petitions for the ensuing year; and any judge so selected shall during that year be deemed to be on the rota for the trial of election petitions:
12. The duties to be performed by the prescribed officer under this

Act with reference to election petitions in Scotland shall be performed by such one or more of the principal clerks of session as may be determined by the lord president of the court of session ; and there shall be awarded to such principal clerk or clerks, in addition to their existing salaries, such remuneration for the performance of the duties imposed on them in pursuance of this Act as the said lord president may, with the consent of the commissioners of the treasury, determine :

13. The judge shall be received at the place where he is about to try an election petition under this Act in the same manner and by the same authorities, as far as circumstances admit, as a judge of the court of justiciary is received at a circuit town, and he shall be attended by such officer or officers as shall be necessary.

14. The travelling and other expenses of the judge, and of the officer or officers in attendance upon him, and all expenses properly incurred in providing the judge with a proper court, shall be defrayed by the commissioners of the treasury out of money to be provided by Parliament :

15. On the trial of an election petition under this Act, the judge shall, subject to the provisions of this Act, have the same powers, jurisdictions and authority as a judge of the court of session presiding at the trial of a civil cause without a jury :

16. Any of Her Majesty's courts of record at Westminster shall in Scotland mean the court of session in Scotland :

17. In lieu of the provisions for the estreating of a recognisance under an election petition, the prescribed officer shall, when otherwise competent under the provisions of this Act, certify that the conditions contained in the bond of caution have not been fulfilled, and it shall then be competent for the party or parties interested to register the said bond, and do diligence upon it as accords of law.

SCHEDULE.

Date of Act.	Title of Act.	Extent of Repeal.
4 & 5 Vict. c. 57 .	An Act for the prevention of Bribery at Elections	The whole Act.
5 & 6 Vict. c. 102 .	An Act for the better Discovery and Prevention of Bribery and Treating at the Election of Members of Parliament	The whole Act.
11 & 12 Vict. c. 98.	An Act to amend the Law for the Trial of Election Petitions	The whole Act.
26 Vict. c. 29 .	An Act to amend and continue the Law relating to Corrupt Practices at Elections of Members of Parliament	Section 8.
28 Vict. c. 8 .	An Act to amend "The Election Petitions Act, 1848," in certain particulars	The whole Act.

THE BALLOT ACT, 1872.*

35 & 36 Vict.
c. 33.

35 & 36 VICT. CHAP. 33.

An Act to Amend the Law relating to Procedure at Parliamentary and Municipal Elections.
[18th July, 1872.]

WHEREAS it is expedient to amend the law relating to procedure at parliamentary and municipal elections:

Be it enacted by the Queen's most Excellent Majesty, by and with the advice and consent of the Lords Spiritual and Temporal, and Commons, in this present Parliament assembled, and by the authority of the same, as follows :—

PART I.

PARLIAMENTARY ELECTIONS.

Procedure at Election.

Nomination of candidates for parliamentary elections.

1. A candidate for election to serve in Parliament for a county or borough shall be nominated in writing. The writing shall be subscribed by two registered electors of such county or borough as proposer and seconder, and by eight other registered electors of the same county or borough as assenting to the nomination, and shall be delivered during the time appointed for the election to the returning officer by the candidate himself, or his proposer or seconder.

If at the expiration of one hour after the time appointed for the election no more candidates stand nominated than there are vacancies to be filled up, the returning officer shall forthwith declare the candidates who may stand nominated to be elected, and return their names to the clerk of the crown in chancery; but if at the expiration of such hour more candidates stand nominated than there are vacancies to be filled up, the returning officer shall adjourn the election and shall take a poll in manner in this Act mentioned.

A candidate may, during the time appointed for the election, but not afterwards, withdraw from his candidature by giving a notice to that effect, signed by him, to the returning officer : Provided that the proposer of a candidate nominated in his absence out of the United Kingdom may withdraw such candidate by a written notice signed by him and delivered to the returning officer, together with a written declaration of such absence of the candidate.

If after the adjournment of an election by the returning officer for the purpose of taking a poll, one of the candidates nominated shall die before the poll has commenced, the returning officer shall, upon being satisfied of the fact of such death, countermand notice of the poll, and all the proceedings with reference to the election shall be commenced afresh in all respects, as if the writ had been received by the returning

---

* The clauses, which are not material for the purposes of this work, are omitted to save space.

APPENDIX.

officer on the day on which proof was given to him of such death: provided that no fresh nomination shall be necessary in the case of a candidate who stood nominated at the time of the countermand of the poll.

2. In the case of a poll at an election the votes shall be given by ballot. The ballot of each voter shall consist of a paper (in this Act called a ballot paper) showing the names and description of the candidates. Each ballot paper shall have a number printed on the back, and shall have attached a counterfoil with the same number printed on the face. At the time of voting, the ballot paper shall be marked on both sides with an official mark, and delivered to the voter within the polling station, and the number of such voter on the register of voters shall be marked on the counterfoil, and the voter having secretly marked his vote on the paper, and folded it up so as to conceal his vote, shall place it in a closed box in the presence of the officer presiding at the polling station (in this Act called the "presiding officer") after having shown to him the official mark at the back. *[Poll at elections.]*

Any ballot paper which has not on its back the official mark, or on which votes are given to more candidates than the voter is entitled to vote for, or on which anything, except the said number on the back, is written or marked by which the voter can be identified, shall be void and not counted.

After the close of the poll the ballot boxes shall be sealed up, so as to prevent the introduction of additional ballot papers, and shall be taken charge of by the returning officer, and that officer shall, in the presence of such agents, if any, of the candidates as may be in attendance, open the ballot boxes, and ascertain the result of the poll by counting the votes given to each candidate, and shall forthwith declare to be elected the candidates or candidate to whom the majority of votes have been given, and return their names to the clerk of the crown in chancery. The decision of the returning officer as to any question arising in respect of any ballot paper shall be final, subject to reversal on petition questioning the election or return.

Where an equality of votes is found to exist between any candidates at an election for a county or borough, and the addition of a vote would entitle any of such candidates to be declared elected, the returning officer, if a registered elector of such county or borough, may give such additional vote, but shall not in any other case be entitled to vote at an election for which he is returning officer.

Offences at Elections.

3. Every person who,—   *[Offences in respect of nomination papers, ballot papers, and ballot boxes.]*
    1. Forges or fraudulently defaces or fraudulently destroys any nomination paper, or delivers to the returning officer any nomination paper, knowing the same to be forged; or
    2. Forges or counterfeits or fraudulently defaces or fraudulently destroys any ballot paper or the official mark on any ballot paper; or
    3. Without due authority supplies any ballot paper to any person; or
    4. Fraudulently puts into any ballot box any paper other than the ballot paper which he is authorised by law to put in; or
    5. Fraudulently takes out of the polling station any ballot paper; or

6. Without due authority destroys, takes, opens, or otherwise interferes with any ballot box or packet of ballot papers then in use for the purposes of the election;

shall be guilty of a misdemeanor, and be liable, if he is a returning officer or an officer or clerk in attendance at a polling station, to imprisonment for any term not exceeding two years, with or without hard labour, and if he is any other person, to imprisonment for any term not exceeding six months, with or without hard labour.

Any attempt to commit any offence specified in this section shall be punishable in the manner in which the offence itself is punishable.

In any indictment or other prosecution for an offence in relation to the nomination papers, ballot boxes, ballot papers, and marking instruments at an election, the property in such papers, boxes, and instruments may be stated to be in the returning officer at such election, as well as the property in the counterfoils.

Infringement of secrecy.

4. Every officer, clerk, and agent in attendance at a polling station shall maintain and aid in maintaining the secrecy of the voting in such station, and shall not communicate, except for some purpose authorised by law, before the poll is closed, to any person any information as to the name or number on the register of voters of any elector who has or has not applied for a ballot paper or voted at that station, or as to the official mark, and no officer, clerk, or agent, and no person whosoever, shall interfere with or attempt to interfere with a voter when marking his vote, or otherwise attempt to obtain in the polling station information as to the candidate for whom any voter in such station is about to vote or has voted, or communicate at any time to any person any information obtained in a polling station as to the candidate for whom any voter in such station is about to vote or has voted, or as to the number on the back of the ballot paper given to any voter at such station. Every officer, clerk, and agent in attendance at the counting of the votes shall maintain and aid in maintaining the secrecy of the voting, and shall not attempt to ascertain at such counting the number on the back of any ballot paper, or communicate any information obtained at such counting as to the candidate for whom any vote is given in any particular ballot paper. No person shall directly or indirectly induce any voter to display his ballot paper after he shall have marked the same, so as to make known to any person the name of the candidate for or against whom he has so marked his vote.

Every person who acts in contravention of the provisions of this section shall be liable, on summary conviction before two justices of the peace, to imprisonment for any term not exceeding six months, with or without hard labour.

Amendment of Law.

Conclusiveness of register of voters.

7. At any election for a county or borough, a person shall not be entitled to vote unless his name is on the register of voters for the time being in force for such county or borough, and every person whose name is on such register shall be entitled to demand and receive a ballot paper and to vote: Provided that nothing in this section shall entitle any person to vote who is prohibited from voting by any statute, or by the common law of Parliament, or relieve such person from any penalties to which he may be liable for voting.

APPENDIX.

Duties of Returning and Election Officers.

8. Subject to the provisions of this Act, every returning officer shall provide such nomination papers, polling stations, ballot boxes, ballot papers, stamping instruments, copies of register of voters, and other things, appoint and pay such officers, and do such other acts and things as may be necessary for effectually conducting an election in manner provided by this Act. <small>General powers and duties of returning officer.</small>

All expenses properly incurred by any returning officer in carrying into effect the provisions of this Act, in the case of any parliamentary election, shall be payable in the same manner as expenses incurred in the erection of polling booths at such election are by law payable.

Where the sheriff is returning officer for more than one county as defined for the purposes of parliamentary elections, he may, without prejudice to any other power, by writing under his hand, appoint a fit person to be his deputy for all or any of the purposes relating to an election in any such county, and may, by himself or such deputy, exercise any powers and do any things which the returning officer is authorised or required to exercise or do in relation to such election. Every such deputy, and also any under sheriff, shall, in so far as he acts as returning officer, be deemed to be included in the term returning officer in the provisions of this Act relating to parliamentary elections, and the enactments with which this part of this Act is to be construed as one.

9. If any person misconducts himself in the polling station, or fails to obey the lawful orders of the presiding officer, he may immediately, by order of the presiding officer, be removed from the polling station by any constable in or near that station, or any other person authorised in writing by the returning officer to remove him; and the person so removed shall not, unless with the permission of the presiding officer, again be allowed to enter the polling station during the day. <small>Keeping of order in station.</small>

Any person so removed as aforesaid, if charged with the commission in such station of any offence, may be kept in custody until he can be brought before the justice of the peace.

Provided that the powers conferred by this section shall not be exercised so as to prevent any elector who is otherwise entitled to vote at any polling station from having an opportunity of voting at such station.

10. For the purpose of the adjournment of the poll, and of every other enactment relating to the poll, a presiding officer shall have the power by law belonging to a deputy returning officer; and any presiding officer and any clerk appointed by the returning officer to attend at a polling station shall have the power of asking the questions, and administering the oath authorised by law to be asked of and administered to voters, and any justice of the peace and any returning officer may take and receive any declaration authorised by this Act to be taken before him. <small>Powers of presiding officer and administration of oaths, &c.</small>

11. Every returning officer, presiding officer, and clerk who is guilty of any wilful misfeasance or any wilful act or omission in contravention of this Act shall, in addition to any other penalty or liability to which <small>Liability of officers for misconduct.</small>

he may be subject, forfeit to any person aggrieved by such misfeasance, act, or omission, a penal sum not exceeding one hundred pounds.

30 & 31 Vict. c. 102.

Section 50 of the Representation of the People Act, 1867 (which relates to the acting of any returning officer, or his partner or clerk, as agent for a candidate), shall apply to any returning officer or officer appointed by him in pursuance of this Act, and to his partner or clerk.

Miscellaneous.

Prohibition of disclosure of vote.

12. No person who has voted at an election shall, in any legal proceeding to question the election or return, be required to state for whom he has voted.

Non-compliance with rules.

13. No election shall be declared invalid by reason of a non-compliance with the rules contained in the first schedule to this Act, or any mistake in the use of forms in the second schedule to this Act, if it appears to the tribunal having cognizance of the question that the election was conducted in accordance with the principles laid down in the body of this Act, and that such non-compliance or mistake did not affect the result of the election.

Use of municipal ballot boxes, &c., for parliamentary election, and *vice versa*.

14. Where a parliamentary borough and municipal borough occupy the whole or any part of the same area, and ballot boxes or fittings for polling stations and compartments provided for such parliamentary borough or such municipal borough may be used in any municipal or parliamentary election in such borough free of charge, and any damage other than reasonable wear and tear caused to the same shall be paid as part of the expenses of the election at which they are so used.

PART II.

MUNICIPAL ELECTIONS.

Application to municipal election of enactments relating to the poll at parliamentary elections.

20. The poll at every contested municipal election shall, so far as circumstances admit, be conducted in the manner which the poll is by this Act directed to be conducted at a contested parliamentary election, and, subject to the modifications expressed in the schedules annexed hereto, such provisions of this Act and of the said schedules as relate to or are concerned with a poll at a parliamentary election, shall apply to a poll at a contested municipal election: Provided as follows:

(1.) The term "returning officer" shall mean the mayor or other officer who, under the law relating to municipal elections, presides at such elections:

(2.) The term "petition questioning the election or return" shall mean any proceeding in which a municipal election can be questioned:

(3.) The mayor shall provide everything which in the case of a parliamentary election is required to be provided by the returning officer for the purpose of a poll:

(4.) All expenses shall be defrayed in manner provided by law with respect to the expenses of a municipal election:

(5.) No return shall be made to the clerk of the Crown in Chancery:

APPENDIX. 291

(6.) Nothing in this Act shall be deemed to authorise the appointment of any agents of a candidate in a municipal election, but if in the case of a municipal election any agent of a candidate is appointed, and a notice in writing of such appointment is given to the returning officer, the provisions of this Act with respect to agents of candidates shall, so far as respects such agent, apply in the case of that election :

(7.) The provisions of this Act with respect to—
    (*a.*) The voting of a returning officer ; and
    (*b.*) The use of a room for taking a poll ; and
    (*c.*) The right to vote of persons whose names are on the register of voters :
shall not apply in the case of a municipal election.

A municipal election shall, except in so far as relates to the taking of the poll in the event of its being contested, be conducted in the manner in which it would have been conducted if this Act had not passed.

21. Assessors shall not be elected in any ward of any municipal borough, and a municipal election need not be held before the assessors or their deputies, but may be held before the mayor, alderman or other returning officer only. *Abolition of ward assessors.*

PART III.

PERSONATION.

24. The following enactments shall be made with respect to personation at parliamentary and municipal elections : *Definition and punishment of personation.*

A person shall for all purposes of the laws relating to parliamentary and municipal elections, be deemed to be guilty of the offence of personation who at an election for a county or borough, or at a municipal election, applies for a ballot paper in the name of some other person, whether that name be that of a person living or dead or of a fictitious person, or who having voted once at any such election applies at the same election for a ballot paper in his own name.

It shall be the duty of the returning officer to institute a prosecution against any person whom he may believe to have been guilty of personation, or of aiding, abetting, counselling, or procuring the commission of the offence of personation by any person at the election for which he is returning officer, and the costs and expenses of the prosecutor and the witnesses in such case, together with compensation for their trouble and loss of time, shall be allowed by the court in the same manner in which courts are empowered to allow the same in cases of felony.

The provisions of the Registration Acts, specified in the third schedule to this Act, shall in England and Ireland respectively apply to personation under this Act in the same manner as they apply to a person who knowingly personates and falsely assumes to vote in the name of another person as mentioned in the said Acts.

25. Where a candidate, on the trial of an election petition claiming the seat for any person, is proved to have been guilty, by himself or by any person on his behalf, of bribery, treating, or undue influence in respect of any person who voted at such election, or where any *Vote to be struck off for bribery, treating, or undue influence.*

person retained or employed for reward by or on behalf of such candidate for all or any of the purposes of such election, as agent, clerk, messenger, or in any other employment, is proved on such trial to have voted at such election, there shall, on a scrutiny, be struck off from the number of votes appearing to have been given to such candidate one vote for every person who voted at such election and is proved to have been so bribed, treated, or unduly influenced, or so retained or employed for reward as aforesaid.

Construction of part of Act.

26. This part of this Act, so far as regards parliamentary elections, shall be construed as one with The Parliamentary Elections Act, 1868, and shall apply to an election for a university or combination of universities.

PART IV.

MISCELLANEOUS.

Application of Act.

30. This Act shall apply to any parliamentary or municipal election which may be held after the passing thereof.

Saving.

31. Nothing in this Act, except Part III. thereof, shall apply to any election for a university or combination of universities.

SCHEDULES.

FIRST SCHEDULE.

PART I.

RULES FOR PARLIAMENTARY ELECTIONS.

Elections.

1. The returning officer shall, in the case of a county election, within two days after the day on which he receives the writ, and in the case of a borough election, on the day on which he receives the writ or the following day, give public notice, between the hours of nine in the morning and four in the afternoon, of the day on which and the place at which he will proceed to an election, and of the time appointed for the election, and of the day on which the poll will be taken in case the election is contested, and of the time and place at which forms of nomination papers may be obtained, and in the case of a county election shall send one of such notices by post, under cover, to the postmaster of the principal post-office of each polling place in the county, endorsed with the words "Notice of election," and the same shall be forwarded free of charge; and the postmaster receiving the same shall forthwith publish the same in the manner in which post-office notices are usually published.

2. The day of election shall be fixed by the returning officer as follows; that is to say, in the case of an election for a county or a district

borough not later than the ninth day after the day on which he receives the writ, with an interval of not less than three clear days between the day on which he gives the notice and the day of election; and in the case of an election for any borough other than a district borough not later than the fourth day after the day on which he receives the writ, with an interval of not less than two clear days between the day on which he gives the notice and the day of election.

3. The place of election shall be a convenient room situate in the town in which such election would have been held if this Act had not passed, or where the election would not have been held in a town, then situate in such town in the county as the returning officer may from time to time determine as being in his opinion most convenient for the electors.

4. The time appointed for the election shall be such two hours between the hours of ten in the forenoon and three in the afternoon as may be appointed by the returning officer, and the returning officer shall attend during those two hours and for one hour after.

5. Each candidate shall be nominated by a separate nomination paper, but the same electors or any of them may subscribe as many nomination papers as there are vacancies to be filled, but no more.

6. Each candidate shall be described in the nomination paper in such manner as in the opinion of the returning officer is calculated to sufficiently identify such candidate; the description shall include his names, his abode, and his rank, profession, or calling, and his surname shall come first in the list of his names. No objection to a nomination paper on the ground of the description of the candidate therein being insufficient, or not being in compliance with this rule, shall be allowed or deemed valid, unless such objection is made by the returning officer, or by some other person, at or immediately after the time of the delivery of the nomination paper.

7. The returning officer shall supply a form of nomination paper to any registered elector requiring the same during such two hours as the returning officer may fix, between the hours of ten in the morning, and two in the afternoon on each day intervening between the day on which notice of the election was given and the day of election, and during the time appointed for the election; but nothing in this Act shall render obligatory the use of a nomination paper supplied by the returning officer, so, however, that the paper be in the form prescribed by this Act.

8. The nomination papers shall be delivered to the returning officer, at the place of election during the time appointed for the election; and the candidate nominated by each nomination paper, and his proposer and seconder, and one other person selected by the candidate, and no person other than aforesaid, shall, except for the purpose of assisting the returning officer, be entitled to attend the proceedings during the time appointed for the election.

9. If the election is contested, the returning officer shall, as soon as practicable after adjourning the election, give public notice of the day on which the poll will be taken, and of the candidates described as in their respective nomination papers, and of the names of the persons who subscribe the nomination paper of each candidate, and of the order in which the names of the candidates will be printed in the ballot paper, and, in the case of an election for a county, deliver to the postmaster of the principal post-office of the town in which is situate the place of election a paper, signed by himself, containing the names of the candidates nominated, and stating the day on which the poll is to be taken,

and the postmaster shall forward the information contained in such paper by telegraph, free of charge, to the several postal telegraph offices situate in the county for which the election is to be held, and such information shall be published forthwith at each such office in the manner in which post-office notices are usually published.

10. If any candidate nominated during the time appointed for the election is withdrawn in pursuance of this Act, the returning officer shall give public notice of the name of such candidate, and the names of the persons who subscribed the nomination paper of such candidate, as well as of the candidates who stood nominated or were elected.

11. The returning officer shall, on the nomination paper being delivered to him, forthwith publish notice of the name of the person nominated as a candidate, and of the names of his proposer and seconder, by placarding or causing to be placarded the names of the candidate and his proposer and seconder in a conspicuous position outside the building in which the room is situate appointed for the election.

12. A person shall not be entitled to have his name inserted in any ballot paper as a candidate unless he has been nominated in manner provided by this Act, and every person whose nomination paper has been delivered to the returning officer during the time appointed for the election shall be deemed to have been nominated in manner provided by this Act, unless objection be made to his nomination paper by the returning officer or some other person before the expiration of the time appointed for the election or within one hour afterwards.

13. The returning officer shall decide on the validity of every objection made to a nomination paper, and his decision, if disallowing the objection, shall be final; but if allowing the same, shall be subject to reversal on petition questioning the election or return.

The Poll.

14. The poll shall take place on such day as the returning officer may appoint, not being in the case of an election for a county or a district borough less than two or more than six clear days, and not being in the case of an election for a borough other than a district borough more than three clear days after the day fixed for the election.

15. At every polling place the returning officer shall provide a sufficient number of polling stations for the accommodation of the electors entitled to vote at such polling place, and shall distribute the polling stations amongst those electors in such a manner as he thinks most convenient, provided that in a district borough there shall be at least one polling station at each contributory place of such borough.

16. Each polling station shall be furnished with such number of compartments, in which the voters can mark their votes screened from observation, as the returning officer thinks necessary, so that at least one compartment be provided for every one hundred and fifty electors entitled to vote at such polling station.

17. A separate room or separate booth may contain a separate polling station, or several polling stations may be constructed in the same room or booth.

18. No person shall be admitted to vote at any polling station except the one allotted to him.

19. The returning officer shall give public notice of the situation of polling stations and the description of voters entitled to vote at each station, and of the mode in which electors are to vote.

20. The returning officer shall provide each polling station with materials for voters to mark the ballot papers, with instruments for stamping thereon the official mark, and with copies of the register of voters, or such part thereof as contains the names of the voters allotted to vote at such station. He shall keep the official mark secret, and an interval of not less than seven years shall intervene between the use of the same official mark at elections for the same county or borough.

21. The returning officer shall appoint a presiding officer to preside at each station, and the officer so appointed shall keep order at his station, shall regulate the number of electors to be admitted at a time, and shall exclude all other persons except the clerks, the agents of the candidates, and the constables on duty.

22. Every ballot paper shall contain a list of the candidates described as in their respective nomination papers, and arranged alphabetically in the order of their surnames, and (if there are two or more candidates with the same surname) of their other names : it shall be in the form set forth in the second schedule to this Act or as near thereto as circumstances admit, and shall be capable of being folded up.

23. Every ballot box shall be so constructed that the ballot papers can be introduced therein, but cannot be withdrawn therefrom, without the box being unlocked. The presiding officer at any polling station, just before the commencement of the poll, shall show the ballot box empty to such persons, if any, as may be present in such station, so that they may see that it is empty, and shall then lock it up, and place his seal upon it in such manner as to prevent its being opened without breaking such seal, and shall place it in his view for the receipt of ballot papers, and keep it so locked and sealed.

24. Immediately before a ballot paper is delivered to an elector, it shall be marked on both sides with the official mark, either stamped or perforated, and the number, name and description of the elector as stated in the copy of the register shall be called out, and the number of such elector shall be marked on the counterfoil, and a mark shall be placed in the register against the number of the elector, to denote that he has received a ballot paper, but without showing the particular ballot paper which he has received.

25. The elector, on receiving the ballot paper, shall forthwith proceed into one of the compartments in the polling station, and there mark his paper, and fold it up so as to conceal his vote, and shall then put his ballot paper, so folded up, into the ballot box ; he shall vote without undue delay, and shall quit the polling station as soon as he has put his ballot paper into the ballot box.

26. The presiding officer, on the application of any voter who is incapacitated by blindness or other physical cause from voting in manner prescribed by this Act, or (if the poll be taken on Saturday) of any voter who declares that he is of the Jewish persuasion, and objects on religious grounds to vote in the manner prescribed in this Act, or of any voter who makes such a declaration as hereinafter mentioned that he is unable to read, shall, in the presence of the agents of the candidates, cause the vote of such voter to be marked on a ballot paper in manner directed by such voter, and the ballot paper to be placed in the ballot box, and the name and number on the register of voters of every voter whose vote is marked in pursuance of this rule, and the reason why it is so marked, shall be entered on a list, in this Act called " the list of votes marked by the presiding officer."

The said declaration, in this Act referred to as " the declaration of inability to read," shall be made by the voter at the time of polling, before the presiding officer, who shall attest it in the form hereinafter mentioned, and no fee, stamp, or other payment shall be charged in respect of such declaration, and the said declaration shall be given to the presiding officer at the time of voting.

27. If a person, representing himself to be a particular elector named on the register, applies for a ballot paper after another person has voted as such elector, the applicant shall, upon duly answering the questions and taking the oath permitted by law to be asked of and to be administered to voters at the time of polling, be entitled to mark a ballot paper in the same manner as any other voter, but the ballot paper (in this Act called a tendered ballot paper) shall be of a colour differing from the other ballot papers, and, instead of being put into the ballot box, shall be given to the presiding officer and endorsed by him with the name of the voter and his number in the register of voters, and set aside in a separate packet, and shall not be counted by the returning officer. And the name of the voter and his number on the register shall be entered on a list, in this Act called the tendered votes list.

28. A voter who has inadvertently dealt with his ballot paper in such manner that it cannot be conveniently used as a ballot paper, may, on delivering to the presiding officer the ballot paper so inadvertently dealt with, and proving the fact of the inadvertence to the satisfaction of the presiding officer, obtain another ballot paper in the place of the ballot paper so delivered up (in this Act called a spoilt ballot paper), and the spoilt ballot paper shall be immediately cancelled.

29. The presiding officer of each station, as soon as practicable after the close of the poll, shall, in the presence of the agents of the candidates, make up into separate packets sealed with his own seal and the seals of such agents of the candidates as desired to affix their seals—
1. Each ballot box in use at his station, unopened but with the key attached; and
2. The unused and spoilt ballot papers, placed together; and
3. The tendered ballot papers; and
4. The marked copies of the register of voters, and the counterfoils of the ballot papers; and
5. The tendered votes list, and the list of votes marked by the presiding officer, and a statement of the number of the voters whose votes are so marked by the presiding officer under the heads "physical incapacity," "Jews," and "unable to read," and the declarations of inability to read;

and shall deliver such packets to the returning officer.

30. The packets shall be accompanied by a statement made by such presiding officer, showing the number of ballot papers entrusted to him, and accounting for them under the heads of ballot papers in the ballot box, unused, spoilt, and tendered ballot papers, which statement is in this Act referred to as the ballot paper account.

Counting Votes.

31. The candidates may respectively appoint agents to attend the counting of the votes.

32. The returning officer shall make arrangements for counting the votes in the presence of the agents of the candidates as soon as practicable after the close of the poll, and shall give to the agents of the

candidates appointed to attend at the counting of the votes notice in writing of the time and place at which he will begin to count the same.

33. The returning officer, his assistants and clerks, and the agents of the candidates, and no other person, except with the sanction of the returning officer, may be present at the counting of the votes.

34. Before the returning officer proceeds to count the votes, he shall, in the presence of the agents of the candidates, open each ballot box, and, taking out the papers therein, shall count and record the numbers thereof, and then mix together the whole of the ballot papers contained in the ballot boxes. The returning officer, while counting and recording the number of ballot papers and counting the votes, shall keep the ballot papers with their faces upwards, and take all proper precautions for preventing any person from seeing the numbers printed on the backs of such papers.

35. The returning officer shall, so far as practicable, proceed continuously with counting the votes, allowing only time for refreshment, and excluding (except so far as he and the agents otherwise agree) the hours between seven o'clock at night and nine o'clock on the succeeding morning. During the excluded time the returning officer shall place the ballot papers and other documents relating to the election under his own seal and the seals of such of the agents of the candidates as desire to affix their seals, and shall otherwise take proper precautions for the security of such papers and documents.

36. The returning officer shall endorse "rejected" on any ballot paper which he may reject as invalid, and shall add to the endorsement "rejection objected to," if an objection be in fact made by any agent to his decision. The returning officer shall report to the clerk of the crown in chancery the number of ballot papers rejected and not counted by him under the several heads of—

1. Want of official mark;
2. Voting for more candidates than entitled to;
3. Writing or mark by which voter could be identified;
4. Unmarked, or void for uncertainty;

and shall on request allow any agent of the candidates, before such report is sent, to copy it.

37. Upon the completion of the counting, the returning officer shall seal up in separate packets the counted and rejected ballot papers. He shall not open the sealed packet of tendered ballot papers or marked copy of the register of voters and counterfoils, but shall proceed, in the presence of the agents of the candidates, to verify the ballot paper account given by each presiding officer by comparing it with the number of ballot papers recorded by him as aforesaid, and the unused and spoilt ballot papers in his possession, and the tendered votes list, and shall reseal each sealed packet after examination. The returning officer shall report to the clerk of the crown in chancery the result of such verification, and shall, on request, allow any agent of the candidates, before such report is sent, to copy it.

38. Lastly, the returning officer shall forward to the clerk of the crown in chancery (in manner in which the poll books are by any existing enactment required to be forwarded to such clerk, or as near thereto as circumstances admit) all the packets of ballot papers in his possession, together with the said reports, the ballot paper accounts, tendered votes lists, lists of votes marked by the presiding officer, statements relating thereto, declarations of inability to read, and packets of counterfoils, and marked copies of registers, sent by each presiding officer, endorsing on each packet a description of its contents and the date of the election to

which they relate, and the name of the county or borough for which such election was held ; and the term poll book in any such enactments shall be construed to include any document forwarded in pursuance of this rule.

39. The clerk of the crown shall retain for a year all documents relating to an election forwarded to him in pursuance of this Act by a returning officer, and then, unless otherwise directed by an order of the House of Commons, or of one of Her Majesty's superior courts, shall cause them to be destroyed.

40. No person shall be allowed to inspect any *rejected ballot papers* in the custody of the clerk of the crown in chancery, except under the order of the House of Commons or under the order of one of Her Majesty's superior courts, to be granted by such court on being satisfied by evidence on oath that the inspection or production of such ballot papers is required for the purpose of instituting or maintaining a prosecution for an offence in relation to ballot papers, or for the purpose of a petition questioning an election or return ; and any such order for the inspection or production *of ballot papers* may be made subject to such conditions as to persons, time, place, and mode of inspection or production as the House or Court making the same may think expedient, and shall be obeyed by the clerk of the crown in chancery. Any power given to a court by this rule may be exercised by any judge of such court at chambers.

41. No person shall, except by order of the House of Commons or any tribunal having cognizance of petitions complaining of undue returns or undue elections, open *the sealed packet of counterfoils* after the same has been once sealed up, or be allowed to inspect any *counted ballot papers* in the custody of the clerk of the crown in chancery ; such order may be made subject to such conditions as to persons, time, place, and mode of opening or inspection as the house or tribunal making the order may think expedient ; provided that on making and carrying into effect any such order, care shall be taken that the mode in which any particular elector has voted shall not be discovered until he has been proved to have voted, and his vote has been declared by a competent court to be invalid.

42. All documents forwarded by a returning officer in pursuance of this Act to the clerk of the crown in chancery, other than ballot papers and counterfoils, shall be open to public inspection at such time and under such regulations as may be prescribed by the clerk of the crown in chancery, with the consent of the Speaker of the House of Commons, and the clerk of the crown shall supply copies of or extracts from the said documents to any person demanding the same on payment of such fees and subject to such regulations as may be sanctioned by the Treasury.

43. Where an order is made for the production by the clerk of the crown in chancery of any document in his possession relating to any specified election, the production by such clerk or his agent of the document ordered, in such manner as may be directed by such order, or by a rule of court having power to make such order, shall be conclusive evidence that such document relates to the specified election ; and any endorsement appearing on any packet of ballot papers produced by such clerk of the crown or his agent shall be evidences of such papers being what they are stated to be by the endorsement. The production from proper custody of a ballot paper purporting to have been used at any election, and of a counterfoil marked with the same printed number and having a number marked thereon in writing, shall be *primâ facie* evidence that the person who voted by such ballot paper was the person who

at the time of such election had affixed to his name in the register of voters at such election the same number as the number written on such counterfoil.

General Provisions.

44. The return of a member or members elected to serve in Parliament for any county or borough shall be made by a certificate of the names of such member or members under the hand of the returning officer endorsed on the writ of election for such county or borough, and such certificate shall have effect and be dealt with in like manner as the return under the existing law, and the returning officer may, if he think fit, deliver the writ with such certificate endorsed to the postmaster of the principal post-office of the place of election, or his deputy, and in that case he shall take a receipt from the postmaster or his deputy for the same; and such postmaster or his deputy, shall then forward the same by the first post, free of charge, under cover to the clerk of the crown, with the words "Election Writ and Return" endorsed thereon.

45. The returning officer shall, as soon as possible, give public notice of the names of the candidates elected, and, in case of a contested election, of the total number of votes given for each candidate, whether elected or not.

46. Where the returning officer is required or authorised by this Act to give any public notice, he shall carry such requirement into effect by advertisements, placards, handbills, or such other means as he thinks best calculated to afford information to the electors.

47. The returning officer may, if he think fit, preside at any polling station, and the provisions of this Act relating to a presiding officer shall apply to such returning officer with the necessary modifications as to things to be done by the returning officer to the presiding officer, or the presiding officer to the returning officer.

48. In the case of a contested election for any county or borough the returning officer may, in addition to any clerks, appoint competent persons to assist him in counting the votes.

49. No person shall be appointed by a returning officer for the purposes of an election who has been employed by any other person in or about the election.

50. The presiding officer may do, by the clerks appointed to assist him, any act which he is required or authorised to do by this Act at a polling station, except ordering the arrest, exclusion, or ejection from the polling station of any person.

51. A candidate may himself undertake the duties which any agent of his if appointed might have undertaken, or may assist his agent in the performance of such duties, and may be present at any place at which his agent may, in pursuance of this Act, attend.

52. The name and address of every agent of a candidate appointed to attend the counting of the votes shall be transmitted to the returning officer one clear day at the least before the opening of the poll; and the returning officer may refuse to admit to the place where the votes are counted any agent whose name and address has not been so transmitted, notwithstanding that his appointment may be otherwise valid and any notice required to be given to an agent by the returning officer may be delivered at or sent by post to such address.

53. If any person appointed an agent by a candidate for the purposes of attending at the polling station or at the counting of the votes dies, or becomes incapable of acting during the time of the election, the

candidate may appoint another agent in his place, and shall forthwith give to the returning officer notice in writing of the name and address of the agent so appointed.

54. Every returning officer, and every officer, clerk or agent authorised to attend at the polling station or at the counting of the votes, shall, before the opening of the poll, make a statutory declaration of secrecy, in the presence, if he is the returning officer, of a justice of the peace, and if he is any other officer or an agent, of a justice of the peace or of the returning officer; but no such returning officer, officer, clerk or agent as aforesaid shall, save as aforesaid, be required as such to make any declaration or take any oath on the occasion of any election.

55. Where in this Act any expressions are used requiring or authorising or inferring that any act or thing is to be done in the presence of the agents of the candidates, such expressions shall be deemed to refer to the presence of such agents of the candidates as may be authorised to attend, and as have in fact attended, at the time and place where such act or thing is being done, and the non-attendance of any agents or agent at such time and place shall not, if such act or thing be otherwise duly done, in anywise invalidate the act or thing done.

56. In reckoning time for the purposes of this Act, Sunday, Christmas Day, Good Friday, and any day set apart for a public fast or public thanksgiving, shall be excluded; and where anything is required by this Act to be done on any day which falls on the above-mentioned days, such thing may be done on the next day, unless it is one of the days excluded as above-mentioned.

57. In this Act—

The expression "district borough" means the borough of Monmouth and any of the boroughs specified in Schedule E. to the Act of the session of the second and third years of the reign of King William the Fourth, chapter 45, intituled "An Act to Amend the Representation of the People in England and Wales;" and—

The expression "polling place" means in the case of a borough, such borough or any part thereof in which a separate booth is required or authorised by law to be required; and

The expression "agents of the candidates," used in relation to a polling station, means agents appointed in pursuance of Section 85 of the Act of the session of the sixth and seventh years of the reign of Her present Majesty, chapter 18.

PART II.

Rules for Municipal Elections.

64. In the application of the provisions of this schedule to municipal elections the following modifications shall be made:—

(*a.*) The expression "register of voters" means the burgess roll of the burgesses of the borough, or, in the case of an election for the ward of a borough, the ward list; and the mayor shall provide true copies of such register for each polling station:

(*b.*) All ballot papers and other documents which, in the case of a parliamentary election, are forwarded to the clerk of the Crown in Chancery shall be delivered to the town clerk of the municipal borough in which the election is held, and shall be kept by him among the records of the borough; and the provisions of Part One of this Schedule with respect to the inspection, production, and destruction of such ballot papers and documents, and to the copies of such documents, shall apply respectively to the ballot papers and documents so in the custody of the town clerk, with these modifications; namely,

(*a.*) An order of the county court having jurisdiction in the borough, or any part thereof, or of any tribunal in which a municipal election is questioned, shall be substituted for an order of the House of Commons, or of one of Her Majesty's Superior Courts; but an appeal from such county court may be had in like manner as in other cases in such county court;

(*b.*) The regulations for the inspection of documents and the fees for the supply of copies of documents of which copies are directed to be supplied, shall be prescribed by the council of the borough with the consent of one of Her Majesty's Principal Secretaries of State; and, subject as aforesaid, the town clerk, in respect of the custody and destruction of the ballot papers and other documents coming into his possession in pursuance of this Act, shall be subject to the directions of the council of the borough.

(*c.*) Nothing in this schedule with respect to the day of the poll shall apply to a municipal election.

"GENERAL RULES (PARLIAMENTARY) M.T., 1868."

I.

The presentation of an election petition shall be made by leaving it at the office of the master nominated by the Chief Justice of the Common Pleas, and such master or his clerk shall (if required) give a receipt, which may be in the following form:—

Received on the   day of   at the master's office a petition touching the election of A.B., a member for   purporting to be signed by [insert the names of petitioners].

C.D., Master's Clerk.

With the petition shall also be left a copy thereof for the master to send to the returning officer pursuant to Section 7 of the Act.

II.

An election petition shall contain the following statements:—

1. It shall state the right of the petitioner to petition within Section 5 of the Act.
2. It shall state the holding and result of the election, and shall briefly state the facts and grounds relied on to sustain the prayer.

III.

The petition shall be divided into paragraphs, each of which, as nearly as may be, shall be confined to a distinct portion of the subject, and every paragraph shall be numbered consecutively, and no costs shall be allowed of drawing or copying any petition not substantially in compliance with this rule, unless otherwise ordered by the court or a judge.

IV.

The petition shall conclude with a prayer, as, for instance that some specified person should be declared duly returned or elected, or that the election should be declared void, or that a return may be enforced (as the case may be), and shall be signed by all the petitioners.

V.

The following form, or one to the like effect, shall be sufficient:—

In the Common Pleas.

"The Parliamentary Elections Act, 1868."

Election for [state the place] holden on the   day of   A.D.

The petition of A. of   [or of A. of   and B. of *as the case may be*] whose names are subscribed.

1. Your petitioner A. is a person who voted [or had a right to vote *as the case may be*] at the above election [or claims to have had a right to be returned at the above election, or was a candidate at the above election]; and your petitioner B. [here state in like manner the right of each petitioner.]

2. And your petitioners state that the election was holden on the day of   A.D.   when A.B., C.D. and E.F. were candidates, and the returning officer has returned A.B. and C.D. as being duly elected.

3. And your petitioners say that [*here state the facts and grounds on which the petitioners rely.*]

Wherefore your petitioners pray that it may be determined that the said A. B. was not duly elected or returned, and that the election was void [*or* that the said E.F. was duly elected and ought to have been returned, *or as the case may be.*]

(Signed)   A.
           B.

VI.

Evidence need not be stated in the petition, but the court or a judge may order such particulars as may be necessary to prevent surprise and unnecessary expense, and to ensure a fair and effectual trial in the same way as in ordinary proceedings in the Court of Common Pleas, and upon such terms as to costs and otherwise as may be ordered.

VII.

When a petitioner claims the seat for an unsuccessful candidate, alleging that he had a majority of lawful votes, the party complaining of or defending the election or return, shall, six days before the day appointed for trial, deliver to the master, and also to the address, if any, given by the petitioners and respondent, as the case may be, a list of the votes intended to be objected to, and of the heads of objection to each such vote, and the master shall allow inspection and office copies of such lists to all parties concerned ; and no evidence shall be given against the validity of any vote, nor upon any head of objection not specified in the list, except by the leave of the court or judge upon such terms as to amendment of the list, postponement of the inquiry and payment of costs as may be ordered.

VIII.

When the respondent in a petition under the Act, complaining of an undue return and claiming the seat for some person, intends to give evidence to prove that the election of such person was undue, pursuant to the 53rd Section of the Act, such respondent shall six days before the day appointed for trial deliver to the master, and also at the address, if any, given by the petitioner, a list of objections to the election upon which he intends to rely, and the master shall allow inspection and office copies of such lists to all parties concerned ; and no evidence shall be given by a respondent of any objection to the election not specified in the list, except by leave of the court or judge, upon such terms as to amendments of the list, postponement of the inquiry and payment of costs, as may be ordered.

IX.

With the petition, petitioners shall leave at the office of the master a writing signed by them or on their behalf, giving the name of some person entitled to practise as an attorney or agent in cases of election petitions whom they authorise to act as their agent, or stating that they act for themselves, as the case may be, and in either case giving an address within three miles from the General Post Office at which notices addressed to them may be left ; and if no such writing be left or address given, then notice of objection to the recognizances and all other notices and proceedings may be given by sticking up the same at the master's office.

X.

Any person returned as a member may at any time after he is returned send or leave at the office of the master a writing signed by him or on his behalf, appointing a person entitled to practise as an attorney or agent in cases of election petitions, to act as his agent in case there should be a petition against him, or stating that he intends to act for himself, and in either case giving an address within three miles from the General Post Office at which notices may be left, and in default of such writing being left in a week after service of the petition, notices and proceedings may be given and served respectively by sticking up the same at the master's office.

XI.

The master shall keep a book or books at his office in which he shall enter all addresses and the names of agents given under either of the preceding rules, which book shall be open to inspection by any person during office hours.

XII.

The master shall upon the presentation of the petition forthwith send a copy of the petition to the returning officer, pursuant to Section 7 of the Act, and shall therewith send the name of the petitioner's agent, if any, and of the address, if any, given as prescribed, and also of the name of the respondent's agent, and the address, if any, given as prescribed, and the returning officer shall forthwith publish those particulars along with the petition.

The cost of publication of this and any other matter required to be published by the returning officer shall be paid by the petitioner or person moving in the matter, and shall form part of the general costs of the petition.

XIII.

The time for giving notice of the presentation of a petition and of the nature of the proposed security shall be five days, exclusive of the day of presentation.

XIV.

Where the respondent has named an agent or given an address, the service of an election petition may be by delivery of it to the agent or by posting it in a registered letter to the address given at such time that, in the ordinary course of post, it would be delivered within the prescribed time.

In other cases the service must be personal on the respondent unless a judge on an application made to him not later than five days after the petition is presented on affidavit showing what has been done, shall be satisfied that all reasonable effort has been made to effect personal service and cause the matter to come to the knowledge of the respondent, including, when practicable, service upon an agent for election expenses, in which case the judge may order that what has been done shall be considered sufficient service, subject to such conditions as he may think reasonable.

XV.

In case of evasion of service, the sticking up a notice in the office of the master of the petition having been presented stating the petitioner, the prayer, and the nature of the proposed security, shall be deemed equivalent to personal service, if so ordered by a judge.

XVI.

The deposit of money by way of security for payment of costs, charges and expenses payable by the petitioner, shall be made by payment into the Bank of England to an account to be opened there by the description of "The Parliamentary Elections Act, 1868, Security Fund," which shall be vested in and drawn upon from time to time by the chief justice of the Common Pleas for the time being, for the purposes for which security is required by the said Act, and a bank-receipt or certificate for the same shall be forthwith left at the master's office.

XVII.

The master shall file such receipt or certificate, and keep a book open to inspection of all parties concerned, in which shall be entered from time to time the amount and the petition to which it is applicable.

XVIII.

The recognizance as security for costs may be acknowledged before a judge at chambers or the master in town, or a justice of the peace in the country.

There may be one recognizance acknowledged by all the sureties, or separate recognizances by one or more, as may be convenient.

XIX.

The recognizance shall contain the name and usual place of abode of each surety, with such sufficient description as shall enable him to be found or ascertained, and may be as follows :—

Be it remembered that on the   day of   in the year of our Lord 18 , before me [name and description] came A. B., of [name and description as above prescribed] and acknowledged himself [or severally acknowledged themselves] to owe to our sovereign lady the Queen the sum of one thousand pounds [or the following sums] (that is to say) the said C. D. the sum of £   , the said E. F., the sum of £   , the said G. H. the sum of £   , and the said J. K., the sum of £   , to be levied on his [or their respective] goods and chattels, land and tenements, to the use of our sovereign lady the Queen, her heirs and successors.

The condition of this recognizance is that if [here insert the names of all the petitioners, and if more than one add, or any of them] shall well and truly pay all costs, charges and expenses in respect of the election petition signed by him [or them] relating to the [here insert the name of the borough, or county] which shall become payable by the said petitioner [or petitioners, or any of them] under the Parliamentary

Elections Act, 1868, to any person or persons, then this recognizance to be void, otherwise to stand in full force.

(Signed)

[*Signatures of sureties.*]

Taken and acknowledged by the above-named [*names of sureties*] on the   day of   at   , before me,

C. D.,

A justice of the peace [*or as the case may be.*]

XX.

The recognizance or recognizances shall be left at the master's office, by or on behalf of the petitioner in like manner as before described for the leaving of a petition forthwith after being acknowledged.

XXI.

The time for giving notice of any objection to a recognizance under the 8th Section of the Act shall be within five days from the date of service of the notice of the petition and of the nature of the security, exclusive of the day of service.

XXII.

An objection to the recognizance must state the ground or grounds thereof, as that the sureties or any, and which of them, are insufficient, or that a surety is dead, or that he cannot be found, or that a person named in the recognizance has not duly acknowledged the same.

XXIII.

Any objection made to the security shall be heard and decided by the master, subject to appeal within five days to a judge, upon summons taken out by either party to declare the security sufficient or insufficient.

XXIV.

Such hearing and decision may be either upon affidavit or personal examination of witnesses, or both, as the master or judge may think fit.

XXV.

If by order made upon such summons the security be declared sufficient, its sufficiency shall be deemed to be established within the meaning of the 9th Section of the said Act, and the petition shall be at issue.

XXVI.

If by order made upon such summons an objection be allowed and the security be declared insufficient, the master or judge shall in such order state what amount he deems requisite to make the security sufficient, and the further prescribed time to remove the objection by deposit shall be within five days from the date of the order, not including the day of the date, and such deposit shall be made in the manner already prescribed.

XXVII.

The costs of hearing and deciding the objection made to the security given shall be paid as ordered by the master or judge, and in default of such order shall form part of the general costs of the petition.

XXVIII.

The costs of hearing and deciding an objection upon the ground of insufficiency of a surety or sureties, shall be paid by the petitioner, and a clause to that effect shall be inserted in the order declaring its sufficiency or insufficiency, unless at the time of leaving the recognizance with the master, there be also left with the master an affidavit of the sufficiency of the surety or sureties sworn by each surety before a justice of the peace, which affidavit any justice of the peace is hereby authorized to take, or before some person authorized to take affidavits in the Court of Common Pleas, that he is seized or possessed of real or personal estate, or both, above what will satisfy his debts of the clear value of the sum for which he is bound by his recognizance, which affidavit may be as follows :—

In the Common Pleas.

"Parliamentary Elections Act, 1868."

I, A. B. of [*as in recognizance*], make oath and say that I am seized or possessed of real [or personal] estate above what will satisfy my debts of the clear value of £

Sworn, &c.

XXIX.

The order of the master for payment of costs shall have the same force as an order made by a judge, and may be made a rule of the Court of Common Pleas, and enforced in like manner as a judge's order.

XXX.

The master shall make out the election list. In it he shall insert the name of the agents of the petitioners and respondent, and the addresses to which notices may be sent, if any. The list may be inspected at the master's office at any time during office hours, and shall be put up for that purpose upon a notice board appropriated to proceedings under the said Act, and headed "Parliamentary Elections Act, 1868."

XXXI.

The time and place of the trial of each election petition shall be fixed by the judges on the rota, and notice thereof shall be given in writing by the master by sticking notice up in his office, sending one copy by the post to the address given by the petitioner, another to the address given by the respondent, if any, and a copy by the post to the sheriff, or in case of a borough having a mayor, to the mayor of that borough, fifteen days before the day appointed for the trial.

The sheriff or mayor, as the case may be, shall forthwith publish the same in the county or borough.

XXXII.

The sticking up of the notice of trial at the office of the master shall be deemed and taken to be notice in the prescribed manner within the meaning of the Act, and such notice shall not be vitiated by any miscarriage of, or relating to, the copy or copies thereof to be sent as already directed.

XXXIII.

The notice of trial may be in the following form :—
"Parliamentary Elections Act, 1868."
Election petition of   county [or borough] of
Take notice, that the above petition [or petitions] will be tried at   on the   day of   and on such other subsequent days as may be needful.
Dated the   day of   .

By order,
(Signed)   A.B.,
The master appointed under the above Act.

XXXIV.

A judge may from time to time, by order made upon the application of a party to the petition, or by notice in such form as the judge may direct to be sent to the sheriff or mayor, as the case may be, postpone the beginning of the trial to such day as he may name, and such notice when received shall be forthwith made public by the sheriff or mayor.

XXXV.

In the event of the judge not having arrived at the time appointed for the trial, or to which the trial is postponed, the commencement of the trial shall *ipso facto* stand adjourned to the ensuing day, and so from day to day.

XXXVI.

No formal adjournment of the court for the trial of an election petition shall be necessary, but the trial is to be deemed adjourned, and may be continued from day to day until the inquiry is concluded ; and in the event of the judge who begins the trial being disabled by illness or otherwise, it may be recommenced and concluded by another judge.

XXXVII.

The application to state a special case may be made by rule in the Court of Common Pleas when sitting, or by a summons before a judge at chambers, upon hearing the parties.

XXXVIII.

The title of the court of record held for the trial of an election petition may be as follows :—
Court for the trial of an election petition for the   [county of   or borough of   *as may be*] between   petitioner and   respondent.
And it shall be sufficient so to entitle all proceedings in that court.

APPENDIX. 309

XXXIX.

An officer shall be appointed for each court for the trial of an election petition, who shall attend at the trial in like manner as the clerks of assize and of arraigns attend at the assize.

XL.

Repealed.

XLI.

The order of a judge to compel the attendance of a person as a witness may be in the following form :—
Court for the trial of an election petition for [complete the title of the court] the   day of   To A.B. [describe the person]   You are hereby required to attend before the above court at [place] on the   day of   at the hour of [or forthwith, as the case may be] to be examined as a witness in the matter of the said petition, and to attend the said court until your examination shall have been completed.
As witness my hand,
A. B.,
Judge of the said court.

XLII.

In the event of its being necessary to commit any person for contempt, the warrant may be as follows :—

At a court holden on   at   for the trial of an election petition for the county [or borough] of   , before Sir Samuel Martin, knight, one of the barons of her Majesty's Court of Exchequer, and one of the judges for the time being for the trial of election petitions in England, pursuant to "The Parliamentary Elections Act, 1868."
Whereas A. B. has this day been guilty, and is by the said court adjudged to be guilty, of a contempt thereof. The said court does therefore sentence the said A. B. for his said contempt to be imprisoned in the   gaol for   calendar months, and to pay to our lady the Queen a fine of £   , and to be further imprisoned in the said gaol until the said fine be paid. And the court further orders that the sheriff of the said county [or as the case may be] and all constables and officers of the peace of any county or place where the said A. B. may be found, shall take the said A. B. into custody and convey him to the said gaol, and there deliver him into the custody of the gaoler thereof, to undergo his said sentence. And the court further orders the said gaoler to receive the said A. B. into his custody, and that he shall be detained in the said gaol in pursuance of the said sentence.

A. D.

Signed the   day of

S. M.

XLIII.

Such warrant may be made out and directed to the sheriff or other person having the execution of process of the superior courts, as the case may be, and to all constables and officers of the peace of the county or place where the person adjudged guilty of contempt may be found, and such warrant shall be sufficient without further particularity, and shall and may be executed by the person to whom it is directed, or any or either of them.

XLIV.

All interlocutory questions and matters, except as to the sufficiency of the security, shall be heard and disposed of before a judge, who shall have the same control over the proceedings under "The Parliamentary Elections Act, 1868," as a judge at chambers in the ordinary proceedings of the superior courts, and such questions and matters shall be heard and disposed of by one of the judges upon the rota, if practicable, and if not, then by any judge at chambers.

XLV.

Notice of an application for leave to withdraw a petition shall be in writing and signed by the petitioners or their agent.

It shall state the ground on which the application is intended to be supported.

The following form shall be sufficient :—

"Parliamentary Elections Act, 1868."
County [or borough] of
      Petition of [*state petitioners*], presented   day of

The petitioner proposes to apply to withdraw his petition upon the following ground [*here state the ground*], and prays that a day may be appointed for hearing his application. Dated this   day of ,
          (Signed)

XLVI.

The notice of application for leave to withdraw shall be left at the master's office.

XLVII.

A copy of such notice of the intention of the petitioner to apply for leave to withdraw his petition shall be given by the petitioner to the respondent, and to the returning officer, who shall make it public in the county or borough to which it relates, and shall be forthwith published by the petitioner in at least one newspaper circulating in the place.

The following may be the form of such notice :—

"Parliamentary Elections Act, 1868."
In the election petition for   in which   is petitioner and   respondent.

Notice is hereby given that the above petitioner has on the day of   lodged at the master's office, notice of an application to withdraw the petition, of which notice the following is a copy—(*set it out.*)

And take notice that, by the rule made by the judges, any person who might have been a petitioner in respect of the said election may, within five days after publication by the returning officer of this notice, give notice in writing of his intention on the hearing to apply for leave to be substituted as a petitioner.

          (Signed)

XLVIII.

Any person who might have been a petitioner in respect of the election to which the petition relates, may, within five days after such notice is published by the returning officer, give notice in writing, signed by him or on his behalf, to the master, of his intention to apply at the hearing to be substituted for the petitioner, but the want of such notice shall not defeat such application if in fact made at the hearing.

XLIX.

The time and place for hearing the application shall be fixed by a judge, and whether before the Court of Common Pleas, or before a judge, as he may deem advisable, but shall not be less than a week after the notice of the intention to apply has been given to the master as hereinbefore provided, and notice of the time and place appointed for the hearing shall be given to such person or persons, if any, as shall have given notice to the master of an intention to apply to be substituted as petitioners, and otherwise in such manner and at such time as the judge directs.

L.

Notice of abatement of a petition, by death of the petitioner or surviving petitioner, under Section 37 of the said Act, shall be given by the party or person interested in the same manner as notice of an application to withdraw a petition; and the time within which application may be made to the court or a judge, by motion or summons at chambers, to be substituted as a petitioner, shall be one calendar month, or such further time as upon consideration of any special circumstances, the court or a judge may allow.

LI.

If the respondent dies or is summoned to Parliament as a peer of Great Britain by a writ issued under the great seal of Great Britain, or if the House of Commons have resolved that his seat is vacant, any person entitled to be a petitioner under the Act in respect of the election to which the petition relates, may give notice of the fact in the county or borough by causing such notice to be published in at least one newspaper circulating therein, if any, and by leaving a copy of such notice signed by him or on his behalf with the returning officer, and a like copy with the master.

LII.

The manner and time of the respondent's giving notice to the court that he does not intend to oppose the petition, shall be by leaving notice thereof in writing at the office of the master, signed by the respondent, six days before the day appointed for trial, exclusive of the day of leaving such notice.

LIII.

Upon such notice being left at the master's office, the master shall forthwith send a copy thereof by the post to the petitioner or his agent and to the sheriff or mayor, as the case may be, who shall cause the same to be published in the county or borough.

LIV.

The time for applying to be admitted as a respondent in either of the events mentioned in the 38th Section of the Act shall be within ten days after such notice is given as hereinbefore directed, or such further time as the court or a judge may allow.

LV.

Costs shall be taxed by the master, or at his request, by any master of a superior court, upon the rule of court or judge's order by which the costs are payable, and costs when taxed may be recovered by execution issued upon the rule of court ordering them to be paid ; or, if payable by the order of a judge, then by making such order a rule of court in the ordinary way, and issuing execution upon such rule against the person by whom the costs are ordered to be paid, or in case there be money in the bank available for the purpose, then to the extent of such money by order of the Chief Justice of the Common Pleas for the time being, upon a duplicate of the rule of court.

The office fees payable for inspection, office copies, enrolment, and other proceedings under the Act, and these rules, shall be the same as those payable, if any, for like proceedings according to the present practice of the Court of Common Pleas.

LVI.

The master shall prepare and keep a roll properly headed for entering the names of all persons entitled to practise as attorney or agent in cases of election petitions, and all matters relating to elections before the court and judges, pursuant to the 57th Section of the said Act ; which roll shall be kept and dealt with in all respects as the roll of attorneys of the Court of Common Pleas, and shall be under the control of that court, as to striking off the roll and otherwise.

LVII.

The entry upon the roll shall be written and subscribed by the attorney or agent, or some attorney authorised by him in writing to sign on his behalf, who shall therein set forth the name, description and address in full.

LVIII.

The master may allow any person upon the roll of attorneys for the time being, and during the present year any person whose name, or the name of whose firm is in the Law List of the present year as a Parliamentary agent to subscribe the roll, and permission to subscribe the roll may be granted to any other person by the court or judge upon affidavit, showing the facts which entitle the applicant to practise as agent according to the principles, practice and rules of the House of Commons in cases of election petitions.

LIX.

An agent employed for the petitioner or respondent shall forthwith leave written notice at the office of the master of his appointment to act as such agent, and service of notices and proceedings upon such agent shall be sufficient for all purposes.

LX.

No proceeding under "The Parliamentary Elections Act, 1868," shall be defeated by any formal objection.

LXI.

Any rule made or to be made in pursuance of the Act, if made in Term time, shall be published by being read by the master in the Court of Common Pleas, and if made out of Term, by a copy thereof being put up at the master's office.

"ADDITIONAL GENERAL RULE (PARLIAMENTARY), Dec., 1868."

That notice of the time and place of the trial of each election petition shall be transmitted by the master to the treasury, and to the clerk of the Crown in Chancery, and that the clerk of the Crown in Chancery shall, on or before the day fixed for the trial, deliver or cause to be delivered to the registrar of the judge who is to try the petition, or his deputy, the poll-books, for which the registrar or his deputy shall give, if required, a receipt. And that the registrar shall keep in safe custody the said poll-books until the trial is over, and then return the same to the Crown office.

"ADDITIONAL GENERAL RULES (PARLIAMENTARY), March, 1869."

I.

All claims at law or in equity to money deposited or to be deposited in the Bank of England for payment of costs, charges and expenses payable by the petitioners pursuant to the 10th General Rule, made the 21st November, 1868, by the judges for the trial of election petitions in England, shall be disposed of by the Court of Common Pleas or a judge.

II.

Money so deposited shall, if and when the same is no longer needed for securing payment of such costs, charges and expenses, be returned or otherwise disposed of as justice may require, by rule of the Court of Common Pleas or order of a judge.

III.

Such rule or order may be made after such notice of intention to apply, and proof that all just claims have been satisfied or otherwise sufficiently provided for as the court or judge may require.

IV.

The rule or order may direct payment either to the party in whose name the same is deposited or to any person entitled to receive the same.

V.

Upon such rule or order being made, the amount may be drawn for by the Chief Justice of the Common Pleas for the time being.

VI.

The draft of the Chief Justice of the Common Pleas for the time being shall, in all cases, be a sufficient warrant to the Bank of England for all payments made thereunder.

Dated the 25th day of March, 1869.

SAMUEL MARTIN. ×
J. S. WILLES. ×
COLIN BLACKBURN. ×

The Judges for the trial of Election Petitions in England.

"ADDITIONAL GENERAL RULES (PARLIAMENTARY), January, 1875."

I.

A copy of every order (other than an order giving further time for delivering particulars, or for costs only), or if the master shall so direct, the order itself or a duplicate thereof, also a copy of every particular delivered, shall be forthwith filed with the master, and the same shall be produced at the trial by the registrar, stamped with the official seal. Such order and particular respectively shall be filed by the party obtaining the same.

II.

The petitioner or his agent shall, immediately after notice of the presentation of a petition and of the nature of the proposed security shall have been served, file with the master an affidavit of the time and manner of service thereof.

III.

The days mentioned in Rules 7 and 8, and in any rule of court or judge's order, whereby particulars are ordered to be delivered, or any act is directed to be done, so many days before the day appointed for trial, are exclusively also of Sunday, Christmas Day, Good Friday, and any day set apart for a public fast or public thanksgiving.

IV.

When the last day for presenting petitions or filing lists of votes or objections, under Rules 7 or 8, or recognizances, or any other matter required to be filed within a given time, shall happen to fall on a holiday, the petition or other matter shall be deemed duly filed if put into the letter box at the master's office at any time during such day; but an affidavit, stating with reasonable precision the time when such delivery was made, shall be filed on the first day after the expiration of the holidays.

V.

Rule 40 is hereby revoked, and in lieu thereof it is ordered that the amount to be paid to any witness whose expenses shall be allowed by the judge shall be ascertained and certified by the registrar; or in the event of his becoming incapacitated from giving such certificate, by the judge.

VI.

After receiving notice of the petitioner's intention to apply for leave to withdraw, or of the respondent's intention not to oppose, or of the abatement of the petition by death, or of the happening of any of the events mentioned in the 38th section of the Act, if such notice be received after notice of trial shall have been given, and before the trial has commenced, the master shall forthwith countermand the notice of trial. The countermand shall be given in the same manner, as near as may be, as the notice of trial.

Dated the 27th day of January, 1875.

G. PIGOTT.
ROBT. LUSH.
GEORGE E. HONYMAN.

Judges for the time being on the rota for the trial of Election Petitions in England.

MUNICIPAL CORPORATIONS ACT, 1882.*

45 & 46 VICT. c. 50.

PART IV.

CORRUPT PRACTICES AND ELECTION PETITIONS.

Corrupt Practices.

77. In this Part—   Definitions.
"Bribery," "treating," "undue influence," and "personation," include respectively anything done before, at, after, or with respect to a municipal election, which if done before, at, after, or with respect to a parliamentary election would make the person doing the same liable to any penalty, punishment, or disqualification for bribery, treating, undue influence, or personation, as the case may be, under any Act for the time being in force with respect to parliamentary elections:

"Candidate" means a person elected, or having been nominated, or having declared himself a candidate for election, to a corporate office:

"Voter" means a burgess or a person who votes or claims to vote at a municipal election:

"Election court" means a court constituted under this Part for the trial of an election petition:

"Municipal election petition" or "election petition" means a petition under this Part complaining of an undue municipal election:

"Parliamentary election petition" means a petition under the Parliamentary Elections Act, 1868:

"Prescribed" means prescribed by general rules made under this Part:

"Borough" and "election" when used with reference to a petition mean the borough and election to which the petition relates:

81. A municipal election shall be wholly avoided by such general corruption, bribery, treating, or intimidation at the election as would by the common law of Parliament avoid a parliamentary election.   Avoidance of election for general corruption.

85. The votes of persons in respect of whom any corrupt practice is proved to have been committed at a municipal election shall be struck off on a scrutiny.   Striking off votes.

86. The enactments for the time being in force for the detection of personation and for the apprehension of persons charged with personation at a parliamentary election shall apply in the case of a municipal election.   Personation.

---

* The sections and parts of sections repealed by the Municipal Elections (Corrupt and Illegal Practices) Act, 1884, are omitted.

318 APPENDIX.

Election Petitions.

Power to question municipal election by petition.

87. (1.) A municipal election may be questioned by an election petition on the ground—

(*a.*) That the election was as to the borough or ward wholly avoided by general bribery, treating, undue influence, or personation; or

(*b.*) That the election was avoided by corrupt practices or offences against this Part committed at the election; or

(*c.*) That the person whose election is questioned was at the time of the election disqualified; or

(*d.*) That he was not duly elected by a majority of lawful votes.

(2.) A municipal election shall not be questioned on any of those grounds except by an election petition.

Presentation of petition.

88. (1.) An election petition may be presented either by four or more persons who voted or had a right to vote at the election, or by a person alleging himself to have been a candidate at the election.

(2.) Any person whose election is questioned by the petition, and any returning officer of whose conduct a petition complains, may be made a respondent to the petition.

(3.) The petition shall be in the prescribed form and shall be signed by the petitioner, and shall be presented in the prescribed manner to the High Court in the Queen's Bench Division, and the prescribed officer shall send a copy thereof to the town clerk, who shall forthwith publish it in the borough.

(4.) It shall be presented within twenty-one days after the day on which the election was held, except that if it complains of the election on the ground of corrupt practices, and specifically alleges that a payment of money or other reward has been made or promised since the election by a person elected at the election, or on his account or with his privity, in pursuance or furtherance of such corrupt practices, it may be presented at any time within twenty-eight days after the date of the alleged payment or promise, whether or not any other petition against that person has been previously presented or tried.

Security for costs.

89. (1.) At the time of presenting an election petition or within three days afterwards, the petitioner shall give security for all costs, charges, and expenses which may become payable by him to any witness summoned on his behalf, or to any respondent.

(2.) The security shall be to such amount, not exceeding five hundred pounds, as the High Court, or a Judge thereof, on summons, directs, and shall be given in the prescribed manner, either by a deposit of money, or by recognisance entered into by not more than four sureties, or partly in one way and partly in the other.

(3.) Within five days after the presentation of the petition the petitioner shall in the prescribed manner serve on the respondent a notice of the presentation of the petition, and of the nature of the proposed security, and a copy of the petition.

(4.) Within five days after service of the notice the respondent may object in writing to any recognisance on the ground that any surety is insufficient or is dead, or cannot be found or ascertained for want of a

APPENDIX.

sufficient description in the recognisance, or that a person named in the recognisance has not duly acknowledged the same.

(5.) An objection to a recognisance shall be decided in the prescribed manner.

(6.) If the objection is allowed, the petitioner may, within a further prescribed time not exceeding five days, remove it by a deposit in the prescribed manner of such sum of money as will, in the opinion of the court or officer having cognisance of the matter, make the security sufficient.

(7.) If no security is given, as prescribed, or any objection is allowed and is not removed, as aforesaid, no further proceedings shall be had on the petition.

90. On the expiration of the time limited for making objections, or, after objection made on the objection being disallowed or removed, whichever last happens, the petition shall be at issue. *Petition at issue.*

91. (1.) The prescribed officer shall as soon as may be make a list, in this Act referred to as the municipal election list, of all election petitions at issue, placing them in the order in which they were presented, and shall keep at his office a copy of this list, open to inspection in the prescribed manner. *Municipal election list.*

(2.) The petitions shall, as far as conveniently may be, be tried in the order in which they stand in the list.

(3.) Two or more candidates may be made respondents to the same petition, and their cases may be tried at the same time, but for the purposes of this part the petition shall be deemed to be a separate petition against each respondent.

(4.) Where more petitions than one are presented relating to the same election, or to elections held at the same time for different wards of the same borough, they shall be bracketed together in the list as one petition, but shall, unless the High Court otherwise directs, stand in the list in the place where the last of them would have stood if it had been the only petition relating to that election.

92. (1.) An election petition shall be tried by an election court consisting of a barrister qualified and appointed as in this section provided, without a jury. *Constitution of election court.*

(2.) A barrister shall not be qualified to constitute an election court if he is of less than fifteen years standing, or is a member of the Commons House of Parliament, or holds any office or place of profit under the Crown, other than that of recorder.

(3.) A barrister shall not be qualified to constitute an election court for trial of an election petition relating to any borough for which he is recorder, or in which he resides, or which is included in a circuit of Her Majesty's judges on which he practises as a barrister.

(4.) As soon as may be after a municipal election list is made out the prescribed officer shall send a copy thereof to each of the judges for the time being on the rota for the trial of parliamentary election petitions.

(5.) If a commissioner to whom the trial of a petition is assigned dies, or declines or becomes incapable to act, the said judges or two of them may assign the trial to be conducted or continued by any other of the commissioners appointed under this section.

320   APPENDIX.

(6.) The election court shall for the purposes of the trial have the same powers and privileges as a judge on the trial of a parliamentary election petition, except that any fine or order of committal by the court may on motion by the person aggrieved be discharged or varied by the High Court, or in vacation by a judge thereof, on such terms, if any, as the High Court or judge thinks fit.

Trial of election petition. **93.** (1.) An election petition shall be tried in open court, and notice of the time and place of trial shall be given in the prescribed manner not less than seven days before the day of trial.

(2.) The place of trial shall be within the borough, except that the High Court may, on being satisfied that special circumstances exist rendering it desirable that the petition should be tried elsewhere, appoint some other convenient place for the trial.

(3.) The election court may in its discretion adjourn the trial from time to time, and from any one place to any other place within the borough or place where it is held.

(4.) At the conclusion of the trial the election court shall determine whether the person whose election is complained of, or any and what other person, was duly elected, or whether the election was void, and shall forthwith certify in writing the determination to the High Court, and the determination so certified shall be final to all intents as to the matters at issue on the petition.

(5.) Where a charge is made in a petition of any corrupt practice or offence against this part having been committed at the election the court shall, in addition to the certificate, and at the same time, report in writing to the High Court as follows :—

(*a.*) Whether any corrupt practice or offence against this part has or has not been proved to have been committed by or with the knowledge and consent of any candidate at the election, and the nature of the corrupt practice or offence ;

(*b.*) The names of all persons (if any) proved at the trial to have been guilty of any corrupt practice or offence against this part ;

(*c.*) Whether any corrupt practices have, or whether there is reason to believe that any corrupt practices have, extensively prevailed at the election in the borough or in any ward thereof.

(6.) The election court may at the same time make a special report to the High Court as to any matters arising in the course of the trial, an account of which ought, in the judgment of the election court, to be submitted to the High Court.

(7.) If, on the application of any party to a petition made in the prescribed manner to the High Court, it appears to the High Court that the case raised by the petition can be conveniently stated as a special case, the High Court may direct the same to be stated accordingly, and any such special case shall be heard before the High Court, and the decision of the High Court shall be final.

(8.) If it appears to the election court on the trial of a petition that any question of law as to the admissibility of evidence, or otherwise, requires further consideration by the High Court, the election court may postpone the granting of a certificate until the question has been determined by the High Court, and for this purpose may reserve any such question, as questions may be reserved by a judge on a trial at nisi prius.

(9.) On the trial of a petition, unless the election court otherwise directs, any charge of a corrupt practice or offence against this part may be gone into, and evidence in relation thereto received before any proof has been given of agency on behalf of any candidate in respect of the corrupt practice or offence.

(10.) On the trial of a petition complaining of an undue election and claiming the office for some person, the respondent may give evidence to prove that that person was not duly elected, in the same manner as if he had presented a petition against the election of that person.

(11.) The trial of a petition shall be proceeded with notwithstanding that the respondent has ceased to hold the office his election to which is questioned by the petition.

(12.) A copy of any certificate or report made to the High Court on the trial of a petition, and, in the case of a decision by the High Court on a special case, a statement of the decision, shall be sent by the High Court to the Secretary of State.

(13.) A copy of any such certificate and a statement of any such decision shall also be certified by the High Court, under the hands of two or more judges thereof, to the town clerk of the borough.

94. (1.) Witnesses at the trial of an election petition shall be summoned and sworn in the same manner, as nearly as circumstances admit, as witnesses at a trial at nisi prius, and shall be liable to the same penalties for perjury. *Witnesses.*

(2.) On the trial the election court may, by order in writing, require any person who appears to the court to have been concerned in the election to attend as a witness, and any person refusing to obey the order shall be guilty of contempt of court.

(3.) The court may examine any person so required to attend or being in court although he is not called and examined by any party to the petition.

(4.) A witness may, after his examination by the court, be cross-examined by or on behalf of the petitioner and respondent or either of them.

(9.) The reasonable expenses incurred by any person in appearing to give evidence at the trial of an election petition, according to the scale allowed to witnesses on the trial of civil actions at the assizes, may be allowed to him by a certificate of the election court or of the prescribed officer, and if the witness was called and examined by the court, shall be deemed part of the expenses of providing a court, but otherwise, shall be deemed costs of the petition.

95. (1.) A petitioner shall not withdraw an election petition without the leave of the election court or High Court on special application, made in the prescribed manner, and at the prescribed time and place. *Withdrawal of petition.*

(2.) The application shall not be made until the prescribed notice of the intention to make it has been given in the borough.

(3.) On the hearing of the application any person who might have been a petitioner in respect of the election may apply to the court to be substituted as a petitioner, and the court may, if he thinks fit, substitute him accordingly.

(4.) If the proposed withdrawal is in the opinion of the court induced by any corrupt bargain or consideration, the court may by order direct that the security given on behalf of the original petitioner shall remain as security for any costs that may be incurred by the substituted petitioner, and that to the extent of the sum named in the security, the original petitioner and his sureties shall be liable to pay the costs of the substituted petitioner.

(5.) If the court does not so direct, then security to the same amount as would be required in the case of a new petition, and subject to the like conditions, shall be given on behalf of the substituted petitioner before he proceeds with his petition and within the prescribed time after the order of substitution.

(6.) Subject as aforesaid, a substituted petitioner shall, as nearly as may be, stand in the same position and be subject to the same liabilities as the original petitioner.

(7.) If a petition is withdrawn, the petitioner shall be liable to pay the costs of the respondent.

(8.) Where there are more petitioners than one, an application to withdraw a petition shall not be made except with the consent of all the petitioners.

Abatement of petition.

96. (1.) An election petition shall be abated by the death of a sole petitioner or of the survivor of several petitioners.

(2.) The abatement of a petition shall not affect the liability of the petitioner or of any other person to the payment of costs previously incurred.

(3.) On the abatement of a petition the prescribed notice thereof shall be given in the borough, and, within the prescribed time after the notice is given, any person who might have been a petitioner in respect of the election may apply to the election court or High Court in the prescribed manner and at the prescribed time and place to be substituted as a petitioner; and the Court may, if it thinks fit, substitute him accordingly.

(4.) Security shall be given on behalf of a petitioner so substituted, as in the case of a new petition.

Withdrawal and substitution of respondents.

97. (1.) If before the trial of an election petition a respondent other than a returning officer—

(*a.*) Dies, resigns, or otherwise ceases to hold the office to which the petition relates; or

(*b.*) Gives the prescribed notice that he does not intend to oppose the petition;

the prescribed notice thereof shall be given in the borough, and within the prescribed time after the notice is given any person who might have been a petitioner in respect of the election may apply to the election court or High Court to be admitted as a respondent to oppose the petition, and shall be admitted accordingly, except that the number of persons so admitted shall not exceed three.

(2.) A respondent who has given the prescribed notice that he does not intend to oppose the petition shall not be allowed to appear or act as a party against the petition in any proceedings thereon.

Costs on election petitions.

98. (1.) All costs, charges, and expenses of and incidental to the presentation of an election petition, and the proceedings consequent thereon, except such as are by this Act otherwise provided for, shall be defrayed by the parties to the petition in such manner and proportions as the election court determines; and in particular any costs, charges, or expenses which in the opinion of the court have been caused by vexatious conduct, unfounded allegations, or unfounded objections on the part either of the petitioner or of the respondent, and any needless expense incurred or caused on the part of petitioner or respondent, may be ordered to be defrayed by the parties by whom it has been incurred or caused, whether they are or not on the whole successful.

(3.) If a petitioner neglects or refuses for three months after demand to pay to any person summoned as a witness on his behalf, or to the respondent, any sum certified to be due to him for his costs, charges, and expenses, and the neglect or refusal is, within one year after the demand, proved to the satisfaction of the High Court, every person who has under this Act entered into a recognisance relating to the petition shall be held to have made default in the recognisance, and the prescribed officer shall thereon certify the recognisance to be forfeited, and it shall be dealt with as a forfeited recognisance relating to a parliamentary election petition.

99. (1.) The town clerk shall provide proper accommodation for holding the election court; and any expenses incurred by him for the purposes of this section shall be paid out of the borough fund or borough rate.

Reception of and attendance on the election court.

(2.) All chief and head constables, superintendents of police, headboroughs, gaolers, constables, and bailiffs shall give their assistance to the election court in the execution of its duties, and if any gaoler or officer of a prison makes default in receiving or detaining a prisoner committed thereto in pursuance of this Part, he shall be liable to a fine not exceeding five pounds for every day during which the default continues.

(3.) The election court may employ officers and clerks as prescribed.

(4.) A shorthand writer shall attend at the trial of an election petition, and shall be sworn by the election court faithfully and truly to take down the evidence given at the trial. He shall take down the evidence at length. A transcript of the notes of the evidence taken by him shall, if the election court so directs, accompany the certificate of the election court. His expenses, according to a prescribed scale, shall be treated as part of the expenses incurred in receiving the court.

100. (1.) The judges for the time being on the rota for the trial of parliamentary election petitions, may from time to time make, revoke, and alter General Rules for the effectual execution of this Part, and of the intention and object thereof, and the regulation of the practice, procedure, and costs of municipal election petitions, and the trial thereof, and the certifying and reporting thereon.

Rules of procedure and jurisdiction.

(2.) All such rules shall be laid before both Houses of Parliament within three weeks after they are made, if Parliament is then sitting, and if not, within three weeks after the beginning of the then next session of Parliament, and shall, while in force, have effect as if enacted in this Act.

(3.) Subject to the provisions of this Act, and of the rules made under it, the principles, practice, and rules for the time being observed in the case of parliamentary election petitions, and in particular the principles and rules with regard to agency and evidence and to a scrutiny, and to the declaring any person elected in the room of any other person declared to have been not duly elected, shall be observed, as far as may be, in the case of a municipal election petition.

(4.) The High Court shall, subject to this Act, have the same powers, jurisdiction, and authority with respect to a municipal election petition and the proceedings thereon as if the petition were an ordinary action within its jurisdiction.

(5.) The duties to be performed by the prescribed officer under this Part shall be performed by the prescribed officer of the High Court.

(6.) The general rules in force at the commencement of this Act with respect to matters within this Part shall, until superseded by rules made under this section, and subject to any amendment thereof by rules so made, have effect, with the necessary modifications, as if made under this section.

<small>Expenses of election court.</small>

101. (1.) The remuneration and allowances to be paid to a commissioner for his services in respect of the trial of an election petition, and to any officers, clerks, or shorthand writers employed under this Part, shall be fixed by a scale made and varied by the election judges on the rota for the trial of parliamentary election petitions, with the approval of the Treasury. The remuneration and allowances shall be paid in the first instance by the Treasury, and shall be repaid to the Treasury, on their certificate, out of the borough fund or borough rate.

(2.) But the election court may in its discretion order that such remuneration and allowances, or the expenses incurred by a town clerk for receiving the election court, shall be repaid, wholly or in part, to the Treasury or the town clerk, as the case may be, in the cases, by the persons, and in the manner following (namely):

(*a.*) When in the opinion of the election court a petition is frivolous and vexatious, by the petitioner:

(*b.*) When in the opinion of the election court a respondent has been personally guilty of corrupt practices at the election, by that respondent.

(3.) An order so made for the repayment of any sum by a petitioner or respondent may be enforced as an order for payment of costs; but a deposit made or security given under this Part shall not be applied for any such repayment until all costs and expenses payable by the petitioner or respondent to any party to the petition have been satisfied.

<small>Acts done pending a petition not invalidated.</small>

102. Where a candidate who has been elected to a corporate office is, by a certificate of an election court or a decision of the High Court, declared not to have been duly elected, acts done by him in execution of the office, before the time when the certificate or decision is certified to the town clerk, shall not be invalidated by reason of that declaration.

<small>Provisions as to elections in the room of persons unseated on petition.</small>

103. Where on an election petition the election of any person to a corporate office has been declared void, and no other person has been declared elected in his room, a new election shall be held to supply the vacancy in the same manner as on a casual vacancy; and, for the purposes of the election, any duties to be performed by a mayor, alderman, or other officer, shall, if he has been declared not elected, be performed by a deputy, or other person who might have acted for him if he had been incapacitated by illness.

104. A person who has voted at a municipal election by ballot shall not in any proceeding to question the election be required to state for whom he has voted. Prohibition of disclosure of vote.

Time.

230. (1.) Where by this Act any limited time from or after any date or event is appointed or allowed for the doing of any act or the taking of any proceeding, then in the computation of that limited time the same shall be taken as exclusive of the day of that date or of the happening of that event, and as commencing at the beginning of the next following day; and the act or proceeding shall be done or taken at the latest on the last day of the limited time as so computed, unless the last day is a Sunday, Christmas Day, Good Friday, or Monday or Tuesday in Easter week, or a day appointed for public fast, humiliation, or thanksgiving, in which case any act or proceeding shall be considered as done or taken in due time if it is done or taken on the next day afterwards, not being one of the days in this section specified. Computation of time.

(2.) Where by this Act any act or proceeding is directed or allowed to be done or taken on a certain day, then if that day happens to be one of the days in this section specified, the act or proceeding shall be considered as done or taken in due time if it is done or taken on the next day afterwards, not being one of the days in this section specified.

(3.) Where by this Act any act or proceeding is directed or allowed to be done or taken within any time not exceeding seven days, the days in this section specified shall not be reckoned in the computation of such time.

CORRUPT AND ILLEGAL PRACTICES PREVENTION ACT, 1883.

46 & 47 Vict. c. 51.

An Act for the Better Prevention of Corrupt and Illegal Practices at Parliamentary Elections.

[25th August, 1883.]

BE it enacted by the Queen's most Excellent Majesty, by and with the advice and consent of the Lords Spiritual and Temporal, and Commons, in this present Parliament assembled, and by the authority of the same, as follows :—

Corrupt Practices.

What is treating.

1. Whereas under Section 4 of the Corrupt Practices Prevention Act, 1854, persons other than candidates at parliamentary elections are not liable to any punishment for treating, and it is expedient to make such persons liable ; be it therefore enacted in substitution for the said Section 4, as follows :—

(1.) Any person who corruptly by himself or by any other person, either before, during, or after an election, directly or indirectly gives or provides, or pays wholly or in part the expense of giving or providing, any meat, drink, entertainment or provision to or for any person, for the purpose of corruptly influencing that person or any other person to give or refrain from giving his vote at the election, or on account of such person or any other person having voted or refrained from voting, or being about to vote or refrain from voting at such election, shall be guilty of treating.

(2.) And every elector who corruptly accepts or takes any such meat, drink, entertainment or provision shall also be guilty of treating.

What is undue influence.

2. Every person who shall directly or indirectly, by himself or by any other person on his behalf, make use of or threaten to make use of any force, violence, or restraint, or inflict or threaten to inflict, by himself or by any other person, any temporal or spiritual injury, damage, harm, or loss upon or against any person in order to induce or compel such person to vote or refrain from voting, or on account of such person having voted or refrained from voting at any election, or who shall by abduction, duress, or any fraudulent device or contrivance impede or prevent the free exercise of the franchise of any elector, or shall thereby compel, induce, or prevail upon any elector either to give or to refrain from giving his vote at any election, shall be guilty of undue influence.

What is corrupt practice.

3. The expression "corrupt practice" as used in this Act means any of the following offences : namely, treating and undue influence, as

defined by this Act, and bribery, and personation, as defined by the enactments set forth in Part III. of the Third Schedule to this Act, and aiding, abetting, counselling, and procuring the commission of the offence of personation, and every offence which is a corrupt practice within the meaning of this Act shall be a corrupt practice within the meaning of the Parliamentary Elections Act, 1868. *31 & 32 Vict. c. 125.*

4. Where upon the trial of an election petition respecting an election for a county or borough the election court, by the report made to the Speaker in pursuance of Section 11 of the Parliamentary Elections Act, 1868, reports that any corrupt practice other than treating or undue influence has been proved to have been committed in reference to such election by or with the knowledge and consent of any candidate at such election, or that the offence of treating or undue influence has been proved to have been committed in reference to such election, by any candidate at such election, that candidate shall not be capable of ever being elected to or sitting in the House of Commons for the said county or borough, and if he has been elected, his election shall be void; and he shall further be subject to the same incapacities as if at the date of the said report he had been convicted on an indictment of a corrupt practice. *Punishment of candidate found, on election petition, guilty personally of corrupt practices. 31 & 32 Vict. c. 125.*

5. Upon the trial of an election petition respecting an election for a county or borough, in which a charge is made of any corrupt practice having been committed in reference to such election, the election court shall report in writing to the Speaker whether any of the candidates at such election has been guilty by his agents of any corrupt practice in reference to such election; and if the report is that any candidate at such election has been guilty by his agents of any corrupt practice in reference to such election, that candidate shall not be capable of being elected to or sitting in the House of Commons for such county or borough for seven years after the date of the report, and if he has been elected his election shall be void. *Punishment of candidate found, on election petition, guilty by agents of corrupt practices.*

6. (1.) A person who commits any corrupt practice other than personation, or aiding, abetting, counselling, or procuring the commission to the offence of personation, shall be guilty of a misdemeanour, and on conviction on indictment shall be liable to be imprisoned, with or without hard labour, for a term not exceeding one year, or to be fined any sum not exceeding two hundred pounds. *Punishment of person convicted on indictment of corrupt practices.*

(2.) A person who commits the offence of personation, or of aiding, abetting, counselling, or procuring the commission of that offence, shall be guilty of felony, and any person convicted thereof, on indictment shall be punished by imprisonment for a term not exceeding two years, together with hard labour.

(3.) A person who is convicted on indictment of any corrupt practice shall (in addition to any punishment as above provided) be not capable during a period of seven years from the date of his conviction:

(*a*.) of being registered as an elector or voting at any election in the United Kingdom, whether it be a parliamentary election or an election for any public office within the meaning of this Act; or

(*b*.) of holding any public or judicial office with the meaning of this Act, and if he holds any such office the office shall be vacated.

(4.) Any person so convicted of a corrupt practice in reference to any election shall also be incapable of being elected to and of sitting in the House of Commons during the seven years next after the date of his conviction, and if at that date he has been elected to the House of Commons his election shall be vacated from the time of such conviction.

Illegal practices.

<small>Certain expenditure to be illegal practice.</small>

7. (1.) No payment or contract for payment shall, for the purpose of promoting or procuring the election of a candidate at any election, be made—

(*a.*) on account of the conveyance of electors to or from the poll, whether for the hiring of horses or carriages, or for railway fares, or otherwise ; or

(*b.*) to an elector on account of the use of any house, land, building, or premises for the exhibition of any address, bill, or notice, or on account of the exhibition of any address, bill, or notice ; or

(*c.*) on account of any committee-room in excess of the number allowed by the First Schedule to this Act.

(2.) Subject to such exception as may be allowed in pursuance of this Act, if any payment or contract for payment is knowingly made in contravention of this section either before, during, or after an election, the person making such payment or contract shall be guilty of an illegal practice, and any person receiving such payment or being a party to any such contract, knowing the same to be in contravention of this Act, shall be guilty of an illegal practice.

(3.) Provided that where it is the ordinary business of an elector as an advertising agent to exhibit for payment bills and advertisements, a payment to or contract with such elector, if made in the ordinary course of business, shall not be deemed to be an illegal practice within the meaning of this section.

<small>Expense in excess of maximum to be illegal practice.</small>

8. (1.) Subject to such exception as may be allowed in pursuance of this Act, no sum shall be paid and no expense shall be incurred by a candidate at an election or his election agent, whether before, during, or after an election, on account of or in respect of the conduct or management of such election, in excess of any maximum amount in that behalf specified in the First Schedule to this Act.

(2.) Any candidate or election agent who knowingly acts in contravention of this section shall be guilty of an illegal practice.

<small>Voting by prohibited persons and publishing of false statements of withdrawal to be illegal.</small>

9. (1.) If any person votes or induces or procures any person to vote at any election, knowing that he or such person is prohibited, whether by this or any other Act from voting at such election, he shall be guilty of an illegal practice.

(2.) Any person who before or during an election knowingly publishes a false statement of the withdrawal of a candidate at such election for the purpose of promoting or procuring the election of another candidate shall be guilty of an illegal practice.

(3.) Provided that a candidate shall not be liable, nor shall his election be avoided, for any illegal practice under this section committed by his agent other than his election agent.

10. A person guilty of an illegal practice, whether under the foregoing sections or under the provisions hereinafter contained in this Act, shall on summary conviction be liable to a fine not exceeding one hundred pounds, and be incapable during a period of five years from the date of his conviction of being registered as an elector or voting at any election (whether it be a parliamentary election or an election for a public office within the meaning of this Act) held for or within the county or borough in which the illegal practice has been committed.

<small>Punishment on conviction of illegal practice.</small>

11. Whereas by sub-section 14 of Section 11 of the Parliamentary Elections Act, 1868, it is provided that where a charge is made in an election petition of any corrupt practice having been committed at the election to which the petition refers, the judge shall report in writing to the speaker as follows :—

<small>Report of election court respecting illegal practice, and punishment of candidate found guilty by such report. 31 & 32 Vict. c. 125.</small>

  (*a*.) "Whether any corrupt practice has or has not been proved to have been committed by or with the knowledge and consent of any candidate at such election, and the nature of such corrupt practice:
  (*b*.) "The names of all persons, if any, who have been proved at the trial to have been guilty of any corrupt practice:
  (*c*.) "Whether corrupt practices have, or whether there is reason to believe corrupt practices have extensively prevailed at the election to which the petition relates":

And whereas it is expedient to extend the said sub-section to illegal practices:

Be it therefore enacted as follows :—

Sub-section 14 of Section 11 of the Parliamentary Elections Act, 1868, shall apply as if that sub-section were herein re-enacted with the substitution of illegal practice within the meaning of this Act for corrupt practice; and upon the trial of an election petition respecting an election for a county or borough, the election court shall report in writing to the speaker the particulars required by the said sub-section as herein re-enacted, and shall also report whether any candidate at such election has been guilty by his agents of any illegal practice within the meaning of this Act in reference to such election, and the following consequences shall ensue upon the report by the election court to the speaker; (that is to say)

<small>31 & 32 Vict., c. 125.</small>

  (a.) If the report is that any illegal practice has been proved to have been committed in reference to such election by or with the knowledge and consent of any candidate at such election, that candidate shall not be capable of being elected to or sitting in the House of Commons for the said county or borough for seven years next after the date of the report, and if he has been elected his election shall be void; and he shall further be subject to the same incapacities as if at the date of the report he had been convicted of such illegal practice; and

  (b.) If the report is that a candidate at such election has been guilty by his agents of any illegal practice in reference to such election, that candidate shall not be capable of being elected to or sitting in the House of Commons for the said county or borough during the Parliament for which the election was held, and if he has been elected, his election shall be void

12. Whereas by the Election Commissioners Act, 1852, as amended by the Parliamentary Elections Act, 1868, it is enacted that where a

<small>Extension of 15 & 16 Vict. c. 57, respecting</small>

election commissioners to illegal practices. 15 & 16 Vict. c. 57. 31 & 32 Vict. c. 57.	joint address of both Houses of Parliament represents to Her Majesty that an election court has reported to the Speaker that corrupt practices have, or that there is reason to believe that corrupt practices have extensively prevailed at an election in any county or borough, and prays Her Majesty to cause inquiry under that Act to be made by persons named in such address (being qualified as therein mentioned), it shall be lawful for Her Majesty to appoint the said persons to be election commissioners for the purpose of making inquiry into the existence of such corrupt practices: And whereas it is expedient to extend the said enactments to the case of illegal practices: Be it therefore enacted as follows:
16 & 16 Vict. c. 57.	When election commissioners have been appointed in pursuance of the Election Commissioners Act, 1852, and the enactments amending the same, they may make inquiries and act and report as if "corrupt practices" in the said Act and the enactments amending the same included illegal practices; and the Election Commissioners Act, 1852, shall be construed with such modifications as are necessary for giving effect to this section, and the expression "corrupt practice" in that Act shall have the same meaning as in this Act.

Illegal Payment, Employment, and Hiring.

Providing of money for illegal practice or payment to be illegal payment.	**13.** Where a person knowingly provides money for any payment which is contrary to the provisions of this Act, or for any expenses incurred in excess of any maximum amount allowed by this Act, or for replacing any money expended in any such payment or expenses, except where the same may have been previously allowed in pursuance of this Act to be an exception, such person shall be guilty of illegal payment.
Employment of hackney carriages, or of carriages and horses kept for hire.	**14.** (1.) A person shall not let, lend, or employ for the purpose of the conveyance of electors to or from the poll, any public stage or hackney carriage, or any horse or other animal kept or used for drawing the same, or any carriage, horse, or other animal which he keeps or uses for the purpose of letting out for hire, and if he lets, lends, or employs such carriage, horse, or other animal, knowing that it is intended to be used for the purpose of the conveyance of electors to or from the poll, he shall be guilty of an illegal hiring. (2.) A person shall not hire, borrow, or use for the purpose of the conveyance of electors to or from the poll any carriage, horse, or other animal which he knows the owner thereof is prohibited by this section to let, lend, or employ for that purpose, and if he does so he shall be guilty of an illegal hiring. (3.) Nothing in this Act shall prevent a carriage, horse, or other animal being let to or hired, employed, or used by an elector, or several electors at their joint cost, for the purpose of being conveyed to or from the poll. (4.) No person shall be liable to pay any duty or to take out a license for any carriage by reason only of such carriage being used without payment or promise of payment for the conveyance of electors to or from the poll at an election.
Corrupt with-	**15.** Any person who corruptly induces or procures any other person

APPENDIX.

to withdraw from being a candidate at an election, in consideration of any payment or promise of payment, shall be guilty of illegal payment, and any person withdrawing, in pursuance of such inducement or procurement, shall also be guilty of illegal payment.

drawal from a candidature.

16. (1.) No payment or contract for payment shall, for the purpose of promoting or procuring the election of a candidate at any election, be made on account of bands of music, torches, flags, banners, cockades, ribbons, or other marks of distinction.

Certain expenditure to be illegal payment.

(2.) Subject to such exception as may be allowed in pursuance of this Act, if any payment or contract for payment is made in contravention of this section, either before, during, or after an election, the person making such payment shall be guilty of illegal payment, and any person being a party to any such contract or receiving such payment shall also be guilty of illegal payment if he knew that the same was made contrary to law.

17. (1.) No person shall, for the purpose of promoting or procuring the election of a candidate at any election, be engaged or employed for payment or promise of payment for any purpose or in any capacity whatever, except for any purposes or capacities mentioned in the first or second parts of the First Schedule to this Act, or except so far as payment is authorised by the first or second parts of the First Schedule to this Act.

Certain employment to be illegal.

(2.) Subject to such exception as may be allowed in pursuance of this Act, if any person is engaged or employed in contravention of this section, either before, during, or after an election, the person engaging or employing him shall be guilty of illegal employment, and the person so engaged or employed shall also be guilty of illegal employment if he knew that he was engaged or employed contrary to law.

18. Every bill, placard, or poster having reference to an election shall bear upon the face thereof the name and address of the printer and publisher thereof; and any person printing, publishing, or posting, or causing to be printed, published, or posted, any such bill, placard, or poster as aforesaid, which fails to bear upon the face thereof the name and address of the printer and publisher, shall, if he is the candidate, or the election agent of the candidate, be guilty of an illegal practice, and if he is not the candidate, or the election agent of a candidate, shall be liable on summary conviction to a fine not exceeding one hundred pounds.

Name and address of printer on placards.

19. The provisions of this Act prohibiting certain payments and contracts for payments, and the payment of any sum, and the incurring of any expense in excess of a certain maximum, shall not affect the right of any creditor, who, when the contract was made or the expense was incurred, was ignorant of the same being in contravention of this Act.

Saving for creditors.

20. (*a*.) Any premises on which the sale by wholesale or retail of any intoxicating liquor is authorised by a licence (whether the licence be for consumption on or off the premises), or

Use of committee room in house for sale of

332 APPENDIX.

Intoxicating liquor or refreshment, or in elementary school, to be illegal hiring.

(*b.*) Any premises where any intoxicating liquor is sold, or is supplied to members of a club, society, or association other than a permanent political club, or

(*c.*) Any premises whereon refreshment of any kind, whether food or drink, is ordinarily sold for consumption on the premises, or

(*d.*) The premises of any public elementary school in receipt of an annual parliamentary grant, or any part of any such premises, or shall not be used as a committee room for the purpose of promoting or procuring the election of a candidate at an election, and if any person hires or uses any such premises or any part thereof for a committee room he shall be guilty of illegal hiring, and the person letting such premises or part, if he knew it was intended to use the same as a committee room, shall also be guilty of illegal hiring :

Provided that nothing in this Section shall apply to any part of such premises which is ordinarily let for the purpose of chambers or offices or the holding of public meetings or of arbitrations, if such part has a separate entrance and no direct communication with any part of the premises on which any intoxicating liquor or refreshment is sold or supplied as aforesaid.

Punishment of illegal payment, employment, or hiring.

21. (1.) A person guilty of an offence of illegal payment, employment or hiring shall, on summary conviction, be liable to a fine not exceeding one hundred pounds.

(2.) A candidate or an election agent of a candidate who is personally guilty of an offence of illegal payment, employment, or hiring shall be guilty of an illegal practice.

Excuse and Exception for Corrupt or Illegal Practice or Illegal Payment, Employment, or Hiring.

Report exonerating candidate in certain cases of corrupt and illegal practice by agents.

22. Where, upon the trial of an election petition respecting an election for a county or borough, the election court report that a candidate at such election has been guilty by his agents of the offence of treating and undue influence, and illegal practice, or of any of such offences, in reference to such election, and the election court further report that the candidate has proved to the court :

(*a.*) That no corrupt or illegal practice was committed at such election by the candidate or his election agent and the offences mentioned in the said report were committed contrary to the orders and without the sanction or connivance of such candidate or his election agent ; and

(*b.*) That such candidate and his election agent took all reasonable means for preventing the commission of corrupt and illegal practices at such election ; and

(*c.*) That the offences mentioned in the said report were of a trivial, unimportant, and limited character ; and

(*d.*) That in all other respects the election was free from any corrupt or illegal practice on the part of such candidate and of his agents ;

then the election of such candidate shall not, by reason of the offences mentioned in such report, be void, nor shall the candidate be subject to any incapacity under this Act.

Power of High Court and election court

23. Where, on application made, it is shown to the High Court or to an election court by such evidence as seems to the Court sufficient :

(*a.*) That any act or omission of a candidate at any election, or of his election agent or of any other agent or person, would, by reason of being a payment, engagement, employment, or contract in contravention of this Act, or being the payment of a sum or the incurring of expense in excess of any maximum amount allowed by this Act, or of otherwise being in contravention of any of the provisions of this Act, be but for this section an illegal practice, payment, employment, or hiring ; and to except innocent act from being illegal practice, &c.

(*b.*) That such act or omission arose from inadvertence or from accidental miscalculation or from some other reasonable cause of a like nature, and in any case did not rise from any want of good faith ; and

(*c.*) That such notice of the application has been given in the county or borough for which the election was held as to the court seems fit ;

and under the circumstances it seems to the court to be just that the candidate and the said election and other agent and person, or any of them, should not be subject to any of the consequences under this Act of the said act or omission, the court may make an order allowing such act or omission to be an exception from the provisions of this Act which would otherwise make the same an illegal practice, payment, employment, or hiring, and thereupon such candidate, agent, or person shall not be subject to any of the consequences under this Act of the said act or omission.

Election Expenses.

24. (1.) On or before the day of nomination at an election, a person shall be named by or on behalf of each candidate as his agent for such election (in this Act referred to as the election agent). Nomination of election agent.

(2.) A candidate may name himself as election agent, and thereupon shall, so far as circumstances admit, be subject to the provisions of this Act both as a candidate and as an election agent, and any reference in this Act to an election agent shall be construed to refer to the candidate acting in his capacity of election agent.

(3.) On or before the day of nomination the name and address of the election agent of each candidate shall be declared in writing by the candidate or some other person on his behalf to the returning officer, and the returning officer shall forthwith give public notice of the name and address of every election agent so declared.

(4.) One election agent only shall be appointed for each candidate, but the appointment, whether the election agent appointed be the candidate himself or not, may be revoked, and in the event of such revocation or his death, whether such event is before, during, or after the election, then forthwith another election agent shall be appointed, and his name and address declared in writing to the returning officer, who shall forthwith give public notice of the same.

25. (1.) In the case of the elections specified in that behalf in the First Schedule to this Act an election agent of a candidate may appoint the number of deputies therein mentioned (which deputies are in this Act referred to as sub-agents), to act within different polling districts. Nomination of deputy election agent as sub-agent.

(2.) As regards matters in a polling district the election agent may act by the sub-agent for that district, and anything done for the purposes of this Act by or to the sub-agent in his district shall be deemed to be done by or to the election agent, and any act or default of a sub-agent which, if he were the election agent, would be an illegal practice or other offence against this Act, shall be an illegal practice and offence against this Act committed by the sub-agent, and the sub-agent shall be liable to punishment accordingly; and the candidate shall suffer the like incapacity as if the said act or default had been the act or default of the election agent.

(3.) One clear day before the polling the election agent shall declare in writing the name and address of every sub-agent to the returning officer, and the returning officer shall forthwith give public notice of the name and address of every sub-agent so declared.

(4.) The appointment of a sub-agent shall not be vacated by the election agent who appointed him ceasing to be election agent, but may be revoked by the election agent for the time being of the candidate, and in the event of such revocation or of the death of a sub-agent another sub-agent may be appointed, and his name and address shall be forthwith declared in writing to the returning officer, who shall forthwith give public notice of the same.

Office of election agent and sub-agent.

26. (1.) An election agent at an election for a county or borough shall have within the county or borough, or within any county of a city or town adjoining thereto, and a sub-agent shall have within his district, or within any county of a city or town adjoining thereto, an office or place to which all claims, notices, writs, summonses, and documents may be sent, and the address of such office or place shall be declared at the same time as the appointment of the said agent to the returning officer, and shall be stated in the public notice of the name of the agent.

(2.) Any claim, notice, writ, summons, or document delivered at such office or place and addressed to the election agent or sub-agent, as the case may be, shall be deemed to have been served on him, and every such agent may in respect of any matter connected with the election in which he is acting be sued in any court having jurisdiction in the county or borough in which the said office or place is situate.

Making of contracts through election agent.

27. (1.) The election agent of a candidate by himself or by his sub-agent shall appoint every polling agent, clerk, and messenger employed for payment on behalf of the candidate at an election, and hire every committee-room hired on behalf of the candidate.

(2.) A contract whereby any expenses are incurred on account of or in respect of the conduct or management of an election shall not be enforceable against a candidate at such election unless made by the candidate himself or by his election agent, either by himself or by his sub-agent; provided that the inability under this section to enforce such contract against the candidate shall not relieve the candidate from the consequences of any corrupt or illegal practice having been committed by his agent.

Payment of expenses through election agent.

28. (2.) Except as permitted by or in pursuance of this Act, no payment and no advance or deposit shall be made by a candidate at an election or by any agent on behalf of the candidate or by any other person at any time, whether before, during, or after such election, in respect of any expenses incurred on account of or in respect of the conduct or management of such election, otherwise than by or through the election agent of the candidate, whether acting in person or by a sub-agent; and all money provided by any person other than the candidate for any expenses incurred on account of or in respect of the conduct or management of the election, whether as gift, loan, advance, or deposit, shall be paid to the candidate or his election agent and not otherwise;

Provided that this section shall not be deemed to apply to a tender of security to or any payment by the returning officer or to any sum disbursed by any person out of his own money for any small expense legally incurred by himself, if such sum is not repaid to him.

(2.) A person who makes any payment, advance, or deposit in contravention of this section, or pays in contravention of this section any money so provided as aforesaid, shall be guilty of an illegal practice.

29. (1.) Every payment made by an election agent, whether by himself or a sub-agent, in respect of any expenses incurred on account of or in respect of the conduct or management of an election, shall, except where less than forty shillings, be vouched for by a bill stating the particulars and by a receipt. *Period for sending in claims and making payments for election expenses.*

(2.) Every claim against a candidate at an election or his election agent in respect of any expenses incurred on account of or in respect of the conduct or management of such election which is not sent in to the election agent within the time limited by this Act shall be barred and shall not be paid; and, subject to such exception as may be allowed in pursuance of this Act, an election agent who pays a claim in contravention of this enactment shall be guilty of an illegal practice.

(3.) Except as by this Act permitted, the time limited by this Act for sending in claims shall be fourteen days after the day on which the candidates returned are declared elected.

(4.) All expenses incurred by or on behalf of a candidate at an election, which are incurred on account of or in respect of the conduct or management of such election, shall be paid within the time limited by this Act and not otherwise; and, subject to such exception as may be allowed in pursuance of this Act, an election agent who makes a payment in contravention of this provision shall be guilty of an illegal practice;

(5.) Except as by this Act permitted, the time limited by this Act for the payment of such expenses as aforesaid shall be twenty-eight days after the day on which the candidates returned are declared elected.

(6.) Where the election court reports that it has been proved to such court by a candidate that any payment made by an election agent in contravention of this section was made without the sanction or connivance of such candidate, the election of such candidate shall not be void, nor shall he be subject to any incapacity under this Act by reason only of such payment having been made in contravention of this section.

(7.) If the election agent in the case of any claim sent in to him within the time limited by this Act disputes it, or refuses or fails to pay it within the said period of twenty-eight days, such claim shall be deemed to be a disputed claim.

(8.) The claimant may, if he thinks fit, bring an action for a disputed claim in any competent court; and any sum paid by the candidate or his agent in pursuance of the judgment or order of such court shall be deemed to be paid within the time limited by this Act, and to be an exception from the provisions of this Act requiring claims to be paid by the election agent.

(9.) On cause shown to the satisfaction of the High Court, such court, on application by the claimant or by the candidate or his election agent, may by order give leave for the payment by a candidate or his election agent of a disputed claim, or of a claim for any such expenses as aforesaid, although sent in after the time in this section mentioned for sending in claims, or although the same was sent in to the candidate and not to the election agent.

(10.) Any sum specified in the order of leave may be paid by the candidate or his election agent, and when paid in pursuance of such leave shall be deemed to be paid within the time limited by this Act.

Reference to taxation of claim against candidates.

30. If any action is brought in any competent court to recover a disputed claim against a candidate at an election, or his election agent, in respect of any expenses incurred on account or in respect of the conduct or management of such election, and the defendant admits his liability, but disputes the amount of the claim, the said amount shall, unless the court, on the application of the plaintiff in the action otherwise directs, be forthwith referred for taxation to the master, official referee, registrar, or other proper officer of the court, and the amount found due on such taxation shall be the amount to be recovered in such action in respect of such claim.

Personal expenses of candidate and petty expenses.

31. (1.) The candidate at an election may pay any personal expenses incurred by him on account of or in connection with or incidental to such election to an amount not exceeding one hundred pounds, but any further personal expenses so incurred by him shall be paid by his election agent.

(2.) The candidate shall send to the election agent within the time limited by this Act for sending in claims a written statement of the amount of personal expenses paid as aforesaid by such candidate.

(3.) Any person may, if so authorised in writing by the election agent of the candidate, pay any necessary expenses for stationery, postage, telegrams, and other petty expenses, to a total amount not exceeding that named in the authority, but any excess above the total amount so named shall be paid by the election agent.

(4.) A statement of the particulars of payments made by any person so authorised shall be sent to the election agent within the time limited by this Act for the sending in of claims, and shall be vouched for by a bill containing the receipt of that person.

Remuneration of election agent and returning officer's expenses.

32. (1.) So far as circumstances admit, this Act shall apply to a claim for his remuneration by an election agent and to the payment thereof in like manner as if he were any other creditor, and if any difference arises respecting the amount of such claim, the claim shall be a disputed claim within the meaning of this Act, and be dealt with accordingly.

38 & 39 Vict. c. 84.

(2.) The account of the charges claimed by the returning officer in the case of a candidate and transmitted in pursuance of Section 4 of the Parliamentary Elections (Returning Officers) Act, 1875, shall be transmitted within the time specified in the said section to the election agent of the candidate, and need not be transmitted to the candidate.

33. (1.) Within thirty-five days after the day on which the candidates returned at an election are declared elected, the election agent of every candidate at that election shall transmit to the returning officer a true return (in this Act referred to as a return respecting election expenses), in the form set forth in the Second Schedule to this Act or to the like effect, containing, as respects that candidate :—

Return and declaration respecting election expenses.

 (a.) A statement of all payments made by the election agent, together with all the bills and receipts (which bills and receipts are in this Act included in the expression "return respecting election expenses");

 (b.) A statement of the amount of personal expenses, if any, paid by the candidate;

 (c.) A statement of the sums paid to the returning officer for his charges, or, if the amount is in dispute, of the sum claimed and the amount disputed;

 (d.) A statement of all other disputed claims of which the election agent is aware;

 (e.) A statement of all the unpaid claims, if any, of which the election agent is aware, in respect of which application has been or is about to be made to the High Court;

 (f.) A statement of all money, securities, and equivalent of money received by the election agent from the candidate or any other person for the purpose of expenses incurred or to be incurred on account of or in respect of the conduct or management of the election, with a statement of the name of every person from whom the same may have been received.

(2.) The return so transmitted to the returning officer shall be accompanied by a declaration made by the election agent before a justice of the peace in the form in the Second Schedule to this Act (which declaration is in this Act referred to as a declaration respecting election expenses).

(3.) Where the candidate has named himself as his election agent, a statement of all money, securities, and equivalent of money paid by the candidate shall be substituted in the return required by this section to be transmitted by the election agent for the like statement of money, securities, and equivalent of money received by the election agent from the candidate; and the declaration by an election agent respecting election expenses need not be made, and the declaration by the candidate respecting election expenses shall be modified as specified in the Second Schedule to this Act.

(4.) At the same time that the agent transmits the said return, or within seven days afterwards, the candidate shall transmit or cause to be transmitted to the returning officer a declaration made by him before a justice of the peace, in the form in the first part of the Second Schedule to this Act (which declaration is in this Act referred to as a declaration respecting election expenses).

(5.) If in the case of an election for any county or borough, the said return and declarations are not transmitted before the expiration of the time limited for the purpose, the candidate shall not, after the expiration of such time, sit or vote in the House of Commons as member for that county or borough until either such return and declarations have been transmitted, or until the date of the allowance of such an authorised excuse for the failure to transmit the same, as in this Act mentioned, and if he sits or votes in contravention of this enactment he shall forfeit one hundred pounds for every day on which he so sits or votes to any person who sues for the same.

(6.) If without such authorised excuse as in this Act mentioned, a candidate or an election agent fails to comply with the requirements of this section, he shall be guilty of an illegal practice.

(7.) If any candidate or election agent knowingly makes the declaration required by this section falsely, he shall be guilty of an offence, and on conviction thereof on indictment shall be liable to the punishment for wilful and corrupt perjury; such offence shall also be deemed to be a corrupt practice within the meaning of this Act.

(8.) When the candidate is out of the United Kingdom at the time when the return is so transmitted to the returning officer, the declaration required by this section may be made by him within fourteen days after his return to the United Kingdom, and in that case shall be forthwith transmitted to the returning officer, but the delay hereby authorised in making such declaration shall not exonerate the election agent from complying with the provisions of this Act as to the return and declaration respecting election expenses.

(9.) Where, after the date at which the return respecting election expenses is transmitted, leave is given by the High Court for any claims to be paid, the candidate or his election agent shall, within seven days after the payment thereof, transmit to the returning officer a return of the sums paid in pursuance of such leave accompanied by a copy of the order of the court giving the leave, and in default he shall be deemed to have failed to comply with the requirements of this section without such authorised excuse as in this Act mentioned.

<small>Authorised excuse for non-compliance with provisions as to return and declaration respecting election expenses</small>

34. (1.) Where the return and declarations respecting election expenses of a candidate at an election for a county or borough have not been transmitted as required by this Act, or being transmitted contain some error or false statement, then—

(a.) if the candidate applies to the High Court or an election court, and shows that the failure to transmit such return and declarations, or any of them, or any part thereof, or any error or false statement therein, has arisen by reason of his illness, or of the absence, death, illness or misconduct of his election agent or sub-agent, or of any clerk or officer of such agent, or by reason of inadvertence or of any reasonable cause of a like nature, and not by reason of any want of good faith on the part of the applicant, or

(b.) if the election agent of the candidate applies to the High Court or an election court, and shows that the failure to transmit the return and declarations which he was required to transmit, or any part thereof, or any error or false statement therein, arose by reason of his illness or of the death or illness of any prior election agent of the candidate, or of the absence, death, illness, or misconduct of any sub-agent, clerk, or officer of an election agent of the candidate, or by reason of inadvertence or of any reasonable cause of a like nature, and not by reason of any want of good faith on the part of the applicant,

the court may, after such notice of the application in the said county or borough, and on production of such evidence of the grounds stated in the application, and of the good faith of the application, and otherwise, as to the court seems fit, make such order for allowing an authorised excuse for the failure to transmit such return and declaration, or for an error or false statement in such return and declaration as to the court seems just.

(2.) Where it appears to the court that any person being or having been election agent or sub-agent has refused or failed to make such return or to supply such particulars as will enable the candidate and his election agent respectively to comply with the provisions of this Act as to the return and declaration respecting election expenses, the court before making an order allowing the excuse as in this section mentioned shall order such person to attend before the court, and on his attendance shall, unless he shows cause to the contrary, order him to make the return and declaration, or to deliver a statement of the particulars required to be contained in the return, as to the court seem just, and to make or deliver the same within such time and to such person and in such manner as the court may direct, or may order him to be examined with respect to such particulars, and may in default of compliance with any such order order him to pay a fine not exceeding five hundred pounds.

(3.) The order may make the allowance conditional upon the making of the return and declaration in a modified form or within an extended time, and upon the compliance with such other terms as to the court seem best calculated for carrying into effect the objects of this Act; and an order allowing an authorised excuse shall relieve the applicant for the order from any liability or consequences under this Act in respect of the matter excused by the order; and where it is proved by the candidate to the court that any act or omission of the election agent in relation to the return and declaration respecting election expenses was without the sanction or connivance of the candidate, and that the candidate took all reasonable means for preventing such act or omission, the court shall relieve the candidate from the consequences of such act or omission on the part of his election agent.

(4.) The date of the order, or if conditions and terms are to be complied with, the date at which the applicant fully complies with them, is referred to in this Act as the date of the allowance of the excuse.

35. (1.) The returning officer at an election, within ten days after he receives from the election agent of a candidate a return respecting election expenses, shall publish a summary of the return in not less than two newspapers circulating in the county or borough for which the election was held, accompanied by a notice of the time and place at which the return and declarations (including the accompanying documents) can be inspected, and may charge the candidate in respect of such publication, and the amount of such charge shall be the sum allowed by the Parliamentary Elections (Returning Officers') Act, 1875. *Publication summary of return of election expenses.*

(2.) The return and declarations (including the accompanying documents) sent to the returning officer by an election agent shall be kept at the office of the returning officer, or some convenient place appointed by him, and shall at all reasonable times during two years next after they are received by the returning officer be open to inspection by any person on payment of a fee of one shilling, and the returning officer shall on demand furnish copies thereof or any part thereof at the price of twopence for every seventy-two words. After the expiration of the said two years the returning officer may cause the said return and declarations (including the accompanying documents) to be destroyed, or, if the candidate or his election agent so require, shall return the same to the candidate. *38 & 39 Vict. c. 84.*

Disqualification of Electors.

36. Every person guilty of a corrupt or illegal practice or of illegal *Prohibition of persons guilty*

340 APPENDIX.

<small>of corrupt or illegal practices, &c., from voting.</small>

employment, payment, or hiring at an election is prohibited from voting at such election, and if any such person votes his vote shall be void.

<small>Prohibition of disqualified persons from voting.
35 & 36 Vict. c. 60.
45 & 46 Vict. c. 50.</small>

37. Every person who, in consequence of conviction or of the report of any election court or election commissioners under this Act, or under the Corrupt Practices (Municipal Elections) Act, 1872, or under Part IV. of the Municipal Corporations Act, 1882, or under any other Act for the time being in force relating to corrupt practices at an election for any public office, has become incapable of voting at any election, whether a parliamentary election or an election to any public office, is prohibited from voting at any such election, and his vote shall be void.

<small>Hearing of person before he is reported guilty of corrupt or illegal practice, and incapacity of person reported guilty.</small>

38. (1.) Before a person, not being a party to an election petition nor a candidate on behalf of whom the seat is claimed by an election petition, is reported by an election court, and before any person is reported by election commissioners, to have been guilty, at an election, of any corrupt or illegal practice, the court or commissioners, as the case may be, shall cause notice to be given to such person, and if he appears in pursuance of the notice, shall give him an opportunity of being heard by himself and of calling evidence in his defence to show why he should not be so reported.

(2.) Every person reported by election commissioners to have been guilty at an election of any corrupt or illegal practice may appeal against such report to the next court of oyer and terminer or gaol delivery held in and for the county or place in which the offence is alleged to have been committed, and such court may hear and determine the appeal; and subject to rules of court such appeal may be brought, heard, and determined in like manner as if the court were a court of quarter sessions and the said commissioners were a court of summary jurisdiction, and the person so reported had been convicted by a court of summary jurisdiction for an offence under this Act, and notice of every such appeal shall be given to the Director of Public Prosecutions in the manner and within the time directed by rules of court, and subject to such rules then within three days after the appeal is brought.

(3.) Where it appears to the Lord Chancellor that appeals under this section are interfering or are likely to interfere with the ordinary business transacted before any courts of oyer and terminer or gaol delivery, he may direct that the said appeals, or any of them, shall be heard by the judges for the time being on the rota for election petitions, and in such case one of such judges shall proceed to the county or place in which the offences are alleged to have been committed, and shall there hear and determine the appeals in like manner as if such judge were a court of oyer and terminer.

(4.) The provisions of the Parliamentary Elections Act, 1868, with respect to the reception and powers of and attendance on an election court, and to the expenses of an election court, and of receiving and accommodating an election court, shall apply as if such judge were an election court.

(5.) Every person who after the commencement of this Act is reported by any election court or election commissioners to have been guilty of any corrupt or illegal practice at an election, shall, whether he obtained a certificate of indemnity or not, be subject to the same incapacity as he would be subject to if he had at the date of such election been convicted of the offence of which he is reported to have been guilty: Provided that a report of any election commissioners inquiring into an election for a county or borough shall not avoid the election of any candidate who has been declared by an election court on the trial of a petition respecting such election to have been duly elected at such election, or render him incapable of sitting in the House of Commons for the said county or borough during the Parliament for which he was elected.

(6.) Where a person who is a justice of the peace is reported by any election court or election commissioners to have been guilty of any corrupt practice in reference to an election, whether he has obtained a certificate of indemnity or not, it shall be the duty of the Director of Public Prosecutions to report the case to the Lord High Chancellor of Great Britain with such evidence as may have been given of such corrupt practice, and where any such person acts as a justice of the peace by virtue of his being, or having been, mayor of a borough, the Lord High Chancellor shall have the same power to remove such person from being a justice of the peace as if he was named in a commission of the peace.

(7.) Where a person who is a barrister or a solicitor, or who belongs to any profession the admission to which is regulated by law, is reported by any election court or election commissioners to have been guilty of any corrupt practice in reference to an election, whether such person has obtained a certificate of indemnity or not, it shall be the duty of the Director of Public Prosecutions to bring the matter before the Inn of Court, High Court, or tribunal having power to take cognisance of any misconduct of such person in his profession, and such Inn of Court, High Court, or tribunal may deal with such person in like manner as if such corrupt practice were misconduct by such person in his profession.

(8.) With respect to a person holding a licence or certificate under the Licensing Acts (in this section referred to as a licensed person) the following provisions shall have effect:

(a.) If it appears to the court by which any licensed person is convicted of the offence of bribery or treating that such offence was committed on his licensed premises, the court shall direct such conviction to be entered in the proper register of licenses.

(b.) If it appears to an election court or election commissioners that a licensed person has knowingly suffered any bribery or treating in reference to any election to take place upon his licensed premises, such court or commissioners (subject to the provisions of this Act as to a person having an opportunity of being heard by himself and producing evidence before being reported) shall report the same; and whether such person obtained a certificate of indemnity or not it shall be the duty of the Director of Public Prosecutions to bring such report before the licensing justices from whom or on whose certificate the licensed person obtained his license, and such licensing justices shall cause such report to be entered in the proper register of licenses.

(c.) Where an entry is made in the register of licenses of any such conviction of or report respecting any licensed person as above in this section mentioned, it shall be taken into consideration by the licensing justices in determining whether they will or will not grant to such person the renewal of his license or certificate, and may be a ground, if the justices think fit, for refusing such renewal.

(9.) Where the evidence showing any corrupt practice to have been committed by a justice of the peace, barrister, solicitor, or other professional person, or any licensed person, was given before election commissioners, those commissioners shall report the case to the Director of Public Prosecutions, with such information as is necessary or proper for enabling him to act under this section.

(10.) This section shall apply to an election court under this Act or under Part IV. of the Municipal Corporations Act, 1882, and the expression election shall be construed accordingly.

List in register of voters of persons incapacitated for voting by corrupt or illegal practices.
45 & 46 Vict. c. 50.

39. (1.) The registration officer in every county and borough shall annually make out a list containing the names and description of all persons who, though otherwise qualified to vote at a parliamentary election for such county or borough respectively, are not capable of voting by reason of having, after the commencement of this Act, been found guilty of a corrupt or illegal practice on conviction or by the report of any election court or election commissioners, whether under this Act or under Part IV. of the Municipal Corporations Act, 1882, or under any other Act for the time being in force relating to a parliamentary election or an election to any public office ; and such officer shall state in the list (in this Act referred to as the corrupt and illegal practices list), the offence of which each person has been found guilty.

(2.) For the purpose of making out such list he shall examine the report of any election court or election commissioners who have respectively tried an election petition or inquired into an election where the election (whether a parliamentary election or an election to any public office) was held in any of the following places ; that is to say—

(a.) If he is the registration officer of a county, in that county, or in any borough in that county ; and

(b.) if he is the registration officer of a borough, in the county in which such borough is situate, or in any borough in that county.

(3.) The registration officer shall send the list to the overseers of every parish within his county or borough, together with his precept, and the overseers shall publish the list together with the list of voters, and shall also in the case of every person in the corrupt and illegal practices list, omit his name from the list of persons entitled to vote, or, as circumstances require, add "objected" before his name in the list of claimants or copy of the register published by them in like manner as is required by law in any other cases of disqualification.

(4.) Any person named in the corrupt and illegal practices list may claim to have his name omitted therefrom, and any person entitled to object to any list of voters for the county or borough may object to the omission of the name of any person from such list. Such claims and objections shall be sent in within the same time and be dealt with in like manner, and any such objection shall be served on the person referred to therein in like manner, as nearly as circumstances admit, as other claims and objections under the enactments relating to the registration of Parliamentary electors.

(5.) The revising barrister shall determine such claims and objections, and shall revise such list in like manner, as nearly as circumstances admit, as in the case of other claims and objections, and of any list of voters.

(6.) Where it appears to the revising barrister that a person not named in the corrupt and illegal practices list is subject to have his name inserted in such list, he shall (whether an objection to the omission of such name from the list has or has not been made, but) after giving such person an opportunity of making a statement to show cause to the contrary, insert his name in such list and expunge his name from any list of voters.

(7.) A revising barrister in acting under this section shall determine only whether a person is incapacitated by conviction or by the report of any election court or election commissioners, and shall not determine whether a person has or has not been guilty of any corrupt or illegal practice.

(8.) The corrupt and illegal practices list shall be appended to the register of electors, and shall be printed and published therewith wherever the same is printed or published.

Proceedings on Election Petition.

40. (1.) Where an election petition questions the return or the election upon an allegation of an illegal practice, then notwithstanding anything in the Parliamentary Elections Act, 1868, such petition, so far as respects such illegal practice, may be presented within the time following (that is to say) : Time for presentation of election petitions alleging illegal practice. 31 & 32 Vict. c. 125.

(*a.*) At any time before the expiration of fourteen days after the day on which the returning officer receives the return and declarations respecting election expenses by the member to whose election the petition relates and his election agent.

(*b.*) If the election petition specifically alleges a payment of money, or some other act to have been made or done since the said day by the member or an agent of the member, or with the privity of the member or his election agent in pursuance or in furtherance of the illegal practice alleged in the petition, the petition may be presented at any time within twenty-eight days after the date of such payment or other act.

(2.) Any election petition presented within the time limited by the Parliamentary Elections Act, 1868, may for the purpose of questioning the return or the election upon an allegation of an illegal practice be amended with the leave of the High Court, within the time within which a petition questioning the return upon the allegation of that illegal practice can under this section be presented. 31 & 32 Vict. c. 125.

(3.) This section shall apply in the case of an offence relating to the return and declarations respecting election expenses in like manner as if it were an illegal practice, and also shall apply notwithstanding that the Act constituting the alleged illegal practice amounted to a corrupt practice.

(4.) For the purposes of this section—

(*a.*) Where the return and declarations are received on different days, the day on which the last of them is received, and

(*b.*) Where there is an authorised excuse for failing to make and transmit the return and declarations respecting election expenses, the date of the allowance of the excuse, or if there was a failure as regards two or more of them, and the excuse was allowed at different times, the date of the allowance of the last excuse,

shall be substituted for the day on which the return and declarations are received by the returning officer.

(5.) For the purpose of this section, time shall be reckoned in like manner as it is reckoned for the purposes of the Parliamentary Elections Act, 1868.

41. (1.) Before leave for the withdrawal of an election petition is Withdrawal of election petition.

granted, there shall be produced affidavits by all the parties to the petition and their solicitors, and by the election agents of all of the said parties who were candidates at the election, but the High Court may on cause shown dispense with the affidavit of any particular person if it seems to the court on special grounds to be just so to do.

(2.) Each affidavit shall state that, to the best of the deponents' knowledge and belief, no agreement or terms of any kind whatsoever has or have been made, and no undertaking has been entered into, in relation to the withdrawal of the petition; but if any lawful agreement has been made with respect to the withdrawal of the petition, the affidavit shall set forth that agreement, and shall make the foregoing statement subject to what appears from the affidavit.

(3.) The affidavits of the applicant and his solicitor shall further state the ground on which the petition is sought to be withdrawn.

(4.) If any person makes any agreement or terms, or enters into any undertaking, in relation to the withdrawal of an election petition, and such agreement, terms, or undertaking is or are for the withdrawal of the election petition in consideration of any payment, or in consideration that the seat shall at any time be vacated, or in consideration of the withdrawal of any other election petition, or is or are (whether lawful or unlawful) not mentioned in the aforesaid affidavits, he shall be guilty of a misdemeanour, and shall be liable on conviction on indictment to imprisonment for a term not exceeding twelve months, and to a fine not exceeding two hundred pounds.

(5.) Copies of the said affidavits shall be delivered to the director of public prosecutions a reasonable time before the application for the withdrawal is heard, and the court may hear the director of public prosecutions or his assistant or other representative (appointed with the approval of the Attorney-General), in opposition to the allowance of the withdrawal of the petition, and shall have power to receive the evidence on oath of any person or persons whose evidence the director of public prosecutions or his assistant, or other representative, may consider material.

(6.) Where in the opinion of the court the proposed withdrawal of a petition was the result of any agreement, terms, or undertaking prohibited by this section, the court shall have the same power with respect to the security as under Section 35 of the Parliamentary Elections Act, 1868, where the withdrawal is induced by a corrupt consideration.

31 & 32 Vict. c. 125.

(7.) In every case of the withdrawal of an election petition the court shall report to the Speaker whether, in the opinion of such court, the withdrawal of such petition was the result of any agreement, terms, or undertaking, or was in consideration of any payment, or in consideration that the seat should at any time be vacated, or in consideration of the withdrawal of any other election petition, or for any other consideration, and, if so, shall state the circumstances attending the withdrawal.

(8.) Where more than one solicitor is concerned for the petitioner or respondent, whether as agent for another solicitor or otherwise, the affidavit shall be made by all such solicitors.

(9.) Where a person not a solicitor is lawfully acting as agent in the case of an election petition, that agent shall be deemed to be a solicitor for the purpose of making an affidavit in pursuance of this section.

Continuation of trial of election petition.

42. The trial of every election petition so far as is practicable, consistently with the interests of justice in respect of such trial, shall be continued *de die in diem* on every lawful day until its conclusion, and

in case the rota of judges for the year shall expire before the conclusion of the trial, or of all the proceedings in relation or incidental to the petition, the authority of the said judges shall continue for the purpose of the said trial and proceedings.

43. (1.) On every trial of an election petition the director of public prosecutions shall by himself or by his assistant, or by such representative as hereinafter mentioned, attend at the trial, and it shall be the duty of such director to obey any directions given to him by the election court with respect to the summoning and examination of any witness to give evidence on such trial, and with respect to the prosecution by him of offenders, and with respect to any person to whom notice is given to attend with a view to report him as guilty of any corrupt or illegal practice. Attendance of director of public prosecutions on trial of election petition and prosecution by him of offenders.

(2.) It shall also be the duty of such director, without any direction from the election court, if it appears to him that any person is able to give material evidence as to the subject of the trial, to cause such person to attend the trial, and with the leave of the court to examine such person as a witness.

(3.) It shall also be the duty of the said director, without any direction from the election court, if it appears to him that any person who has not received a certificate of indemnity has been guilty of a corrupt or illegal practice, to prosecute such person for the offence before the said court, or if he thinks it expedient in the interests of justice before any other competent court.

(4.) Where a person is prosecuted before an election court for any corrupt or illegal practice, and such person appears before the court, the court shall proceed to try him summarily for the said offence, and such person, if convicted thereof upon such trial, shall be subject to the same incapacities as he is rendered subject to under this Act upon conviction, whether on indictment or in any other proceeding for the said offence; and further, may be adjudged by the court, if the offence is a corrupt practice, to be imprisoned, with or without hard labour, for a term not exceeding six months or to pay a fine not exceeding two hundred pounds, and if the offence is an illegal practice to pay such fine as is fixed by this Act for the offence;

Provided that, in the case of a corrupt practice, the court, before proceeding to try summarily any person, shall give such person the option of being tried by a jury.

(5.) Where a person is so prosecuted for any such offence, and either he elects to be tried by a jury or he does not appear before the court, or the court thinks it in the interests of justice expedient that he should be tried before some other court, the court, if of opinion that the evidence is sufficient to put the said person upon his trial for the offence, shall order such person to be prosecuted on indictment or before a court of summary jurisdiction, as the case may require, for the said offence; and in either case may order him to be prosecuted before such court as may be named in the order; and for all purposes preliminary and of and incidental to such prosecution the offence shall be deemed to have been committed within the jurisdiction of the court so named.

(6.) Upon such order being made,
 (a.) if the accused person is present before the court, and the offence is an indictable offence, the court shall commit him to take his trial, or cause him to give bail to appear and take his trial for the said offence; and

(*b.*) if the accused person is present before the court, and the offence is not an indictable offence, the court shall order him to be brought before the court of summary jurisdiction before whom he is to be prosecuted, or cause him to give bail to appear before that court ; and

(*c.*) if the accused person is not present before the court, the court shall as circumstances require issue a summons for his attendance, or a warrant to apprehend him and bring him before a court of summary jurisdiction, and that court, if the offence is an indictable offence, shall, on proof only of the summons or warrant and the identity of the accused, commit him to take his trial, or cause him to give bail to appear and take his trial for the said offence, or, if the offence is punishable on summary conviction, shall proceed to hear the case, or if such court be not the court before whom he is directed to be prosecuted, shall order him to be brought before that court.

(7.) The director of public prosecutions may nominate, with the approval of the Attorney-General, a barrister or solicitor of not less than ten years standing, to be his representative for the purpose of this section, and that representative shall receive such remuneration as the Commissioners of Her Majesty's Treasury may approve. There shall be allowed to the director and his assistant or representative, for the purposes of this section, such allowance for expenses as the Commissioners of Her Majesty's Treasury may approve.

(8.) The costs incurred in defraying the expenses of the director of public prosecutions under this section (including the remuneration of his representative) shall, in the first instance, be paid by the Commissioners of Her Majesty's Treasury, and so far as they are not in the case of any prosecution paid by the defendant shall be deemed to be expenses of the election court ; but if for any reasonable cause it seems just to the court so to do, the court shall order all or part of the said costs to be repaid to the Commissioners of Her Majesty's Treasury by the parties to the petition, or such of them as the court may direct.

Power to election court to order payment by county or borough or individual of costs of election petition.

44. (1.) Where upon the trial of an election petition respecting an election for a county or borough it appears to the election court that a corrupt practice has not been proved to have been committed in reference to such election by or with the knowledge and consent of the respondent to the petition, and that such respondent took all reasonable means to prevent corrupt practices being committed on his behalf, the court may make one or more orders with respect to the payment either of the whole or such part of the costs of the petition as the court may think right as follows :—

(*a.*) if it appears to the court that corrupt practices extensively prevailed in reference to the said election, the court may order the whole or part of the costs to be paid by the county or borough ; and

(*b.*) if it appears to the court that any person or persons is or are proved, whether by providing money or otherwise, to have been extensively engaged in corrupt practices, or to have encouraged or promoted extensive corrupt practices in reference to such election, the court may, after giving such person or persons an opportunity of being heard by counsel or solicitor and examining and cross-examining witnesses to show cause why the order should not be made, order the whole or part of the costs to be paid by that person, or those persons or any of them, and may order that if the costs cannot be recovered from one or more of such persons they shall be paid by some other of such persons or by either of the parties to the petition.

(2.) Where any person appears to the court to have been guilty of the offence of a corrupt or illegal practice, the court may, after giving such person an opportunity of making a statement to show why the order should not be made, order the whole or any part of the costs of or incidental to any proceeding before the court in relation to the said offence or to the said person to be paid by the said person.

(3.) The rules and regulations of the Supreme Court of Judicature with respect to costs to be allowed in actions, causes, and matters in the High Court shall in principle and so far as practicable apply to the costs of petition and other proceedings under the Parliamentary Elections Act, 1868, and under this Act, and the taxing officer shall not allow any costs, charges or expenses on a higher scale than would be allowed in any action, cause, or matter in the High Court on the higher scale, as between solicitor and client.

Miscellaneous.

45. Where information is given to the Director of Public Prosecutions that any corrupt or illegal practices have prevailed in reference to any election, it shall be his duty, subject to the regulations under the Prosecution of Offences Act, 1879, to make such inquiries and institute such prosecutions as the circumstances of the case appear to him to require. Inquiry by director of public prosecutions into alleged corrupt or illegal practices.

46. Where a person has, either before or after the commencement of this Act, become subject to any incapacity under the Corrupt Practices Prevention Acts or this Act by reason of a conviction or of a report of any election court or election commissioners, and any witness who gave evidence against such incapacitated person upon the proceeding for such conviction or report is convicted of perjury in respect of that evidence, the incapacitated person may apply to the High Court, and the court, if satisfied that the conviction or report so far as respects such person was based upon perjury, may order that such incapacity shall thenceforth cease, and the same shall cease accordingly. Removal of incapacity on proof that it was procured by perjury.

47. (1.) Every county shall be divided into polling districts, and a polling place shall be assigned to each district in such manner that, so far as is reasonably practicable, every elector resident in the county shall have his polling place within a distance not exceeding three miles from his residence, so nevertheless that a polling district need not in any case be constituted containing less than one hundred electors. Amendment of law as to polling districts and polling places.

(2.) In every county the local authority who have power to divide that county into polling districts shall from time to time divide the county into polling districts, and assign polling places to those districts, and alter those districts and polling places in such manner as may be necessary for the purpose of carrying into effect this section.

(3.) The power of dividing a borough into polling districts vested in a local authority by the Representation of the People Act, 1867, and the enactments amending the same, may be exercised by such local authority from time to time, and as often as the authority think fit, and the said power shall be deemed to include the power of altering any polling district, and the said local authority shall from time to time, where necessary for the purpose of carrying this section into effect, divide the borough into polling districts in such manner that :—

    (*a.*) Every elector resident in the borough, if other than one hereinafter mentioned, shall be enabled to poll within a distance not exceeding one mile from his residence, so nevertheless that a polling district need not be constituted containing less than three hundred electors ; and

    (*b.*) Every elector resident in the boroughs of East Retford, Shoreham, Cricklade, Much Wenlock, and Aylesbury, shall be enabled to poll within a distance not exceeding three miles from his residence, so nevertheless that a polling district need not be constituted containing less than one hundred electors.

(4.) So much of Section 5 of the Ballot Act, 1872, and the enactments amending the same as in force and is not repealed by this Act, shall apply as if the same were incorporated in this section.

(5.) The expenses incurred by the local authority of a county or borough under this or any other Act in dividing their county or borough into polling districts, and, in the case of a county, assigning polling places to such districts, and in altering any such districts or polling places, shall be defrayed in like manner as if they were expenses incurred by the registration officer in the execution of the enactments respecting the registration of electors in such county or borough, and those enactments, so far as is consistent with the tenor thereof, shall apply accordingly.

Conveyance of voters by sea in certain cases.

48. Where the nature of a county is such that any electors residing therein are unable at an election for such county to reach their polling place without crossing the sea or a branch or arm thereof, this Act shall not prevent the provision of means for conveying such electors by sea to their polling place, and the amount of payment for such means of conveyance may be in addition to the maximum amount of expenses allowed by this Act.

Election commissioners not to inquire into elections before the passing of this Act.

49. Notwithstanding the provisions of the Act 15 and 16 Vict. cap. 57, or any amendment thereof, in any case where, after the passing of this Act, any commissioners have been appointed, on a joint address of both Houses of Parliament, for the purpose of making inquiry into the existence of corrupt practices in any election, the said commissioners shall not make inquiries concerning any election that shall have taken place prior to the passing of this Act, and no witness called before such commissioners, or at any election petition after the passing of this Act, shall be liable to be asked or bound to answer any question for the purpose of proving the commission of any corrupt practice at or in relation to any election prior to the passing of this Act : Provided that nothing herein contained shall affect any proceedings that shall be pending at the time of such passing.

Legal Proceedings.

Trial in Central Criminal Court of indictment.

50. Where an indictment as defined by this Act for any offence under the Corrupt Practices Prevention Acts or this Act is instituted in the High Court, or is removed into the High Court by a writ of certiorari issued at the instance of the Attorney-General, and the Attorney-General suggests on the part of the Crown that it is expedient for the purposes of justice that the indictment should be tried in the Central Criminal Court, or if a special jury is ordered, that it should be tried before a judge and jury at the Royal Courts of Justice, the High Court may, if it think fit, order that such indictment shall be so tried upon such terms as the court may think just, and the High Court may make such orders as appear to the court necessary or proper for carrying into effect the order for such trial. *for corrupt practice at instance of Attorney-General.*

51. (1.) A proceeding against a person in respect of the offence of a corrupt or illegal practice, or any other offence under the Corrupt Practices Prevention Act, or this Act, shall be commenced within one year after the offence was committed, or if it was committed in reference to an election with respect to which an inquiry is held by election commissioners shall be commenced within one year after the offence was committed, or within three months after the report of such commissioners is made, whichever period last expires, so that it be commenced within two years after the offence was committed, and the time so limited by this section shall, in the case of any proceeding under the Summary Jurisdiction Acts for any such offence, whether before an election court or otherwise, be substituted for any limitation of time contained in the last-mentioned Acts. *Limitation of time for prosecution of offence.*

(2.) For the purposes of this section the issue of a summons, warrant, writ, or other process shall be deemed to be a commencement of a proceeding, where the service or execution of the same on or against the alleged offender is prevented by the absconding or concealment or act of the alleged offender, but save as aforesaid the service or execution of the same on or against the alleged offender, and not the offence thereof, shall be deemed to be the commencement of the proceeding.

52. Any person charged with a corrupt practice may, if the circumstances warrant such finding, be found guilty of an illegal practice (which offence shall for that purpose be an indictable offence), and any person charged with an illegal practice may be found guilty of that offence, notwithstanding that the act constituting the offence amounted to a corrupt practice, and a person charged with illegal payment, employment, or hiring, may be found guilty of that offence, notwithstanding that the Act constituting the offence amounted to a corrupt or illegal practice. *Persons charged with corrupt practice may be found guilty of illegal practice.*

53. (1.) Sections 10, 12, and 13 of the Corrupt Practices Prevention Act, 1854, and Section 6 of the Corrupt Practices Prevention Act, 1863 (which relate to prosecutions for bribery and other offences under those Acts), shall extend to any prosecution on indictment for the offence of any corrupt practice within the meaning of this Act, and to any action for any pecuniary forfeiture for an offence under this Act, in like manner as if such offence were bribery within the meaning of those Acts, and such indictment or action were the indictment or action in those sections mentioned, and an order under the said Section 10 may be made on the defendant; but the Director of Public Prosecutions, or any person instituting any prosecution in his behalf, or by direction of an *Application of enactments of 17 & 18 Vict. c. 102, and 26 & 27 Vict. c. 29, relating to prosecutions for bribery. 17 & 18 Vict. c. 102. 26 & 27 Vict. c. 29.*

election court, shall not be deemed to be a private prosecutor, nor required under the said sections to give any security.

(2.) On any prosecution under this Act, whether on indictment or summarily, and whether before an election court or otherwise, and in any action for a pecuniary forfeiture under this Act, the person prosecuted or sued, and the husband or wife of such person, may, if he or she think fit, be examined as an ordinary witness in the case.

(3.) On any such prosecution or action as aforesaid it shall be sufficient to allege that the person charged was guilty of an illegal practice, payment, employment, or hiring within the meaning of this Act, as the case may be, and the certificate of the returning officer at an election that the election mentioned in the certificate was duly held, and that the person named in the certificate was a candidate at such election, shall be sufficient evidence of the facts therein stated.

Prosecution on summary conviction, and appeal to quarter sessions.

54. (1.) All offences under this Act punishable on summary conviction may be prosecuted in manner provided by the Summary Jurisdiction Acts.

(2.) A person aggrieved by a conviction by a Court of Summary Jurisdiction for an offence under this Act may appeal to general or quarter sessions against such conviction.

Application of Summary Jurisdiction and Indictable Offences Acts to proceedings before election courts.

55. (1.) Except that nothing in this Act shall authorise any appeal against a summary conviction by an election court, the Summary Jurisdiction Act shall, so far as is consistent with the tenor thereof, apply to the prosecution of an offence summarily before an election court, in like manner as if it were an offence punishable only on summary conviction, and accordingly the attendance of any person may be enforced, the case heard and determined, and any summary conviction by such court be carried into effect and enforced, and the costs thereof paid, and the record thereof dealt with under those Acts in like manner as if the court were a Petty Sessional Court for the county or place in which such conviction took place.

(2.) The enactments relating to charges before justices against persons for indictable offences shall, so far as is consistent with the tenor thereof, apply to every case where an election court orders a person to be prosecuted on indictment in like manner as if the court were a justice of the peace.

Exercise of jurisdiction of High Court, and making of rules of court.

56. (1.) Subject to any rules of court, any jurisdiction vested by this Act in the High Court may, so far as it relates to indictments or other criminal proceedings, be exercised by any judge of the Queen's Bench Division, and in other respects may either be exercised by one of the judges for the time being on the rota for the trial of election petitions, sitting either in court or at chambers, or may be exercised by a master of the Supreme Court of Judicature in manner directed by and subject to an appeal to the said judges:

Provided that a master shall not exercise jurisdiction in the case either of an order declaring any act or omission to be an exception from the provisions of this Act with respect to illegal practices, payments, employments, or hirings, or of an order allowing an excuse in relation to a return or declaration respecting election expenses.

(2.) Rules of court may from time to time be made, revoked, and altered for the purposes of this Act, and of the Parliamentary Elections

Act, 1868, and the Acts amending the same, by the same authority by whom rules of court for procedure and practice in the Supreme Court of Judicature can for the time being be made.

57. (1.) The Director of Public Prosecutions, in performing any duty under this Act, shall act in accordance with the regulations under the Prosecution of Offences Act, 1879, and subject thereto in accordance with the directions (if any) given to him by the Attorney-General ; and any assistant or representative of the Director of Public Prosecutions, in performing any duty under this Act, shall act in accordance with the said regulations and directions, if any, and with the directions given to him by the Director of Public Prosecutions.

(2.) Subject to the provisions of this Act, the costs of any prosecution on indictment for an offence punishable under this Act, whether by the Director of Public Prosecutions or his representative, or by any other person, shall, so far as they are not paid by the defendant, be paid in like manner as costs in the case of a prosecution for felony are paid.

Director of public prosecutions and expenses of prosecutions, 42 & 43 Vict. c. 22.

58. (1.) Where any costs or other sums (not being costs of a prosecution on indictment) are, under an order of an election court, or otherwise under this Act, to be paid by a county or borough, the Commissioners of Her Majesty's Treasury shall pay those costs or sums, and obtain repayment of the amount so paid, in like manner as if such costs and sums were expenses of Election Commissioners paid by them, and the Election Commissioners' Expenses Acts, 1869 and 1871, shall apply accordingly as if they were herein re-enacted and in terms made applicable to the above-mentioned costs and sums.

(2.) Where any costs or other sums are, under the order of an election court or otherwise under this Act, to be paid by any person, those costs shall be a simple contract debt due from such person to the person or persons to whom they are to be paid, and if payable to the Commissioners of Her Majesty's Treasury shall be a debt to Her Majesty, and in either case may be recovered accordingly.

Recovery of costs payable by county or borough or by person.

32 & 33 Vict. c. 21.
34 & 35 Vict. c. 61.

Supplemental Provisions, Definitions, Savings, and Repeals.

59. (1.) A person who is called as a witness respecting an election before any election court shall not be excused from answering any question relating to any offence at or connected with such election, on the ground that the answer thereto may criminate or tend to criminate himself or on the ground of privilege ;

Provided that—

(a.) a witness who answers truly all questions which he is required by the election court to answer shall be entitled to receive a certificate of indemnity under the hand of a member of the court stating that such witness has so answered : and

(b.) an answer by a person to a question put by or before any election court shall not, except in the case of any criminal proceeding for perjury in receipt of such evidence, be in any proceeding, civil or criminal, admissible in evidence against him :

(2.) Where a person has received such a certificate of indemnity in relation to an election, and any legal proceeding is at any time instituted

Obligation of witness to answer, and certificate of indemnity.

against him for any offence under the Corrupt Practices Prevention Acts or this Act committed by him previously to the date of the certificate at or in relation to the said election, the court having cognisance of the case shall on proof of the certificate stay the proceeding, and may in their discretion award to the said person such costs as he may have been put to in the proceeding.

(3.) Nothing in this section shall be taken to relieve a person receiving a certificate of indemnity from any incapacity under this Act or from any proceeding to enforce such incapacity (other than a criminal prosecution).

(4.) This section shall apply in the case of a witness before any election commissioners, in like manner as if the expression " election court " in this section included election commissioners.

(5.) Where a solicitor or person lawfully acting as agent for any party to an election petition respecting any election for a county or borough has not taken any part or been concerned in such election, the election commissioners inquiring into such election shall not be entitled to examine such solicitor or agent respecting matters which came to his knowledge by reason only of his being concerned as solicitor or agent for a party to such petition.

Submission of report of election court or commissioners to Attorney-General.

60. An election court or election commissioners, when reporting that certain persons have been guilty of any corrupt or illegal practice, shall report whether those persons have or not been furnished with certificates of indemnity; and such report shall be laid before the Attorney-General (accompanied in the case of the commissioners with the evidence on which such report is based), with a view to his instituting or directing a prosecution against such persons as have not received certificates of indemnity, if the evidence should, in his opinion, be sufficient to support a prosecution.

Breach of duty by officer.
35 & 36 Vict. c. 33.

6 Vict. c. 18.

61. (1.) Section 11 of the Ballot Act, 1872, shall apply to a returning officer or presiding officer or clerk who is guilty of any wilful misfeasance or wilful act or omission in contravention of this Act in like manner as if the same were in contravention of the Ballot Act, 1872.

(2.) Section 97 of the Parliamentary Registration Act, 1843, shall apply to every registration officer who is guilty of any wilful misfeasance or wilful act of commission or omission contrary to this Act in like manner as if the same were contrary to the Parliamentary Registration Act, 1843.

Publication and service of notices.
35 & 36 Vict. c. 33.

62. (1.) Any public notice required to be given by the returning officer under this Act shall be given in the manner in which he is directed by the Ballot Act, 1872, to give a public notice.

(2.) Where any summons, notice, or document is required to be served on any person with reference to any proceeding respecting an election for a county or borough, whether for the purpose of causing him to appear before the High Court or any election court, or election commissioners, or otherwise, or for the purpose of giving him an opportunity of making a statement, or showing cause, or being heard by himself, before any court or commissioners, for any purpose of this Act, such summons, notice, or document may be served either by delivering the same to such person, or by leaving the same at, or sending the same by post by a registered letter to, his last known place of abode in the said county or borough, or if the proceeding is before any court or commissioners, in such other manner as the court or commissioners may direct, and in proving such service by post it shall be sufficient to prove that the letter was prepaid, properly addressed, and registered with the post-office.

(3.) In the form of notice of a Parliamentary election set forth in the second schedule to the Ballot Act, 1872, the words "or any illegal practice," shall be inserted after the words "or other corrupt practices," and the words the "Corrupt and Illegal Practices Prevention Act, 1883," shall be inserted after the words "Corrupt Practices Prevention Act, 1854."

63. (1.) In the Corrupt Practices Prevention Acts, as amended by this Act, the expression "candidate at an election," and the expression "candidate," respectively mean, unless the context otherwise requires, any person elected to serve in Parliament at such election, and any person who is nominated as a candidate at such election, or is declared by himself or by others to be a candidate, on or after the day of the issue of the writ for such election, or after the dissolution or vacancy in consequence of which such writ has been issued ; *Definition of candidate, and saving for persons nominated without consent.*

(2.) Provided that where a person has been nominated as a candidate or declared to be a candidate by others, then—

(a.) If he was so nominated or declared without his consent, nothing in this Act shall be construed to impose any liability on such person, unless he has afterwards given his assent to such nomination or declaration, or has been elected ; and

(b.) If he was so nominated or declared, either without his consent or in his absence, and he takes no part in the election, he may, if he thinks fit, make the declaration respecting election expenses contained in the second part in the second schedule to this Act, and the election agent shall, so far as circumstances admit, comply with the provisions of this Act with respect to expenses incurred on account of or in respect of the conduct or management of the election in like manner as if the candidate had been nominated or declared with his consent.

64. In this Act, unless the context otherwise requires— *General interpretation of terms.*

The expression "election" means the election of a member or members to serve in Parliament :

The expression "election petition" means a petition presented in pursuance of the Parliamentary Elections Act, 1868, as amended by this Act : *31 & 32 Vict. c. 125.*

The expression "election court" means the judges presiding at the trial of an election petition, or, if the matter comes before the High Court, that court :

The expression "election commissioners" means commissioners appointed in pursuance of the Election Commissioners Act, 1852, and the enactments amending the same : *15 & 16 Vict. c. 57.*

The expression "High Court" means Her Majesty's High Court of Justice in England :

The expressions "court of summary jurisdiction," "petty sessional court," and "Summary Jurisdiction Acts," have the same meaning as in the Summary Jurisdiction Act, 1879 : *42 & 43 Vict. c. 49.*

The expression "the Attorney-General" includes the Solicitor-General in cases where the office of the Attorney-General is vacant or the Attorney-General is interested or otherwise unable to act:

The expression "registration officer" means the clerk of the peace in a county, and the town clerk in a borough, as respectively defined by the enactments relating to the registration of parliamentary electors:

The expression "elector" means any person whose name is for the time being on the register roll or book containing the names of the persons entitled to vote at the election with reference to which the expression is used:

The expression "register of electors" means the said register roll or book:

The expression "polling agent" means an agent of the candidate appointed to attend at a polling station in pursuance of the Ballot Act, 1872, or of the Acts therein referred to or amending the same:

35 & 36 Vict. c. 33.

The expression "person" includes an association or body of persons, corporate or unincorporate, and where any act is done by any such association or body, the members of such association or body who have taken part in the commission of such act shall be liable to any fine or punishment imposed for the same by this Act:

The expression "committee room" shall not include any house or room occupied by a candidate at an election as a dwelling, by reason only of the candidate there transacting business with his agents in relation to such election; nor shall any room or building be deemed to be a committee room for the purposes of this Act by reason only of the candidate or any agent of the candidate addressing therein electors, committee men or others:

The expression "public office" means any office under the Crown or under the charter of a city or municipal borough, or under the Acts relating to municipal corporations or to the poor law, or under the Elementary Act, 1870, or under the Public Health Act, 1875, or under any Acts amending the above-mentioned Acts, or under any other Acts for the time being in force (whether passed before or after the commencement of this Act) relating to local government, whether the office is that of mayor, chairman, alderman, councillor, guardian, member of a board, commission, or other local authority in any county, city, borough, union, sanitary district, or other area, or is the office of clerk of the peace, town clerk, clerk or other officer under a council, board, commission, or other authority, or is any other office, to which a person is elected or appointed under any such charter or Act as above-mentioned, and includes any other municipal or parochial office; and the expressions "election," "election petition," "election court," and "register of electors," shall, where expressed to refer to an election for any such public office, be construed accordingly:

33 & 34 Vict. c. 75.
38 & 39 Vict. c. 55.

The expression "judicial office" includes the office of justice of the peace and revising barrister:

The expression "personal expenses," as used with respect to the expenditure of any candidate in relation to any election, includes the reasonable travelling expenses of such candidate, and the reasonable expenses of his living at hotels or elsewhere for the purposes of and in relation to such election:

APPENDIX.

The expression "indictment" includes information:
The expression "costs" includes costs, charges and expenses:
The expression "payment" includes any pecuniary or other reward; and the expressions "pecuniary reward" and "money" shall be deemed to include any office, place, or employment, and any valuable security or other equivalent for money, and any valuable consideration, and expressions referring to money shall be construed accordingly:
The expression "Licensing Acts" means the Licensing Acts, 1872 to 1874:
Other expressions have the same meaning as in the Corrupt Practices Prevention Acts.

65. (1.) The enactments described in the Third Schedule to this Act are in this Act referred to as the Corrupt Practices Prevention Acts. *Short titles.*

(2.) The Acts mentioned in the Fourth Schedule to this Act are in this Act referred to and may be cited respectively by the short titles in that behalf in that schedule mentioned.

(3.) This Act may be cited as the Corrupt and Illegal Practices Prevention Act, 1883.

(4.) This Act and the Corrupt Practices Prevention Acts may be cited together as the Corrupt Practices Prevention Acts, 1854 to 1883.

66. The Acts set forth in the Fifth Schedule to this Act are hereby repealed as from the commencement of this Act to the extent in the third column of that schedule mentioned, provided that this repeal or the expiration of any enactment not continued by this Act shall not revive any enactment which at the commencement of this Act is repealed, and shall not affect anything duly done or suffered before the commencement of this Act, or any right acquired or accrued, or any incapacity incurred before the commencement of this Act, and any person subject to any incapacity under any enactment hereby repealed or not continued shall continue subject thereto, and this Act shall apply to him as if he had become so subject in pursuance of the provisions of this Act. *Repeal of Acts.*

67. This Act shall come into operation on the fifteenth day of October, One thousand eight hundred and eighty-three, which day is in this Act referred to as the commencement of this Act. *Commencement of Act.*

Application of Act to Scotland.

68. This Act shall apply to Scotland, with the following modifications: *Application of Act to Scotland.*

(1.) The following expressions shall mean as follows:
The expression "misdemeanour" shall mean crime and offence:
The expression "indictment" shall mean criminal letters:
The expression "solicitor" shall mean enrolled law agent:
The expression "revising barrister" shall mean sheriff:
The expression "barrister" shall mean advocate:
The expression "petty sessional court" shall mean sheriff court:
The expression "quarter sessions" shall mean the Court of Justiciary:

The expression "registration officer" shall mean an assessor under the enactments relating to the registration of Parliamentary voters :

The expression "municipal borough" shall include royal burgh and burgh of regality and burgh of barony :

The expression "Acts relating to municipal corporations" shall include the General Police and Improvement (Scotland) Act, 1862, and any other Act relating to the constitution and government of burghs in Scotland :

The expression "mayor" shall mean provost or chief magistrate

The expression "alderman" shall mean bailie :

The expression "Summary Jurisdiction Acts" shall mean the Summary Jurisdiction (Scotland) Acts 1864 and 1881 and any Acts amending the same.

(2.) The provisions of this Act with respect to polling districts and the expenses of dividing a county or borough into polling districts shall not apply to Scotland.

(3.) The provisions respecting the attendance at the trial of an election petition of a representative of the Director of Public Prosecutions shall not apply to Scotland, and in place thereof the following provisions shall have effect :

(a.) At the trial of every election petition in Scotland Her Majesty's advocate shall be represented by one of his deputes or by the procurator-fiscal of the sheriff court of the district, who shall attend such trial as part of his official duty, and shall give all necessary assistance to the judge with respect to the citation of witnesses and recovery of documents :

(b.) If the judge shall grant a warrant for the apprehension, commitment, or citation of any person suspected of being guilty of a corrupt or illegal practice, the case shall be reported to Her Majesty's advocate in order that such person may be brought to trial before the High Court of Justiciary or the sheriff, according to the nature of the case :

(c.) It shall be the duty of the advocate depute or, in his absence, the procurator-fiscal, if it appears to him that a corrupt or illegal practice within the meaning of this Act has been committed by any person who has not received a certificate of indemnity, to report the case to Her Majesty's Advocate in order to such person being brought to trial before the proper court, although no warrant may have been issued by the judge.

(4.) The jurisdiction of the High Court of Justice under this Act shall, in Scotland, be exercised by one of the Divisions of the Court of Session, or by a judge of the said court to whom the same may be remitted by such division, and subject to an appeal thereto, and the Court of Session shall have power to make Acts of sederunt for the purposes of this Act.

(5.) Court of Oyer and Terminer shall mean a circuit court of Justiciary, and the High Court of Justiciary shall have powers to make Acts of adjournal regulating the procedure in appeals to the circuit court under this Act.

(6.) All offences under this Act punishable on summary conviction may be prosecuted in the sheriff court in manner provided by the Summary Jurisdiction Acts, and all necessary jurisdictions are hereby conferred on sheriffs.

(7.) The authority given by this Act to the Director of public prosecutions in England shall in Scotland be exercised by Her Majesty's advocate, and the reference to the Prosecution of Offences Act, 1879, shall not apply.

(8.) The expression "Licensing Acts" shall mean "the Public Houses Acts Amendment (Scotland) Act, 1862," and "The Publicans' Certificates (Scotland) Act, 1876," and the Acts thereby amended and therein recited. 25 & 26 Vict. c. 35.
39 & 40 Vict. c. 26.

(9.) The expression "Register of Licenses" shall mean the register kept in pursuance of Section 12 of the Act of the ninth year of the reign of King George the Fourth, chapter 58.

(10.) The references to the Public Health Act, 1875, and to the Elementary Education Act, 1870, shall be construed to refer to the Public Health (Scotland) Act, 1867, and to the Elementary Education (Scotland) Act, 1872.

(11.) Any reference to the Parliamentary Elections Returning Officers Act, 1875, shall not apply.

(12.) The provision with respect to the registration officer sending the corrupt and illegal practices list to overseers and the dealing with such list by overseers shall not apply, and in lieu thereof it is hereby enacted that the assessor shall in counties include the names of such persons in the list of persons who have become disqualified, and in boroughs shall omit the names of such persons from the list of persons entitled to vote.

(13.) The power given by this Act to the Lord Chancellor in England shall in Scotland, except so far as relates to the justices of the peace, be exercised by the Lord Justice General.

(14.) Any reference to the Attorney-General shall refer to the Lord Advocate.

(15.) The provisions with respect to the removal of cases to the Central Criminal Court or to the trial of cases at the Royal Courts of Justice shall not apply.

(16.) Section 38 of the County Voters Registration (Scotland) Act, 1861, shall be substituted for Section 97 of the Parliamentary Registration Act, 1843, where reference is made to that section in this Act. 24 & 25 Vict. c. 83.

(17.) The provision of this Act with regard to costs shall not apply to Scotland, and instead thereof the following provision shall have effect :

> The costs of petitions and other proceedings under "The Parliamentary Elections Act, 1868," and under this Act, shall, subject to any regulations which the Court of Session may make by Act of sederunt, be taxed as nearly as possible according to the same principles as costs between agent and client are taxed in a cause in that court, and the auditor shall not allow any costs, charges, or expenses, on a higher scale.

Application of Act to Ireland.

69. This Act shall apply to Ireland, with the following modifications : Application of Act to Ireland.

(1.) No person shall be tried for any offence against this Act under any of the provisions of "the Prevention of Crime (Ireland) Act, 1882." 45 & 46 Vict. c. 25.

(2.) The expression "Summary Jurisdiction Acts" means, with reference to the Dublin Metropolitan Police District, the Acts regulating the powers and duties of justices of the peace and of the police in such district; and with reference to other parts of Ireland means the Petty Sessions (Ireland) Act, 1851, and any Acts amending the said Act.

14 & 15 Vict. c. 93.

(3.) Section one hundred and three of the Act of the Session of the thirteenth and fourteenth years of the reign of Her present Majesty, chapter sixty-nine, shall be substituted for section ninety-seven of the Parliamentary Registration Act, 1843, where reference is made to that section in this Act.

(4.) The provision with respect to the registration officer sending the corrupt and illegal practices list to overseers and the dealing with such list by overseers shall not apply, and in lieu thereof it is hereby enacted that the registration officer shall, after making out such list, himself publish the same in the manner in which he publishes the lists referred to in the twenty-first and the thirty-third sections of the Act of the Session of the thirteenth and fourteenth years of the reign of Her present Majesty, chapter sixty-nine; and shall also in the case of every person in the corrupt and illegal practices list enter "objected to" against his name in the register and lists made out by such registration officer in like manner as he is by law required to do in other cases of disqualification.

(5.) The Supreme Court of Judicature in Ireland shall be substituted for the Supreme Court of Judicature.

(6.) The High Court of Justice in Ireland shall be substituted for the High Court of Justice in England.

(7.) The Lord High Chancellor of Ireland shall be substituted for the Lord High Chancellor of Great Britain.

(8.) The Attorney-General for Ireland shall be substituted for the Director of Public Prosecutions, and the reference to the prosecution of the Offences Act, 1879, shall not apply.

(9.) The provisions of this Act relative to polling districts shall not apply to Ireland, but in the county of the town of Galway there shall be a polling station at Barna, and at such other places within the parliamentary borough of Galway as the town commissioners may appoint.

(10.) Any reference to Part IV. of the Municipal Corporations Act, 1882, shall be construed to refer to the Corrupt Practices (Municipal Elections) Act, 1872.

(11.) Any reference to the Licensing Acts shall be construed to refer to the Licensing Acts (Ireland), 1872-1874.

41 & 42 Vict. c. 52.

(12.) The Public Health (Ireland) Act, 1878, shall be substituted for the Public Health Act, 1875.

(13.) The provisions with respect to the removal of cases to the Central Criminal Court, or to the trial of cases at the Royal Courts of Justice, shall not apply to Ireland.

Continuance.

Continuance.

70. This Act shall continue in force until the thirty-first day of December one thousand eight hundred and eighty-four, and no longer, unless continued by Parliament; and such of the Corrupt Practices Prevention Acts as are referred to in Part One of the Third Schedule to this Act shall continue in force until the same day, and no longer, unless continued by Parliament.

[Continued by 47 & 48 Vict. c. 53, until December 31, 1885.]

SCHEDULES.

FIRST SCHEDULE.

PART I.

PERSONS LEGALLY EMPLOYED FOR PAYMENT.

(1.) One election agent and no more.

(2.) In counties one deputy election agent (in this Act referred to as a sub-agent) to act within each polling district and no more.

(3.) One polling agent in each polling station and no more.

(4.) In a borough one clerk and one messenger, or if the number of electors in the borough exceeds five hundred, a number of clerks and messengers not exceeding in number one clerk and one messenger for every complete five hundred electors in the borough, and if there is a number of electors over and above any complete five hundred or complete five hundreds of electors, then one clerk and one messenger may be employed for such number, although not amounting to a complete five hundred.

(5.) In a county for the central committee-room one clerk and one messenger, or if the number of electors in the county exceeds five thousand, then a number of clerks and messengers not exceeding in number one clerk and one messenger for every complete five thousand electors in the county; and if there is a number of electors over and above any complete five thousand or complete five thousands of electors, then one clerk and one messenger may be employed for such number, although not amounting to a complete five thousand.

(6.) In a county a number of clerks and messengers not exceeding in number one clerk and one messenger for each polling district in the county, or where the number of electors in a polling district exceeds five hundred one clerk and one messenger for every complete five hundred electors in the polling district, and if there is a number of electors over and above any complete five hundred or complete five hundreds of electors, then one clerk and one messenger may be employed for such number, although not amounting to a complete five hundred: Provided always, that the number of clerks and messengers so allowed in any county may be employed in any polling district where their services may be required.

(7.) Any such paid election agent, sub-agent, polling agent, clerk, and messenger may or may not be an elector but may not vote.

(8.) In the case of the boroughs of East Retford, Shoreham, Cricklade, Much Wenlock, and Aylesbury, the provisions of this part of this schedule shall apply as if such borough were a county.

PART II.

LEGAL EXPENSES IN ADDITION TO EXPENSES UNDER PART I.

(1.) Sums paid to the returning officer for his charges not exceeding the amount authorised by the Act 38 & 39 Vict. c. 84.

(2.) The personal expenses of the candidate.

(3.) The expenses of printing, the expenses of advertising, and the expenses of publishing, issuing, and distributing addresses and notices.

(4.) The expenses of stationery, messages, postage, and telegrams.

(5.) The expenses of holding public meetings.

(6.) In a borough the expenses of one committee-room and if the number of electors in the borough exceeds five hundred then of a number of committee-rooms not exceeding the number of one committee-room for every complete five hundred electors in the borough, and if there is a number of electors over and above any complete five hundred or complete five hundreds of electors, then of one committee-room for such number, although not amounting to a complete five hundred.

(7.) In a county the expenses of a central committee-room, and in addition of a number of committee-rooms not exceeding in number one committee-room for each polling district in the county, and where the number of electors in a polling district exceeds five hundred one additional committee-room may be hired for every complete five hundred electors in such polling district over and above the first five hundred.

Part III.

Maximum for Miscellaneous Matters.

Expenses in respect of miscellaneous matters other than those mentioned in Part I. and Part II. of this schedule not exceeding in the whole the maximum amount of two hundred pounds, so nevertheless that such expenses are not incurred in respect of any matter or in any manner constituting an offence under this or any other Act, or in respect of any matter or thing, payment for which is expressly prohibited by this or any other Act.

Part IV.

Maximum Scale.

(1.) In a borough the expenses mentioned above in Parts I., II., and III. of this Schedule, other than personal expenses and sums paid to the returning officer for his charges, shall not exceed in the whole the maximum amount in the scale following:—

If the number of electors on the register—	The maximum amount shall be—
Does not exceed 2,000	£350.
Exceeds 2,000	£380, and an additional £30 for every complete 1,000 electors above 2,000.
Provided that in Ireland if the number of electors on the register—	The maximum amount shall be—
Does not exceed 500	£200.
Exceeds 500, but does not exceed 1,000	£250.
Exceeds 1,000, but does not exceed 1,500	£275.

(2.) In a county the expenses mentioned above in Parts I., II., and III. of this Schedule, other than personal expenses and sums paid to the returning officer for his charges, shall not exceed in the whole the maximum amount in the scale following :—

If the number of electors on the register— The maximum amount shall be—.
Does not exceed 2,000 £650 in England and Scotland, and £500 in Ireland.
Exceeds 2,000 . . £710 in England and Scotland, and £540 in Ireland, and an additional £60 in England and Scotland, and £40 in Ireland, for every complete 1,000 electors above 2,000.

Part V.

General.

(1.) In the case of the boroughs of East Retford, Shoreham, Cricklade, Much Wenlock and Aylesbury, the provisions of Parts II., III., and IV. of this schedule shall apply as if such borough were a county.

(2.) For the purposes of this schedule the number of electors shall be taken according to the enumeration of the electors in the register of electors.

(3). Where there are two or more joint candidates at an election the maximum amount of expenses mentioned in Parts III. and IV. of this schedule shall, for each of such joint candidates, be reduced by one-fourth, or if there are more than two joint candidates, by one-third.

(4.) Where the same election agent is appointed by or on behalf of two or more candidates at an election, or where two or more candidates, by themselves or any agent or agents, hire or use the same committee-rooms for such election, or employ or use the services of the same sub-agents, clerks, messengers, or polling agents at such election, or publish a joint address or joint circular or notice at such election, those candidates shall be deemed for the purposes of this enactment to be joint candidates at such election.

Provided that—

(*a.*) The employment and use of the same committee-room, sub-agent, clerk, messenger, or polling agent, if accidental or casual, or of a trivial and unimportant character, shall not be deemed of itself to constitute persons joint candidates.

(*b.*) Nothing in this enactment shall prevent candidates from ceasing to be joint candidates.

(*c.*) Where any excess of expenses above the maximum allowed for one of two or more joint candidates has arisen owing to his having ceased to be a joint candidate, or to his having become a joint candidate after having begun to conduct his election as a separate candidate, and such ceasing or beginning was in good faith, and such excess is not more than under the circumstances is reasonable, and the total expenses of such candidate do not exceed the maximum amount allowed for a separate candidate, such excess shall be deemed to have arisen from a reasonable cause within the meaning of the enactments respecting the allowance by the High Court or Election Court of an exception from the provisions of this Act which would otherwise make an act an illegal practice, and the candidate and his election agent may be relieved accordingly from the consequences of having incurred such excess of expenses.

SECOND SCHEDULE.

PART I.

FORM OF DECLARATIONS AS TO EXPENSES.

Form for Candidate.

I, , having been a candidate at the election for the county [*or* borough] of on the day of , do hereby solemnly and sincerely declare that I have examined the return of election expenses [about to be] transmitted by my election agent [*or if the candidate is his own election agent,* " by me "] to the returning officer at the said election, a copy of which is now shown to me and marked , and to the best of my knowledge and belief that return is correct;

And I further solemnly and sincerely declare that, except as appears from that return, I have not, and to the best of my knowledge and belief no person, nor any club, society, or association, has on my behalf, made any payment, or given, promised, or offered any reward, office, employment, or valuable consideration, or incurred any liability on account of or in respect of the conduct or management of the said election;

And I further solemnly and sincerely declare that I have paid to my election agent [*if the candidate is also his own election agent, leave out* " to my election agent "] the sum of pounds and no more for the purpose of the said election, and that, except as specified in the said return, no money, security, or equivalent for money has to my knowledge or belief been paid, advanced, given, or deposited by anyone to or in the hands of my election agent [*or if the candidate is his own election agent,* " myself "] or any other person for the purpose of defraying any expenses incurred on my behalf on account of or in respect of the conduct or management of the said election;

And I further solemnly and sincerely declare that I will not, except so far as I may be permitted by law, at any future time make or be party to the making or giving of, any payment, reward, office, employment, or valuable consideration for the purpose of defraying any such expenses as last mentioned, or provide or be party to the providing of any money, security, or equivalent for money for the purpose of defraying any such expenses.

Signature of declarant . *C.D.*

Signed and declared by the above-named declarant on the day of   , before me.

(Signed)   E.F.
Justice of the Peace for

Form for Election Agent.

I,   , being election agent to   , candidate at the election for the county [or borough] of   , on the   day of   , do hereby solemnly and sincerely declare that I have examined the return of election expenses about to be transmitted by me to the returning officer at the said election, and now shown to me and marked   , and to the best of my knowledge and belief that return is correct ;

And I hereby further solemnly and sincerely declare that, except as appears from that return, I have not and to the best of my knowledge and belief no other person, nor any club, society, or association has on behalf of the said candidate made any payment, or given, promised, or offered any reward, office, employment, or valuable consideration, or incurred any liability on account of or in respect of the conduct or management of the said election ;

And I further solemnly and sincerely declare that I have received from the said candidate   pounds and no more [or nothing] for the purpose of the said election, and that, except as specified in the said return sent to me, no money, security, or equivalent for money has been paid, advanced, given, or deposited by any one to me or in my hands, or, by the best of my knowledge and belief, to or in the hands of any other person for the purpose of defraying any expenses incurred on behalf of the said candidate on account of, or in respect of the conduct or management of the said election.

Signature of declarant   A.B.

Signed and declared by the above-named declarant on the day of   before me.

(Signed)   E.F.
Justice of the Peace for

FORM OF RETURN OF ELECTION EXPENSES.

I, *A.B.*, being election agent to *C.D.*, candidate at the election for the county [or borough] of   on the   day of   , make the following return respecting election expenses of the said candidate at the said election [*or where the candidate has named himself as election agent*, " I, *C.D.*, candidate at the election for " the county [or borough] of   on the   day of "   , acting as my election agent, make the following " return respecting my election expenses at the said election "].

Receipts.

Received of [*the above-named candidate*] [*or where the candidate is his own election agent*, " Paid by me "]   . . . .   £

Received of *J.K.* . . . .
[*Here set out the name and description of every person, club, society, or association, whether the candidate or not, from whom any money, securities, or equivalent of money was received in respect of expenses incurred on account of or in connexion with or incidental to the above election, and the amount received from each person, club, society, or association separately.*]

Expenditure.

Paid to *E.F.*, the returning officer for the said county [or borough], for his charges at the said election . . . . £

Personal expenses of the said *C.D.*, paid by himself [or *if the candidate is his own election agent,* "Paid by me as candidate"] . . . . £

  Do.   do.   paid by me [or *if the candidate is his own election agent, add* "acting as election agent"] . . . . £

Received by me for my services as election agent at the said election [or *if the candidate is his own election agent, leave out this item*] . . . . £

Paid to *G.H.* as sub-agent of the polling district of . £
[*The name and description of each sub-agent and the sum paid to him must be set out separately.*]

Paid to   as polling agent   . £
Paid to   as clerk for   days services   . £
Paid to   as messenger for   days services   £

[*The names and descriptions of every polling agent, clerk, and messenger, and the sum paid to each, must be set out separately either in the account or in a separate list annexed to and referred to in the account, thus,* "Paid to polling agent (or *as the case may be*) as per annexed list £   ."]

Paid to the following persons in respect of goods supplied or work and labour done :
  To *P.Q.* (printing) . . . . . . £
  To *M.N.* (advertising) . . . . . £
  To *R.S.* (stationery) . . . . . £

[*The name and description of each person, and the nature of the goods supplied, or the work and labour done by each, must be set out separately either in the account or in a separate list annexed to and referred to in the account.*]

Paid for postage . . . . £
Paid for telegrams . . . . . . £
Paid for the hire of rooms as follows :—
  For holding public meetings . . . £
  For committee-rooms . . . . . £

[*A room hired for a public meeting or for a committee-room must be named or described so as to identify it; and the name and description of every person to whom*

APPENDIX.

any *payment was made for each such room, together with the amount paid, must be set out separately either in the account or in a separate list annexed to and referred to in the account.*]

Paid for miscellaneous matters, namely— . . . £

[*The name and description of each person to whom any sum is paid, and the reason for which it was paid to him, must be set out separately either in the account or in a separate list annexed to and referred to in the account.*]

In addition to the above, I am aware, as election agent for *C.D.*, [*or if the candidate is his own election agent, leave out* "as election agent for *C.D.*"] of the following disputed and unpaid claims; namely—
Disputed claims.

    By *T.U.* for . . . . £

[*Here set out the name and description of each person whose claim is disputed, the amount of the claim, and the goods, work, or other matter on the ground of which the claim is based.*]

Unpaid claims allowed by the High Court to be paid after the proper time or in respect of which application has been or is about to be made to the High Court.

    By *M.O.* for . . . . £

[*Here state the name and description of each person to whom any such claim is due, and the amount of the claim, and the goods, work, and labour or other matter on account of which the claim is due.*]

                          (Signed)   *A.B.*

Part II.

Form of Declaration as to Expenses.

Form for candidate where declared a candidate or nominated in his absence and taking no part in the election.

I,   , having been nominated [*or* having been declared by others] in my absence [to be] a candidate at the election for the county or borough of   held on the   day of   , do hereby solemnly and sincerely declare that I have taken no part whatever in the said election.

And I further solemnly and sincerely declare that [*or* with the exception of   ] I have not, and no person, club, society, or association at my expense has, made any payment or given, promised, or offered, any reward, office, employment, or valuable consideration, or incurred any liability on account of or in respect of the conduct or management of the said election.

APPENDIX.

And I further solemnly and sincerely declare that [or with the exception of   ] I have not paid any money or given any security or equivalent for money to the person acting as my election agent at the said election, or to any other person, club, society, or association on account of or in respect of the conduct or management of the said election, and that [or with the exception of   ] I am entirely ignorant of any money security or equivalent for money having been paid, advanced, given, or deposited by any one for the purpose of defraying any expenses incurred on account of or in respect of the conduct or management of the said election.

And I further solemnly and sincerely declare that I will not, except so far as I may be permitted by law, at any future time make or be party to the making or giving of any payment, reward, office, employment, or valuable consideration for the purpose of defraying any such expenses as last mentioned, or provide or be party to the providing of any money, security, or equivalent of money for the purpose of defraying any such expenses.

Signature of declarant   C.D.

Signed and declared by the above-named declarant on the day of   , before me,
(Signed)   E.F.
Justice of the Peace for

THIRD SCHEDULE.

CORRUPT PRACTICES PREVENTION ACTS.

Session and Chapter.	Title of Act.	Enactments referred to as being the Corrupt Practices Prevention Act.
	PART I. *Temporary.*	
17 & 18 Vict. c. 102 .	The Corrupt Practices Prevention Act, 1854.	The whole Act so far as unrepealed.
26 & 27 Vict. c. 29 .	An Act to amend and continue the law relating to corrupt practices at elections of Members of Parliament.	The whole Act so far as unrepealed.
31 & 32 Vict. c. 125 .	The Parliamentary Elections Act, 1868.	The whole Act so far as unrepealed.
35 & 36 Vict. c. 33 .	The Ballot Act, 1872.	Part III. so far as unrepealed.
42 & 43 Vict. c. 75 .	The Parliamentary Elections and Corrupt Practices Act, 1879.	The whole Act so far as unrepealed.

APPENDIX.

Session and Chapter.	Title of Act.	Enactments referred to as being the Corrupt Practices Prevention Acts.
	PART TWO. *Permanent.*	
30 & 31 Vict. c. 102.	The Representation of the People Act, 1867.	Sections eleven forty-nine, and fifty.
31 & 32 Vict. c. 48.	The Representation of the People (Scotland) Act, 1868.	Sections eight and forty-nine.
31 & 32 Vict. c. 49.	The Representation of the People (Ireland) Act, 1868.	Sections eight and thirteen.
44 & 45 Vict. c. 40.	The Universities Elections Amendment (Scotland) Act, 1881.	Sub-section seventeen of section two.

PART THREE.

ENACTMENTS DEFINING THE OFFENCES OF BRIBERY AND PERSONATION.

[The full text of all these enactments is given in the body of the work. See pp. 3, 4, 5].

FOURTH SCHEDULES.

SHORT TITLES.

Session and Chapter.	Long Title.	Short Title.
15 & 16 Vict. c. 57.	An Act to provide for more effectual inquiry into the existence of corrupt practices at the election of Members to serve in Parliament.	Election Commissioners Act, 1852.
26 & 27 Vict. c. 29.	An Act to amend and continue the law relating to corrupt practices at elections of Members of Parliament.	The Corrupt Practices Prevention Act, 1863.

APPENDIX.

FIFTH SCHEDULE.

Enactments Repealed.

Note.—Portions of Acts which have already been specifically repealed are in some instances included in the repeal in this Schedule in order to preclude henceforth the necessity of looking back to previous Acts.

A description or citation of a portion of an Act is inclusive of the words, section, or other part first or last mentioned, or otherwise referred to as forming the beginning or as forming the end of the portion comprised in the description or citation.

Session and Chapter.	Title or Short Title.	Extent of Repeal.
60 Geo. 3. & 1 Geo. 4 c. 11.	An Act for the better regulation of polls, and for making further provision touching the election of Members to serve in Parliament for Ireland.	Section thirty-six.
1 & 2 Geo. 4. c. 58.	An Act to regulate the expenses of election of Members to serve in Parliament for Ireland.	The whole Act except section three.
4 Geo. 4. c. 55.	An Act to consolidate and amend the several Acts now in force so far as the same relate to the election and return of Members to serve in Parliament for the counties of cities and counties of towns in Ireland.	Section eighty-two.
17 & 18 Vict. c. 102.	The Corrupt Practices Prevention Act, 1854.	Section one. Section two, from "and any person so offending" to "with full costs of suit." Section three, from "and any person so offending" to the end of the section. Section four. Section five. Section six.

APPENDIX.

Session and Chapter.	Title or Short Title.	Extent of Repeal.
17 & 18 Vict. c. 102 .	The Corrupt Practices Prevention Act, 1854.	Section seven, from "and all payments" to the end of the section. Section nine, section fourteen, section twenty-three, section thirty-six, section thirty-eight, from "and the words personal expenses" to the end of the section, and section thirty-nine and Schedule A.
21 & 22 Vict. c. 87. .	An Act to continue and amend the Corrupt Practices Prevention Act, 1854.	The whole Act.
26 & 27 Vict. c. 29 .	An Act to amend and continue the law relating to corrupt practices at elections of Members of Parliament.	The whole Act, except section six.
30 & 31 Vict. c. 102.	The Representation of the People Act, 1867,	Section thirty-four, from "and in other boroughs the justices" to "greater part thereof is situate" and section thirty-six.
31 & 32 Vict. c. 48 .	The Representation of the People (Scotland) Act, 1868.	Section twenty-five.
31 & 32 Vict. c. 49 .	The Representation of the People (Ireland) Act, 1868.	Section twelve.
31 & 32 Vict. c. 58. .	The Parliamentary Electors Registration Act, 1868.	Section eighteen, from "the power of dividing their county" to the end of the section.
31 & 32 Vict. c. 125 .	The Parliamentary Elections Act, 1868.	So much of section three as relates to the definitions of "candidate." Section sixteen.

Session and Chapter.	Title or Short Title.	Extent of Repeal.
31 & 32 Vict. c. 125 .	The Parliamentary Elections Act, 1868.	Section thirty-three.
		Section thirty-six.
		Section forty-one, from "but according to the same principles" to "the High Court of Chancery."
		Section forty-three.
		Section forty-five.
		Section forty-six.
		Section forty-seven.
		Section fifty-eight, from "The principles" down to "in the court of session," being sub-section sixteen.
35 & 36 Vict. c. 33.	The Ballot Act, 1872.	Section five, from the beginning down to "one hundred registered electors."
		Section twenty-four, from "The offence of personation, or of aiding," to "hard labour," and from "The offence of personation shall be deemed to be" to the end of the section.
42 & 43 Vict. c. 75.	The Parliamentary Elections and Corrupt Practices Act, 1879.	Section three and schedule.
43 Vict. c. 18.	The Parliamentary Elections and Corrupt Practices Act, 1880.	The whole Act, except sections one and three.

MUNICIPAL ELECTIONS (CORRUPT AND ILLEGAL PRACTICES) ACT, 1884.

47 & 48 VICT. c. 70.

An Act for the better Prevention of Corrupt and Illegal Practices at Municipal and other Elections.

14th August, 1884.

BE it enacted by the Queen's most Excellent Majesty, by and with the advice and consent of the Lords Spiritual and Temporal, and Commons, in this present Parliament assembled, and by the authority of the same as follows ; (that is to say,)

1. This Act may be cited as the Municipal Elections (Corrupt and Illegal Practices) Act, 1884. *Short title.*

Corrupt Practices.

2. (1.) The expression "corrupt practice" in this Act means any of the following offences, namely, treating, undue influence, bribery, and personation as defined by the enactments set forth in Part One of the Third Schedule to this Act, and aiding, abetting, counselling and procuring the commission of the offence of personation. *Definition and punishment of corrupt practice at municipal election.*

(2.) A person who commits any corrupt practice in reference to a municipal election shall be guilty of the like offence, and shall on conviction be liable to the like punishment, and subject to the like incapacities, as if the corrupt practice had been committed in reference to a parliamentary election.

3. (1.) Where upon the trial of an election petition respecting a municipal election for a borough or ward of a borough it is found by the report of an election court made in pursuance of section ninety-three of the Municipal Corporations Act, 1882, that any corrupt practice, other than treating and undue influence, has been proved to have been committed in reference to such election by or with the knowledge and consent of any candidate at such election, or that the offence of treating or undue influence has been proved to have been committed in reference to such election by any candidate at such election, that candidate shall not be capable of ever holding a corporate office in the said borough, and if he has been elected his election shall be void ; and he shall further be subject to the same incapacities as if at the date of the said report he had been convicted of a corrupt practice. *Incapacity of candidate reported guilty of corrupt practice. 45 & 46 Vict. c. 50.*

(2.) Upon the trial of an election petition respecting a municipal election for a borough or ward of a borough in which a charge is made of any corrupt practice having been committed in reference to such election, the election court shall report in writing to the High Court whether any of the candidates at such election has been guilty by his agents of any corrupt practice in reference to such election, and if the report is that any candidate at such election has been guilty by his agents of a corrupt practice in reference to such election, that candidate shall not be capable of being elected to or holding any corporate office in the said borough, during a period of three years from the date of the report, and if he has been elected, his election shall be void.

Illegal Practices.

<small>Certain expenditure to be illegal practice.</small>

4. (1.) No payment or contract for payment shall, for the purpose of promoting or procuring the election of a candidate at a municipal election, be made—

(a.) on account of the conveyance of electors to or from the poll whether for the hiring of horses or carriages, or for railway fares or otherwise ; or

(b.) to an elector on account of the use of any house, land, building, or premises for the exhibition of any address, bill, or notice, or on account of the exhibition of any address, bill, or notice ; or

(c.) on account of any committee room in excess of the number allowed by this Act (that is to say), if the election is for a borough one committee room for the borough, and if the election is for a ward one committee room for the ward, and if the number of electors in such borough or ward exceeds two thousand, one additional committee room for every two thousand electors and incomplete part of two thousand electors, over and above the said two thousand.

(2.) Subject to such exception as may be allowed in pursuance of this Act, if any payment or contract for payment is knowingly made in contravention of this section either before, during, or after a municipal election, the person making such payment or contract shall be guilty of an illegal practice, and any person receiving such payment or being a party to any such contract, knowing the same to be in contravention of this Act, shall also be guilty of an illegal practice.

(3.) Provided that where it is the ordinary business of an elector as an advertising agent to exhibit for payment bills and advertisements, a payment to or contract with such elector if made in the ordinary course of business, shall not be deemed to be an illegal practice within the meaning of this section.

<small>Expense in excess of maximum to be illegal practice.</small>

5. (1.) Subject to such exception as may be allowed in pursuance of this Act, no sum shall be paid and no expense shall be incurred by or on behalf of a candidate at an election, whether before, during, or after an election, on account of or in respect of the conduct or management of such election, save that in the case of an election of a councillor a sum may be paid and expense incurred not in excess of the maximum amount following ; (that is to say,)

The sum of twenty-five pounds, and, if the number of electors in the borough or ward exceeds five hundred, an additional amount of threepence for each elector above the first five hundred electors.

(2.) Any candidate or agent of a candidate or person who knowingly acts in contravention of this section shall be guilty of an illegal practice.

(3.) Where there are two or more joint candidates at an election the maximum amount of expenses shall, for each of such joint candidates, be reduced by one fourth, or if there are more than two joint candidates by one third.

(4.) Where two or more candidates at the election, by themselves or any agent or agents, hire or use the same committee rooms for such election, or employ or use the services of the same clerks, messengers, or polling agent at such election, or publish a joint address or joint circular or notice at such election, those candidates shall be deemed for the purposes of this enactment to be joint candidates at such election: Provided that—

  (*a.*) The employment and use of the same committee room, clerk, messenger, or polling agent, if accidental or casual, or of a trivial and unimportant character, shall not be deemed of itself to constitute persons joint candidates.

  (*b.*) Nothing in this enactment shall prevent candidates from ceasing to be joint candidates:

  (*c.*) Where any excess of expenses above the maximum allowed for one of two or more joint candidates has arisen owing to his having ceased to be a joint candidate, or to his having become a joint candidate after having begun to conduct his election as a separate candidate, and such ceasing or beginning was in good faith, and such excess is not more than under the circumstances is reasonable, and the total expenses of such candidate do not exceed the maximum amount allowed for a separate candidate, such excess shall be deemed to have arisen from a reasonable cause within the meaning of the enactments respecting the allowance by the High Court or election court of an exception from the provisions of this Act which would otherwise make an act an illegal practice, and the candidate may be relieved accordingly from the consequences of having incurred such excess of expenses.

6. (1.) If any person votes or induces or procures any person to vote at a municipal election, knowing that he or such person is prohibited, whether by this or any other Act, from voting at such election, he shall be guilty of an illegal practice. *Voting by prohibited persons and publishing of false statements of withdrawal to be illegal.*

(2.) Any person who before or during a municipal election knowingly publishes a false statement of the withdrawal of a candidate at such election for the purpose of promoting or procuring the election of another candidate shall be guilty of an illegal practice.

(3.) Provided that a candidate shall not be liable, nor shall his election be avoided, for any illegal practice under this section committed without his knowledge and consent.

7. A person guilty of an illegal practice in reference to a municipal election, shall on summary conviction be liable to a fine not exceeding one hundred pounds and be incapable during a period of five years from the date of his conviction of being registered as an elector or voting at any election (whether it be a parliamentary election or an election for a public office within the meaning of this Act) held for or within the borough in which the illegal practice has been committed. *Punishment on conviction of illegal practice.*

APPENDIX.

Incapacity of candidate reported guilty of illegal practice. 45 & 46 Vict. c. 50.

8. (1.) An illegal practice within the meaning of this Act shall be deemed to be an offence against Part Four of the Municipal Corporations Act, 1882, and a petition alleging such illegal practice may be presented and tried accordingly.

(2.) Upon the trial of an election petition respecting a municipal election for a borough or ward of a borough in which a charge is made of any illegal practice having been committed in reference to such election, the election court shall report in writing to the High Court whether any of the candidates at such election has been guilty by himself or his agents of an illegal practice in reference to such election, and if the report is that a candidate at such election has been guilty by himself or his agents of an illegal practice in reference to such election, the candidate shall not be capable of being elected to or of holding any corporate office in the said borough during the period for which he was elected to serve, or for which if elected he might have served, and if he was elected, his election shall be void; and, if the report is that such candidate has himself been guilty of such illegal practice, he shall also be subject to the same incapacities as if at the date of the report he had been convicted of such illegal practice.

Illegal Payment, Employment, and Hiring.

Providing of money for illegal practice or payment to be illegal payment.

9. Where a person knowingly provides money for any payment which is contrary to the provisions of this Act, or for any expenses incurred in excess of any maximum amount allowed by this Act, or for replacing any money expended in any such payment, except where the same may have been previously allowed in pursuance of this Act to be an exception, such person shall be guilty of illegal payment.

Employment of hackney carriages, or of carriages and horses kept for hire.

10. (1.) A person shall not let, lend, or employ for the purpose of the conveyance of electors to or from the poll at a municipal election, any public stage or hackney carriage, or any horse or other animal kept or used for drawing the same, or any carriage, horse, or other animal which he keeps or uses for the purpose of letting out for hire, and if he lets, lends, or employs such carriage, horse, or other animal, knowing that it is intended to be used for the purpose of the conveyance of electors to or from the poll, he shall be guilty of illegal hiring.

(2.) A person shall not hire, borrow, or use for the purpose of the conveyance of electors to or from the poll any carriage, horse, or other animal which he knows the owner thereof is prohibited by this section to let, lend, or employ for that purpose, and if he does so he shall be guilty of illegal hiring.

(3.) Nothing in this Act shall prevent a carriage, horse, or other animal being let to or hired, employed, or used by an elector, or several electors at their joint cost, for the purpose of conveying him or them to or from the poll.

(4.) No person shall be liable to pay any duty or to take out a license for any carriage by reason only of such carriage being used without payment or promise of payment for the conveyance of electors to or from the poll at an election.

Corrupt withdrawal from a candidature.

11. Any person who corruptly induces or procures any other person to withdraw from being a candidate at a municipal election, in consideration of any payment or promise of payment, shall be guilty of illegal payment, and any person withdrawing in pursuance of such inducement or procurement shall also be guilty of illegal payment.

12. (1.) No payment or contract for payment shall, for the purpose of promoting or procuring the election of a candidate at a municipal election, be made on account of bands of music, torches, flags, banners, cockades, ribbons, or other marks of distinction. *Certain expenditure to be illegal payment.*

(2.) Subject to such exception as may be allowed in pursuance of this Act, if any payment or contract for payment is made in contravention of this section, either before, during, or after an election, the person making such payment shall be guilty of illegal payment, and any person being a party to any such contract or receiving such payment shall also be guilty of illegal payment if he knew that the same was made contrary to law.

13. (1.) No person shall, for the purpose of promoting or procuring the election of a candidate at a municipal election, be engaged or employed for payment or promise of payment for any purpose or in any capacity whatever, except as follows (that is to say), *Certain employment to be illegal.*

(a.) a number of persons may be employed, not exceeding two for a borough or ward, and if the number of electors in such borough or ward exceeds two thousand one additional person may be employed for every thousand electors and incomplete part of a thousand electors over and above the said two thousand, and such persons may be employed as clerks and messengers, or in either capacity ; and

(b.) one polling agent may be employed in each polling station :

Provided that this section shall not apply to any engagement or employment for carrying into effect a contract bonâ fide made with any person in the ordinary course of business.

(2.) Subject to such exception as may be allowed in pursuance of this Act, if any person is engaged or employed in contravention of this section, either before, during, or after an election, the person engaging or employing him shall be guilty of illegal employment, and the person so engaged or employed shall also be guilty of illegal employment if he knew that he was engaged or employed in contravention of this Act.

(3.) A person legally employed for payment under this section may or may not be an elector, but may not vote.

14. Every bill, placard, or poster having reference to a municipal election shall bear upon the face thereof the name and address of the printer and publisher thereof ; and any person printing, publishing, or posting, or causing to be printed, published, or posted, any such bill, placard, or poster as aforesaid, which fails to bear upon the face thereof the name and address of the printer and publisher, shall, if he is a candidate, be guilty of an illegal practice, and if he is not the candidate, shall be liable on summary conviction to a fine not exceeding one hundred pounds. *Name and address of printer on placards.*

15. The provisions of this Act prohibiting certain payments and contracts for payments, and the payment of any sum, and the incurring of any expense, in excess of a certain maximum, shall not *Saving for creditors.*

affect the right of any creditor who, when the contract was made or the expense was incurred, was ignorant of the same being in contravention of this Act.

<small>Use of certain premises for committee rooms or meetings to be illegal hiring.</small>

16. (1.) (a.) Any premises, which are licensed for the sale of any intoxicating liquor for consumption on or off the premises, or on which refreshment of any kind (whether food or drink) is ordinarily sold for consumption on the premises, or

(b.) Any premises where any intoxicating liquor is supplied to members of a club, society, or association, or any part of any such premises,

shall not, for the purpose of promoting or procuring the election of a candidate at a municipal election, be used either as a committee room or for holding a meeting, and if any person hires or uses any such premises or any part thereof in contravention of this section he shall be guilty of illegal hiring, and the person letting or permitting the use of such premises or part thereof, if he knew it was intended to use the same, in contravention of this section, shall also be guilty of illegal hiring.

(2.) Provided that nothing in this section shall apply to any part of such premises which is ordinarily let for the purpose of chambers or offices or the holding of public meetings or of arbitrations, if such part has a separate entrance and no direct communication with any part of the premises on which any intoxicating liquor or refreshment is sold or supplied as aforesaid.

<small>Punishment of illegal payment, employment, or hiring.</small>

17. (1.) A person guilty of an offence of illegal payment, employment, or hiring shall, on summary conviction, be liable to a fine not exceeding one hundred pounds.

(2.) Where an offence of illegal payment, employment, or hiring is committed by a candidate, or with his knowledge and consent, such candidate shall be guilty of an illegal practice.

<small>Avoidance of election for extensive illegal practices, &c.</small>

18. Where upon the trial of an election petition respecting a municipal election for a borough or ward of a borough it is found by the election court that illegal practices or offences of illegal payment, employment, or hiring, committed in reference to such election for the purpose of promoting the election of a candidate at that election, have so extensively prevailed that they may be reasonably supposed to have affected the result of that election, the election court shall report such finding to the High Court, and the election of such candidate, if he has been elected, shall be void, and he shall not, during the period for which he was elected to serve, or for which, if elected, he might have served, be capable of being elected to or holding any corporate office in the said borough.

Excuse and Exception for Corrupt or Illegal Practice or Illegal Payment, Employment or Hiring.

<small>Report exonerating candidate in certain cases of corrupt and</small>

19. Where, upon the trial of an election petition respecting a municipal election, the election court reports that a candidate at such election has been guilty by his agents of the offence of treating and

undue influence, and illegal practice, or of any of such offences, in reference to such election, and the election court further report that the candidate has proved to the court— *Illegal practice by agents.*

- (*a.*) That no corrupt or illegal practice was committed at such election by the candidate or with his knowledge or consent, and the offences mentioned in the said report were committed without the sanction or connivance of such candidate ; and
- (*b.*) That all reasonable means for preventing the commission of corrupt and illegal practices at such election were taken by and on behalf of the candidate ; and
- (*c.*) That the offences mentioned in the said report were of a trivial, unimportant, and limited character ; and
- (*d.*) That in all other respects the election was free from any corrupt or illegal practice on the part of such candidate, and of his agents ;

then the election of such candidate shall not, by reason of the offences mentioned in such report, be void, nor shall the candidate be subject to any incapacity under this Act.

20. Where, on application made, it is shown to the High Court or to a municipal election court by such evidence as seems to the Court sufficient— *Power of High Court and election court to except innocent act from being illegal practice, &c.*

- (*a.*) That any act or omission of a candidate at a municipal election for a borough or ward of a borough, or of any agent or other person, would, by reason of being in contravention of any of the provisions of this Act, be but for this section an illegal practice, payment, employment, or hiring ; and
- (*b.*) that such act or omission arose from inadvertence or from accidental miscalculation or from some other reasonable cause of a like nature, and in any case did not arise from any want of good faith ; and
- (*c.*) that such notice of the application has been given in the said borough as to the Court seems fit ;

and under the circumstances it seems to the Court to be just that the said candidate, agent and person, or any of them, should not be subject to any of the consequences under this Act of the said act or omission, the Court may make an order allowing such act or omission to be an exception from the provisions of this Act which would otherwise make the same an illegal practice, payment, employment, or hiring, and thereupon such candidate, agent, or person shall not be subject to any of the consequences under this Act of the said act or omission.

21. (1.) Every claim against any person in respect of any expenses incurred by or on behalf of a candidate at an election of a councillor on account of or in respect of the conduct or management of such election shall be sent in within fourteen days after the day of election, and if not so sent in shall be barred and not paid, and all expenses incurred as aforesaid shall be paid within twenty-one days after the day of election, and not otherwise, and any person who makes a payment in contravention of this section, except where such payment is allowed as provided by this section, shall be guilty of an illegal practice, but if such payment was made without the sanction or connivance of the candidate, the election of such candidate shall not be void, nor shall he be subject to any incapacity under this Act by reason only of such payment having been made in contravention of this section. *Sending in claims and making payments for election expenses.*

(2.) Every agent of a candidate at an election of a councillor shall, within twenty-three days after the day of election, make a return to the candidate in writing of all expenses incurred by such agent on account of or in respect of the conduct or management of such election, and if he fails so to do shall be liable, on summary conviction, to a fine not exceeding fifty pounds.

(3.) Within twenty-eight days after the day of election of a councillor every candidate at such election shall send to the town clerk a return of all expenses incurred by such candidate or his agents on account of or in respect of the conduct or management of such election, vouched (except in the case of sums under twenty shillings) by bills stating the particulars and receipts, and accompanied by a declaration by the candidate made before a justice in the form set forth in the Fourth Schedule to this Act, or to the like effect.

(4.) After the expiration of the time for making such return and declaration the candidate, if elected, shall not, until he has made the return and declaration (in this Act referred to as the return and declaration respecting election expenses), or until the date of the allowance of such authorised excuse, as is mentioned in this Act, sit or vote in the council, and if he does so shall forfeit fifty pounds for every day on which he so sits or votes to any person who sues for the same.

(5.) If the candidate without such authorised excuse as is mentioned in this Act fails to make the said return and declaration he shall be guilty of an illegal practice, and if he knowingly makes the said declaration falsely he shall be guilty of an offence, and on conviction thereof on indictment shall be liable to the punishment for wilful and corrupt perjury, and such offence shall also be deemed to be a corrupt practice within the meaning of this Act.

(6.) The county court for the district in which the election was held, or the High Court, or an election court, may, on application either of the candidate or a creditor, allow any claim to be sent in and any expense to be paid after the time limited by this section, and a return of any sum so paid shall forthwith after payment be sent to the town clerk.

(7.) If the candidate applies to the High Court or an election court, and shows that the failure to make the said return and declaration, or either of them, or any error or false statement therein, has arisen by reason of his illness or absence, or of the absence, death, illness, or misconduct of any agent, clerk, or officer, or by reason of inadvertence, or of any reasonable cause of a like nature, and not by reason of any want of good faith on the part of the applicant, the court may, after such notice of the application and on production of such evidence of the grounds stated in the application, and of the good faith of the applicant, and otherwise as to the court seems fit, make such order for allowing the authorised excuse for the failure to make such return and declaration, or for an error or false statement in such return or declaration, as to the court seems just.

(8.) The order may make the allowance conditional upon compliance with such terms as to the court seems calculated for carrying into effect the objects of this Act, and the order shall relieve the applicant from any liability or consequences under this Act in respect of the matters excused by the order.

(9.) The date of the order, or if conditions and terms are to be complied with, the date at which the applicant fully complies with them, is referred to in this Act as the date of the allowance of the excuse.

(10.) The return and declaration sent in pursuance of this Act to the town clerk shall be kept at his office, and shall at all reasonable times during the twelve months next after they are received by him be open to inspection by any person on payment of the fee of one shilling, and the town clerk shall, on demand, furnish copies thereof or of any part thereof at the price of twopence for every seventy-two words.

(11.) After the expiration of the said twelve months the town clerk may cause the return and declaration to be destroyed, or if the candidate so require shall return the same to him.

Disqualification of Electors.

22. Every person guilty of a corrupt or illegal practice or of illegal employment, payment, or hiring at a municipal election is prohibited from voting at such election, and if any such person votes his vote shall be void, and shall be struck off on a scrutiny. *Prohibition of persons guilty of offences from voting.*

23. So much of sections thirty-seven and thirty-eight of the Corrupt and Illegal Practices Prevention Act, 1883, as is set forth in Part Two of the Third Schedule to this Act, shall apply as part of this Act. *Application of ss. 37 & 38 of 46 & 47 Vict. c. 51.*

24. (1.) The town clerk in every municipal borough shall annually in July make out a list containing the names and description of all persons who, though otherwise qualified to be enrolled as burgesses of such borough, have under this Act, or under the Corrupt and Illegal Practices Prevention Act, 1883, or under any other Act for the time being in force relating to a parliamentary election or an election to any public office, become after the commencement of this Act, by reason of conviction of a corrupt or illegal practice, or of the report of any election court or election commissioners, incapable of voting at a municipal election in such borough or any ward thereof, and the town clerk shall state in the list (in this Act referred to as the corrupt and illegal practices list) the offence of which each person has been found guilty. *List in burgess roll of persons incapacitated for voting by corrupt or illegal practices*

(2.) For the purpose of making out such list he shall examine the report of any election court or election commissioners who have respectively tried an election petition or inquired into an election where the election (whether a parliamentary election or an election to any public office) was held in the said borough or in the county in which such borough is situate.

(3.) The town clerk of any municipal borough shall, not less than fourteen days before the first day appointed by law for the publication of the parish burgess lists in such borough, send the corrupt and illegal practices lists to the overseers of every parish wholly or partly within the borough, and the overseers shall publish that list together with the parish burgess lists, and shall also, in the case of every person in the corrupt and illegal practices list, omit his name from the list of persons entitled to be enrolled as burgesses or to be elected councillors, or, as circumstances require, add "objected" before his name in the list of claimants published by them, in like manner as is required by law in any other cases of disqualification.

(4.) Any person named in the corrupt and illegal practices list may claim to have his name omitted therefrom, and any person entitled to object to any parish burgess list may object to the omission of the name of any person from such first-mentioned list. Such claims and objections shall be sent in within the same time and be dealt with in like manner, and any such objection shall be served on the person referred to therein in like manner, as nearly as circumstances admit, as other claims and objections under the enactments relating to the enrolment of burgesses.

(5.) The revising authority shall determine such claims and objections and shall revise such list in like manner, as nearly as circumstances admit, as in the case of other claims and objections and of any parish burgess list and list of persons entitled to be elected councillors.

(6.) Where it appears to the revising authority that a person not named in the list is subject to have his name inserted in the corrupt and illegal practices list, he shall (whether an objection to the omission of such name from the list has or has not been made, but) after giving such person an opportunity of making a statement to show cause to the contrary, insert his name in that list and expunge his name from any list of burgesses or of persons entitled to be elected councillors.

(7.) A revising authority in acting under this section shall determine only whether a person is incapacitated by conviction or by the report of any election court or election commissioners, and shall not determine whether a person has or has not been guilty of any corrupt or illegal practice.

(8.) The corrupt and illegal practices list shall be appended to the burgess roll, and shall be printed and published therewith wherever the same is printed or published.

(9.) Any town clerk or overseer who fails to comply with the provisions of this section shall be liable to the like fine as he is liable to under section seventy-five of the Municipal Corporations Act, 1882, for any neglect or refusal in relation to a parish burgess list as therein mentioned.

45 & 46 Vict., c. 50.

Proceedings on Election Petitions.

Petition for illegal practice.

25. (1.) A municipal election petition complaining of the election on the ground of an illegal practice may be presented at any time before the expiration of fourteen days after the day on which the town clerk receives the return and declaration respecting election expenses by the candidate to whose election the petition relates, or where there is an authorised excuse for failing to make the return and declaration then within the like time after the date of the allowance of the excuse.

Time for presentation of petition alleging illegal practices.

(2.) A municipal election petition, complaining of the election on the ground of an illegal practice, and specifically alleging a payment of money or other act made or done since the election by the candidate elected at such election, or by an agent of the candidate, or with the privity of the candidate, in pursuance or in furtherance of such illegal practice, may be presented at any time within twenty-eight days after the date of such payment or act, whether or not any other petition against that person has been previously presented or tried.

(3.) Any election petition presented within the time limited by the Municipal Corporations Act, 1882, may, for the purpose of complaining of the election upon an allegation of an illegal practice, be amended with the leave of the High Court within the time within which a petition complaining of the election on the ground of that illegal practice can, under this section, be presented.

(4.) This section shall apply notwithstanding the illegal practice is also a corrupt practice.

45 & 46 Vict. c. 50.

26. (1.) Before leave for the withdrawal of a municipal election petition is granted, there shall be produced affidavits by all the parties to the petition and their solicitors, but the High Court may on cause shown dispense with the affidavit of any particular person if it seems to the court on special grounds to be just so to do.

Withdrawal of election petition.

(2.) Each affidavit shall state that, to the best of the deponent's knowledge and belief, no agreement or terms of any kind whatsoever has or have been made, and no undertaking has been entered into, in relation to the withdrawal of the petition; but if any lawful agreement has been made with respect to the withdrawal of the petition, the affidavit shall set forth that agreement, and shall make the foregoing statement subject to what appears from the affidavit.

(3.) The affidavits of the applicant and his solicitor shall further state the ground on which the petition is sought to be withdrawn.

(4.) If any person makes any agreement or terms, or enters into any undertaking, in relation to the withdrawal of an election petition, and such agreement, terms, or undertaking is or are for the withdrawal of the election petition in consideration of any payment, or in consideration that the seat shall at any time be vacated, or in consideration of the withdrawal of any other election petition, or is or are (whether lawful or unlawful) not mentioned in the aforesaid affidavits, he shall be guilty of a misdemeanor, and shall be liable on conviction on indictment to imprisonment for a term not exceeding twelve months, and to a fine not exceeding two hundred pounds.

(5.) Copies of the said affidavits shall be delivered to the Director of Public Prosecutions a reasonable time before the application for the withdrawal is heard, and the court may hear the Director of Public Prosecutions or his assistant or other representative (appointed with the approval of the Attorney-General), in opposition to the allowance of the withdrawal of the petition, and shall have power to receive the evidence on oath of any person or persons whose evidence the Director of Public Prosecutions or his assistant, or other representative, may consider material.

(6.) Where in the opinion of the court the proposed withdrawal of a petition was the result of any agreement, terms, or undertaking prohibited by this section, the court shall have the same power with respect to the security as under section ninety-five of the Municipal Corporations Act, 1882, where the withdrawal is induced by a corrupt consideration.

45 & 46 Vict. c. 50.

(7.) In every case of the withdrawal of an election petition, by leave of the election court such court shall report in writing to the High Court whether, in the opinion of such election court, the withdrawal of such petition was the result of any agreement, terms, or undertaking, or was in consideration of any payment, or in consideration that the seat should at any time be vacated, or in consideration of the withdrawal of any other election petition, or for any other consideration, and if so, shall state the circumstances attending the withdrawal.

(8.) Where more than one solicitor is concerned for the petitioner or respondent, whether as agent for another solicitor or otherwise, the affidavit shall be made by all such solicitors.

Continuation trial of election petition.

27. The trial of every municipal election petition shall, so far as is practicable consistently with the interests of justice in respect of such trial, be continued de die in diem on every lawful day until its conclusion.

Attendance of Director of Public Prosecutions on trial of election petition, and prosecution by him of offenders.

28. (1.) On every trial of a municipal election petition the Director of Public Prosecutions shall by himself or his assistant, or by such representative as hereinafter mentioned, attend at the trial, and it shall be the duty of such Director to obey any directions given to him by the election court with respect to the summoning and examination of any witness to give evidence on such trial, and with respect to the prosecution by him of offenders, and with respect to any person to whom notice is given to attend with a view to report him as guilty of any corrupt or illegal practice.

(2.) It shall also be the duty of such Director, without any direction from the election court, if it appears to him that any person is able to give material evidence as to the subject of the trial, to cause such person to attend the trial, and with the leave of the court to examine such person as a witness.

(3.) It shall also be the duty of the said Director, without any direction from the election court, if he thinks it expedient in the interests of justice so to do, to prosecute, either before the said court or before any other competent court, any person who has not received a certificate of indemnity and who appears to him to have been guilty of a corrupt or illegal practice at a municipal election.

(4.) Where a person is prosecuted before an election court for any corrupt or illegal practice, and such person appears before the court, the court shall proceed to try him summarily for the said offence, and such person, if convicted thereof upon such trial, shall be subject to the same incapacities as he is subject to under this or any other Act, upon conviction, whether on indictment or in any other proceeding for the said offence; and further, may be adjudged by the court, if the offence is a corrupt practice, to be imprisoned, with or without hard labour, for a term not exceeding six months or to pay a fine not exceeding two hundred pounds, and if the offence is an illegal practice, to pay such fine as is fixed by this Act for the offence:

Provided that, in the case of a corrupt practice, the court, before proceeding to try summarily any person, shall give such person the option of being tried by a jury.

(5.) Where a person is so prosecuted for any such offence, and either he elects to be tried by a jury or he does not appear before the court, or the court thinks it in the interests of justice expedient that he should be tried before some other court, the court, if of opinion that the evidence is sufficient to put the said person upon his trial for the offence, shall order such person to be prosecuted on indictment or before a court of summary jurisdiction, as the case may require, for the said offence; and in either case may order him to be prosecuted before such court as may be named in the order; and for all purposes preliminary and of and incidental to such prosecution the offence shall be deemed to have been committed within the jurisdiction of the court so named.

(6.) Upon such order being made,

(a.) If the accused person is present before the court, and the offence is an indictable offence, the court shall commit him to take his trial, or cause him to give bail to appear and take his trial for the said offence ; and

(b.) If the accused person is present before the court, and the offence is not an indictable offence, the court shall order him to be brought before the court of summary jurisdiction before whom he is to be prosecuted, or cause him to give bail to appear before that court ; and

(c.) If the accused person is not present before the court, the court shall as circumstances require issue a summons for his attendance, or a warrant to apprehend him, and bring him before a court of summary jurisdiction, and that court, if the offence is an indictable offence, shall, on proof only of the summons or warrant and the identity of the accused, commit him to take his trial, or cause him to give bail to appear and take his trial for the said offence, or if the offence is punishable on summary conviction, shall proceed to hear the case, or if such court be not the court before whom he is directed to be prosecuted shall order him to be brought before that court.

(7.) Any order or act of an election court under this section shall not be subject to be discharged or varied under sub-section six of section ninety-two of the Municipal Corporations Act, 1882. *45 & 46 Vict. c. 50.*

(8.) The Director of Public Prosecutions may nominate, with the approval of the Attorney-General, any barristers or solicitors of not less than ten years' standing, one of whom shall, when required, act as the representative for the purposes of this section of such Director, and when so acting shall receive such remuneration as the Treasury may approve. There shall be allowed to the Director and his assistant or representative, for the purposes of this section, such allowance for expenses as the Treasury may approve.

(9.) The costs incurred in defraying the expenses of the Director of Public Prosecutions under this section (including the remuneration of his representatives) shall, in the first instance, be paid by the Treasury, and so far as they are not in the case of any prosecution paid by the defendant, shall be deemed to be expenses of the election court, and shall be paid as the expenses of that court are directed by section one hundred and one of the Municipal Corporations Act, 1882, to be paid ; but if for any reasonable cause it seems just to the court so to do, the court shall order all or part of the said costs to be repaid to the Treasury by the parties to the petition, or such of them as the court may direct. *45 & 46 Vict. c. 50.*

29. (1.) Where upon the trial of a municipal election petition it appears to the election court that a corrupt practice has not been proved to have been committed in reference to the election by or with the knowledge and consent of the respondent to the petition, and that such respondent took all reasonable means to prevent corrupt practices being committed on his behalf, the court may make one or more orders with respect to the payment either of the whole or such part of the costs of the petition as the court may think right as follows : *Power to election court to order payment by borough or individual of costs of election petition.*

(a.) If it appears to the court that corrupt practices extensively prevailed in reference to the said election, the court may order the whole or part of the costs to be paid by the borough ; and

(*b.*) If it appears to the court that any person or persons is or are proved, whether by providing money or otherwise, to have been extensively engaged in corrupt practices, or to have encouraged or promoted extensive corrupt practices in reference to such election, the court may, after giving such person or persons an opportunity of being heard by counsel or solicitor and of examining and cross-examining witnesses to show cause why the order should not be made, order the whole or part of the costs to be paid by that person, or those persons or any of them, and may order that if the costs cannot be recovered from one or more of such persons they shall be paid by some other of such persons or by either of the parties to the petition.

(2.) Where any person appears to the court to have been guilty of the offence of a corrupt or illegal practice, the court may, after giving such person an opportunity of making a statement to show why the order should not be made, order the whole or any part of the costs of or incidental to any proceeding before the court in relation to the said offence or to the said person to be paid by the said person to such person or persons as the court may direct.

(3.) The rules and regulations of the Supreme Court of Judicature with respect to costs to be allowed in actions, causes, and matters in the High Court shall in principle and so far as practicable apply to the costs of petition and other proceedings under Part Four of the Municipal Corporations Act, 1882, and this Act, and the taxing officer shall not allow any costs, charges, or expenses on a higher scale than would be allowed in any action, cause or matter in the High Court on the higher scale, as between solicitor and client.

45 & 46 Vict. c. 50.

Miscellaneous.

General provisions as to prosecution of offences under this Act.

30. Subject to the other provisions of this Act, the procedure for the prosecution of a corrupt or illegal practice or any illegal payment, employment, or hiring committed in reference to a municipal election, and the removal of any incapacity incurred by reason of a conviction or report relating to any such offence, and the duties of a Director of Public Prosecutions in relation to any such offence, and all other proceedings in relation thereto (including the grant to a witness of a certificate of indemnity), shall be the same as if such offence had been committed in reference to a parliamentary election ; and sections forty-five and forty-six and sections fifty to fifty-seven (both inclusive) and sections fifty-nine and sixty of the Corrupt and Illegal Practices Prevention Act, 1883, shall apply accordingly as if they were re-enacted in this Act with the necessary modifications, and with the following additions :—

46 & 47 Vict. c. 51.

(*a.*) Where the Director of Public Prosecutions considers that the circumstances of any case require him to institute a prosecution before any court other than an election court for any offence other than a corrupt practice committed in reference to a municipal election in any borough, he may, by himself or his assistant, institute such prosecution before any court of summary jurisdiction in the county in which the said borough is situate or to which it adjoins, and the offence shall be deemed for all purposes to have been committed within the jurisdiction of such court ; and

(b.) General rules for the purposes of Part Four of the Municipal Corporations Act, 1882, shall be made by the same authority as rules of Court under the said sections ; and 45 & 46 Vict. c. 50.

(c.) The giving or refusal to give a certificate of indemnity to a witness by the election court shall be final and conclusive. s. 94. (7.)

31. If any person, in consequence of conviction or of the report of an election court under this Act, becomes not capable of being elected to or sitting in the House of Commons, or of being elected to or holding any public or judicial office, and such person, at the date of the said conviction or report, has been so elected or holds any such office, then his seat or office, as the case may be, shall be vacated as from that date. Person incapacitated by conviction or report to vacate seat or office.

32. (1). Where any costs of a petition are, under an order of a municipal election court, to be paid by a borough, such costs shall be paid out of the borough fund or borough rate. Payment and recovery of costs.

(2.) Where any costs or other sums are, under the order of an election court or otherwise under this Act, to be paid by any person, those costs shall be a simple contract debt due from such person to the person or persons to whom they are to be paid, and if payable to the Treasury shall be a debt to Her Majesty, and in either case may be recovered accordingly.

33. Where any summons, notice, or document is required to be served on any person with reference to any proceeding respecting a municipal election in any borough or ward of a borough, whether for the purpose of causing him to appear before the High Court or any election court, or otherwise, or for the purpose of giving him an opportunity of making a statement, or showing cause, or being heard by himself, before any such court, for any purpose of this Act, such summons, notice, or document may be served either by delivering the same to such person, or by leaving the same at, or sending the same by post by a registered letter to, his last known place of abode in the said borough, or, if the proceeding is before any court, in such other manner as the court may direct, and in proving such service by post it shall be sufficient to prove that the letter was prepaid, properly addressed, and registered with the post office. Service of notices.

34. In this Act expressions have the same meaning as in the Municipal Corporations Act, 1882, and in the Corrupt and Illegal Practices Prevention Act, 1883 ; except that the words "borough," "election petition," "election court," and "candidate," shall, unless the context otherwise requires, have the meaning given by the Municipal Corporations Act, 1882, and not the meaning given by the Corrupt and Illegal Practices Prevention Act, 1883 ; and except that "election" shall, unless the context otherwise requires, mean a municipal election. Definitions. 45 & 46 Vict. c. 50. 46 & 47 Vict. c. 51.

For the purposes of this Act the number of electors shall be taken according to the enumeration of the electors in the burgess roll.

Application to City of London of Act and of Part Four of 45 & 46 Vict. c. 50.

35. This Act and Part Four of the Municipal Corporations Act, 1882, shall apply to a municipal election in the city of London, subject as follows:—

(1.) For the purpose of such application "municipal election" means an election to the office of mayor, alderman, common councilman, or sheriff, and includes the election of any officer elected by the mayor, aldermen, and liverymen in common hall, and the expression "corporate office" includes each of the aforesaid offices, and the expression "borough" shall be deemed to apply to the said city:

(2.) The expression "burgess" means, in relation to each municipal election, any person entitled to vote at such election:

(3.) Any costs or expenses directed to be paid out of the borough fund or borough rate shall, if incurred in respect of the election of an alderman or common councilman for any ward, be paid out of the ward rate of that ward, and in any other case shall be paid by the chamberlain of the said city out of the city's cash:

30 Vict. c. 1.

(4.) The enactments relating to personation, polling agents, and disclosure of votes shall not apply, save that if any person commits any offence under the City of London Municipal Elections Amendment Act, 1867, in relation to the declaration required by that Act to be made at the poll, he shall, in addition, be deemed guilty of a corrupt practice under this Act:

(5.) A vacancy in any office created by the decision of an election court shall be filled by a new election, and every summoning officer is hereby authorised and required to summon the electors for such election:

(6.) In the case of an election of an alderman and common councilman a sum may be paid and expense incurred not in excess of the maximum fixed by this Act for the election of a councillor.

(7.) In the case of an election by liverymen in common hall a sum may be paid and expenses incurred, if a poll be not demanded, not exceeding forty pounds, and, if a poll be demanded, then not exceeding two hundred and fifty pounds, and, in the event of a poll being demanded, such poll shall take place on the third day after the demand for a poll be made, unless such third day be a Sunday, in which case the poll shall take place on the fourth day, and the poll shall last for one day only and commence at the hour of eight in the morning and close at six in the evening.

(8.) The town clerk shall send the corrupt and illegal practices list, when made out by him, to the ward clerk of each ward not less than fourteen days before the day on which the list of persons entitled to vote in such ward is required to be made out, and the aldermen and common councilmen of each ward shall omit from such last-mentioned list the names of all persons mentioned in the corrupt and illegal practices list, and the corrupt and illegal practices list shall be printed and appended to every copy of the list of persons entitled to vote in such ward.

Application of Act to other Elections.

36. (1.) Subject as hereinafter mentioned, the provisions of this Act and of Part Four of the Municipal Corporations Act, 1882, as amended by this Act, shall extend to elections for the offices mentioned in the first column of the First Schedule to this Act as if re-enacted herein and in terms made applicable thereto, and petitions may be presented and tried, and offences prosecuted and punished, and incapacities incurred in reference to each such election accordingly. Application of this Act and Part Four of 45 & 46 Vict. c. 50, to other elections.

Provided that in the application of the said provisions to any such election :

(a.) The area, officer, and rate mentioned opposite to the office in the second, third, and fourth columns of the said schedule, shall be deemed to be substituted for the borough or ward, town clerk, and borough fund or rate respectively.

(b.) The expression "corporate office" in the said provisions shall mean an office mentioned in the said schedule, and in relation to the election of a guardian of a union includes any such office in the union, and "a municipal election" shall mean an election to such office, and the expressions "municipal election court," "municipal election list," and "municipal election petition" shall be constructed accordingly.

(c.) No corrupt and illegal practices list shall be made for any such election.

(d.) Vacancies created by the decision of an election court shall be filled by a new election.

(e.) A petition relating to the election of a guardian of a union may be tried at any place within the union.

(f.) Nothing in the said provisions shall render it unlawful to hold a meeting for the purpose of promoting or procuring the election of a candidate to any office mentioned in the said schedule on any licensed or other premises not situate in an urban sanitary district or in the Metropolis ;

(g.) Where the poll at any election to an office in the said schedule is taken by means of voting papers, such of the said provisions as relate to personation, polling agents, disclosure of votes and conveyance of voters, shall not apply ; but any offence in relation to voting papers or to personation or to voting at such election which is punishable on summary conviction (that is to say), the offences mentioned in section three of the Poor Law Amendment Act, 1851, and in rule sixty-nine of Schedule Two to the Public Health Act, 1875, shall, without prejudice to the punishment under such section and rule of a person guilty of such offence, be deemed to be an illegal practice within the meaning of the said provisions. 14 & 15 Vict. c. 105. 38 & 39 Vict. c. 55.

(h.) The Local Government Board shall have the same power as heretofore under section eight of the Poor Law Amendment Act, 1842, to determine any question arising as to the right of a person to act as guardian, except that the Board shall not have power— 5 & 6 Vict. c. 67.

    (a.) To determine, until after the expiration of twenty-one days after the election of a person as guardian, any question which can be determined upon an election petition under this section; nor

(b.) To determine any question which is raised by an election petition under this section, and is either awaiting decision or has been decided by an election court; nor—

(c.) To determine any question of general corruption, or of any corrupt or illegal practice, except so far as appears to such Board necessary for determining the validity of any vote.

(2.) The judges for the time being on the rota for the trial of parliamentary election petitions, or any two of those judges, may annually appoint as many barristers, not exceeding five, as they may think necessary to be commissioners for the trial of election petitions under Part Four of the Municipal Corporations Act, 1882, and this Act, and shall from time to time assign the petitions (whether relating to a municipal election or to any other election to which this Act extends) to be tried by each commissioner.

Exemption from provisions as to maximum expenses.

37. The provisions of this Act which prohibit the payment of any sum, and the incurring of any expense by or on behalf of a candidate at an election, on account of, or in respect of, the conduct or management of the election, and those which relate to the time for sending in and paying claims, and those which relate to the maximum amount of election expenses, or the return or declaration respecting election expenses, shall not apply to any of the elections mentioned in the First Schedule to this Act.

Repeal.

Repeal of Acts.

38. The Acts specified in the Second Schedule to this Act are hereby repealed as from the commencement of this Act to the extent in the third column of that schedule mentioned, but such repeal shall not affect anything duly done or suffered, or any right acquired or accrued, or any incapacity incurred, before the commencement of this Act; and any person subject to any incapacity under any enactment hereby repealed, or under any enactment for which such repealed enactment was substituted, shall continue subject thereto, and this Act shall apply to him as if he had become so subject in pursuance of the provisions of this Act.

Commencement of Act.

39. This Act shall come into operation on the first day of October, one thousand eight hundred and eighty-four, which day is in this Act referred to as the commencement of this Act.

Extent of Act.

Act not to extend to Scotland or Ireland.

40. This Act shall not extend to Scotland or Ireland.

Duration of Act.

41. This Act shall continue in force to the end of the year one thousand eight hundred and eighty-six, and no longer.

SCHEDULES.

FIRST SCHEDULE.

Section 36.

ELECTIONS TO WHICH THIS ACT EXTENDS.

In England.

Office.	Area.	Officer.	Rate.
Member of local board, as defined by the Public Health Act, 1875.	Local Government district or ward of such district.	Clerk to the local board, or person performing like duties.	The general district rate.
Member of Improvement Commissioners, as defined by the Public Health Act, 1875.	Improvement Act district or ward of such district.	Clerk to the Improvement Commissioners or person performing like duties.	The general district rate or other rate out of which the expenses of the Improvement Commissioners are payable.
Guardian elected under the Poor Law Amendment Act, 1834.	Parish or ward of a parish or united parishes.	Clerk to the guardians, or person performing like duties.	The poor rate of the parish or united parishes.
Member of school board.	School district or division of the metropolis.	Returning officer of school board.	The school fund.

SECOND SCHEDULE.

ENACTMENTS REPEALED.

Section 39.

A description or citation of a portion of an Act is inclusive of the words, section, or other part first and last mentioned, or otherwise referred to as forming the beginning or as forming the end of the portion comprised in the description or citation.

As to England.

33 & 34 Vict. c. 75.	The Elementary Education Act, 1870.	Section thirty-three.
45 & 46 Vict. c. 50	The Municipal Corporations Act, 1882.	Section seventy-seven, from "corrupt practice" down to "or personation," and from "canvasser" down to "candidate at a municipal election."
		Section seventy-eight.
		Section seventy-nine.
		Section eighty.
		Section eighty-two.
		Section eighty-three.
		Section eighty-four.
		Section ninety-two, sub-section four, from "and those judges" down to the end of the sub-section.
		Section ninety-four, sub-sections five, six, seven, and eight.
		So much of section ninety-eight, sub-section two, as relates to the principles of taxation.

APPENDIX.

THIRD SCHEDULE.

Section 2.

PART I.

Enactments defining Corrupt Practices.

[These are set out in full in the body of the work. See Part I., chapter I.]

PART II.

Section 23.

Enactments relating to Disqualification of Electors.

The Corrupt and Illegal Practices Prevention Act, 1883, 46 & 47 Vict. c. 51, sections 37 and 38.

S. 37. Every person who, in consequence of conviction or of the report of any election court or election commissioners under this Act, or under the Corrupt Practices (Municipal Elections) Act, 1872, or under Part Four of the Municipal Corporations Act, 1882, or under any other Act for the time being in force relating to corrupt practices at an election for any public office, has become incapable of voting at any election, whether a parliamentary election or an election to any public office, is prohibited from voting at any such election, and his vote shall be void. *Prohibition of disqualified persons from voting. 35 & 36 Vict. c. 60. 45 & 46 Vict. c. 50.*

S. 38. (1.) Before a person, not being a party to an election petition nor a candidate on behalf of whom the seat is claimed by an election petition, is reported by an election court ° ° ° to have been guilty, at an election, of any corrupt or illegal practice, the court ° ° ° shall cause notice to be given to such person, and if he appears in pursuance of the notice, shall give him an opportunity of being heard by himself and of calling evidence in his defence to show why he should not be so reported. *Hearing of person before he is reported guilty of corrupt or illegal practice, and incapacity of person reported guilty.*

° ° ° ° °

(5.) Every person who, after the commencement of this Act, is reported by any election court ° ° ° to have been guilty of any corrupt or illegal practice at an election, shall, whether he obtained a certificate of indemnity or not, be subject to the same incapacity as he would be subject to if he had at the date of such election been convicted of the offence of which he is reported to have been guilty ° °

(6.) Where a person who is a justice of the peace is reported by any election court ° ° ° to have been guilty of any corrupt practice in reference to an election, whether he has obtained a certificate of indemnity or not, it shall be the duty of the Director of Public Prosecutions to report the case to the Lord High Chancellor of Great Britain, with such evidence as may have been given of such corrupt practice, and where any such person acts as a justice of the peace by virtue of his being or having been mayor of a borough, the Lord High Chancellor shall have the same power to remove such person from being a justice of the peace as if he was named in a commission of the peace.

(7.) Where a person who is a barrister or a solicitor, or who belongs to any profession the admission to which is regulated by law, is reported by any election court ° ° ° to have been guilty of any corrupt practice in reference to an election, whether such person has obtained a certificate of indemnity or not, it shall be the duty of the Director of Public Prosecutions to bring the matter before the Inn of Court, High Court, or tribunal having power to take cognizance of any misconduct of such person in his profession, and such Inn of Court, High Court, or tribunal may deal with such person in like manner as if such corrupt practice were misconduct by such person in his profession.

(8.) With respect to a person holding a license or certificate under the Licensing Acts (in this section referred to as a licensed person) the following provisions shall have effect :—

(*a*.) If it appears to the court by which any licensed person is convicted of the offence of bribery or treating that such offence was committed on his licensed premises, the court shall direct such conviction to be entered in the proper register of licenses :

(*b*.) If it appears to an election court ° ° ° that a licensed person has knowingly suffered any bribery or treating in reference to any election to take place upon his licensed premises, such court ° ° ° (subject to the provisions of this Act as to a person having an opportunity of being heard by himself and producing evidence before being reported) shall report the same, and, whether such person obtained a certificate of indemnity or not, it shall be the duty of the Director of Public Prosecutions to bring such report before the licensing justices from whom or on whose certificate the licensed person obtained his license, and such licensing justices shall cause such report to be entered in the proper register of licenses.

(*c*.) Where an entry is made in the register of licenses of any such conviction of or report respecting any licensed person as above in this section mentioned, it shall be taken into consideration by the licensing justices in determining whether they will or will not grant to such person the renewal of his license or certificate, and may be a ground, if the justices think fit, for refusing such renewal.

° • ◡ • ◦

FOURTH SCHEDULE.

Section 2L.

Form of Declaration by Candidate as to Expenses.

I,   , having been a candidate at the election of councillor for the borough [or ward] of   , on the   day of   [and my agents do hereby solemnly and sincerely declare that I have paid   ] for my expenses at the said election, and that, except as aforesaid, I have not, and to the best of my knowledge and belief, no person, nor any club, society, or association, has on my behalf, made any payment, or given, promised, or offered any reward, office, employment, or valuable consideration, or incurred any liability on account of or in respect of the conduct or management of the said election.

And I further solemnly and sincerely declare that, except as aforesaid, no money, security, or equivalent for money, has to my knowledge or belief been paid, advanced, given or deposited by anyone to or in the hands of myself, or any other person, for the purpose of defraying any expenses incurred on my behalf on account of or in respect of the conduct or management of the said election.

And I further solemnly and sincerely declare that I will not at any future time make or be a party to the making or giving of any payment, reward, office, employment, or valuable consideration for the purpose of defraying any such expenses as last mentioned, or provide or be a party to the providing of any money, security, or equivalent for money for the purpose of defraying any such expenses.

                 Signature of declarant   C.D.

Signed and declared by the above-named declarant on the   day of   , before me
                 (Signed)   E.F.
                 Justice of the peace for

1883.

GENERAL RULES

FOR THE EFFECTUAL EXECUTION OF PART IV. OF "THE MUNICIPAL CORPORATIONS ACT, 1882,"

MADE BY

Sir CHARLES EDWARD POLLOCK, Knight;
Sir HENRY MANISTY, Knight; and
Sir HENRY CHARLES LOPES, Knight;

THE JUDGES FOR THE TIME BEING ON THE ROTA FOR THE TRIAL OF PARLIAMENTARY ELECTION PETITIONS.

1. The presentation of a Municipal Election Petition shall be made by leaving it at the office of the Master for the time being nominated as prescribed officer under the Parliamentary Elections Act, 1868, and such Master or his clerk shall (if required) give a receipt which may be in the following form :—

Received on the   day of   at the Master's office a petition touching the election of *A.B.*, alderman, councillor [&c., *as the case may be*] for the borough of   purporting to be signed by [*insert the names of petitioners*].

C.D., Master's Clerk.

With the petition shall also be left a copy thereof for the Master to send to the town clerk, pursuant to section 88, sub-section (3) of the Act.

2. A municipal election petition shall contain the following statements :—

(1.) It shall state the right of the petitioner or petitioners to petition within section 88, sub-section (1), of the Act.

(2.) It shall state the holding and result of the election, and shall briefly state the facts and grounds relied on to sustain the prayer.

3. The petition shall be divided into paragraphs, each of which, as nearly as may be, shall be confined to a distinct portion of the subject, and every paragraph shall be numbered consecutively, and no costs shall be allowed of drawing or copying any petition not substantially in compliance with this rule, unless otherwise ordered by the High Court or a judge thereof.

4. The petition shall conclude with a prayer, as for instance, that

some specified person should be declared duly returned or elected, or that the election should be declared void, or that a return may be enforced, (as the case may be,) and shall be signed by all the petitioners.

5. The following form, or one to the like effect, shall be sufficient :—

In the High Court of Justice,
"The Municipal Corporations Act, 1882."
Election for [*state the place and office for which election held*] holden on the   day of   A.D.
The petition of *A.* of   [*or* of *A.* of
, and *B.* of
as *the case may be*] whose names are subscribed.

1. Your petititioner A. is a person who voted [*or* had a right to vote, *as the case may be,*] at the above election, [*or* was a candidate at the above election] ; and your petitioner *B.* [*here state in like manner the right of each petitioner*].
2. And your petitioners state that the election was holden on the   day of   A.D.   , when *A.B., C.D.,* and *E.F.* were candidates, and that *A.B.* and *C.D.* have been in the usual manner declared to be duly elected.
3. And your petitioners say that [*here state the facts and grounds on which the petitioners rely*].

Wherefore your petitioners pray that it may be determined that the said *A.B.* was not duly elected, and that the election was void [*or* that the said *E.F.* was duly elected and ought to have been returned, *or as the case may be*].

(Signed)
A.
B.

6. Evidence need not be stated in the petition, but the High Court or a judge thereof may order such particulars as may be necessary to prevent surprise and unnecessary expense, and to insure a fair and effectual trial in the same way as in ordinary proceedings in the said High Court, and upon such terms as to costs and otherwise as may be ordered.

7. When a petitioner claims the office for an unsuccessful candidate, alleging that he had a majority of lawful votes, the party complaining of or defending the election shall, six days before the day appointed for trial, deliver to the Master and also at the address, if any given by the petitioners and respondents, as the case may be, a list of the votes intended to be objected to, and the heads of objection to each such vote, and the Master shall allow inspection and office copies of such lists to all parties concerned ; and no evidence shall be given against the validity of any vote, nor upon any head of objection not specified in the list, except by leave of the High Court or a judge thereof, upon such terms as to amendment of the list, postponement of the inquiry, and payment of costs, as may be ordered.

8. When the respondent in a petition under the Act complaining of an undue election, and claiming the office for some person, intends to give evidence to prove that the election of such person was undue, pursuant to the 93rd section of the Act, sub-section 10, such respondent shall, six days before the day appointed for trial, deliver to the Master, and also at the address, if any, given by the petitioner, a list of the objections to the election upon which he intends to rely, and the Master

shall allow inspection and office copies of such lists to all parties concerned; and no evidence shall be given by a respondent of any objection to the election not specified in the list, except by leave of the High Court or a judge thereof, upon such terms as to amendment of the list, postponement of the inquiry, and payment of costs, as may be ordered.

9. With the petition the petitioner or petitioners shall leave at the office of the Master a writing, signed by him or them or on his or their behalf, giving the name of some person entitled to practice as a solicitor in the High Court of Justice whom he or they authorise to act as his or their agent, or stating that he or they for himself or themselves, as the case may be, and in either case giving an address, within three miles from the General Post Office, at which notices addressed to him or them may be left; and if no such writing be left or address given, then notice of objection to the recognizances, and all other notices and proceedings may be given by sticking up the same at the Master's office.

10. Any person elected to any municipal office may at any time after he is elected send to or leave at the office of the Master a writing, signed by him or on his behalf, appointing a person entitled to practise as a solicitor in the High Court of Justice, to act as his agent in case there should be a petition against him, or stating that he intends to act for himself, and in either case giving an address within three miles from the General Post Office at which notices may be left, and in default of such writing being left in a week after service of the petition, notices and proceedings may be given and served respectively by sticking up the same at the Master's office.

11. The Master shall keep a book or books at his office in which he shall enter all addresses and the names of agents given under either of the preceding rules, which book shall be open to inspection by any person during office hours.

12. The Master shall, upon the presentation of the petition, forthwith send a copy of the petition to the town clerk, pursuant to section 88 of the Act, sub-section (3), and shall therewith send the name of the petitioner's agent, if any, and the address, if any, given as prescribed, and also the name of the respondent's agent, and the address, if any, given as prescribed, and the town clerk shall forthwith publish those particulars along with the petition.

The cost of publication of this and any other matter required to be published by the town clerk shall be paid by the petitioner or person moving in the matter, and shall form part of the general costs of the petition.

13. The time for giving notice of the presentation of a petition and of the nature of the proposed security, shall be five days, exclusive of the day of presentation.

14. Where the respondent has named an agent or given an address, the service of a municipal election petition may be by delivery of it to the agent, or by posting it in a registered letter to the address given at such time that, in the ordinary course of post, it would be delivered within the prescribed time.

In other cases the service must be personal on the respondent, unless a judge of the High Court, on an application made to him not later than five days after the petition is presented on affidavit, showing what has been done, shall be satisfied that all reasonable effort has been made to effect personal service and cause the matter to come to the knowledge of the respondent, in which case the judge may order that what has been done shall be considered sufficient service, subject to such conditions as he may think reasonable. An agent employed for the petitioner or respondent shall forthwith leave written notice at the office of the Master of his appointment to act as such agent, and service of notices and proceedings upon such agent shall be sufficient for all purposes.

15. In case of evasion of service the sticking up a notice in the office of the Master of the petition having been presented, stating the petitioner, the prayer, and the nature of the proposed security, shall be deemed equivalent to personal service if so ordered by a judge.

16. The deposit of money by way of security for payment of costs, charges, and expenses, payable by the petitioner, shall be made by payment into the Bank of England to an account to be opened there by the description of " The Municipal Corporations Act, 1882, Security Fund," which shall be vested in and drawn upon from time to time by the Lord Chief Justice of England for the time being for the purposes for which security is required by the said Act, and a bank receipt or certificate for the same shall be forthwith left at the Master's office.

17. The Master shall file such receipt or certificate, and keep a book open to inspection of all parties concerned, in which shall be entered from time to time the amount and the petition to which it is applicable.

18. All claims at law or in equity to money so deposited or to be deposited in the Bank of England shall be disposed of by the High Court of Justice or a judge thereof.

19. Money so deposited shall, if, and when the same is no longer needed for securing payment of such costs, charges, and expenses, be returned or otherwise disposed of as justice may require, by rule of the High Court, or order of a judge thereof.

20. Such rule or order may be made after such notice of intention to apply, and proof that all just claims have been satisfied or otherwise sufficiently provided for, as the Court or judge may require.

21. The rule or order may direct payment either to the party in whose name the same is deposited, or to any person entitled to receive the same.

22. Upon such rule or order being made, the amount may be drawn for by the Lord Chief Justice of England for the time being.

23. The draft of the Lord Chief Justice of England for the time being shall in all cases be a sufficient warrant to the Bank of England for all payments made thereunder.

24. The recognizance as security for costs may be acknowledged before a judge of the High Court or the Master in town, or a justice of the peace in the country.

There may be one recognizance acknowledged by all the sureties, or separate recognizances by one or more, as may be convenient.

25. The recognizance shall contain the name and usual place of abode of each surety, with such sufficient description as shall enable him to be found or ascertained, and may be as follows :—

Be it remembered that on the   day of   , in the year of our Lord 18   , before me [*name and description*] came *A.B.*, of [*name and description as above prescribed*] and acknowledged himself [*or* severally acknowledged themselves] to owe to our Sovereign Lady the Queen the sum of five hundred pounds [*or* the following sums], (that is to say) the said *C.D.* the sum of £   , the said *E.F.* the sum of £   , the said *G.H.* the sum of £   , and the said *J.K.* the sum of £   , to be levied on his [*or* their respective] goods and chattels, lands, and tenements, to the use of our said Sovereign Lady the Queen, her heirs and successors.

The condition of this recognizance is that if [*here insert the names of all the petitioners, and if more than one, add*, or any of them] shall well and truly pay all costs, charges, and expenses in respect of the election petition signed by him [*or* them] relating to the [*here insert the name of the borough*] which shall become payable by the petitioner [*or* petitioners, or any of them] under the Municipal Corporations Act, 1882, to any person or persons, then this recognizance to be void, otherwise to stand in full force.

Signed,

[*Signature of sureties.*]

Taken and acknowledged by the above-named [*name of sureties*] on the   at   , before me,

C.D.

A justice of the peace [*or, as the case may be*].

26. The recognizance or recognizances shall be left at the Master's office, by or on behalf of the petitioner in like manner as before prescribed for the leaving of a petition forthwith after being acknowledged.

The security may (unless the High Court or a judge thereof shall otherwise order on summons), be given to any amount not less than £300; but the High Court or a judge thereof may, on summons taken out within five days from the service of the notice of the nature and amount of the security, order that the same shall be increased within a time to be fixed in the order by further security to be given in the manner directed by the Act, for a further amount, not exceeding with the amount for which security shall have been already given £500. And in default of compliance with such order, no further proceedings shall be had on the petition.

27. The time for giving notice of any objection to a recognizance under the 89th section of the Act, sub-section (4), shall be within five days from the date of service of the notice of the petition and of the nature of the security, exclusive of the day of service, or in case of further security within five days after service of notice of the nature thereof, exclusive of the day of such service.

28. An objection to the recognizance must state the ground or grounds thereof, as that the sureties, or any and which of them, are insufficient, or that a surety is dead, or that he cannot be found, or that a person named in the recognizance has not duly acknowledged the same.

29. Any objection made to the security shall be heard and decided by the Master, subject to appeal within five days to a judge, upon summons taken out by either party to declare the security sufficient or insufficient.

30. Such hearing and decision may be either upon affidavit or personal examination of witnesses, or both, as the Master or judge may think fit.

31. If an objection be allowed and the security be declared insufficient, the Master or judge shall in his order state what amount he

deems requisite to make the security sufficient, and the further prescribed time to remove the objection by deposit shall be within five days from the date of the order, not including the day of the date, and such deposit shall be made in the manner already prescribed.

32. The costs of hearing and deciding the objections made to the security given shall be paid as ordered by the Master or judge, and in default of such order shall form part of the general costs of the petition.

33. The costs of hearing and deciding an objection upon the ground of insufficiency of a surety or sureties, shall be paid by the petitioner, and a clause to that effect shall be inserted in the order declaring its sufficiency or insufficiency, unless at the time of leaving the recognizance with the Master there be also left with the Master an affidavit of the sufficiency of the surety or sureties sworn by each surety before a justice of the peace, which affidavit any justice of the peace is hereby authorised to take, or before some person authorised to take affidavits in the High Court of Justice that he is seized or possessed of real or personal estate, or both, above what will satisfy his debts, of the clear value of the sum for which he is bound by his recognizance, which affidavit may be as follows :

In the High Court of Justice.
 Municipal Corporations Act, 1882.
I *A.B.*, of [*as in recognizance*] make oath and say that I am seized or possessed of real [*or* personal] estate above what will satisfy my debts, of the clear value of £

                Sworn, &c.

34. The order of the Master for payment of costs shall have the same force as an order made by a judge, and may be enforced in like manner as a judge's order in an ordinary proceeding in the High Court of Justice.

35. A copy of every order (other than an order giving further time for delivering particulars, or for costs only), or, if the Master shall so direct, the order itself or a duplicate thereof, also a copy of every particular delivered, shall be forthwith filed with the Master, and the same shall be produced at the trial by the Registrar, stamped with the official seal. Such order shall be filed by the party obtaining the same, and such particular by the party delivering the same.

36. The petitioner or his agent shall, immediately after notice of the presentation of a petition and of the nature of the proposed security shall have been served, file with the Master an affidavit of the time and manner of service thereof.

37. The days mentioned in rules 7 and 8, and in any rule of court or judge's order, whereby particulars are ordered to be delivered, or any act is directed to be done, so many days before the day appointed for trial, shall be reckoned exclusively of the day of delivery, or of doing the act ordered and the day appointed for trial, and exclusively also of Sunday, Christmas Day, Good Friday, and any day set apart for a public fast or public thanksgiving.

38. When the last day for presenting petitions, or filing lists of votes or objections, under rules 7 and 8, or recognizances, or any other matter required to be filed within a given time, shall happen to fall on a holiday, the petition or other matter shall be deemed duly filed if put into the letter box at the Master's office at any time during such day; but an affidavit, stating with reasonable precision the time when such delivery was made, shall be filed on the first day after the expiration of the holidays.

39. The Master shall make out the municipal election list. In it he shall insert the names of the agents of the petitioners and respondents, and the addresses to which notices may be sent, if any. The list may be inspected at the Master's office at any time during office hours, and shall be put up for that purpose upon a notice board appropriated to proceedings under the said Act, and headed "Municipal Election List."

40. The time of the trial of each municipal election petition shall be fixed by the election judges on the rota or any one of them, who shall signify the same to the Master, and notice thereof shall be given in writing by the Master by sticking notice up in his office, sending one copy by post to the address given by the petitioner, another to the address given by the respondent, if any, and a copy by the post to the town clerk of the borough to which the petition relates, fifteen days before the day appointed for the trial.

The town clerk shall forthwith publish the same in the borough.

41. The sticking up of the notice of trial at the office of the Master shall be deemed and taken to be notice in the prescribed manner within the meaning of the Act, and such notice shall not be vitiated by any miscarriage of or relating to the copy or copies thereof to be sent as already directed.

42. The notice of trial may be in the following form:—

Municipal Corporations Act, 1882.

Election petition of
Borough of

Take notice that the above petition [or petitions] will be tried at
on the
day of   and on such other subsequent
days as may be needful.

Dated the   day of
Signed, by order,
A.B.,
The Master appointed under the above Act.

43. A judge may from time to time, by order made upon the application of a party to the petition, or by notice in such form as the judge may direct to be sent to the town clerk, postpone the beginning of the trial to such day as he may name, and such notice when received shall be forthwith made public by the town clerk.

44. In the event of the barrister to whom the trial of the petition is assigned not having arrived at the time appointed for the trial, or to which the trial is postponed, the commencement of the trial shall *ipso facto* stand adjourned for the ensuing day, and so from day to day.

45. No formal adjournment of the court for the trial of a municipal election petition shall be necessary, but the trial is to be deemed adjourned, and may be continued from day to day until the inquiry is concluded.

46. After receiving notice of the petitioner's intention to apply for leave to withdraw, or of the respondent's intention not to oppose, or of the abatement of the petition by death, or of the happening of any of the events mentioned in the 97th section of the Act, if such notice be received after notice of trial shall have been given, and before the trial has commenced, the Master shall forthwith countermand the notice of trial. The countermand shall be given in the same manner, as near as may be, as the notice of trial.

47. If all the respondents shall give notice of their intention not to oppose the petition, and no other person shall be admitted as a respondent, the High Court of Justice, or a Judge, may either declare the election void or direct the trial to proceed. Notice of such order shall be forthwith given by the Master to the town clerk, and if the election be declared void the office shall be deemed to be vacant from the first day (not being a *dies non*) after the date of such order.

The court or judge may also make such order as to costs as may be just.

48. The application to state a special case may be made by motion in the High Court of Justice, or by a summons before a judge thereof.

49. The title of the court held for the trial of a municipal election petition may be as follows :—

"Court for the trial of a municipal election petition for the borough of [*or be*] between .... *as may* petitioner and .... respondent,"

and it shall be sufficient so to entitle all proceedings in that court.

50. An officer shall be appointed for each court for the trial of a municipal election petition by the election judges, at the time that they assign the petition to the barrister; such officer shall attend at the trial in like manner as the clerks of assize and arraigns attend at the assizes.

Such officer may be called the registrar of that court. He, by himself, or in case of need, his sufficient deputy, shall perform all the functions incident to the officer of a court of record, and also such duties as may be prescribed of him.

51. The Commissioner may appoint a proper person to act as crier and officer of the court.

52. The shorthand writer to attend at the trial of a petition shall be the shorthand writer to the House of Commons for the time being or his deputy, and the Master shall send a copy of the notice of trial to the said shorthand writer to the House of Commons.

53. The amount to be paid to any witness whose expenses shall be allowed by the Commissioner trying the petition shall be ascertained and certified by the registrar; or in the event of his becoming incapacitated from giving such certificate, by the Commissioner.

54. The order of the court to compel the attendance of a person as a witness may be in the following form :—

Court for the trial of a municipal election petition for [*complete the title of the Court*] the .... day of ....

To *A.B.* [*describe the person*]. You are hereby required to attend before the above court at [*place*] on .... day of .... at the hour of [*or forthwith, as the case may be*], to be examined as a witness in the matter of the said petition, and to attend the said court until your examination shall have been completed.

As witness my hand, *A.B.*,

The Commissioner to whom the trial of the said petition is assigned.

55. In the event of its being necessary to commit any person for contempt, the warrant may be as follows :—

At a court holden on .... at

for the trial of a municipal election petition for the borough of   before *A.B.*, one of the barristers appointed for the trial of municipal election petitions, pursuant to "The Municipal Corporations Act, 1882."

Whereas *C.D.* has this day been guilty, and is by the said court adjudged to be guilty, of a contempt thereof. The said court does therefore sentence the said *C.D.* for his said contempt to be imprisoned in the   gaol for   calendar months [*or as may be*] and to pay to our Lady the Queen a fine of £   , and to be further imprisoned in the said gaol until the said fine be paid, and the court further orders that the sheriff of the borough [*if any or as the case may be*], and all constables and officers of the peace of any county, borough or place where the said *C.D.* may be found, shall take the said *C.D.* into custody and convey him to the said gaol, and there deliver him into the custody of the gaoler thereof, to undergo his said sentence: and the court further orders the said gaoler to receive the said *C.D.* into his custody, and that he shall be detained in the said gaol in pursuance of the said sentence.

A.B.

Signed the   day of

A.B.

56. Such warrant may be made out and directed to the sheriff or other person having the execution of process of the High Court as the case may be, and to all constables and officers of the peace of the county, borough, or place where the person adjudged guilty of contempt may be found, and such warrant shall be sufficient without further particularity, and shall and may be executed by the persons to whom it is directed or any or either of them.

57. All interlocutory questions and matters, except as to the sufficiency of the security, shall be heard and disposed of before a judge, who shall have the same control over the proceedings under the Municipal Corporations Act, 1882, as a judge in the ordinary proceedings of the High Court, and such questions and matters shall be heard and disposed of by any judge of the High Court.

58. Notice of an application for leave to withdraw a petition shall be in writing and signed by the petitioners or their agent.

It shall state the ground on which the application is intended to be supported.

The following form shall be sufficient:—

Municipal Corporations Act, 1882.

Borough of   Petition of [*state petitioners*] presented   day of

The petitioner proposes to apply to withdraw his petition upon the following ground [*here state the ground*], and prays that a day may be appointed for hearing his application.

Dated this   day of

(Signed)

59. The notice of application for leave to withdraw shall be left at the Master's office.

60. A copy of such notice of the intention of the petitioner to apply for leave to withdraw his petition shall be given by the petitioner to the respondent, and to the town clerk, who shall cause the same to be published in the borough to which it relates.

The following may be the form of such notice:—

Municipal Corporations Act, 1882.

In the election petition for   in which   is petitioner and   respondent.

Notice is hereby given, that the above petitioner has on the   day of   lodged at the master's office notice of an application to withdraw the petition, of which notice the following is a copy [*set it out*].

And take notice that by the rule made by the judges, any person who might have been a petitioner in respect of the said election may, within five days after publication by the town clerk of this notice, give notice in writing of his intention on the hearing to apply for leave to be substituted as a petitioner.

(Signed)

61. Any person who might have been a petitioner in respect of the election to which the petition relates, may, within five days after such notice is published by the returning officer, give notice, in writing, signed by him or on his behalf, to the Master of his intention to apply at the hearing to be substituted for the petitioner, but the want of such notice shall not defeat such application, if in fact made at the hearing.

62. The time and place for hearing the application shall be fixed by a judge, and whether before the High Court, or before a judge, as he may deem advisable, but shall not be less than a week after the notice of the intention to apply has been given to the Master as hereinbefore provided, and notice of the time and place appointed for the hearing shall be given to such person or persons, if any, as shall have given notice to the Master of an intention to apply to be substituted as petitioners, and otherwise in such manner and at such time as the court or judge directs.

63. Notice of abatement of a petition, by death of the petitioner or surviving petitioner, under section 96, sub-section 1, of the said Act, shall be given by the party or person interested in the same manner as a notice of an application to withdraw a petition, and the time within which application may be made to the High Court, or a judge thereof, by motion or summons at chambers, to be substituted as a petitioner, shall be one calendar month, or such further time as upon consideration of any special circumstances the High Court or a judge thereof may allow.

64. If the respondent dies, any person entitled to be a petitioner under the Act in respect of the election to which the petition relates, may give notice of the fact in the borough by causing such notice to be published in at least one newspaper circulating therein, if any, and by leaving a copy of such notice signed by him or on his behalf with the town clerk, and a like copy with the Master.

65. The manner of the respondent's giving notice that he does not intend to oppose the petition shall be by leaving notice thereof in writing at the office of the Master signed by the respondent.

66. Upon such notice being left at the Master's office, the Master shall forthwith send a copy thereof by the post to the petitioner or his agent, and to the town clerk, who shall cause the same to be published in the borough.

67. The time for applying to be admitted as a respondent in either of the events mentioned in the 97th section of the Act shall be within ten

days after such notice is given as hereinbefore directed, or such further time as the High Court or a judge thereof may allow.

68. Costs shall be taxed by the Master, or at his request by any Master of the superior court upon the rule of court or judge's order by which the costs are payable, and costs when taxed may be recovered in like manner as if payable under a rule of court, judgment, or order of a judge in the ordinary proceedings in the High Court of Justice, or in case there be money in the Bank available for the purpose, then to the extent of such money by order of the Lord Chief Justice of England for the time being.

The office fees payable for inspection, office copies, enrolment, and other proceedings under the Act and these rules, shall be the same as those payable, if any, for like proceedings according to the present practice of the High Court of Justice.

69. No proceedings under the Municipal Corporations Act, 1882, shall be defeated by any formal objection.

70. Any rule made or to be made in pursuance of the Act shall be published by a copy thereof being put up at the Master's office.

Dated the 17th day of April, 1883.

C. E. POLLOCK.
H. MANISTY.
HENRY C. LOPES,

The judges for the time being on the rota for the trial of Parliamentary Election Petitions.

INDEX.

ABATEMENT of petition, 173.
ACTION for disputed claims, 153.
ADMISSION, by agent, 210.
ADMISSION, by witness, 204,
ADDRESS, contract for exhibition of, when illegal practice, 70.
ADVERTISEMENTS for claims, 149.
ADVERTISING AGENT may be paid for bill posting, &c., 70.
" AFFECT THE ELECTION," meaning of, 107.
AGREEMENT by one candidate to pay expenses of another, not bribery, 38.
AGENCY.
    Proof of at trial, 203.
    A question of fact, 115.
    In case of joint candidature, 127.
    When it begins and ends, 129, 210.
    Constituted by employment or recognition, 114.
AGENT convicted of corruption, employment of, avoids election, 98.
AGENTS,
    Of candidate, 109 *et seq*.
    Candidate liable for acts of, 109.
    Sub-agents, extent of their authority, 110.
    Number of unpaid, not limited, 111.
    Authority to canvass, effect of, 112.
    Limitations of their authority, 112.
    Disobedient, candidate liable for, 113.
    Implied, how constituted, 114.
    Need not be paid, 115.
    Canvassing does not necessarily constitute agency, 116.
    Nor being on a large committee, 116.
    Sufficient evidence of being, what is, 117.
    May act by sub-agents, 119.
    Members of political associations, how far, 119 *et seq*.
    Effect of repudiation by candidate, 123.
    Candidate using political association makes its officers, 125.
    Responsibility of candidates for, when treacherous, 128.

AGENTS,
    When agency begins, 129.
    And ends, 129.
    With limited authority, candidate how far bound, 113.
ALDERMAN, election of, application of law to, 258, 259.
ALIENS, cannot vote, 87, 200.
AMENDMENT of particulars, 182, 183.
AMENDMENT of petition, 177.
AMOUNT of bribe immaterial, 11.
APPOINTMENT of election agent, 131.
ASSESSOR, election of, application of law to, 258.
ASSOCIATIONS,
    Political, 119.
    Political, repudiation of, 122.
    Political, effect of subscriptions to, by candidates, 124.
ATTEMPTS, to corrupt, 8, 45.
    To intimidate, 62.
AUDITOR ELECTIVE, application of law to, 258

BALLOT,
    Test, bribery and treating at, 15, 46.
    Advertising to be a sham, 63.
BALLOT ACT,
    Effect of violation of, 2.
BALLOT papers, when examined, 200.
BALLOT papers ill-marked, disallowed, 199.
BALLOT papers, inspection of, 194.
BANDS and banners, payments for, illegal, 80
BANK-book, proof of, 209.
BARRISTER'S court money, payment of, when bribery, 22.
BARRISTERS, special punishment of, 235.
BETS on election, 40.

INDEX.

BILL posting, contracts for, when illegal practice, 70 et seq.
BILLS to bear printer's name, 88.
BOROUGHS, maximum expenditure in, 111.
BRIBERY,
  By agent, avoids election, 1.
  Statutory definition of, 4, 5, 6.
  Need not be direct, 9.
  Time when done, how far material, 11.
  Effect of, when done after election, 12.
  Amount given in, immaterial, 11.
  Form of, immaterial, 16.
  Committed, although vote not affected, 8.
  By colourable payments, 9, 16, 20.
  At municipal election may avoid parliamentary election, 13, 14.
  At test ballot, 15.
  At former election, 16.
  After election, 12.
  By profuse household expenditure, 23.
  By charitable gifts, 29, 37.
  By purchasing influence, 27, 28, 37.
  By paying wages, 34.
  By paying travelling expenses, 21.
  No relief from consequences of, 11, 51.
  General, 101.

CABS, when illegal to hire, 77.
CANDIDATE, expenses of, agreement by another candidate to pay, 40.
CANDIDATE,
  Bribery by, 4 et seq.
  Illegal practices by, 67 et seq.
  Illegal payment by, 76.
  Personal expenses of, 142.
  Election expenses of, 137.
  Subscriptions to pay expenses of, 149.
  To make declaration of purity, 155.
  Declaration by, when abroad, 156.
  False declaration by, 158.
  Liable for acts of agents, 110.
CANVASS, authority to effect of, 112.
  Authority to effect of, 112.
CANVASS BOOK, contents, how proved, 209.
CANVASSERS, colourable payments to, bribery, 6, 19.
CANVASSING, illegitimate, 57.
CERTIFICATE of judges, effect of, 208.
CHANGE of Election Agent, 133.
CHARITIES, subscriptions to, 31, 32.
CHARITABLE gifts, 29, 38.
CHILDREN, payments to, may be bribery, 9.
CITY OF LONDON, application of Acts to, 267, 268.
CLAIMS for expenses, when to be sent in, 150.

CLAIMS for expenses, when to be paid, 152.
CLAIMS for seat, withdrawal of, 178, 179.
CLERICAL organisation, when candidate responsible for, 126.
CLERGYMEN, intimidation by, 61.
  Special punishment of, 235.
CLERKS, to be appointed by Election Agent, 136.
  Colourable payments to, bribery, 16, 19.
  Number allowed, 81, 82.
CLUBS, when use of, as Committee Rooms, prohibited, 83, 94.
COALS, gifts to electors, 35.
COALITION of candidates, bribery before, effect of, 127.
COCKADES, payments for, illegal, 80.
COLOURABLE payments, bribery, 9, 16, 20.
COMMISSION to examine witness, 184.
COMMITTEE, election, agency of, 116.
COMMITTEE ROOM, what is, 72.
COMMITTEE ROOMS,
  Hiring of, when bribery, 20.
  Excessive number of, contracts for, 71.
  Number allowed, 71.
  What are, 72.
  In what places illegal, 79.
COMMON COUNCILMAN, application of Acts to, 267.
CONSTITUENCY when ordered to pay costs, 216, 225.
CONVEYANCE OF VOTERS,
  Contracts or payment for, an illegal practice, 67.
  By sea, 80.
  To poll when bribery, 20, 22.
CONVICTS may not vote, 87.
"CORRUPTLY," meaning of, 43.
CORRUPT AGENT, employment of, 7, 98.
CORRUPT PRACTICES,
  Defined, 3.
  How punished, 233 et seq.
CORRUPTION, general, 101 et seq.
COSTS,
  On election petitions, 213, 224.
  Usually follow the event, 213.
  Exceptions to the rule where petition succeeds, 214, 215.
  Exceptions to the rule where petition fails, 215.
  When returning officer in fault, 215.
  Agreement not to ask for, 215.
  Where constituency or town may be ordered to pay, 216, 226.
  Where persons (not parties to petition), to pay, 216, 217.

INDEX. 407

COSTS,
　Where third persons (ordered to pay), 216, 217.
　Expenses of witnesses, 218.
　Taxation of, 218.
　To be taxed on a liberal scale, 219.
　Counsel's fees, 220, 221.
　Instructions for brief, 222.
　Number of witnesses allowed, 222.
　When to be incurred, 223.
　How recovered, 224.
　Payment out of security fund, 225.

COUNCILLOR, expenditure at election of, 159.
　Return and declaration of expenses by, 162.
　Penalties for sitting before return of expenses, 162.
　Applications for relief by, 169.

COUNSEL, fees of, 220, 221.

COUNTERFOILS, inspection of, 194.

COUNTIES, conveyance of voters by sea where legal, 80.

COUNTIES, maximum expenditure in, 146.

COUNTY COUNCIL ELECTIONS, application of Act of 1884 to, 159, 160, 170, 265, 266.

COURT,
　Attendance of director of public prosecutions at election court, 186.
　By what Courts offenders tried and punished, 227 et seq.
　Election commissioners and their powers, 227.
　Effect of their report, 228.
　Appeal from election commissioners, 236.
　Report of election court, 237.
　Effect of report of election court, 238.
　Power of election, to try offenders, 240.
　Sentences by election, 241.
　Trial by Court of summary jurisdiction, 246.
　Time for prosecuting before any, 247.
　Appeal from summary jurisdiction, 249.
　Prosecutions before assize, 250.
　Venue may be changed, 250.
　Actions in civil, for penalties, 254.
　Witnesses ordered out of court, 202.

CRIMINAL LAW, offences against. See *Punishments*.

CUSTOM, withdrawal of, 60.

DECEASED PERSONS, statements by, 210.

DECLARATION, false, 66.

DECLARATION OF ELECTION EXPENSES, 156.
　By election agent, 156.

DEFINITION OF BRIBERY, 4, 6.

DENTISTS, special punishment of, 235.

DEMURRABLE PETITION, 176.

DIRECTOR of public prosecutions, his duties at trial of petition. 186
　Prosecution by, 229 et seq.

DISCOVERY, 181.

DISCREDITING one's witness, 203, 205.

DISPUTED CLAIM,
　Action for, 153.
　May be taxed, 154.

DISSENTING MINISTERS,
　Intimidation by, 62.
　Intimidation of, 61.

DOCTORS, special punishment of, 235.

DOCUMENTS, production of, 209.

DRUNKENNESS, general, evidence of general treating, 102.

ECCLESIASTICS,
　Limits of their influence, 61.
　Undue influence by, 61.
　May select candidate, 61.
　And canvass for him, 62.

ELECTION, formal proof of, 202, 212.
　Illegal practices, by avoiding election, 76.
　His appointment and duties, 131.
　Who should be appointed, 131.
　Should be a solicitor, 131.
　When to be appointed. 132, 133.
　When to be named, 132.
　And to whom to be named, 133.
　Notice of appointment of, 133.
　May be changed, 133.
　Sub-agents of, 134.
　Offices of, 134.
　Service of documents on, 135.
　Remuneration of, 151.
　To pay election expenses, 136.
　To make return of election expenses, 154.
　To make declaration, 155.

ELECTION COMMISSIONERS, 233.

ELECTION COMMITTEE, agency of, 120.

ELECTION COURT (Parliamentary), 237.

ELECTION COURT (Municipal), 243.

ELECTION EXPENSES,
　Subscriptions towards, 40.
　Should be estimated in advance, 141.
　What need not be estimated or returned, 141.
　What are, 141.
　What kinds are allowable, 142.
　Maximum amount allowed, 144.
　Scale of, in boroughs and counties, 144, 146.

ELECTION EXPENSES,
  In case of joint candidature restricted, 147.
  Relief in case of limit being exceeded, 148.
  To be paid by election agent, 149.
  Claims for, to be sent to election agent, 149.
  When to be sent in, 150.
  Late claims for barred, 151.
  When to be paid, 152.
  Leave to pay out of time, how obtained, 152.
  Return of, 154.
  Declaration, verifying return of, 155.

ELECTION PETITION. See *Petition*.

ELECTION, avoided at common law, when, 101.

EMPLOYERS, intimidation by, 60.

EMPLOYMENT OF VOTERS,
  When bribery, 16, 19.

EMPLOYMENT OF CORRUPT AGENT avoids election, 98.
  When personal, 98, 99.

EQUALITY OF VOTES, 198.

ESTIMATE OF ELECTION EXPENSES, 141.

EVENT, costs usually follow, 213.
  May be distributive, 213.

EVIDENCE,
  Admissions, 210.
  Cogent, of mere offer required, 8.
  Of agency, what is sufficient, 111.
  Of general corruption, 102.

EVIDENCE ON ELECTION PETITIONS,
  Not to be stated in petition, 181.
  How procured, 184.
  Rewards for legality of, 185.
  Rules of common law generally apply, 201.
  Exceptions, 201, 202.
  Witnesses ordered out of court, 202.
  Improper rejection or admission, 203.
  Discrediting witness, 203, 204.
  Cross examining hostile witness, 204.
  Use of witness's previous statements, 204.
  Admission by witness, 205.
  Court may require proof of agency first, 206.
  Political opinions of witness, 207.
  Of acts done at previous elections, 207.
  Of acts done at municipal elections, 208.
  Admissions by agent after poll, 210.
  Production of documents, 209.
  Unstamped documents, 209.
  On municipal election petitions, 212.

EXPENDITURE,
  Lavish household, not necessarily bribery, 30.

EXPENSES,
  Election, through whom to be paid, 72.
  As to petty expenses, 137.
  Of Election. See *Election Expenses*.
  Municipal election, 159.

FALSE DECLARATION,
  Punishment of, 158.
  Avoids election, 68.
  A corrupt practice, 68.

FILING PETITION, 176.

FLYS, payment for, illegal, 78.

FORFEITURE OF THE SEAT,
  How caused, 1, 2.

FORM OF BRIBE immaterial, 16.

FORM OF SUMMONS, for particulars, 181.

FORM OF PETITIONS, 193.

FRAUDULENT devices to impede voting, 63.

FREEMEN'S ADMISSION FEES,
  Payment of, when bribery, 24.

GENERAL
  Corruption, 101.
  Bribery, 101.
  Treating, 102.
  Intimidation, 103.
  Intimidation, effect of on poll, 104.
  What amounts to, 103, 104.

GIFTS,
  To non-electors, may be bribery, 9.
  To children, may be bribery, 9.
  To women, may be bribery, 10.

GUARDIANS, poor law, elections of, law applicable to, 263.

HACKNEY CARRIAGES, when illegal to hire, 78.

HIRING, illegal, what is, 77 *et seq.*

HIRING, illegal, by candidate or any agent, 77.

HOLIDAY, giving, when bribery, 25, 27.

HOTELS not to be used as committee rooms, 83.

HOUSEHOLD EXPENDITURE, lavish, not necessarily bribery, 28.

HOSPITALITY, not necessarily treating, 51, 52.

HOSTILE WITNESS, examination of, 204.

ILLEGAL,
  Employments, 78.
  Hirings, 78.
  Payments, 76.
  Practices, prevalence of, 106.

INDEX.

ILLEGAL PRACTICES.
    Avoiding the seat if done by any agent, 67.
    Avoiding the seat if done by election agent, 76 *et seq.*
    Do not necessarily avoid election, 75.

INFANTS MAY NOT VOTE, 87, 200.

IMPLIED PROMISE TO TREAT, 50.

IMPROVEMENT COMMISSIONERS, application of law to, 260.

INDIVIDUALS GUILTY, payment of costs of, petition by, 216, 225.

INFLUENCE,
    Purchase of, may be bribery, 39.
    Undue. See *Undue Influence*.

INSPECTION,
    Of documents, 181.
    Of ballot papers, 194.

INSTRUCTIONS FOR BRIEF, costs of, 222.

INTERROGATORIES not allowed, 181.

INTIMIDATION. See *Undue Influence*.

IRISH CONSTITUENCIES, expenditure allowed in, 141.

JOINT CANDIDATURE,
    Agency in case of, 127.
    Expenses restricted in case of, 147.
    What is, 147.
    Severance of, 147.
    Relief against excessive expenditure in, 148.

JOINT COST, conveyance to the poll at, 79.

JUSTICE OF PEACE, special punishment of, 231.

LANDLORDS,
    Undue influence by, 58.
    May select their tenants, 58.

LEGITIMATE INFLUENCE, 57.

LENDING CARRIAGES for conveyance of voters, when illegal, 79.

LIABILITY,
    Of candidate for agents, 109 *et seq.*
    Of candidate for political associations, 121.

LICENSED PREMISES may not be used as committee rooms, 83.

LISTS OF OBJECTIONS, 195.

LIVERY STABLE KEEPER, payments to, for carriages, &c., 77.

LOCAL BOARD ELECTIONS, application of law to, 260.

Locus standi of elector at trial, 197.

LONDON,
    Act applied to municipal elections, 267.
    City of, expenses at municipal elections in, 267.

LORD MAYOR OF LONDON, act applied to election of, 267.

LOSS OF TIME, payments for, 21.

LUNATIC, vote of, bad. 200.

MAXIMUM,
    Expenditure, 85, 91, 141, 146.

MAYOR, election of, application of law to, 258.

MESSENGERS,
    Colourable payments to, bribery, 16, 19.
    To be appointed by election agent, 136.
    By whom paid, 136.
    Number allowed, 81, 82.

MISCELLANEOUS EXPENSES limited, 141.

MISCONDUCT OF REGISTRATION OFFICER, 256.

MOB VIOLENCE, effect of, 104.

MONEY,
    Provided for election to be paid to election agent, 149.

MOTIVE OR DONOR, test of bribery, 8, 36.

MUNICIPAL ELECTIONS,
    Effect of bribery at, 13, 14.
    Effect of treating at, 46.
    Declaration of election expenses at, 162.
    Committee rooms allowed in, 90, 95.
    Election agent at, not provided for, 160.
    Expenses at, how regulated, 159.
    Expenses at, none except in election of Councillors, 159.
    Illegal payments, hirings and employments at, 90.
    Illegal practices which avoid, 90.
    Maximum expenditure upon, 91, 159.
    Prevalence of illegal practices, 106 *et seq.*
    Political clubs not always to be used at, 94.
    School rooms may be used as committee rooms, 95.
    Seat, how forfeited, 2.
    Relief, applications for, 169 *et seq.*
    Return of election expenses at, 160.
    Voters prohibited from voting at, 95.
    Bribery at, effect on parliamentary election, 208.

MUNICIPAL ELECTION COURT, 243.

MUNICIPAL ELECTION EXPENSES, 159.

MUNICIPAL ELECTION PETITIONS, 169 *et seq.*
    What elections questioned by, 189.
    On what grounds, 189.
    By whom to be presented, 190.
    When to be presented, 190.
    Security for costs of, 191.
    Expenses of witnesses upon, 192.
    Relief at trial of, 192.
    Evidence, 201.

410 INDEX.

NON-ELECTORS,
  Gifts to may be bribery, 9, 31.
  Treating may be corrupt treating, 16.
NOTICE OF TRIAL, 177.
NOTICE of appointment of election agent, 133.

OBJECTIONS TO RETURN, particulars of, 183.
OFFENCES. See *Punishments*.
OFFENDERS,
  Their detection and punishment, 227.
  By what courts punished, 233 *et seq*.
OFFER,
  Corrupt, may be bribery, 8, 15.
OFFICE, offer of an, bribery, 28.
OPERATIVE, threats, to avoid an election, must be, 59.
ORANGE LODGE, subscriptions to, 31.

PAID AGENTS,
  Excessive number of, 81.
  May not vote, 86.
PAIRING, voting after, 63.
PARTICULARS,
  How obtained, 181.
  When ordered, 182.
  How framed, 182, 183.
  Amendment of, 183.
PARTICULARS of objections, obtainable by petitioner, 183.
PAYMENTS to voters, when bribery, 16, 21.
PAYMENTS, illegal, 76 *et seq*.
PEERS may not vote, 87.
PENALTIES, suits for, 251.
PERSONATION, 64.
  Defined, 64.
  Innocent, 65.
  Offence of, when complete, 65.
  No relief against, 54.
PERSONAL EXPENSES OF CANDIDATE,
  What are, 142.
  To be returned, 150.
PETITION,
  Who may present, 172 *et seq*.
  When to be presented, 173.
  How abated, 173.
  Practice on filing, 175.
  Service of, 176.
  Security for costs of, 176.
  Objections to the security, 177.
  Payments into court, how made, 177.
  Amendment of, 178.
  Formal objections to, 178.
  Notice of trial, 180.
  Withdrawal of, 178, 180.
  Corrupt bargain to withdraw, 179.
  Practice on withdrawal of, 180.
  Withdrawing opposition to, 180.

PETITION,
  Discovery and interrogatories, in aid of, 181.
  Special case upon, 180, 188.
  Inspection of ballot papers, 181.
  Particulars, delivery of, 181.
  Objections, particulars of, 183.
  Production of telegrams, 184.
  Commission to examine witness on, 184.
  Offering rewards for evidence, 185.
  Relief on hearing of, 187, 188.
  Taxation of witnesses' expenses, 189.
PETTY EXPENSES OF VOLUNTEERS, 137.
PLACARDS,
  Excessive payments for, when bribery, 19.
  Contracts for, when illegal practices, 70.
POLICEMEN may vote at Parliamentary elections, 87.
  Not at Municipal elections, 96, 200.
POLITICAL ASSOCIATIONS, candidate when responsible for, 121.
POLITICAL CLUB, premises of, may be used as committee rooms, 83.
  Not always in Municipal elections, 94.
POLITICAL SOCIETIES, treating, 52.
POLLING AGENTS, to be appointed by election agent, 136.
POSTERS issued without printer's name, 88.
PRACTICES, illegal, by candidate or election agent, 76.
PRACTICE. See *Petition, Relief, Scrutiny, and Criminal Law*.
PRACTICE on application for relief, 164.
PRACTICE on election petitions, 172.
PRACTICE on a scrutiny, 193.
PRIESTS, undue influence by, 61.
PREVALENCE of illegal practices, hirings, &c. (Municipal), 106.
PRODUCTION of documents, 209.
PROFUSION before elections, 27, 28.
PROHIBITED PAYMENTS, 76, 140.
PROMISES, difficulty in getting evidence of, 206.
PROCEDURE. See *Petition, Scrutiny, Relief, and Criminal Law*.
PROSECUTIONS, director of public, his functions, 229.
  Private, 230.
PUBLIC HOUSES,
  Opening, 48.
  Not to be used for committee rooms, 83.
PUBLIC MEETINGS, expenses of, 139, 143.
PUNISHMENTS, 233 *et seq*.
  By what courts awarded, 234 *et seq*.
  Effect of report of commissioners, 234.

INDEX. 411

PUNISHMENTS,
  Of barristers reported, 235.
  Of solicitors reported, 235.
  Of doctors, dentists, and clergymen reported, 235.
  Before report, party to be heard, 236.
  Appeal upon report, 236.
  By election court, 237.
  Of candidate guilty by his agent, 238.
  Of candidate guilty of corrupt practices, 238.
  Effect of report of election court upon other persons, 239.
  Committal for trial by election court, 240.
  By a court of summary jurisdiction, 246.
  By the court of assize, 250.

QUO WARRANTO, when available, 259, 264.

RAILWAY FARE, payment of, when bribery, 21.
  " " " when illegal practice, 67.
RATES, corrupt payment of, bribery, 6, 25.
RECOVERY OF COSTS, 224.
RECOGNISANCE, objections to, 177.
RECRIMINATORY EVIDENCE, 193, 196.
REFRESHMENTS TO AGENTS, 47.
REGISTER, inspection of, 194.
  " how far conclusive of right to vote, 198.
REGISTRAR, taxation of witnesses, expenses, 189.
REGISTRATION COURT, payments for attending, when bribery, 23, 24, 25.
REGISTRATION EXPENSES, 140.
REGISTRATION OFFICER, misconduct of, 256.
RELIEF,
  Against consequences of treating or undue influence, 53.
  None after bribery or personation, 54.
  Against consequences of illegal practices, 74.
RELIEF BY THE COURT,
  Against effect of excessive expenditure, 148.
  Procedure to obtain, 164.
  Applications for, 164.
  Parties to be heard on, 164.
  On default concerning return of election expenses, 165.
  Should be sought without delay, 165.
  How obtained when agent in default, 167.
  On hearing of petition, 187.
REPORT OF JUDGE, effect of, 208.
REPUDIATION OF AGENTS, 129.

RETAINER TO COUNSEL, 222.
RETIREMENT OF CANDIDATE, procuring, when illegal practice, 80.
RETURNING OFFICER'S VOTE, 87.
  " " CHARGES, 151.
RETURN OF ELECTION EXPENSES, 154.
REVIEWING TAXATION, 220.
REVISING BARRISTER'S COURT,
  Payment for attendance at, 22.
  Treating for attendance at, 46.
REWARDS FOR EVIDENCE, 186.
RIBBONS, payment for, 80.
RIOTING, general effect of, 104.
ROOMS. See *Committee Rooms*.

SCALE OF EXPENDITURE AT ELECTION ALLOWED, 141.
SCHOOL BOARD ELECTIONS, law applicable to, 264.
SCHOOLROOM, when use of, as committee room allowed, 84, 95.
SCRUTINY, where votes come off on a, 198.
SCRUTINY LISTS, 194.
SCRUTINY OF VOTES,
  When made, 193.
  Recriminatory case upon, 193.
  Practice where claimed, 196.
  Delivery of scrutiny lists, 195.
  And list of objections, 195.
  Inspection of ballot papers, 194.
  Order of proceeding at trial, 196.
  Elector has no *locus standi*, 197.
  Register, how far conclusive on, 198.
  Ballot papers ill marked, 199.
  Votes struck off, 199.
  When ballot papers examined, 200.
  Practice as to tendered votes, 201.
SEA CONVEYANCE OF VOTERS, when legal, 80.
SECURITY FOR COSTS OF PETITION, 177 *et seq*, 224.
SECRECY OF BALLOT, 200, 206.
SERVICE OF NOTICES AND DOCUMENTS, 135.
  " ELECTION NOTICES, 135.
  " PETITION, 176.
SHERIFF OF CITY OF LONDON, Act applied to, 267.
SOLICITOR AND CLIENT, costs as between, 219.
SOLICITOR should be chosen as election agent, 132.
SOLICITORS, special punishment of, 235.
SPECIAL CASE 182.

SPIRITUAL INTIMIDATION, 61 et seq.
SUB-AGENTS,
  How and when appointed, 134.
  Revocation of their appointment, 134.
  Candidate's liability for, 134.
  Offices of, 136.
  Service of notices on, 136.
  Relief for default of, 167.
  Extent of their authority, 110.
SUBPŒNAS for witnesses, 185.
SUBSCRIPTIONS,
  To charities, 30.
  Towards candidates' expenses, legal, 40.
  Towards candidates' election expenses, how to be paid, 149.
SUITS for penalties, 234.
SUMMONS for particulars, 181.

TAVERNS not to be used as committee rooms, 81.
TAXATION of costs, 213, 225.
TAXATION of disputed claims, 154.
TENDERED VOTES, 201.
TERMINATION of agency, 129.
TEST BALLOT,
  Bribery at, 15.
  Treating at, 46.
THREATS, when undue influence, 59, 62.
TIME FOR FILING PETITIONS,
  How reckoned, 175, 191.
  For delivering scrutiny lists, 195.
  For delivering lists of objections, 195.
TORCHES, payments for, illegal, 80.
TOWN CLERK, documents in custody of, 213.
TRAVELLING EXPENSES,
  Payment of, when bribery, 21, 22.
  Payment of, now always illegal, 22.
TREACHERY BY AGENT, 128.
TREATING, 41.
  On the nomination or polling day, 41.
  Statutory definitions of, 42.
  Must be done corruptly, 43.
  Must be done to influence the vote, 44.
  Offer to treat is not, 46.
  But may be bribery, 46.
  Non-electors may avoid election, 46.
  At municipal elections, 46.
  At revision courts, 47.
  By refreshments to agents, 47.
  By opening public houses, 48.
  After election, 49.
  Amount of, when immaterial, 49.
  Relief where trivial, 49, 53.
  Conditions on which relief granted, 53.
  General treating, 102.
  By agent, avoids election, 41.

UNDUE INFLUENCE, 56, 64
  Defined, 56.
  Antiquity of law against, 56.
  By illegitimate canvassing, 57.
  Compared with bribery, 58.
  By bottling voters, 58.
  By landlords, 58, 59.
  By employers, 60.
  By workpeople, 60.
  Withdrawal of custom, 60.
  Spiritual intimidation, 61.
  Attempts to use, avoid election, 62.
  Hasty words not, 62.
  Relief against consequences of, 63.
UNIVERSITIES, corrupt payment of members' fees, bribery, 7.

VALUE of bribe immaterial, 11.
VIOLENCE, general, 103.
VOLUNTARY AGENTS,
  Number of, unlimited, 111.
  Candidate liable for, 111.
  Repudiation of, 123.
VOTE if not free is bad, 56.
VOTERS, bottling, 58.
VOTES struck off on scrutiny, 199 et seq.
VOTING, when illegal, 85.
  Who are prohibited from, 86 et seq.
  Who prohibited at municipal elections, 95.
VOTING cards, when a fraudulent device, 63.

WARD, corrupt, not liable to pay costs, 225.
WAGERS on result of election, 40.
WATCHERS, colourable payments to, bribery, 16-19.
WITHDRAWAL,
  Of custom, undue influence by, 60.
  Loss by, should be substantial, 60.
WITHDRAWAL OF PETITION, 178.
WITNESS,
  Commission to examine, 184.
  Attendance of, 184, 185.
  Admissions by, 205.
WITNESSES,
  May be called by the Court, 211.
  May be called by the Public Prosecutor, 212.
WITNESSES' EXPENSES, 189.
  On what scale allowed, 223.
WORDS, hasty, not undue influence, 62.
WORKPEOPLE,
  Holiday to, may be bribery, 25, 26.
  Intimidation of, 60.
  Intimidation by, 60.
WOMEN,
  Gifts to, may amount to bribery, 10.
  Treating, may amount to bribery, 46.
  May not vote, 87.

WATERLOW & SONS LIMITED,
STATIONERS AND PRINTERS.

ELECTION WORK.

WATERLOW & SONS LIMITED

Undertake every class of Printing and Stationery connected with Parliamentary, County or Municipal Elections, and with the large resources at their command can fulfil orders entrusted to them with the utmost despatch.

CANDIDATES' ADDRESSES, POSTERS, NOTICES, CIRCULARS, CARDS OF SOLICITATION AND DIRECTIONS, POLLING CARDS, BALLOT BOOKS, BALLOT PAPERS, &c., &c.

THE ELECTION ADDRESSES OF CANDIDATES PRINTED OR LITHOGRAPHED (FAC-SIMILE) IN A FEW HOURS, AND THE ENVELOPES OR WRAPPERS ADDRESSED FROM THE REGISTER, AND POSTED WITH THE UTMOST DESPATCH.

WATERLOW & SONS LIMITED,
LONDON WALL, LONDON, E.C.

WATERLOW & SONS LIMITED,
STATIONERS AND PRINTERS.

LIST OF FORMS, BOOKS, &c.,
REQUIRED BY PRESIDING & RETURNING OFFICERS, CANDIDATES & ELECTION AGENTS.

These Forms have been settled by H. Stephen, Esq., and H. E. Miller, Esq., Barristers-at-Law, Authors of the "County Council Compendium."

1.	Appointment of Deputy Returning Officer	1/- per doz.
2.	Writ to Mayor of Borough to elect County Councillor, parchment	1/- each.
2a.	Do. do. do. do. when divided into Wards	1/- ,,
3.	Notice of Election, Poster	7/6 per 100.
4.	Nomination Form	1/6 per doz.
4a.	Notice of Withdrawal	1/- ,,
5.	Suggestions for filling up Nomination Papers	1/- ,,
6.	Notice of Nomination, Poster	7/6 per 100.
7.	Notice of Objection to Nomination	1/- per doz.
8.	Notice of Poll and Polling Districts, Poster	7/6 per 100.
9.	Appointment of Presiding Officer, Polling Clerks, &c.	1/6 per doz.
10.	Appointment of Election Agent	1/- ,,
11.	Notification of Appointment of Election Agent	1/- ,,
12.	Forms of Appointment of Sub-Agents	1/- ,,
13.	Instructions to Sub-Agents	2/- ,,
14.	Notification to Returning Officer of appointment of Sub-Agents	1/6 ,,
14a.	Appointment of Messengers and Clerks	1/- ,,
15.	Form of Hire of Committee Rooms	1/- ,,
15a.	Authority to Pay Petty Expenses	1/- ,,
15b.	Return of Canvass from District Committee to Central Committee	6/- per 100.
15c.	Return of Canvass to District Committee by Canvassers	6/- ,,
16.	Instructions for Presiding Officers, Poll Clerks, &c.	1/6 per doz.
17.	Instructions to Agents attending Polling Stations	2/6 ,,
18.	Notice of Counting Votes	1/- ,,
19.	Appointment of Agent for Counting Votes	1/6 ,,
20.	Notification to Returning Officer of appointment of Agents for Counting Votes	2/- ,,
21.	Appointment of Agents to detect personation	1/6 ,,
22.	Notification to Returning Officer of appointment of same	1/- ,,
23.	Return of persons elected	1/6 ,,
24.	Notice to Candidate of his Election	2/- ,,
25.	Declaration on acceptance of office	1/6 ,,
26.	Declaration of Secrecy	1/6 ,,
27.	Questions to be put	2/- ,,
28.	Declaration of inability to read	1/6 ,,
29.	List of Tendered Votes	1/6 ,,
30.	List of Votes marked by the Presiding Officer	1/6 ,,
30a.	Ballot Paper Account	1/6 ,,
31.	Admission Card to Polling Stations	5/- per 100.
32.	Form of Card to be used in Counting Ballot Papers	6/- ,,
33.	Declaration of Expenses	1/6 per doz.
34.	Notice of allotment of Polling Stations, Poster	7/6 per 100.
35.	Notice of Situation of Polling Stations and guidance for Voting, Poster	7/6 ,,
36.	Notice of Election of Councillors unopposed, Poster	7/6 ,,
37.	Returning Officer's Notice of Election after contest, Poster	7/6 ,,
38.	Caution to Electors as to Corrupt Practices, Poster	7/6 ,,
39.	Caution to Electors as to Offences against the Ballot Act, Poster	7/6 ,,
40.	Caution as to disturbance in Polling Stations, Poster	7/6 ,,
41.	Ballot Papers, in books with counterpart, numbered, and with Candidates' Names, *at a few hours' notice*	To order.
42.	Direction Slips "Way In" "Way Out," Gummed Paper or Index Hands	6d. per doz.
43.	Order Book	2/6 each.
44.	Notice of Polling Place	To order.

These Forms and Books are kept in Stock, and sent off immediately on receipt of Order, Special Forms Printed to Order at few hours' notice.

WATERLOW & SONS LIMITED,
LONDON WALL, LONDON, E.C.

WATERLOW & SONS LIMITED,
STATIONERS AND PRINTERS.

LIST OF
STATIONERY, &c.,
FOR
POLLING STATIONS.

In Packets. Price 5s. 6d. each, or £3 per doz.

Four large Envelopes endorsed for Papers, Books, viz. :—

1. The Unused and Spoilt Ballot Papers.
2. The Tendered Ballot Papers.
3. The Marked Copies of the Register of Voters, and the Counterfoils of the Ballot Papers.
4. The Tendered Votes List and the List of Votes marked by Presiding Officer.

Tape for fastening up Ballot Box.

Sealing Wax.

Eight Indelible Pencils for use of Voters.

Six Sheets of Blotting Paper.

Six Sheets Large Brown Paper.

Twelve Sheets Note Paper and Envelopes.

Six Pencils, Six Penholders and Pens.

One Bottle of Ink and Inkstand.

One Ball of Twine.

One Pentateuch.

One New Testament.

WATERLOW & SONS LIMITED,
LONDON WALL, LONDON, E.C.

WATERLOW & SONS LIMITED,
STATIONERS AND PRINTERS.

THE ELECTION AGENT'S CASH BOOK
(COPYRIGHT),

Ruled and Printed with Headings, suitable for every description of outlay, with a Summary at end of every 16 pages, enabling the Election Agent to ascertain at a glance the Expenditure incurred up to any given time.

(A) 54 leaves, super-royal 4to, bound limp roan and lettered ... **12s. 6d.**
(B) 72   ditto   ditto   ditto   ... **16s. 0d.**

A large number of these Books were used at the last General Election and gave great satisfaction.

CANVASSING BOOKS
6s. PER 100.
Specimen sent free on application.

WHITE POST CARDS
7d. PER DOZEN.

These Cards are very much superior to the Ordinary Buff Cards. They can be had in Sheets of 42 on for convenience of printing large quantities for Elections and similar purposes. Specimens sent on application.

STATIONERY AND ALL OTHER REQUISITES
FOR
ELECTION AGENTS AND PRESIDING OFFICERS
SUPPLIED AT A DAY'S NOTICE.

WATERLOW & SONS LIMITED,
LONDON WALL, LONDON, E.C.

WATERLOW & SONS LIMITED,
STATIONERS AND PRINTERS.

BALLOT BOXES.

These Boxes are made of Japanned Metal with Handles and Tumbler Locks. Three Seals are placed on the front, and one with slit and slide cover on the top, for sealing up, thus effectually preventing any tampering with the contents, or the introduction or withdrawal of papers after the seals are affixed.

Japanned Metal—	Each.	Doz.
To take 500 Voting Papers ...	10s. 6d. ...	£6.
To take 1,000 ditto ...	15s. 0d. ...	£8. 10s.

PERCUSSION PRESS.

Fitted with a word of 3 or 4 letters, embossing the Paper on both sides.

5s. 6d. each.   £3. per doz.

LEVER PRESS.

A strong powerful Press. Fitted with a word of 3 or 4 letters, or a design.

7s. 6d. each.   £4. 5s. per doz.

DUPLEX PRESS.

A slight pressure on the handle produces a coloured impression on both sides of the paper. Fitted with an ordinary word of 3 or 4 letters, or a design.

8s. 6d. each.   £4. 15s. per doz.

PERFORATING PRESS.

This is the best and most effectual press for cancelling Voting Papers.

Fitted with a word of 3 or 4 letters, or a design of between 50 and 60 pinholes.

10s. each.   £5. 8s. per doz.

Any of the above altered for future Elections at a charge of from 3s. each.

WATERLOW & SONS LIMITED,
LONDON WALL, LONDON, E.C.

WATERLOW & SONS LIMITED,
STATIONERS AND PRINTERS.

JUST PUBLISHED.

THE LAW RELATING TO
CORRUPT PRACTICES
AT
PARLIAMENTARY, MUNICIPAL
AND
OTHER ELECTIONS,
AND
THE PRACTICE ON ELECTION PETITIONS,

With an Appendix of Statutes, Rules, and Forms:

BY

MILES WALKER MATTINSON
AND
STUART CUNNINGHAM MACASKIE,
OF GRAY'S INN, BARRISTERS-AT-LAW.

THIRD EDITION. Demy 8vo. In Cloth, 10s.

WATERLOW & SONS LIMITED,
LONDON WALL, LONDON, E.C.

WATERLOW & SONS LIMITED,
STATIONERS AND PRINTERS.

Opinions of the Press
ON PREVIOUS EDITIONS OF THE WORK BY
MESSRS. MATTINSON & MACASKIE,
ON

"The Law Relating to Corrupt Practices."

"Invaluable to Electioneerers and Party Agents. . . . . . We recommend it not only to every Election Agent but to every Candidate."—*Whitehall Review.*

"The difficult topic of Agency in particular is fully and clearly treated. . . . The greater scope and careful workmanship of this book make any comparison with other books yet published out of the question."—*Law Times.*

"It is compiled upon an easy intelligible plan, and has evidently been very carefully prepared. . . . An invaluable guide to the Statutory standard of Parliamentary probity."—*Globe.*

"A complete guide to the Election Law, and written with such a masterful grasp of the subject and lucidity rarely to be found in law books."—*Wednesbury Herald.*

"Gentlemen about to embark in the adventures of Electioneering had better get this book promptly and study it carefully."—*Western Times.*

"A valuable *résumé* of the law under which future Elections will have to be conducted."—*Daily Chronicle.*

"A valuable, explicit, and carefully compiled compendium of Election Law."—*Tower Hamlets Independent.*

"To Agents and Candidates the information will be specially valuable, for the writers point out, especially in the matter of the use of Conveyances and of the hire of Committee Rooms, not only what is forbidden, but what is permissible."—*Brighton Daily Post.*

"It is of the most complete and explanatory character."—*Cornishman.*

WATERLOW & SONS LIMITED,
LONDON WALL, LONDON, E.C.

WATERLOW & SONS LIMITED,
STATIONERS AND PRINTERS.

TABLE OF CORRUPT AND ILLEGAL PRACTICES WHICH VITIATE THE ELECTION.

By M. W. MATTINSON and S. C. MACASKIE,
Barristers-at-Law.

ON LINEN-LINED CARD.

PRICES: 1 copy, 2d.; 50 copies, 6s.; 100 copies, 10s.; 250 copies, £1. 2s. 6d.; 500 copies, £2; 1,000 copies, £3. 15s.; or printed on stout cardboard 11 by 17, suitable for affixing to the walls of committee rooms, Price 6d. each.

The Law relating to the management of

PARLIAMENTARY, COUNTY COUNCIL AND MUNICIPAL ELECTIONS.

A hand-book of the Law relating to the machinery of Elections.
By HENRY STEPHEN, Esq., of the Middle Temple, *Barrister-at-Law.*
Second Edition. In Cloth, 1s.

THE FRANCHISE ACTS, 1884-5:
BEING THE
REPRESENTATION OF THE PEOPLE ACT, 1884;
REGISTRATION ACT, 1885;
PARLIAMENTARY ELECTION (REDISTRIBUTION) ACT, 1884;
WITH INTRODUCTIONS AND NOTES.
By MILES WALKER MATTINSON,
Barrister-at-Law.
Joint Author of "MATTINSON AND MACASKIE ON CORRUPT PRACTICES."
In Boards, 2s. 6d.

THE ELECTORAL BOUNDARIES OF THE UNITED KINGDOM.
Being Schedules 5, 6 and 7 of the Parliamentary Elections (Redistribution) Act, 1885. WITH INDEX.
In Boards, 2s. 6d.

WATERLOW & SONS LIMITED,
LONDON WALL, LONDON, E.C.

www.ingramcontent.com/pod-product-compliance
Lightning Source LLC
Chambersburg PA
CBHW051726300426
44115CB00007B/477